THE LITERARY COMPANION TO MEDICINE

THE LITERARY COMPANION TO MEDICINE

An anthology of prose and poetry

collected by

Richard Gordon

SINCLAIR-STEVENSON

First published in Great Britain in 1993
by Sinclair-Stevenson
an imprint of Reed Consumer Books Ltd
Michelin House, 81 Fulham Road, London SW3 6RB
and Auckland, Melbourne, Singapore and Toronto

A CIP catalogue record for this book
is available at the British Library
ISBN 1 85619 335 7

Typeset by CentraCet, Cambridge
Printed in England by Clays Ltd, St Ives plc

CONTENTS

INTRODUCTION: WHY MEDICINE?

'MEDICINE, THAT SUBDIVISION of the humanities.' The compliment which Thomas Mann paid us in 1924 would a hundred years earlier have sounded ridiculous.

Until the middle of the nineteenth century, medicine was a brutal confrontation between doctor and patient of bleeding and blistering; a squalor of purging and puking; the screaming endurance of amputation and of wanton surgical slashing; the everyday terror of pestilence; the melancholy resignation to lifelong deformity; the shrugging at fettered madness and the joyful embarkation upon doubly perilous childbirth. It was an exciting panorama of pain and death, which leant itself to the writing of vivid tragedy, or of broad comedy, as conveniently as warfare.

The discovery of anaesthesia in Boston in 1846, and of surgical antisepsis by Lord Lister in 1865, drained from hospitals the agony and mortality of the battlefield. In the 1840s, official uneasiness towards each summer's water-borne epidemics – which flushed citizens from the filthy infective streets into the crammed pestiferous churchyards – set cleanliness dogging the heels of godliness. Masterful Miss Nightingale in the Crimean War of 1854 gentrified nursing. In 1876 came the discovery of every germ having its own disease, even if nobody had the slightest idea how to cure them. All this turned medicine under Queen Victoria into a respectable occupation for intelligent gentlemen.

The Law and the Church were until then the only trees rooted in the rich, blood-soaked European soil upon which the flowers of its culture blossomed. The likely lad had no other branches to climb. He needed to rise to the top of the tree to command the landscape, whether he was not particularly devout like Wolsey, nor utterly honest like Bacon. Now medicine sprang forth like a beanstalk, and the doctor, a technician jangling the keys of Heaven and Hell, newly embroidered with learning, illuminated with re-lit Greek ideals, emboldened by effectiveness, harnessed by respectability when loosed in society, castrated by ethics when permitted into shameless intimacy, shot up like Jack to become a literary hero.

The first was George Eliot's Dr Lydgate in *Middlemarch*, written in 1871 but set in 1829, when 'the heroic times of copious bleeding and blistering had not yet departed . . . in spite of venerable colleges which used great efforts to secure purity of knowledge by making it scarce'. The practitioner arose from the tradesmen's entrance in the semi-basement to the door up the front steps. Instead of using the 'potticary', as in the days of Queen Charlotte, ladies consulted the doctor. Hospitals were busily refounding their medical schools, elevating their ruffianly apprentices in bloodstained jackets into students just like the classicists and philosophers, while Dickens was having such fun with Benjamin Allen and Bob Sawyer.

'I do not know a better training for a writer than to spend some years in the medical profession', prescribed Somerset Maugham in 1938. He had qualified at St Thomas's Hospital in 1897, and made a medical student the hero of his first success, *Of Human Bondage*. Maugham recalled appreciatively at Cap Ferrat the St Thomas's wards, which had usefully presented him with life in the raw and the observation of every emotion of mankind, where he saw people suffer and die and glimpsed 'the gallantry that made a man greet the prognosis of death with an ironic joke because he was too proud to let those about him see the terror of his soul', as he so expertly put it. Jean-Paul Sartre agreed: 'Doctors, priests, magistrates, and officers know men as thoroughly as if they had made them.' So did Dr Anton Chekhov, who qualified in Moscow in 1884: 'It seems to me that as a doctor I have described the sickness of the soul correctly.' Chekhov practised sporadically, out of duty and kindness, and maintained that medicine was his wife and literature his mistress – but as C. P. Snow mentioned, 'It was the mistress who kept him'.

Medicine means life and death, deliverance and despair, hope and fright, mystery and mechanics. It is a microscope trained upon life's fundamentals, eagerly focused by novelists since the 1820s. Readership is guaranteed. There may be doubters about the soul, but no one can deny the existence of the body, and everyone wants to know the terrible things that can happen to it.

Since the discovery of chemotherapy in Germany in 1933, and of penicillin in Oxford in 1941, medicine has undergone a sea-change. Doctors can now do something to cure their patients. Therapy and technique have advanced astoundingly, increasing medical drama and adding an exciting variety of props. All successful literature about medicine over the past half-century has become film and television, proving how medicine expresses the stark facts of life with the drama of lightning flashes.

Selecting an anthology, like selecting a Test team, incites outrage at the dropping of favourites. Maugham is slighted because his medical story *Sanatorium* is better done by Thomas Mann, and Chekhov deserves to be seen rather than read. This compilation is mostly about doctors, and partly by doctors, who generally write about doctors. There is medical gossip about the authors, and about the characters – which was not always apparent to their creators. The most popular medical literature has been overlooked, because its volumes are so widely scattered that you can take one from the library when you return this.

CHARLES DICKENS

Benjamin Allen and Bob Sawyer, quintessential medical students, shared digs in Lant Street, which you can find easily today just south of the Thames by London Bridge. It is five minutes' walk from Guy's Hospital and round the corner from the last galleried tavern in London, the 1677 George (which got into *Little Dorrit*). Nearby is White Hart Yard, once offering the White Hart Inn to which Mr Pickwick with Mr Wardle pursued Mr Jingle – who had eloped with the Wardle spinster aunt – and felicitously encountered its 'boots', Sam Weller.

Charles John Huffam Dickens (1812–70) himself lived in Lant Street. The family home the previous Christmastide had been in respectable Gower Street, Bloomsbury, beside University College Hospital (where the first operation under anaesthesia in Europe was performed, twenty-three years later). In February, Dickens's father was locked up in Marshalsea Prison for debt. After a brief move round the corner, Charles Dickens took lodgings in Lant Street with landlord Archibald Russell, an Insolvency Court official (who got into *The Old Curiosity Shop*). Dickens had the back attic overlooking a timber yard, his bed and bedding was sent in, he slept on the floor, and 'thought it was Paradise'. He breakfasted with his family in the New Marshalsea Prison just over Borough High Street, went back to prison for his supper, and stayed until the bell expelled visitors at ten o'clock. During the day he worked in Warren's blacking warehouse, across the Thames at Hungerford Market. He was twelve years old. In recompense, Lant Street now has a primary school named after him.

From Dickens's warm embrace of medical students' idiosyncrasies, he could himself have walked the wards of Bartholomew's with student Jack Hopkins. He assuredly mixed with them while knocking about London, as a reporter at Doctors' Commons or working on the *Morning Chronicle* in the 1830s. At the time, he must have encountered the prototype Buzfuz.

The three medical activities in Dickens's life were: chairing fund-raising hospital dinners; growing so furious over Parliament's neglecting the 1854 cholera epidemic that he urged, in *Household Words*, a worker's revolt (but he soon got over it); and attending to his fellow victims when he escaped death in a railway crash on 6 June 1865. He was returning with his mistress, the actress Ellen Ternan, from a holiday in Boulogne, when the Folkestone boat train thundered down unexpectedly between Ashford and Tonbridge upon the platelayers, who were busily removing the track. Calmly unscrewing his brandy flask (he never travelled without it) and filling his top hat with water, Dickens usefully applied both to the injured and dying. This left him with an understandable neurosis about rail travel.

From childhood, Dickens suffered attacks of left-sided abdominal pain, perhaps colic from a kidney stone, for which he took the antispasmodic henbane. From his twenties, Dickens suffered painful *tic douloureux*, spasmodic neuralgia of the trigeminal nerve in the face. In his fifties, he developed a swollen and painful left foot, suspected as the gout prevalent among the meat-eating and port-drinking classes, but diagnosed in 1867 as an infective erysipelas by Sir Henry Thompson (a fashionable surgeon who operated successfully six years later for bladder stones on the exiled Emperor Napoleon III in Chislehurst, who annoyingly died three days later). Like many Victorians, Dickens regularly swallowed tincture of opium to cheer himself up.

Dickens had bleeding piles and an anal fissure – dreadfully painful – which was operated upon by a rectal expert in the autumn of 1840, before the arrival of anaesthesia from Boston. By 1869 he was complaining of poor memory, and on 17 April of that year, in Chester on one of his reading tours, he suffered the first of his 'TIAs' – transient strokes. He suddenly became giddy, uncertain with his left hand, unsteady on his left leg. He consulted old Sir Thomas Watson, physician at the Middlesex Hospital, who put him off public reading. In 1866 he had already been diagnosed as suffering 'degeneration of some functions of the heart', probably a disturbance of its rhythm, for which he took the reasonable prescription of iron, quinine and digitalis.

One evening, at home in Gad's Hill, he felt ill over dinner, announced that he was going to London, and lost consciousness. The local doctor administered enemas, the family applied hot bricks to his cooling feet, the specialist summoned from London diagnosed 'unmistakable symptoms of brain haemorrhage' and sent a bill for twenty guineas. Dickens's breathing developed the mortal periodic gasping recorded by Hippocrates; at ten past six next morning he died. It was exactly five years after the rail smash.

From Pickwick Papers

THERE IS A repose about Lant Street, in the Borough, which sheds a gentle melancholy upon the soul. There are always a good many houses to let in the street: it is a bye-street too, and its dulness is soothing. A house in Lant Street would not come within the denomination of a first-rate residence, in the strict acceptation of the term; but it is a most desirable spot nevertheless. If a man wished to abstract himself from the world – to remove himself from within the reach of temptation – to place himself beyond the possibility of any inducement to look out of the window – he should by all means go to Lant Street.

In this happy retreat are colonised a few clear-starchers, a sprinkling of journeymen bookbinders, one or two prison agents for the Insolvent Court, several small housekeepers who are employed in the Docks, a handful of mantua-makers, and a seasoning of jobbing tailors. The majority of the inhabitants either direct their energies to the letting of furnished apartments, or devote themselves to the healthful and invigorating pursuit of mangling. The chief features in the still life of the street are green shutters, lodging-bills, brass door-plates, and bell-handles; the principal specimens of animated nature, the pot-boy, the muffin youth, and the baked-potato man. The population is migratory, usually disappearing on the verge of quarter-day, and generally by night. His Majesty's revenues are seldom collected in this happy valley; the rents are dubious; and the water communication is very frequently cut off.

Mr Bob Sawyer embellished one side of the fire, in his first-floor front, early on the evening for which he had invited Mr Pickwick; and Mr Ben Allen the other. The preparations for the reception of visitors appeared to be completed. The umbrellas in the passage had been heaped into the little corner outside the back-parlour door; the bonnet and shawl of the landlady's servant had been removed from the bannisters; there was not more than two pairs of pattens on the street-door mat, and a kitchen candle, with a very long snuff, burnt cheerfully on the edge of the staircase window. Mr Bob Sawyer had himself purchased the spirits at a wine vaults in High Street, and had returned home preceding the bearer thereof, to preclude the possibility of their delivery at the wrong house. The punch was ready made in a red pan in the bed-room; a little table, covered with a green baize cloth, had been borrowed from the parlour, to play at cards on; and the glasses of the establishment, together with those which had been borrowed for the occasion from the public-house, were all drawn up in a tray, which was deposited on the landing outside the door.

Notwithstanding the highly satisfactory nature of all these arrangements, there was a cloud on the countenance of Mr Bob Sawyer, as he sat by the fireside. There was a sympathising expression, too, in the features of Mr Ben Allen, as he gazed intently on the coals; and a tone of melancholy in his voice, as he said, after a long silence:

'Well, it *is* unlucky she should have taken it in her head to turn sour, just on this occasion. She might at least have waited till to-morrow.'

'That's her malevolence, that's her malevolence,' returned Mr Bob Sawyer, vehemently. 'She says that if I can afford to give a party I ought to be able to pay her confounded "little bill".'

'How long has it been running?' inquired Mr Ben Allen. A bill, by the bye, is the most extraordinary locomotive engine that the genius of man ever produced. It would keep on running during the longest lifetime, without ever once stopping of its own accord.

'Only a quarter, and a month or so,' replied Mr Bob Sawyer.

Ben Allen coughed hopelessly, and directed a searching look between the two top bars of the stove.

'It'll be a deuced unpleasant thing if she takes it into her head to let out, when those fellows are here, won't it?' said Mr Ben Allen at length.

'Horrible,' replied Bob Sawyer, 'horrible.'

A low tap was heard at the room door. Mr Bob Sawyer looked expressively at his friend, and bade the tapper come in; whereupon a dirty slipshod girl in black cotton stockings, who might have passed for the neglected daughter of a superannuated dustman in very reduced circumstances, thrust in her head, and said,

'Please, Mister Sawyer, Missis Raddle wants to speak to *you.*'

Before Mr Bob Sawyer could return any answer, the girl suddenly disappeared with a jerk, as if somebody had given her a violent pull behind; this mysterious exit was no sooner accompished, than there was another tap at the door – a smart pointed tap, which seemed to say, 'Here I am, and in I'm coming.'

Mr Bob Sawyer glanced at his friend with a look of abject apprehension, and once more cried 'Come in.'

The permission was not at all necessary, for, before Mr Bob Sawyer had uttered the words, a little fierce woman bounced into the room, all in a tremble with passion, and pale with rage.

'Now, Mr Sawyer,' said the little fierce woman, trying to appear very calm, 'if you'll have the kindness to settle that little bill of mine, I'll thank you, because I've got my rent to pay this afternoon, and my landlord's awaiting below now.' Here the little woman rubbed her hands, and looked steadily over Mr Bob Sawyer's head, at the wall behind him.

'I am very sorry to put you to any inconvenience, Mrs Raddle,' said Bob Sawyer, deferentially, 'but –'

'Oh, it isn't any inconvenience,' replied the little woman, with a shrill titter. 'I didn't want it particular before today; leastways, as it has to go to my landlord directly, it was as well for you to keep it as me. You promised me this afternoon, Mr Sawyer, and every gentleman as has ever lived here, has kept his word, sir, as of course anybody as calls himself a gentleman, does.' Mrs Raddle tossed her head, bit her lips, rubbed her hands harder, and looked at the wall more steadily than ever. It was plain to see, as Mr Bob Sawyer remarked in a style of eastern allegory on a subsequent occasion, that she was 'getting the steam up'.

'I am very sorry, Mrs Raddle,' said Bob Sawyer with all imaginable humility, 'but the fact is, that I have been disappointed in the City to-day.' – Extraordinary place that City. An astonishing number of men always *are* getting disappointed there.

'Well, Mr Sawyer,' said Mrs Raddle, planting herself firmly on a purple cauliflower in the Kidderminster carpet, 'and what's that to me, sir?'

'I – I – have no doubt, Mrs Raddle,' said Bob Sawyer, blinking this last question, 'that before the middle of next week we shall be able to set outselves quite square, and go on, on a better system, afterwards.'

This was all Mrs Raddle wanted. She had bustled up to the apartment of the unlucky Bob Sawyer, so bent upon going into a passion, that, in all probability, payment would have rather disappointed her than otherwise. She was in excellent order for a little relaxation of the kind: having just exchanged a few introductory compliments with Mr R. in the front kitchen.

'Do you suppose, Mr Sawyer,' said Mrs Raddle, elevating her voice for the information of the neighbours, 'do you suppose that I'm a-going day after day to let a fellar occupy my lodgings as never thinks of paying his rent, nor even the very money laid out for the fresh butter and lump sugar that's bought for his breakfast, and the very milk that's took in, at the street door? Do you suppose a hard-working and industrious woman as has lived in this street for twenty year (ten year over the way, and nine year and three quarter in this very house) has nothing else to do but to work herself to death after a parcel of lazy idle fellars, that are always smoking and drinking, and lounging, when they ought to be glad to turn their hands to anything that would help 'em to pay their bills? Do you –'

'My good soul,' interposed Mr Benjamin Allen, soothingly.

'Have the goodness to keep your observashuns to yourself, I beg,' said Mrs Raddle, suddenly arresting the rapid torrent of her speech, and addressing the third party with impressive slowness and solemnity. 'I am not aweer, sir, that you have any right to address your conversation to me. I don't think I let these apartments to you, sir.'

'No, you certainly did not,' said Mr Benjamin Allen.

'Very good, sir,' responded Mrs Raddle, with lofty politeness. 'Then p'raps, sir, you'll confine yourself to breaking the arms and legs of the poor people in the hospitals, and keep yourself *to* yourself, sir, or there may be some persons here as will make you, sir.'

'But you are such an unreasonable woman,' remonstrated Mr Benjamin Allen.

'I beg your parding, young man,' said Mrs Raddle, in a cold perspiration of anger. 'But will you have the goodness just to call me that again, sir?'

'I didn't make use of the word in any invidious sense, ma'am,' replied Mr Benjamin Allen, growing somewhat uneasy on his own account.

'I beg your parding, young man,' demanded Mrs Raddle in a louder and more imperative tone. 'But who do you call a woman? Did you make that remark to me, sir?'

'Why, bless my heart!' said Mr Benjamin Allen.

'Did you apply that name to me, I ask of you, sir?' interrupted Mrs Raddle, with intense fierceness, throwing the door wide open.

'Why, of course I did,' replied Mr Benjamin Allen.

'Yes, of course you did,' said Mrs Raddle, backing gradually to the door, and raising her voice to its loudest pitch, for the special behoof of Mr Raddle in the kitchen. 'Yes, of course you did! And everybody knows that they may safely insult me in my own 'ouse while my husband sits sleeping down-stairs, and taking no more notice than if I was a dog in the streets. He ought to be ashamed of himself (here Mrs Raddle sobbed) to allow his wife to be treated in this way by a parcel of young cutters and carvers of live people's bodies, that disgraces the lodgings (another sob), and leaving her exposed to all manner of abuse; a base, faint-hearted, timorous wretch, that's afraid to come up-stairs, and face the ruffinly creatures – that's afraid – that's afraid to come!' Mrs Raddle paused to listen whether the repetition of the taunt had roused her better half; and, finding that it had not been successful, proceeded to descend the stairs with sobs innumerable: when there came a loud double knock at the street door: whereupon she burst into an hysterical fit of weeping, accompanied with dismal moans, which was prolonged until the knock had been repeated six times, when, in an uncontrollable burst of mental agony, she threw down all the umbrellas, and disappeared into the back parlour, closing the door after her with an awful crash.

'Does Mr Sawyer live here?' said Mr Pickwick, when the door was opened.

'Yes,' said the girl, 'first floor. It's the door straight afore you, when you gets to the top of the stairs.' Having given this instruction, the handmaid, who had been brought up among the aboriginal inhabitants of Southwark, disappeared, with the candle in her hand, down the kitchen stairs: perfectly satisfied that she had done everything that could possibly be required of her under the circumstances.

Mr Snodgrass, who entered last, secured the street door, after several ineffectual efforts, by putting up the chain; and the friends stumbled up-stairs, where they were received by Mr Bob Sawyer, who had been afraid to go down, lest he should be waylaid by Mrs Raddle.

'How are you?' said the discomfited student. 'Glad to see you, – take care of the glasses.' This caution was addressed to Mr Pickwick, who had put his hat in the tray.

'Dear me,' said Mr Pickwick, 'I beg your pardon.'

'Don't mention it, don't mention it,' said Bob Sawyer. 'I'm rather confined for room, here, but you must put up with all that, when you come to see a young bachelor. Walk in. You've seen this gentleman before, I think?' Mr Pickwick shook hands with Mr Benjamin Allen, and his friends followed his example. They had scarcely taken their seats when there was another double knock.

'I hope that's Jack Hopkins!' said Mr Bob Sawyer. 'Hush. Yes, it is. Come up, Jack; come up.'

A heavy footstep was heard upon the stairs, and Jack Hopkins presented himself. He wore a black velvet waistcoat, with thunder-and-lightning buttons; and a blue striped shirt, with a white false collar.

'You're late, Jack?' said Mr Benjamin Allen.

'Been detained at Bartholomew's,' replied Hopkins.

'Anything new?'

'No, nothing particular. Rather a good accident brought into the casualty ward.'

'What was that, sir?' inquired Mr Pickwick.

'Only a man fallen out of a four pair of stairs' window; – but it's a very fair case – very fair case indeed.'

'Do you mean that the patient is in a fair way to recover?' inquired Mr Pickwick.

'No,' replied Hopkins, carelessly. 'No, I should rather say he wouldn't. There must be a splendid operation though, to-morrow – magnificent sight if Slasher does it.'

'You consider Mr Slasher a good operator?' said Mr Pickwick.

'Best alive,' replied Hopkins. 'Took a boy's leg out of the socket last week – boy ate five apples and a ginger-bread cake – exactly two minutes after it was all over, boy said he wouldn't lie there to be made game of, and he'd tell his mother if they didn't begin.'

'Dear me!' said Mr Pickwick, astonished.

'Pooh! That's nothing, that ain't,' said Jack Hopkins. 'Is it, Bob?'

'Nothing at all,' replied Mr Bob Sawyer.

'By the bye, Bob,' said Hopkins, with a scarcely perceptible glance at Mr Pickwick's attentive face, 'we had a curious accident last night. A child was brought in, who had swallowed a necklace.'

'Swallowed what, sir?' interrupted Mr Pickwick.

'A necklace,' replied Jack Hopkins. 'Not all at once, you know, that would be too much – *you* couldn't swallow that, if the child did – eh, Mr Pickwick, ha! ha!' Mr Hopkins appeared highly gratified with his own pleasantry; and continued. 'No, the way was this. Child's parents were poor people who lived in a court. Child's eldest sister bought a necklace; common necklace, made of large black wooden beads. Child, being fond of toys, cribbed the necklace, hid it, played with it, cut the string, and swallowed a bead. Child thought it capital fun, went back next day, and swallowed another bead.'

'Bless my heart,' said Mr Pickwick, 'what a dreadful thing! I beg your pardon, sir. Go on.'

'Next day, child swallowed two beads; the day after that, he treated himself to three, and so on, till in a week's time he had got through the necklace – five-and-twenty beads in all. The sister, who was an industrious girl, and seldom treated herself to a bit of finery, cried her eyes out, at the loss of the necklace; looked high and low for it; but, I needn't say, didn't find it. A few days afterwards, the family were at dinner – baked shoulder of mutton, and potatoes under it – the child, who wasn't hungry, was playing about the room, when suddenly there was heard a devil of a noise, like a small hailstorm. 'Don't do that, my boy,' said the father. 'I ain't a doin' nothing,' said the child. 'Well, don't do it again,' said the father. There was a short silence, and then the noise began again, worse than ever. 'If you don't mind what I say, my boy,' said the father, 'you'll find yourself in bed, in something less than a pig's whisper.' He gave the child a shake to make him obedient, and such a rattling ensued as nobody ever heard before. 'Why, dam'me, it's *in* the child!' said the father, 'he's got the croup in the wrong place!' 'No I haven't, father,' said the child, beginning to cry, 'it's the necklace; I swallowed it, father.' – The father caught the child up, and ran with him to the hospital: the beads in the boy's stomach rattling all the way with the jolting; and the people looking up in the air, and down in the cellars, to see where the unusual sound came from. He's in the hospital now,' said Jack Hopkins, 'and he makes such a devil of a noise when he walks about, that they're obliged to muffle him in a watchman's coat, for fear he should wake the patients!'

'That's the most extraordinary case I ever heard of,' said Mr Pickwick, with an emphatic blow on the table.

'Oh, that's nothing,' said Jack Hopkins; 'is it, Bob?'

'Certainly not,' replied Bob Sawyer.

'Very singular things occur in our profession, I can assure you, sir,' said Hopkins.

'So I should be disposed to imagine,' replied Mr Pickwick. . . .

Shiftless students make ingenious doctors.

But, as the pavements of Bristol are not the widest or cleanest upon earth, so its streets are not altogether the straightest or least intricate; Mr Winkle, being greatly puzzled by their manifold windings and twistings, looked about him for a decent shop in which he could apply afresh, for counsel and instruction.

His eye fell upon a newly-painted tenement which had been recently converted into something between a shop and a private-house, and which a red lamp, projecting over the fan-light of the street-door, would have sufficiently announced as the residence of a medical practitioner, even if the word 'Surgery' had not been inscribed in golden characters on a wainscot ground, above the window of what, in times bygone, had been the front parlour. Thinking this an eligible place wherein to make his inquiries, Mr Winkle stepped into the little shop where the gilt-labelled drawers and bottles were; and finding nobody there, knocked with a half-crown on the counter, to attract the attention of anybody who might happen to be in the back parlour, which he judged to be the innermost and peculiar sanctum of the establishment, from the repetition of the word surgery on the door – painted in white letters this time, by way of taking off the monotony.

At the first knock, a sound, as of persons fencing with fire-irons, which had until now been very audible, suddenly ceased; at the second, a studious-looking young gentleman in green spectacles, with a very large book in his hand, glided quietly into the shop, and stepping behind the counter, requested to know the visitor's pleasure.

'I am sorry to trouble you, sir,' said Mr Winkle, 'but will you have the goodness to direct me to –'

'Ha! ha! ha!' roared the studious young gentleman, throwing the large book up into the air, and catching it with great dexterity at the very moment when it threatened to smash to atoms all the bottles on the counter. 'Here's a start!'

There was, without doubt; for Mr Winkle was so very much astonished at the extraordinary behaviour of the medical gentleman, that he involuntarily retreated towards the door, and looked very much disturbed at his strange reception.

'What, don't you know me?' said the medical gentleman.

Mr Winkle murmured, in reply, that he had not that pleasure.

'Why, then,' said the medical gentleman, 'there are hopes for me yet; I may attend half the old women in Bristol if I've decent luck. Get out, you mouldy old villain, get out!' With this adjuration, which was addressed to the large book, the medical gentleman kicked the volume with remarkable agility to the further end of the shop, and, pulling off his green spectacles, grinned the identical grin of Robert Sawyer, Esquire, formerly of Guy's Hospital in the Borough, with a private residence in Lant Street.

'You don't mean to say you weren't down upon me!' said Mr Bob Sawyer, shaking Mr Winkle's hand with friendly warmth.

'Upon my word I was not,' replied Mr Winkle, returning the pressure.

'I wonder you didn't see the name,' said Bob Sawyer, calling his friend's attention to the outer door, on which, in the same white paint, were traced the words 'Sawyer, late Nockemorf.'

'It never caught my eye,' returned Mr Winkle.

'Lord, if I had known who you were, I should have rushed out, and caught you in my arms,' said Bob Sawyer; 'but upon my life, I thought you were the King's-taxes.'

'No!' said Mr Winkle.

'I did, indeed,' responded Bob Sawyer, 'and I was just going to say that I wasn't at home, but if you'd leave a message I'd be sure to give it to myself; for he don't know me; no more does the Lighting and Paving. I think the Church-rates guesses who I am, and I know the Waterworks does, because I drew a tooth of his when I first came down here. But come in, come in!' Chattering in this way, Mr Bob Sawyer pushed Mr Winkle into the back room, where, amusing himself by boring little circular caverns in the chimney-piece with a red-hot poker, sat no less a person than Mr Benjamin Allen.

'Well!' said Mr Winkle. 'This is indeed a pleasure I did not expect. What a very nice place you have here!'

'Pretty well, pretty well,' replied Bob Sawyer. 'I *passed*, soon after that precious party, and my friends came down with the needful for this business; so I put on a black suit of clothes, and a pair of spectacles, and came here to look as solemn as I could.'

'And a very snug little business you have, no doubt?' said Mr Winkle, knowingly.

'Very,' replied Bob Sawyer. 'So snug, that at the end of a few years you might put all the profits in a wine glass, and cover 'em over with a gooseberry leaf.'

'You cannot surely mean that?' said Mr Winkle. 'The stock itself –'

'Dummies, my dear boy,' said Bob Sawyer; 'half the drawers have nothing in 'em, and the other half don't open.'

'Nonsense!' said Mr Winkle.

'Fact – honour!' returned Bob Sawyer, stepping out into the shop, and demonstrating the veracity of the assertion by divers hard pulls at the little gilt knobs on the counterfeit drawers. 'Hardly anything real in the shop but the leeches, and *they* are second-hand.'

'I shouldn't have thought it!' exclaimed Mr Winkle, much surprised.

'I hope not,' replied Bob Sawyer, 'else where's the use of appearances, eh? But what will you take? Do as we do? That's right. Ben, my fine fellow, put your hand into the cupboard, and bring out the patent digester.'

Mr Benjamin Allen smiled his readiness, and produced from the closet at his elbow a black bottle half full of brandy.

'You don't take water, of course?' said Bob Sawyer.

'Thank you,' replied Mr Winkle. 'It's *rather* early. I should like to qualify it, if you have no objection.'

'None in the least, if you can reconcile it to your conscience,' replied Bob Sawyer; tossing off, as he spoke, a glass of the liquor with great relish. 'Ben, the pipkin!'

Mr Benjamin Allen drew forth, from the same hiding-place, a small brass pipkin, which Bob Sawyer observed he prided himself upon, particularly because it looked so business-like. The water in the professional pipkin having been made to boil, in course of time, by various little shovelsfull of coal, which Mr Bob Sawyer took out of a practicable window-seat, labelled 'Soda Water,' Mr Winkle adulterated his brandy; and the conversation was becoming general when it was interrupted by the entrance into the shop of a boy, in a sober grey livery and a gold-laced hat, with a small covered basket under his arm: whom Mr Bob Sawyer immediately hailed with, 'Tom, you vagabond, come here.'

The boy presented himself accordingly.

'You've been stopping to over all the posts in Bristol, you idle young scamp!' said Mr Bob Sawyer.

'No, sir, I haven't,' replied the boy.

'You had better not!' said Mr Bob Sawyer, with a threatening aspect. 'Who do you suppose will ever employ a professional man, when they see his boy playing at marbles in the gutter, or flying the garter in the horse-road? Have you no feeling for your profession, you groveller? Did you leave all the medicine?'

'Yes, sir.'

'The powders for the child, at the large house with the new family, and the pills to be taken four times a day at the ill-tempered old gentleman's with the gouty leg?'

'Yes, sir.'

'Then shut the door, and mind the shop.'

'Come,' said Mr Winkle, as the boy retired, 'things are not quite so bad as you would have me believe, either. There is *some* medicine to be sent out.'

Mr Bob Sawyer peeped into the shop to see that no stranger was within hearing, and leaning forward to Mr Winkle, said, in a low tone:

'He leaves it all at the wrong houses.'

Mr Winkle looked perplexed, and Bob Sawyer and his friend laughed.

'Don't you see?' said Bob. 'He goes up to a house, rings the area bell, pokes a packet of medicine without a direction into the servant's hand,

and walks off. Servant takes it into the dining-parlour; master opens it, and reads the label: "Draught to be taken at bed-time – pills as before – lotion as usual – *the* powder. From Sawyer's, late, Nockemorf's. Physicians' prescriptions carefully prepared," and all the rest of it. Shows it to his wife – *she* reads the label; it goes down to the servants – *they* read the label. Next day, boy calls: "Very sorry – his mistake – immense business – great many parcels to deliver – Mr Sawyer's compliments – late Nockemorf." The name gets known, and that's the thing, my boy, in the medical way. Bless your heart, old fellow, it's better than all the advertising in the world. We have got one four-ounce bottle that's been to half the houses in Bristol, and hasn't done yet.'

'Dear me, I see,' observed Mr Winkle; 'what an excellent plan!'

'Oh, Ben and I have hit upon a dozen such,' replied Bob Sawyer, with great glee. 'The lamplighter has eighteen-pence a week to pull the night-bell for ten minutes every time he comes round; and my boy always rushes into church, just before the psalms, when the people have got nothing to do but look about 'em, and calls me out, with horror and dismay depicted on his countenance. "Bless my soul," everybody says, "somebody taken suddenly ill! Sawyer, late Nockemorf, sent for. What a business that young man has!"'

At the termination of this disclosure of some of the mysteries of medicine, Mr Bob Sawyer and his friend, Ben Allen, threw themselves back in their respective chairs, and laughed boisterously.

(1836–37)

On 21 October 1854 Florence Nightingale sailed from Dover for Scutari with thirty-nine women, most of whom she later described as 'too old, weak, drunken, dirty, thick-witted or dishonest to be anything else but nurses'. The nurse's job was despised below the activities of household maids who emptied their masters' chamber-pots and slop-buckets. She was an occasional servant, hired for lying-in and laying-out, a woman usefully hardened against the mess and indelicacy of the illnesses which struck mankind in between these two events. Sara Gamp was shortly killed off in St Thomas's Hospital School for Nurses by Miss Nightingale, who recreated the nurse to be as respectable as the governess, and who thought Dickens a sentimentalist.

From Martin Chuzzlewit

Mr Pecksniff had been to the undertaker, and was now upon his way to another officer in the train of mourning: a female functionary, a nurse, and watcher, and performer of nameless offices about the persons of the dead: whom he had recommended. Her name, as Mr Pecksniff gathered from a scrap of writing in his hand, was Gamp; her residence in Kingsgate Street, High Holborn. So Mr Pecksniff, in a hackney cab, was rattling over Holborn stones, in quest of Mrs Gamp.

This lady lodged at a bird-fancier's, next door but one to the celebrated mutton-pie shop, and directly opposite to the original cat's-meat warehouse; the renown of which establishments was duly heralded on their respective fronts. It was a little house, and this was the more convenient; for Mrs Gamp being, in her highest walk of art, a monthly nurse, or, as her sign-board boldly had it, 'Midwife,' and lodging in the first-floor front, was easily assailable at night by pebbles, walking-sticks, and fragments of tobacco-pipe: all much more efficacious than the street-door knocker, which was so constructed as to wake the street with ease, and even spread alarms of fire in Holborn, without making the smallest impression on the premises to which it was addressed.

It chanced on this particular occasion, that Mrs Gamp had been up all the previous night, in attendance upon a ceremony to which the usage of gossips has given that name which expresses, in two syllables, the curse pronounced on Adam. It chanced that Mrs Gamp had not been regularly engaged, but had been called in at a crisis, in consequence of her great repute, to assist another professional lady with her advice; and thus it happened that, all points of interest in the case being over, Mrs Gamp had come home again to the bird-fancier's, and gone to bed. So, when Mr Pecksniff drove up in the hackney cab, Mrs Gamp's curtains were drawn close, and Mrs Gamp was fast asleep behind them.

If the bird-fancier had been at home, as he ought to have been, there would have been no great harm in this; but he was out, and his shop was closed. The shutters were down certainly; and in every pane of glass there was at least one tiny bird in a tiny bird-cage, twittering and hopping his little ballet of despair, and knocking his head against the roof: while one unhappy goldfinch, who lived outside a red villa with his name on the door, drew the water for his own drinking, and mutely appealed to some good man to drop a farthing's worth of poison in it. Still, the door was shut. Mr Pecksniff tried the latch, and shook it, causing a cracked bell inside to ring most mournfully; but no one came. The bird-fancier was an easy shaver also, and a fashionable hair-dresser also; and perhaps he had been sent for, express, from the court end of the town, to trim a lord, or cut and curl a lady; but however that might be, there, upon his own ground, he was not; nor was there any more distinct trace of him to assist the imagination of an inquirer, than a professional print or emblem of his calling (much favoured in the trade), representing a hair-dresser of easy manners curling a lady of distinguished fashion, in the presence of a patent upright grand pianoforte.

Noting these circumstances, Mr Pecksniff, in the innocence of his heart, applied himself to the knocker; but at the first double knock, every window in the street became alive with female heads; and before he could repeat the performance, whole troops of married ladies (some about to trouble Mrs Gamp themselves, very shortly) came flocking round the steps, all crying out with one accord, and with uncommon interest, 'Knock at the winder, sir, knock at the winder. Lord bless you, don't lose no more time than you can help; knock at the winder!'

Acting upon this suggestion, and borrowing the driver's whip for the purpose, Mr Pecksniff soon made a commotion among the first-floor flower-pots, and roused Mrs Gamp, whose voice – to the great satisfaction of the matrons – was heard to say, 'I'm coming.'

'He's as pale as a muffin,' said one lady, in allusion to Mr Pecksniff.

'So he ought to be, if he's the feelings of a man,' observed another.

A third lady (with her arms folded) said she wished he had chosen any other time for fetching Mrs Gamp, but it always happened so with *her*.

It gave Mr Pecksniff much uneasiness to find, from these remarks, that he was supposed to have come to Mrs Gamp upon an errand touching – not the close of life, but the other end. Mrs Gamp herself was under the same impression, for, throwing open the window, she cried behind the curtains, as she hastily attired herself:

'Is it Mrs Perkins?'

'No!' returned Mr Pecksniff, sharply. 'Nothing of the sort.'

'What, Mr Whilks!' cried Mrs Gamp. 'Don't say it's you, Mr Whilks, and that poor creetur Mrs Whilks with not even a pincushion ready. Don't say it's you, Mr Whilks!'

'It isn't Mr Whilks,' said Pecksniff. 'I don't know the man. Nothing of the kind. A gentleman is dead; and some person being wanted in the house, you have been recommended by Mr Mould the undertaker.'

As she was by this time in a condition to appear, Mrs Gamp, who had a face for all occasions, looked out of the window with her mourning countenance, and said she would be down directly. But the matrons took it very ill, that Mr Pecksniff's mission was of so unimportant a kind; and the lady with her arms folded rated him in good round terms, signifying that she would be glad to know what he meant by terrifying delicate females 'with his corpses'; and giving it as her opinion that he was quite ugly enough to know better. The other ladies were not at all behind-hand in expressing similar sentiments; and the children, of whom some scores had now collected, hooted and defied Mr Pecksniff quite savagely. So, when Mrs Gamp appeared, the unoffending gentleman was glad to hustle her with very little ceremony into the cabriolet, and drive off, overwhelmed with popular execration.

Mrs Gamp had a large bundle with her, a pair of pattens, and a species of gig umbrella; the latter article in colour like a faded leaf, except where a circular patch of a lively blue had been dexterously let in at the top. She was much flurried by the haste she had made, and laboured under the most erroneous views of cabriolets, which she appeared to confound with mail-coaches or stage-waggons, inasmuch as she was constantly endeavouring for the first half mile to force her luggage through the little front window, and clamouring to the driver to 'put it in the boot.' When she was disabused of this idea, her whole being resolved itself into an absorbing anxiety about her pattens, with which she played innumerable games at quoits, on Mr Pecksniff's legs. It was not until they were close upon the house of mourning that she had enough composure to observe:

'And so the gentleman's dead, sir! Ah! The more's the pity.' She didn't even know his name. 'But it's what we must all come to. It's as certain as being born, except that we can't make our calculations as exact. Ah! Poor dear!'

She was a fat old woman, this Mrs Gamp, with a husky voice and a moist eye, which she had a remarkable power of turning up, and only showing the white of it. Having very little neck, it cost her some trouble to look over herself, if one may say so, at those to whom she talked. She wore a very rusty black gown, rather the worse for snuff, and a shawl and bonnet to correspond. In these dilapidated articles of dress she had, on principle, arrayed herself, time out of mind, on such occasions as the present; for this at once expressed a decent amount of veneration for the deceased, and invited the next of kin to present her with a fresher suit of weeds: an appeal so frequently successful, that the very fetch and ghost of Mrs Gamp, bonnet and all, might be seen hanging up, any hour in the day, in at least a dozen of the second-hand clothes shops about Holborn. The face of Mrs Gamp – the nose in particular – was somewhat red and swollen, and it was difficult to enjoy her society without becoming conscious of a smell of spirits. Like most persons who have attained to great eminence in their profession, she took to hers very kindly; insomuch, that setting aside her natural predilections as a woman, she went to a lying-in or a laying-out with equal zest and relish.

'Ah!' repeated Mrs Gamp; for it was always a safe sentiment in cases of mourning. 'Ah dear! When Gamp was summoned to his long home, and I see him a-lying in Guy's Hospital with a penny-piece on each eye, and his wooden leg under his left arm, I thought I should have fainted away. But I bore up.'

If certain whispers current in the Kingsgate Street circles had any truth in them, she had indeed borne up surprisingly; and had exerted such uncommon fortitude, as to dispose of Mr Gamp's remains for the benefit of science. But it should be added, in fairness, that this had happened twenty years before; and that Mr and Mrs Gamp had long been separated, on the ground of incompatibility of temper in their drink.

'You have become indifferent since then, I suppose?' said Mr Pecksniff. 'Use is second nature, Mrs Gamp.'

'You may well say second nater, sir,' returned that lady. 'One's first ways is to find sich things a trial to the feelings, and so is one's lasting custom. If it wasn't for the nerve a little sip of liquor gives me (I never was able to do more than taste it), I never could go through with what I sometimes has to do. "Mrs Harris," I says, at the very last case as ever I acted in, which it was but a young person, "Mrs Harris," I says, "leave the bottle on the chimney-piece, and don't ask me to take none, but let me put my lips to it when I am so dispoged, and then I will do what I'm engaged to do, according to the best of my ability." "Mrs Gamp," she says, in answer, "if ever there was a sober creetur to be got at eighteen pence a day for working people, and three and six for gentlefolks – night watching,"' said Mrs Gamp, with emphasis, '"being a extra charge – you are that inwallable person." "Mrs Harris," I says to her, "don't name the charge, for if I could afford to lay all my feller creeturs out for nothink, I would gladly do it, sich is the love I bears 'em. But what I always says to them as has the management of matters, Mrs Harris:"' here she kept her eye on Mr Pecksniff: '"be they gents or be they ladies, is, don't ask me whether I won't take none, or whether I will, but leave the bottle on the chimney-piece, and let me put my lips to it when I am so dispoged."'

The conclusion of this affecting narrative brought them to the house. In the passage they encountered Mr Mould the undertaker: a little elderly gentleman, bald, and in a suit of black; with a note-book in his hand, a massive gold watch-chain dangling from his fob, and a face in which a queer attempt at melancholy was at odds with a smirk of satisfaction; so that he looked as a man might, who, in the very act of smacking his lips over choice old wine, tried to make believe it was physic.

'Well, Mrs Gamp, and how are *you*, Mrs Gamp?' said this gentleman, in a voice as soft as his step.

'Pretty well, I thank you, sir,' dropping a curtsey.

'You'll be very particular here, Mrs Gamp. This is not a common case, Mrs Gamp. Let everything be very nice and comfortable, Mrs Gamp, if you please,' said the undertaker, shaking his head with a solemn air.

'It shall be, sir,' she replied, curtseying again. 'You knows me of old, sir, I hope.'

'I hope so, too, Mrs Gamp,' said the undertaker; 'and I think so, also.' Mrs Gamp curtseyed again. 'This is one of the most impressive cases, sir,' he continued, addressing Mr Pecksniff, 'that I have seen in the whole course of my professional experience.'

'Indeed, Mr Mould!' cried that gentleman.

'Such affectionate regret, sir, I never saw. There is no limitation, there is positively NO limitation:' opening his eyes wide, and standing on tiptoe: 'in point of expense! I have orders, sir! to put on my whole establishment of mutes; and mutes come very dear, Mr Pecksniff; not to mention their drink. To provide silver-plated handles of the very best description, ornamented with angels' heads from the most expensive dies. To be perfectly profuse in feathers. In short, sir, to turn out something absolutely gorgeous.'

'My friend Mr Jonas [Jonas Chuzzlewit, the corpse's son] is an excellent man,' said Mr Pecksniff.

'I have seen a good deal of what is filial in my time, sir,' retorted Mould, 'and what is unfilial too. It is our lot. We come into the knowledge of those secrets. But anything so filial as this; anything so honourable to human nature; so calculated to reconcile all of us to the world we live in; never yet came under my observation. It only proves, sir, what was so forcibly observed by the lamented theatrical poet – buried at Stratford – that there is good in everything.'

(1843–44)

ANTHONY TROLLOPE

The Victorian grave was a conspicuous consumer. How enjoyably solemn, the panoply of the pall! Black horses tossing sable plumes, engraved-glass showcase hearses, black crape weepers trailing from black silk hats, the widow veiled profusely in black muslin, the crafted gloom of the mutes, the laurels and lilies, new black cotton gloves all round, the cold buffet and port. Before the technology of mass-entertainment, life and death had to provide their own.

Death in Dickens is dramatic. New Yorkers crammed a Manhattan pier in 1841, shouting at an incoming steamer cargoed with the latest episode of *Old Curiosity Shop* to discover if Little Nell had gone. Anthony Trollope (1815–82) was unfashionably as unexcitable about death as Shakespeare. The death of terrifying Mrs Proudie, wife of the Bishop of Barchester, is as casual as Polonius's end behind the arras.

And as unpremeditated. While *The Last Chronicle of Barset* was running in *Cornhill* magazine in 1867, Trollope was undergoing his daily self-punishment of words in the Athenaeum Club in Pall Mall. Against the steady scratching of his pen, two unobservant clerics were expressing, across the fireplace, their weariness towards the whole diocese of Barset's recurrent characters. One clergyman contemptuously belittled Mrs Proudie. Trollope rose irritably from the writing-table. 'I am her author,' he confounded the startled pair. 'If you do not care for Mrs Proudie, very well. I shall dispose of her within the week.' He clapped on his hat and took a hansom to his other club, the Garrick, by Leicester Square, where he settled himself down again and killed her.

In *The Last Chronicle*, Mr Crawley, the difficult perpetual curate of Hogglestock, is committed on bail by Silverbridge magistrates for trial at Barchester assizes for stealing a £20 cheque (he was not guilty). Mrs Proudie wishes to settle his hash by dispatching Mr Thumble from the Palace to take over the church services and clerical duties of Hogglestock. The monumentally henpecked Bishop dares for once to object. Mr Thumble goes to Hogglestock.

Mrs Proudie is an interesting case of cadaveric spasm. This is a rigidity which sometimes grips the body at the instant of death, a spasm which makes murderers clasp their guns and fallen soldiers still to sight their rifles. Dr Filgrave had, strictly, no professional obligation to share with the Bishop his diagnosis of Mrs Proudie's cardiac condition, nor to impart plainly his depressing prognosis. Perhaps he felt that, as he could do nothing to treat her complaint, it was best not to fuss over it. It is odd that the Bishop seemingly did not recognise his wife's illness. Perhaps he felt guilty at acknowledging so wicked a friend.

From The Last Chronicle of Barset

SOME HOUR OR two before Mr Thumble's return Mrs Proudie returned to her husband, thinking it better to let him know what she had done. She resolved to be very firm with him, but at the same time she determined not to use harsh language, if it could be avoided. 'My dear,' she said, 'I have arranged with Mr Thumble.' She found him on this occasion sitting at his desk with papers before him, with a pen in his hand; and she could see at a glance that nothing had been written on the paper. What would she have thought had she known that when he placed the sheet before him he was proposing to consult the archbishop as to the propriety of his resignation! He had not, however, progressed so far as to write even the date of his letter.

'You have done what?' said he, throwing down the pen.

'I have arranged with Mr Thumble as to going out to Hogglestock,' said she firmly. 'Indeed he has gone already.' Then the bishop jumped up from his seat, and rang the bell with violence. 'What are you going to do?' said Mrs Proudie.

'I am gong to depart from here,' said he. 'I will not stay here to be the mark of scorn for all men's fingers. I will resign the diocese.'

'You cannot do that,' said the wife.

'I can try, at any rate,' said he. Then the servant entered. 'John,' said he, addressing the man, 'let Mr Thumble know the moment he returns to the palace that I wish to see him here. Perhaps he may not come to the palace. In that case let word be sent to his house.'

Mrs Proudie allowed the man to go before she addressed her husband again. 'What do you mean to say to Mr Thumble when you see him?'

'That is nothing to you.'

She came up to him and put her hand upon his shoulder, and spoke to him very gently. 'Tom,' she said, 'is that the way in which you speak to your wife?'

'Yes, it is. You have driven me to it. Why have you taken upon yourself to send that man to Hogglestock?'

'Because it was right to do so. I came to you for instructions, and you would give none.'

'I should have given what instructions I pleased in proper time. Thumble shall not go to Hogglestock next Sunday.'

'Who shall go, then?'

'Never mind. Nobody. It does not matter to you. If you will leave me now I shall be obliged to you. There will be an end of all this very soon, – very soon.'

Mrs Proudie after this stood for a while thinking what she would say; but she left the room without uttering another word. As she looked at him a hundred different thoughts came into her mind. She had loved him dearly, and she loved him still; but she knew now, – at this moment felt absolutely sure, – that by him she was hated! In spite of all her roughness and temper, Mrs Proudie was in this like other women, – that she would fain have been loved had it been possible. She had always meant to serve him. She was conscious of that! conscious also in a way that, although she had been industrious, although she had been faithful, although she was clever, yet she had failed. At the bottom of her heart she knew that she had been a bad wife. And yet she had meant to be a pattern wife! She had meant to be a good Christian; but she had so exercised her Christianity that not a soul in the world loved her, or would endure her presence if it could be avoided! She had sufficient insight to the minds and feelings of those around her to be aware of this. And now her husband had told her that her tyranny to him was so overbearing that he must throw up his great position, and retire to an obscurity that would be exceptionally disgraceful to them both, because he could no longer endure the public disgrace which her conduct brought upon him in his high place before the world! Her heart was too full for speech; and she left him, very quietly closing the door behind her.

She was preparing to go up to her chamber, with her hand on the banisters and with her foot on the stairs, when she saw the servant who had answered the bishop's bell. 'John,' she said, 'when Mr Thumble comes to the palace, let me see him before he goes to my lord.'

'Yes, ma'am,' said John, who well understood the nature of these quarrels between his master and his mistress. But the commands of the mistress were still paramount among the servants, and John proceeded on his mission with the view of accomplishing Mrs Proudie's behests. Then Mrs Proudie went upstairs to her chamber, and locked her door.

Mr Thumble returned to Barchester that day, leading the broken-down cob; and a dreadful walk he had. He was not good at walking, and before he came near Barchester had come to entertain a violent hatred for the beast he was leading. The leading of a horse that is tired, or in pain, or lame, or even stiff in his limbs, is not pleasant work. The brute will not accommodate his paces to the man, and will contrive to make his head very heavy on the bridle. And he will not walk on the part of the road which the man intends for him, but will lean against the man, and will make himself altogether very disagreeable. It may be understood, therefore, that Mr Thumble was not in a good humour when he entered the palace yard. Nor was he altogether quiet in his mind as to the injury which he had done to the animal. 'It was the brute's fault,' said Mr Thumble. 'It comes generally of not knowing how to ride 'em,' said the groom. For Mr Thumble, though he often had a horse out of the episcopal stables, was not ready with his shillings to the man who waited upon him with the steed.

He had not, however, come to any satisfactory understanding respecting the broken knees when the footman from the palace told him he was wanted. It was in vain that Mr Thumble pleaded that he was nearly dead with fatigue, that he had walked all the way from Hogglestock and must go home to change his clothes. John was peremptory with him, insisting that he must wait first upon Mrs Proudie and then upon the bishop. Mr Thumble might perhaps have turned a deaf ear to the latter command, but the former was one which he felt himself bound to obey. So he entered the palace, rather cross, very much soiled as to his outer man; and in this condition went up a certain small staircase which was familiar to him, to a small parlour which adjoined Mrs Proudie's room, and there awaited the arrival of the lady. That he should be required to wait some quarter of an hour was not surprising to him; but when half an hour was gone, and he remembered himself of his own wife at home, and of the dinner which he had not yet eaten, he ventured to ring the bell. Mrs Proudie's own maid, Mrs Draper by name, came to him and said that she had knocked twice at Mrs Proudie's door, and would knock again. Two minutes after that she returned, running into the room with her arms extended, and exclaiming, 'Oh, heavens, sir; mistress is dead!' Mr Thumble, hardly knowing what he was about, followed the woman into the bedroom, and there he found himself standing awestruck before the corpse of her who had so lately been the presiding spirit of the palace.

The body was still resting on its legs, leaning against the end of the side of the bed, while one of the arms was close clasped round the bed-post. The mouth was rigidly close, but the eyes were open as though staring at him. Nevertheless there could be no doubt from the first glance that the woman was dead. He went up close to it, but did not dare to touch it. There was no one as yet there but he and Mrs Draper; – no one else knew what had happened.

'It's her heart,' said Mrs Draper.

'Did she suffer from heart-complaint?' he asked.

'We suspected it, sir, though nobody knew it. She was very shy of talking about herself.'

'We must send for the doctor at once,' said Mr Thumble. 'We had better touch nothing till he is here.' Then they retreated and the door was locked.

In ten minutes everybody in the house knew it except the bishop; and in twenty minutes the nearest apothecary with his assistant were in the room, and the body had been properly laid upon the bed. Even then the husband had not been told, – did not know either his relief or his loss. It was now past seven, which was the usual hour for dinner at the palace, and it was probable that he would come out of his room among the servants, if he were not summoned. When it was proposed to Mr Thumble that he should go in to him and tell him, he positively declined, saying that the sight which he had just seen and the exertions of the day together, had so unnerved him, that he had not physical strength for the task. The apothecary, who had been summoned in a hurry, had escaped, probably being equally unwilling to be the bearer of such a communication. The duty therefore fell to Mrs Draper, and under the pressing instance of the other servants she descended to her master's room. Had it not been that the hour of dinner had come, so that the bishop could not have been left much longer to himself, the evil time would have been still postponed.

She went very slowly along the passage, and was just going to pause ere she reached the room, when the door was opened and the bishop stood close before her. It was easy to be seen that he was cross. His hands and face were unwashed and his face was haggard. In these days he would not even go through the ceremony of dressing himself before dinner. 'Mrs Draper,' he said, 'why don't they tell me that dinner is ready? Are they going to give me any dinner?' She stood a moment without answering him, while the tears streamed down her face. 'What is the matter?' said he. 'Has your mistress sent you here?'

'Oh, laws!' said Mrs Draper, – and she put out her hands to support him if such support should be necessary.

'What is the matter?' he demanded angrily.

'Oh, my lord; – bear it like a Christian. Mistress isn't no more.' He leaned back against the door-post, and she took hold of him by the arm. 'It was the heart, my lord. Dr Filgrave hisself has not been yet; but that's what it was.' The bishop did not say a word, but walked back to his chair before the fire. . . .

He saw Dr Filgrave twice, both before and after the doctor had been upstairs. There was no doubt, Dr Filgrave said, that it was as Mrs Draper had surmised. The poor lady was suffering, and had for years been suffering, from heart-complaint. To her husband she had never said a word on the subject. To Mrs Draper a word had been said now and again, – a word when some moment of fear would come, when some sharp stroke of agony would tell of danger. But Mrs Draper had kept the secret of her mistress, and none of the family had known that there was aught to be feared. Dr Filgrave, indeed, did tell the bishop that he had dreaded all along exactly that which had happened. He had said the same to Mr Rerechild, the surgeon, when they two had had a consultation together at the palace on the occasion of a somewhat alarming birth of a grandchild. But he mixed up this information with so much medical Latin, and was so pompous over it, and the bishop was so anxious to be rid of him, that his words did not have much effect. What did it all matter? The thorn was gone, and the wife was dead, and the widower must balance his gain and loss as best he might.

(1866–67)

Queenie Leavis saw *The Symbolic Function of the Doctor in Victorian Novels* as 'either wise family friend or humorously as a self-important old humbug'. She discerned: 'He was necessarily outside class, privileged to tell the truth to the upper classes and handle them impartially, frequently having to be let into secrets not even revealed to the family lawyer.'

Trollope had not got the measure of doctors as he had of clerics, but doctors then were less regimented and less important. His GPs are amusing old codgers like Dr Filgrave, who in *Dr Thorne* nine years earlier was Dr Fillgrave (prolific authors cannot be pernickety). Dr Fillgrave was 'five feet five; and he had a little round abdominal protuberance, which an inch and a half added to the heels of his boots hardly enabled him to carry off as well as he himself would have wished . . . the great feature of his face was his mouth. The amount of secret medical knowledge of which he could give assurance by the pressure of those lips was truly wonderful.' A persistent medical tic. Dr Filgrave made £6,000 a year out of Barchester.

Dr Thorne himself was emphatically different, 'proud, arrogant, contradictory, headstrong'. The decoration on the mantelpiece of his den was a child's skull, and during a contentious conversation with the grand Lady Arabella – it was about the ponderous amours of the younger characters – he toyed idly with a pair of adult femurs. When their exchanges of anguished politeness grew warmer, 'he began to walk about, still holding the two bones like a pair of dumb-bells'. Like George Eliot's Dr Lydgate, Dr Thorne felt himself superior to the values of the everyday drawing-room. He had a weakness for large mugs of tea.

Dr Thorne is Trollope's most genial and sporadically humorous book. The Countess de Courcey foreshadows Lady Bracknell: 'Degree!' she crushes a nephew opting for pursuing his studies instead of an heiress. 'Why, Frank, I am talking to you of your prospects in life, of your future position, of that on which everything hangs, and you tell me of your degree!' Frank is a cheerful, Bertie Woosterish, Cambridge undergraduate in love with Dr Thorne's penniless niece Mary, who is the heiress – which is entirely unknown all round, remember this is Trollope – of the alcoholic, self-made millionaire baronet Sir Roger Scatcherd, who is a difficult patient. Sir Roger 'had been making a week of it', after landing the contract for cutting the Panama Canal (presciently, twenty-two years before de Lesseps did).

From Doctor Thorne

'WHY DO YOU take it then? Why do you do it? Your life is not like his. Oh, Scatcherd! Scatcherd!' and the doctor prepared to pour out the flood of his eloquence in beseeching this singular man to abstain from his well-known poison.

'Is that all you know of human nature, doctor? Abstain. Can you abstain from breathing, and live like a fish does under water?'

'But Nature has not ordered you to drink, Scatcherd.'

'Habit is second nature, man; and a stronger nature than the first. And why should I not drink? What else has the world given me for all that I have done for it? What other resource have I? What other gratification?'

'Oh, my God! Have you not unbounded wealth? Can you not do anything you wish? be anything you choose?'

'No,' and the sick man shrieked with an energy that made him audible all through the house. 'I can do nothing that I would choose to do; be nothing that I would wish to be! What can I do? What can I be? What gratification can I have except the brandy bottle? If I go among gentlemen, can I talk to them? If they have anything to say about a railway, they will ask me a question: if they speak to me beyond that, I must be dumb. If I go among my workmen, can they talk to me? No; I am their master, and a stern master. They bob their heads and shake in their shoes when they see me. Where are my friends? Here!' said he, and he dragged a bottle from under his very pillow. 'Where are my amusements? Here!' and he brandished the bottle almost in the doctor's face. 'Where is my one resource, my one gratification, my only comfort after all my toils? Here, doctor; here, here, here!' and, so saying, he replaced his treasure beneath his pillow.

There was something so horrifying in this, that Dr Thorne shrank back amazed, and was for a moment unable to speak. . . .

Sir Roger impulsively sends for Dr Fillgrave instead.

When Dr Fillgrave was first shown into Sir Roger's dining-room, he walked up and down the room for a while with easy, jaunty step, with his hands joined together behind his back, calculating the price of the furniture, and counting the heads which might be adequately entertained in a room of such noble proportions; but in seven or eight minutes an air of impatience might have been seen to suffuse his face. Why could he not be shown up into the sick man's room? What necessity could there be for keeping him there, as though he were some apothecary with a box of leeches in his pocket? He then rang the bell, perhaps a little violently. 'Does Sir Roger know that I am here?' he said to the servant. 'I'll tell my lady,' said the man, again vanishing.

For five minutes more he walked up and down, calculating no longer the value of the furniture, but rather that of his own importance. He was not wont to be kept waiting in this way; and though Sir Roger Scatcherd was at present a great and a rich man, Dr Fillgrave had remembered him a very small and a very poor man. He now began to think of Sir Roger as the stone-mason, and to chafe somewhat more violently at being so kept by such man.

When one is impatient, five minutes is as the duration of all time, and a quarter of an hour is eternity. At the end of twenty minutes the step of Dr Fillgrave up and down the room had become very quick, and he had just made up his mind that he would not stay there all day to the serious detriment, perhaps fatal injury, of his other expectant patients. His hand was again on the bell, and was about to be used with vigour, when the door opened and Lady Scatcherd entered.

The door opened and Lady Scatcherd entered; but she did so very slowly, as though she were afraid to come into her own dining-room. We must go back a little and see how she had been employed during those twenty minutes.

'Oh, laws!' Such had been her first exclamation on hearing that the doctor was in the dining-room. She was standing at the time with her housekeeper in a small room in which she kept her linen and jam, and in which, in company with the same housekeeper, she spent the happiest moments of her life.

'Oh laws! now, Hannah, what shall we do?'

'Send 'un up at once to the master, my lady! let John take 'un up.'

'There'll be such a row in the house, Hannah; I know there will.'

'But sure-ly didn't he send for 'un? Let the master have the row himself, then; that's what I'd do, my lady,' added Hannah, seeing that her ladyship still stood trembling in doubt, biting her thumbnail.

'You couldn't go up to the master yourself, could you now, Hannah?' said Lady Scatcherd in her most persuasive tone.

'Why, no,' said Hannah, after a little deliberation; 'no, I'm afeard I couldn't.'

'Then I must just face it myself.' And up went the wife to tell her lord that the physician for whom he had sent had come to attend his bidding.

In the interview which then took place the baronet had not indeed been violent, but he had been very determined. Nothing on earth, he said, should induce him to see Dr Fillgrave and offend his dear old friend Thorne.

'But, Roger,' said her ladyship, half-crying, or rather pretending to cry in her vexation, 'what shall I do with the man? How shall I get him out of the house?'

'Put him under the pump,' said the baronet; and he laughed his peculiar low guttural laugh, which told so plainly of the havoc which brandy had made in his throat.

'That's nonsense, Roger; you know I can't put him under the pump. Now you are ill, and you'd better see him just for five minutes. I'l make it all right with Dr Thorne.'

'I'd be d— if I do, my lady.' All the people about Boxall Hill called poor Lady Scatcherd 'my lady,' as if there was some excellent joke in it; and so, indeed, there was.

'You know you needn't mind nothing he says, nor yet take nothing he sends: and I'll tell him not to come no more. Now do 'ee see him, Roger.'

But there was no coaxing Roger over now, or indeed ever: he was a wilful, headstrong, masterful man; a tyrant always, though never a cruel one, and accustomed to rule his wife and household as despotically as he did his gangs of workmen. Such men it is not easy to coax over.

'You go down and tell him I don't want him, and won't see him, and that's an end of it. If he chose to earn his money why didn't he come yesterday when he was sent for? I'm well now and don't want him; and what's more, I won't have him. Winterbones [his confidential clerk, also a drunkard], lock the door.'

So Winterbones, who during this interview had been at work at his little table, got up to lock the door, and Lady Scatcherd had no alternative but to pass through it before the last edict was obeyed.

Lady Scatcherd, with slow step, went downstairs and again sought counsel with Hannah, and the two, putting their heads together, agreed that the only cure for the present evil was to be found in a good fee. So Lady Scatcherd, with a five-pound note in her hand, and trembling in every limb, went forth to encounter the august presence of Dr Fillgrave.

As the door opened, Dr Fillgrave dropped the bell-rope which was in his hand, and bowed low to the lady. Those who knew the doctor well would have known from his bow that he was not well pleased; it was as much as though he said, 'Lady Scatcherd, I am your most obedient humble servant; at any rate it appears that it is your pleasure to treat me as such.'

Lady Scatcherd did not understand all this; but she perceived at once that the man was angry.

'I hope Sir Roger does not find himself worse,' said the doctor. 'The morning is getting on; shall I step up and see him?'

'Hem! ha! oh! Why, you see, Dr Fillgrave, Sir Roger finds hisself vastly better this morning, vastly so.'

'I'm very glad to hear it, very; but as the morning is getting on, shall I step up to see Sir Roger?'

'Why, Dr Fillgrave, sir, you see, he finds hisself so much hisself this morning, that he a'most thinks it would be a shame to trouble you.'

'A shame to trouble me!' This was a sort of shame which Dr Fillgrave did not at all comprehend. 'A shame to trouble me! Why, Lady Scatcherd –'

Lady Scatcherd saw that she had nothing for it but to make the whole matter intelligible. Moreover, seeing that she appreciated more thoroughly the smallness of Dr Fillgrave's person than she did the peculiar greatness of his demeanour, she began to be a shade less afraid of him than she had thought she should have been.

'Yes, Dr Fillgrave; you see, when a man like he gets well, he can't abide the idea of doctors: now yesterday, he was all for sending for you; but today he comes to hisself, and don't seem to want no doctor at all.'

Then did Dr Fillgrave seem to grow out of his boots, so suddenly did he take upon himself sundry modes of expansive altitude; – to grow out of his boots and to swell upwards, till his angry eyes almost looked down on Lady Scatcherd, and each erect hair bristled up towards the heavens.

'This is very singular, very singular, Lady Scatcherd; very singular, indeed; very singular; quite unusual. I have come here from Barchester, at some considerable inconvenience, at some very considerable inconvenience, I may say, to my regular patients; and – and – and – I don't know that anything so very singular ever occurred to me before.' And then Dr Fillgrave, with a compression of his lips which almost made the poor woman sink into the ground, moved towards the door.

Then Lady Scatcherd bethought her of her great panacea. 'It isn't about the money, you know, doctor,' said she; 'of course Sir Roger don't expect you to come here with post-horses for nothing.' In this, by the by, Lady Scatcherd did not stick quite close to veracity, for Sir Roger, had he known it, would by no means have assented to any payment; and the note which her ladyship held in her hand was taken from her own private purse. 'It ain't at all about the money, doctor'; and then she tendered the bank-note, which she thought would immediately make all things smooth.

Now Dr Fillgrave dearly loved a five-pound fee. What physician is so unnatural as not to love it? He dearly loved a five-pound fee; but he loved his dignity better. He was angry also; and like all angry men, he loved his grievance. He felt that he had been badly treated; but if he took the money he would throw away his right to indulge any such feeling. At that moment his outraged dignity and his cherished anger were worth more to him than a five-pound note. He looked at it with wishful but still averted eyes, and then sternly refused the tender.

'No, madam,' said he; 'no, no'; and with his right hand raised with his eye-glasses in it, he motioned away the tempting paper. 'No; I should have been happy to have given Sir Roger the benefit of any medical skill I may have, seeing that I was specially called in –'

'But, doctor; if the man's well, you know –'

'Oh, of course; if he's well, and does not choose to see me, there's an end of it. Should he have any relapse, as my time is valuable, he will perhaps oblige me by sending elsewhere. Madam, good morning. I will, if you will allow me, ring for my carriage – that is, post-chaise.'

'But, doctor, you'll take the money; you must take the money; indeed you'll take the money,' said Lady Scatcherd, who had now become really unhappy at the idea that her husband's unpardonable whim had brought this man with post-horses all the way from Barchester, and that he was to be paid nothing for his time nor costs.

'No, madam, no. I could not think of it. Sir Roger, I have no doubt, will know better another time. It is not a question of money; not at all.'

'But it is a question of money, doctor; and you really shall, you must.' And poor Lady Scatcherd, in her anxiety to acquit herself at any rate of any pecuniary debt to the doctor, came to personal close quarters with him, with the view of forcing the note into his hands.

'Quite impossible, quite impossible,' said the doctor, still cherishing his grievance, and valiantly rejecting the root of all evil. 'I shall not do anything of the kind, Lady Scatcherd.'

'Now, doctor, do 'ee; to oblige me.'

'Quite out of the question.' And so, with his hands and hat behind his back, in token of his utter refusal to accept any pecuniary accommodation of his injury, he made his way backward to the door, her ladyship perseveringly pressing him in front. So eager had been the attack on him, that he had not waited to give his order about the post-chaise, but made his way at once towards the hall.

'Now, do 'ee take it, do 'ee,' pressed Lady Scatcherd.

'Utterly out of the question,' said Dr Fillgrave, with great deliberation, as he backed his way into the hall. As he did so, of course he turned round – and he found himself almost in the arms of Dr Thorne.

As Burley must have glared at Bothwell when they rushed together in that dread encounter on the mountain side; as Achilles may have glared at Hector when at last they met, each resolved to test in fatal conflict the prowess of the other, so did Dr Fillgrave glare at his foe from Greshamsbury, when, on turning round on his exalted heel, he found his nose on a level with the top button of Dr Thorne's waistcoat.

(1858)

Sir Roger's only son shortly dies from the same complaint ('It was found to be necessary that the internment should be made very quickly, as the body was already nearly destroyed by alcohol'), which awards Mary with surprising millions and allows Frank to kill two birds with one stone.

Trollope himself died from the same complaint as his creation Mrs Proudie.

From the British Medical Journal

MR ANTHONY TROLLOPE'S illness, which terminated fatally on Wednesday night, presents many points of medical interest. In January last he consulted Dr Murrell for shortness of breath on exertion, and other symptoms which had been attributed to angina pectoris. On inquiry, it was found that there had been no true anginal attack, but an examination disclosed the existence of an aortic diastolic murmur. It was decided that Mr Trollope should take a rest, and he accordingly went to Ireland for a holiday. In October he returned to town, and resumed his literary labours. On November 3rd he was suddenly seized with aphasia and paralysis of the right arm and leg, evidently due to embolism. At first there was great mental excitement, which was with difficulty subdued by the free administration of bromide of sodium. For some days he was able to utter only a few simple words, which served to express his wants, but, little by little, the power of language returned and the paralysed limbs regained power. Last week he had so far recovered as to take outdoor exercise, and there was every prospect of a speedy restoration to health. On Saturday last there was some return of the mental irritability, and it was apparent that further changes were taking place in the brain-substance. He gradually became comatose, and for the last three days of his life took nothing by mouth, with the exception of a little iced water. Predigested foods were used in the form of enemata, and suppositories of peptones were found useful. The immediate cause of death was congestion of the lungs.

(1882)

HERMAN MELVILLE

Herman Melville (1819–91) was an unruly sailor before the mast. He jumped ship in the Marquesas Islands in mid-Pacific on 9 July 1842, was captured by cannibals, but was offered pot luck rather than forming it, escaped after four weeks, wrote about it in *Typee: a Peep at Polynesian Life* (1846) and enjoyed a smash success as 'the man who had lived among cannibals'.

Melville had first sailed as a nineteen-year-old hand aboard the *Highlander*, bound for Liverpool, an experience which became *Redburn, His First Voyage* (1849). He had deserted in the Pacific the forecastle of the New England whaler *Acushnet*, and on 9 August he signed on to the Australian whaler *Lucy Ann*; six weeks later he mutinied in Tahiti. The mutineers were jailed in the Papeete *calabooza* and restrained *en masse* in a twenty-foot-long stocks, under the amiable wardenship of a fearsomely voracious, six-foot-tall ('as big round as a hogshead'), old Tahitian, 'Captain Bob'.

Melville collusively escaped from the *calabooza* with the dubious ship's doctor 'Long Ghost', and wrote beautifully comically about the Tahitians – incorrigibly impulsive, immoral and indolent – in *Omoo* (1847), 'a wanderer'. This won priceless wrathful publicity for sending up the fierce unChristian antagonism between C. of E. and RC missionaries: 'Pity it was, they couldn't marry – pity for the ladies of the island, I mean, and the cause of morality; for what business had the ecclesiastical old bachelors, with such a set of trim little native handmaidens? These damsels were their first converts; and devoted ones they were'.

Melville later sailed in another Pacific whaler, *Charles and Henry*, then served as ordinary seaman aboard the frigate USS *United States* out of Honolulu. He was paid off on 14 October 1844 in Boston, went home to mother in Troy, New York, and settled down to write about everything.

The *United States* gave him the material for *White-Jacket, or The World in a Man-of-War*, which appeared in 1850, the year before *Moby-Dick*. *White-Jacket* cocks a sharp eye at the US Navy: its account of Surgeon of the Fleet Cadwallader Cuticle's operation at sea is the funniest surgical satire in print. In 1852, Melville went serious with *Pierre, or The Ambiguities*, lost his baffled audience, in 1866 became a New York customs officer and remained one for nineteen years. He died with the *Press* obituary: 'Even his own generation had long thought him dead'. He enjoyed a highly successful posthumous collaboration in *Billy Budd* (1924) with Benjamin Britten in 1950.

From White-Jacket

CADWALLADER CUTICLE, MD., and Honorary Member of the most distinguished Colleges of Surgeons both in Europe and America, was our Surgeon of the Fleet. Nor was he at all blind to the dignity of his position; to which, indeed, he was rendered peculiarly competent, if the reputation he enjoyed was deserved. He had the name of being the foremost surgeon in the Navy, a gentleman of remarkable science and a veteran practitioner.

He was a small, withered man, nearly, perhaps quite, sixty years of age. His chest was shallow, his shoulders bent, his pantaloons hung round skeleton legs, and his face was singularly attenuated. In truth, the corporeal vitality of this man seemed, in a good degree, to have died out of him. He walked abroad, a curious patchwork of life and death, with a wig, one glass eye, and a set of false teeth, while his voice was husky and thick; but his mind seemed undebilitated as in youth; it shone out of his remaining eye with basilisk brilliancy.

Like most old physicians and surgeons who have seen much service, and have been promoted to high professional place for their scientific attainments, this Cuticle was an enthusiast in his calling. In private, he had once been heard to say, confidentially, that he would rather cut off a man's arm than dismember the wing of the most delicate pheasant. . . .

Next morning, at the appointed hour, the surgeons arrived in a body. They were accompanied by their juniors, young men ranging in age from nineteen years to thirty. Like the senior surgeons, these young gentlemen were arrayed in their blue navy uniforms, displaying a profusion of bright buttons, and several broad bars of gold lace about the wristbands. As in honour of the occasion, they had put on their best coats; they looked exceedingly brilliant.

The whole party immediately descended to the half-deck, where preparations had been made for the operation. A large garrison-ensign was stretched across the ship by the mainmast, so as completely to screen the space behind. This space included the whole extent aft to the bulkhead of the commodore's cabin, at the door of which the marine orderly paced, in plain sight, cutlass in hand.

Upon two gun-carriages, dragged amidships, the death-board (used for burials at sea) was horizontally placed, covered with an old royal-stun'-sail. Upon this occasion, to do duty as an amputation-table, it was widened by an additional plank. Two match-tubs, near by, placed one upon another, at either end supported another plank, distinct from the table, whereon was exhibited an array of saws and knives of various and peculiar shapes and sizes; also, a sort of steel, something like the dinner-table implement, together with long needles, crooked at the end for taking up the arteries, and large darning-needles, thread, and beeswax, for sewing up a wound.

At the end nearest the larger table was a tin basin of water, surrounded by small sponges, placed at mathematical intervals. From the long horizontal pole of a great-gun rammer – fixed in its usual place overhead – hung a number of towels, with 'US' marked in the corners.

All these arrangements had been made by the 'surgeon's steward', a person whose important functions in a man-of-war will, in a future chapter, be entered upon at large. Upon the present occasion, he was bustling about, adjusting and readjusting the knives, needles, and carver, like an over-conscientious butler fidgeting over a dinner-table just before the convivialists enter.

But by far the most striking object to be seen behind the ensign was a human skeleton, whose every joint articulated with wires. By a rivet at the apex of the skull, it hung dangling from a hammock-hook fixed in a beam above. Why this object was here will presently be seen; but why it was placed immediately at the foot of the amputation-table, only Surgeon Cuticle can tell.

While the final preparations were being made, Cuticle stood conversing with the assembled surgeons and assistant surgeons, his invited guests.

'Gentlemen,' said he, taking up one of the glittering knives, and artistically drawing the steel across it; 'Gentlemen, though these scenes are very unpleasant, and in some moods, I may say, repulsive to me – yet how much better for our patient to have the contusions and lacerations of his present wound – with all its dangerous symptoms – converted into a clean incision, free from these objections, and occasioning so much less subsequent anxiety to himself and the surgeon! Yes,' he added, tenderly feeling the edge of his knife, 'amputation is our only resource. Is it not so, Surgeon Patella?' turning toward that gentleman, as if relying upon some sort of an assent, however clogged with conditions.

'Certainly,' said Patella, 'amputation is your only resource, Mr Surgeon of the Fleet; that is, I mean, if you are fully persuaded of its necessity.'

The other surgeons said nothing, maintaining a somewhat reserved air, as if conscious that they had no positive authority in the case, whatever might be their own private opinions; but they seemed willing to behold, and, if called upon, to assist at the operation, since it could not now be averted.

The young men, their assistants, looked very eager, and cast frequent glances of awe upon so distinguished a practitioner as the venerable Cuticle.

'They say he can drop a leg in one minute and ten seconds from the moment the knife touches it,' whispered one of them to another.

'We shall see,' was the reply; and the speaker clapped his hand to his fob, to see if his watch would be forthcoming when wanted.

'Are you all ready here?' demanded Cuticle, now advancing to his steward; 'have not those fellows got through yet?' pointing to three men of the carpenter's gang, who were placing bits of wood under the gun-carriages supporting the central table.

'They are just through, sir,' respectfully answered the steward, touching his hand to his forehead, as if there were a cap-front there.

'Bring up the patient, then,' said Cuticle.

'Young gentlemen,' he added, turning to the row of assistant surgeons, 'seeing you here reminds me of the classes of students once under my instruction at the Philadelphia College of Physicians and Surgeons. Ah, those were happy days!' he sighed, applying the extreme corner of his handkerchief to his glass eye. 'Excuse an old man's emotions, young gentlemen; but when I think of the numerous rare cases that then came under my treatment, I cannot but give way to my feelings. The town, the city, the metropolis, young gentlemen, is the place for you students; at least in these dull times of peace, when the Army and Navy furnish no inducements for a youth ambitious of rising in our honourable profession. Take an old man's advice, and if the war now threatening between the States and Mexico should break out, exchange your Navy commissions for commissions in the Army. From having no military marine herself, Mexico has always been backward in furnishing subjects for the amputation-tables of foreign navies. The cause of science has languished in her hands. The Army, young gentlemen, is your best school; depend upon it. You will hardly believe it, Surgeon Bandage,' turning to that gentleman, 'but this is my first important case of surgery in a nearly three years' cruise. I have been almost wholly confined in this ship to doctor's practice – prescribing for fevers and fluxes. True, the other day a man fell from the mizzen-topsail-yard; but that was merely an aggravated case of dislocations, and bones splintered and broken. No one, sir, could have made an amputation of it, without severely contusing his conscience. And mine – I may say it, gentlemen, without ostentation – is peculiarly susceptible.'

And so saying, the knife and carver touchingly dropped to his sides, and he stood for a moment fixed in a tender reverie. But a commotion being heard beyond the curtain, he started, and, briskly crossing and recrossing the knife and carver, exclaimed, 'Ah, here comes our patient; surgeons, this side of the table, if you please; young gentlemen, a little further off, I beg. Steward, take off my coat – so; my neckerchief now; I must be perfectly unencumbered, Surgeon Patella, or I can do nothing whatever.'

These articles being removed, he snatched off his wig, placing it on the gun-deck capstan; then took out his set of false teeth, and placed it by the side of the wig; and, lastly, putting his forefinger to the inner angle of his blind eye, spirted out the glass optic with professional dexterity, and deposited that, also, next to the wig and false teeth.

Thus divested of nearly all inorganic appurtenances, what was left of the surgeon slightly shook itself, to see whether anything more could be spared to advantage.

'Carpenter's mates,' he now cried, 'will you never get through with that job?'

'Almost through, sir – just through,' they replied, staring round in search of the strange, unearthly voice that addressed them; for the absence of his teeth had not at all improved the conversational tones of the surgeon of the fleet.

With natural curiosity these men had purposely been lingering, to see all they could; but now, having no further excuse, they snatched up their hammers and chisels, and – like the stage-builders decamping from a public meeting at the eleventh hour, after just completing the rostrum in time for the first speaker – the carpenter's gang withdrew.

The broad ensign now lifted, revealing a glimpse of the crowd of man-of-war's-men outside, and the patient, borne in the arms of two of his messmates, entered the place. He was much emaciated, weak as an infant, and every limb visibly trembled, or rather jarred, like the head of a man with the palsy. As if an organic and involuntary apprehension of death had seized the wounded leg, its nervous motions were so violent that one of the messmates was obliged to keep his hand upon it.

The top-man was immediately stretched upon the table, the attendants steadying his limbs, when, slowly opening his eyes, he glanced about at the glittering knives and saws, the towels and sponges, the armed sentry at the commodore's cabin-door, the row of eager-eyed students, the meagre death's-head of a Cuticle, now with his shirt sleeves rolled up upon his withered arms and knife in hand, and, finally, his eye settled in horror upon the skeleton, slowly vibrating and jingling before him, with the slow, slight roll of the frigate in the water.

'I would advise perfect repose of your every limb, my man,' said Cuticle, addressing him; 'the precision of an operation is often impaired by the inconsiderate restlessness of the patient. But if you consider, my good fellow,' he added, in a patronizing and almost sympathetic tone, and slightly pressing his hand on the limb, 'if you consider how much better it is to live with three limbs than to die with four, and especially if you but knew to what torments both sailors and soldiers were subjected before the time of Celsus, owing to the lamentable ignorance of surgery then prevailing, you would certainly thank God from the bottom of your heart that *your* operation has been postponed to the period of this enlightened age, blessed with a Bell, a Brodie, and a Lally. My man, before Celsus's time, such was the general ignorance of our noble science, that, in order to prevent the excessive effusion of blood, it was deemed indispensable to operate with a red-hot knife' – making a professional movement toward the thigh – 'and pour scalding oil upon the parts' – elevating his elbow, as if with a teapot in his hand – 'still further to sear them, after amputation had been performed.'

'He is fainting!' said one of his messmates; 'quick! some water!' The steward immediately hurried to the top-man with the basin.

Cuticle took the top-man by the wrist, and feeling it awhile, observed, 'Don't be alarmed, men,' addressing the two messmates; 'he'll recover presently; this fainting very generally takes place.' And he stood for a moment, tranquilly eyeing the patient.

Now the surgeon of the fleet and the top-man presented a spectacle which, to a reflecting mind, was better than a churchyard sermon on the mortality of man.

Here was a sailor, who, four days previous, had stood erect – a pillar of life – with an arm like a royal-mast, and a thigh like a windlass. But the slightest conceivable finger-touch of a bit of crooked trigger had eventuated in stretching him out, more helpless than an hour-old babe, with a blasted thigh, utterly drained of its brawn. And who was it that now stood over him like a superior being, and, as if clothed himself with the attributes of immortality, indifferently discoursed of carving up his broken flesh, and thus piecing out his abbreviated days? Who was it, that, in capacity of surgeon, seemed enacting the part of a Regenerator of life? The withered, shrunken, one-eyed, toothless, hairless Cuticle; with a trunk half dead – a *memento mori* to behold!

And while in those soul-sinking and panic-striking premonitions of speedy death which almost invariably accompany a severe gun-shot wound, even with the most intrepid spirits; while thus drooping and dying, this once robust top-man's eye was now waning in his head like a Lapland moon being eclipsed in clouds – Cuticle, who for years had still lived in his withered tabernacle of a body – Cuticle, no doubt sharing in the common self-delusion of old age – Cuticle must have felt his hold of life as secure as the grim hug of a grizzly bear. Verily, life is more awful than death; and let no man, though his live heart beat in him like a cannon – let him not hug his life to himself; for, in the predestinated necessities of things, that bounding life of his is not a whit more secure than the life of a man on his deathbed. Today we inhale the air with expanding lungs, and life runs through us like a thousand Niles; but tomorrow we may collapse in death, and all our veins be dry as the Brook Kedron in a drought.

'And now, young gentlemen,' said Cuticle, turning to the assistant surgeons, 'while the patient is coming to, permit me to describe to you the highly interesting operation I am about to perform.'

'Mr Surgeon of the Fleet,' said Surgeon Bandage, 'if you are about to lecture, permit me to present you with your teeth; they will make your discourse more readily understood.' And so saying, Bandage, with a bow, placed the two semicircles of ivory into Cuticle's hands.

'Thank you, Surgeon Bandage,' said Cuticle, and slipped the ivory into its place.

'In the first place, now, young gentlemen, let me direct your attention to the exellent preparation before you. I have had it unpacked from its case, and set up here from my stateroom, where it occupies the spare berth; and all this for your express benefit, young gentlemen. This skeleton I procured in person from the Hunterian Department of the

Royal College of Surgeons in London. It is a masterpiece of art. But we have no time to examine it now. Delicacy forbids that I should amplify at a juncture like this' – casting an almost benignant glance toward the patient, now beginning to open his eyes; 'but let me point out to you upon this thigh-bone' – disengaging it from the skeleton, with a gentle twist – 'the precise place where I propose to perform the operation. *Here*, young gentlemen, *here* is the place. You perceive it is very near the point of articulation with the trunk.'

'Yes,' interposed Surgeon Wedge, rising on his toes, 'yes, young gentlemen, the point of articulation with the *acetabulum* of the *os innominatum*.'

'Where's your *Bell on Bones*, Dick?' whispered one of the assistants to the student next to him. 'Wedge has been spending the whole morning over it, getting out the hard names.'

'Surgeon Wedge,' said Cuticle, looking round severely, 'we will dispense with your commentaries, if you please, at present. Now, young gentlemen, you cannot but perceive, that the point of operation being so near the trunk and the vitals, it becomes an unusually beautiful one, demanding a steady hand and a true eye; and, after all, the patient may die under my hands.'

'Quick, steward! water, water; he's fainting again!' cried the two messmates.

'Don't be alarmed for your comrade, men,' said Cuticle, turning round. 'I tell you it is not an uncommon thing for the patient to betray some emotion upon these occasions – most usually manifested by swooning; it is quite natural it should be so. But we must not delay the operation. – Steward, that knife – no, the next one – there, that's it. He is coming to, I think' – feeling the top-man's wrist. 'Are you all ready, sir?'

This last observation was addressed to one of the *Neversink*'s assistant surgeons, a tall, lank, cadaverous young man, arrayed in a sort of shroud of white canvass, pinned about his throat, and completely enveloping his person. He was seated on a match-tub – the skeleton swinging near his head – at the foot of the table, in readiness to grasp the limb, as when a plank is being severed by a carpenter and his apprentice.

'The sponges, steward,' said Cuticle, for the last time taking out his teeth, and drawing up his shirt sleeve still further. Then, taking the patient by the wrist, 'Stand by, now, you messmates; keep hold of his arms; pin him down. Steward, put your hand on the artery; I shall commence as soon as his pulse begins to – *now, now*!' Letting fall the wrist, feeling the thigh carefully, and bowing over it an instant, he drew the fatal knife unerringly across the flesh. As it first touched the part, the row of surgeons simultaneously dropped their eyes to the watches in their hands, while the patient lay, with eyes horribly distended, in a kind of waking trance. Not a breath was heard; but as the quivering flesh parted in a long, lingering gash, a spring of blood welled up between the living walls of the wound, and two thick streams, in opposite directions, coursed down the thigh. The sponges were instantly dipped in the purple pool; every face present was pinched to a point with suspense; the limb writhed; the man shrieked; his messmates pinioned him; while round and round the leg went the unpitying cut.

'The saw!' said Cuticle.

Instantly it was in his hand.

Full of the operation, he was about to apply it, when, looking up, and turning to the assistant surgeons, he said, 'Would any of you young gentlemen like to apply the saw? A splendid subject!'

Several volunteered; when, selecting one, Cuticle surrendered the instrument to him, saying, 'Don't be hurried, now; be steady.'

While the rest of the assistants looked upon their comrade with glances of envy, he went rather timidly to work; and Cuticle, who was earnestly regarding him, suddenly snatched the saw from his hand. 'Away, butcher! you disgrace the profession. Look at *me*!'

For a few moments the thrilling rasping sound was heard; and then the top-man seemed parted in twain at the hip, as the leg slowly slid into the arms of the pale, gaunt man in the shroud, who at once made away with it, and tucked it out of sight under one of the guns.

'Surgeon Sawyer,' now said Cuticle, courteously turning to the surgeon of the *Mohawk*, 'would you like to take up the arteries? They are quite at your service, sir.'

'Do, Sawyer; be prevailed upon,' said Surgeon Bandage.

Sawyer complied; and while, with some modesty, he was conducting the operation, Cuticle, turning to the row of assistants, said, 'Young gentlemen, we will now proceed with our illustration. Hand me that bone, steward.' And taking the thigh-bone in his still bloody hands, and holding it conspicuously before his auditors, the surgeon of the fleet began:

'Young gentlemen, you will perceive that precisely at this spot – *here* – to which I previously directed your attention – at the corresponding spot precisely – the operation has been performed. About here, young gentlemen, *here*' – lifting his hand some inches from the bone – 'about *here* the great artery was. But you noticed that I did not use the tourniquet; I never do. The forefinger of my steward is far better than a tourniquet, being so much more manageable, and leaving the smaller veins uncompressed. But I have been told, young gentlemen, that a certain Seignior Seignioroni, a surgeon of Seville, has recently invented an admirable substitute for the clumsy, old-fashioned tourniquet. As I understand it, it is something like a pair of *callipers*, working with a small Archimedes screw – a very clever invention, according to all accounts. For the padded points at the end of the arches' – arching his forefinger and thumb – 'can be so worked as to approximate in such a way, as to – but you don't attend to me, young gentlemen,' he added, all at once starting.

Being more interested in the active proceedings of Surgeon Sawyer, who was now threading a needle to sew up the overlapping of the stump, the young gentlemen had not scrupled to turn away their attention altogether from the lecturer.

A few moments more, and the top-man, in a swoon, was removed below into the sick-bay. As the curtain settled again after the patient had disappeared, Cuticle, still holding the thigh-bone of the skeleton in his ensanguined hands, proceeded with his remarks upon it; and having concluded them, added, 'Now, young gentlemen, not the least interesting consequence of this operation will be the finding of the ball, which, in case of non-amputation, might have long eluded the most careful search. That ball, young gentlemen, must have taken a most circuitous route. Nor, in cases where the direction is oblique, is this at all unusual. Indeed, the learned Henner gives us a most remarkable – I had almost said an incredible – case of a soldier's neck, where the bullet, entering at the part called Adam's Apple –'

'Yes,' said Surgeon Wedge, elevating himself, 'the *pomum Adami*.'

'Entering the point called *Adam's Apple*,' continued Cuticle, severely emphasizing the last two words, 'ran completely round the neck, and, emerging at the same hole it had entered, shot the next man in the ranks. It was afterward extracted, says Henner, from the second man, and pieces of the other's skin were found adhering to it. But examples of foreign substances being received into the body with a ball, young gentlemen, are frequently observed. Being attached to a United States ship at the time, I happened to be near the spot of the battle of Ayacucho, in Peru. The day after the action, I saw in the barracks of the wounded a trooper, who having been severely injured in the brain, went crazy, and, with his own holster-pistol, committed suicide in the hospital. The ball drove inward a portion of his woollen night-cap –'

'In the form of a *cul-de-sac*, doubtless,' said the undaunted Wedge.

'For once, Surgeon Wedge, you use the only term that can be employed; and let me avail myself of this opportunity to say to you, young gentlemen, that a man of true science' – expanding his shallow chest a little – 'uses but a few hard words, and those only when none other will answer his purpose; whereas the smatterer in science' – slightly glancing toward Wedge – 'thinks, that by mouthing hard words he proves that he understands hard things. Let this sink deep in your minds, young gentlemen; and, Surgeon Wedge' – with a stiff bow – 'permit me to submit the reflection to yourself. Well, young gentlemen, the bullet was afterward extracted by pulling upon the external parts of the *cul-de-sac* – a simple, but exceedingly beautiful operation. There is a fine example, somewhat similar, related in Guthrie; but, of course, you must have met with it, in so well-known a work as his *Treatise upon Gun-shot Wounds*. When, upward of twenty years ago, I was with Lord Cochrane, then admiral of the fleets of this very country' – pointing shoreward, out of a port-hole – 'a sailor of the vessel to which I was attached, during the blockade of Bahia, had his leg –.' But by this time the fidgets had completely taken possession of his auditors, especially of the senior surgeons; and turning upon them abruptly he added, 'But I will not detain you longer, gentlemen' – turning round upon all the surgeons – 'your dinners must be waiting you on board your respective ships. But, Surgeon Sawyer, perhaps you may desire to wash your hands before you go. There is the basin, sir; you will find a clean towel on the rammer. For myself, I seldom use them' – taking out his handkerchief. 'I must leave you now, gentlemen,' – bowing. 'Tomorrow, at ten, the limb will be upon the table, and I shall be happy to see you all upon the occasion. Who's there?' turning to the curtain, which then rustled.

'Please, sir,' said the steward, entering, 'the patient is dead.'

'The body, also, gentlemen, at ten precisely,' said Cuticle, once more turning round upon his guests. 'I predicted that the operation might prove fatal; he was very much run down. Good morning'; and Cuticle departed.

(1850)

SIR FREDERICK TREVES

When King Edward VII developed acute appendicitis on 24 June 1902, it was most awkward for everybody. He was due to be crowned two days later in Westminster Abbey. The royal foreigners were already pouring into London, the royal chefs were already plucking the quails and partridges, the royal presence was pressingly felt in beflagged streets throughout his Kingdom and across his perpetually sunlit Empire. Sir Frederick Treves (1853–1923), from the London Hospital in the East End, saved His Majesty's life by cancelling the Coronation, and submitting the King instead to an appendicectomy upstairs at Buckingham Palace. The operation was then uncommon, underrated by Treves's fellow surgeons, and risky.

This made Treves the King's official surgeon and a baronet. But in 1908 he retired aged fifty-five to enjoy his remaining fifteen years travelling and writing, after World War One living sunnily in the South of France. He had begun producing books in 1900, rising every morning at six o'clock at No. 6 Wimpole Street for the day's literary work before the surgical. Sir Frederick was a native of Dorset, a handsome, square-faced man with an upswept moustache finer than Kaiser William's, a keen rugger player and bicyclist, who became a consultant surgeon aged only thirty-one. He founded the British Red Cross Society and held the certificate of a master mariner, permitting him, should he care to, to command any vessel afloat flying the Red Ensign. Thomas Hardy scattered his ashes in Dorchester cemetery.

Treves is best remembered for *The Elephant Man*, published in the year of his death, which was a hit in the West End and on Broadway fifty years later. The true story started in December 1886, when an empty greengrocer's shop opposite the London Hospital advertised a freak show at tuppence a look. The freak was a man resembling an elephant. Treves was then Lecturer in Anatomy at the London Hospital, and gave a shilling for a private view. He found a little man with a vast, misshapen head, a mass like an elephant's trunk sprouting from his brow, a stump like a tusk jutting from his upper jaw, his nose a shapeless lump, the back of both his head and his body drooping with sacks of flesh under skin 'the surface of which was comparable to brown cauliflower'. The freak was huddled under a blanket, warmed by a brick on a gas-jet, barefoot, naked but for a pair of tattered dress-suit trousers, and ordered about like a dog.

This was John Merrick, aged twenty-one. Treves examined him in the hospital and wrote a paper on his deformities for the British Medical Journal. Two years later, the police brought to the London Hospital a horrible vagrant: Merrick, clutching Treves's cherished visiting-card. Treves manipulated hospital bureaucracy to install Merrick in an attic overlooking a yard where the iron beds were refurbished ('Bedstead Square'). He mastered his patient's spluttering speech and talked to him for two hours on Sunday mornings (surgery was more leisurely under Queen Victoria). He found behind the expressionless face a shy, sensitive and intelligent young man, who was an eager reader, particularly of romantic fiction. Merrick got into the papers. In no time at all, the Princess of Wales came to see him, and the society ladies of London were sending him their photographs. All visitors to his attic conscientiously treated him as a normal human being – except for one new nurse who dropped his dinner-tray, shrieked and fled.

Treves was surprised when Merrick desired a smart silver-fitted dressing-bag for Christmas, until he reasoned that a man who is a monster must fantasise that he is a dandy, a gallant, a 'nut'. In 1890 Merrick was found dead in bed, from defying his deformities by attempting to sleep on his back like everyone else. The Elephant Man had suffered from neurofibromatosis, an inherited disease passed by a dominant gene, in which non-malignant tumours grew from the sheaths of the nerves running through his skin and the skin itself suffered darkening. Ninety years after his death, X-rays of Merrick's skeleton displayed that he had also fibrous dysplasia, a linked genetic disorder, which gave him softened, cystic bones, and growths on his skull; and that he suffered a tuberculous hip-joint, too.

The Elephant Man's combination of horror and pathos is irresistible, its effect heightened by the story's unsentimental telling. Treves's style is concise and unruffled, expectedly from a profession where human misery must be assuaged without emotion, mercy expressed realistically, and pity becomes practical.

Treves wrote also *A Manual of Surgery* and *The Pathology, Diagnosis and Treatment of Obstruction of the Intestine.*

The following story illustrates the danger of over-confidence in both surgery and marriage.

The Idol with Hands of Clay

THE GOOD SURGEON is born, not made. He is a complex product in any case, and often something of a prodigy. His qualities cannot be expressed by diplomas nor appraised by university degrees. It may be possible to ascertain what he knows, but no examination can elicit what he can do. He must know the human body as a forester knows his wood; must know it even better than he must know the roots and branches of every tree, the source and wanderings of every rivulet, the banks of every alley, the flowers of every glade. As a surgeon, moreover, he must be learned in the moods and troubles of the wood, must know of the wild winds that may rend it, of the savage things that lurk in its secret haunts, of the strangling creepers that may throttle its sturdiest growth, of the rot and mould that may make dust of its very heart. As an operator, moreover, he must be a deft handicraftsman and a master of touch.

He may have all these acquirements and yet be found wanting; just as a man may succeed when shooting at a target, but fail when faced by a charging lion. He may be a clever manipulator and yet be mentally clumsy. He may even be brilliant, but Heaven help the poor soul who has to be operated upon by a brilliant surgeon. Brilliancy is out of place in surgery. It is pleasing in the juggler who plays with knives in the air, but it causes anxiety in an operating theatre.

The surgeon's hands must be delicate, but they must also be strong. He needs a lacemaker's fingers and a seaman's grip. He must have courage, be quick to think and prompt to act, be sure of himself and captain of the venture he commands. The surgeon has often to fight for another's life. I conceive of him, then, not as a massive Hercules wrestling ponderously with Death for the body of Alcestis, but as a nimble man in doublet and hose who, over a prostrate form, fights Death with a rapier.

These reflections were the outcome of an incident which had set me thinking of the equipment of a surgeon and of what is needed to fit him for his work. The episode concerned a young medical man who had started practice in a humble country town. His student career had been meritorious and indeed distinguished. He had obtained an entrance scholarship at his medical school, had collected many laudatory certificates, had been awarded a gold medal and had become a Fellow of the Royal College of Surgeons. His inclination was towards surgery. He considered surgery to be his *métier.* Although circumstances had condemned him to the drab life of a family doctor in a little town, he persisted that he was, first and foremost, a surgeon, and, indeed, on his door-plate had inverted the usual wording and had described himself as 'surgeon and physician'. In his hospital days he had assisted at many operations, but his opportunities of acting as a principal had been few and insignificant. In a small practice in a small town surgical opportunities are rare. There was in the place a cottage hospital with six beds, but it was mostly occupied by medical cases, by patients with rheumatism or pneumonia, by patients who had to submit to the surgical indignity of being poulticed and of being treated by mere physic. Cases worthy of a Fellow of the Royal College of Surgeons were very few, and even these seldom soared in interest above an abscess or a broken leg.

Just before the young doctor settled down to practise he married. It was a very happy union. The bride was the daughter of a neighbouring farmer. She had spent her life in the country, was more familiar with the ways of fowls and ducks than with the ways of the world, while a sunbonnet became her better than a Paris toque. She was as pretty as the milkmaid of a pastoral picture with her pink-and-white complexion, her laughing eyes and her rippled hair.

Her chief charm was her radiant delight in the mere joy of living. The small world in which she moved was to her always in the sun, and the sun was that of summer. There was no town so pretty as her little town, and no house so perfect as 'the doctor's' in the High Street. 'The doctor's' was a Georgian house with windows of many panes, with a fanlight like a surprised eyebrow over the entry and a self-conscious brass knocker on the door. The house was close to the pavement, from which it was separated by a line of white posts connected by loops of chains. Passers-by could look over the low green wooden blinds into the dining-room and see the table covered with worn magazines, for the room was intended to imitate a Harley Street waiting-room. They could see also the bright things on the sideboard, the wedding-present biscuit box, the gong hanging from two cow-horns and the cup won at some hospital sports. To the young wife there never was such a house, nor such furniture, nor such ornaments, nor, as she went about with a duster from room to room, could there be a greater joy than that of keeping everything polished and bright.

Her most supreme adoration, however, was for her husband. He was so handsome, so devoted, and so amazingly clever. His learning was beyond the common grasp, and the depths of his knowledge unfathomable. When a friend came in at night to smoke a pipe she would sit silent and open-mouthed, lost in admiration of her husband's dazzling intellect. How glibly he would talk of metabolism and blood-pressure; how marvellously he endowed common things with mystic significance when he discoursed upon the value in calories of a pound of steak, or upon the vitamins that enrich the common bean, or even the more common cabbage. It seemed to her that behind the tiny world she knew there was a mysterious universe with which her well-beloved was as familiar as was she with the contents of her larder.

She was supremely happy and content, while her husband bestowed upon her all the affection of which he was capable. He was naturally vain, but her idolatry made him vainer. She considered him wonderful, and he was beginning to think her estimate had some truth in it. She was so proud of him that she rather wearied her friends by the tale of his achievements. She pressed him to allow her to have his diploma and his more florid certificates framed and hung up in the consulting room, but he had said with chilling superiority that such things 'were not done', so that she could only console herself by adoring the modesty of men of genius.

One day this happy, ever-busy lady was seized with appendicitis. She had had attacks in her youth, but they had passed away. This attack, although not severe, was graver, and her husband determined, quite wisely, that an operation was necessary. He proposed to ask a well-known surgeon in a neighbouring city to undertake this measure. He told his wife, of course, of his intention, but she would have none of it. 'No,' she said, 'she would not be operated on by stuffy old Mr Heron. He was no good. She could not bear him even to touch her. If an operation was necessary no one should do it but her husband. He was so clever, such a surgeon, and so up-to-date. Old Heron was a fossil and behind the times. No! Her clever Jimmy should do it and no one else. She could trust no one else. In his wonderful hands she would be safe, and would be running about again in the garden in no time. What was the use of a fine surgeon if his own wife was denied his precious help!'

The husband made no attempt to resist her wish. He contemplated the ordeal with dread, but was so influenced by her fervid flattery that he concealed from her the fact that the prospect made him faint of heart and that he had even asked himself: 'Can I go through with it?'

He told me afterwards that his miserable vanity decided him. He could not admit that he lacked either courage or competence. He saw, moreover, the prospect of making an impression. The town people would say: 'Here is a surgeon so sure of himself that he carries out a grave operation on his own wife without a tremor.' Then, again, his assistant would be his fellow-practitioner in the town. How impressed he would be by the operator's skill, by his coolness, by the display of the latest type of instrument, and generally by his very advanced methods. It was true that it was the first major operation he had ever undertaken, but he no longer hesitated. He must not imperil his wife's faith in him nor fail to realize her conception of his powers. As he said to me more than once, it was his vanity that decided him.

He read up the details of the operation in every available manual he possessed. It seemed to be a simple procedure. Undoubtedly in nine cases out of ten it *is* a simple measure. His small experience, as an onlooker, had been limited to the nine cases. He had never met with the tenth. He hardly believed in it. The operation as he had watched it at the hospital seemed so simple, but he forgot that the work of expert hands does generally appear simple.

The elaborate preparations for the operation – made with anxious fussiness and much clinking of steel – were duly completed. The lady was brought into the room appointed for the operation and placed on the table. She looked very young. Her hair, parted at the back, was arranged in two long plaits, one on either side of her face, as if she were a schoolgirl. She had insisted on a pink bow at the end of each plait, pleading that they were cheerful. She smiled as she saw her husband standing in the room looking very gaunt and solemn in his operating dress – a garb of linen that made him appear half-monk, half-mechanic. She held her hand towards him, but he said he could not take it as his own hand was sterilized. Her smile vanished for a moment at the rebuke, but came back again as she said: 'Now don't look so serious, Jimmy; I am not the least afraid. I know that with you I am safe and that you will make me well, but be sure you are by my side when I awake, for I want to see you as I open my eyes. Wonderful boy!'

The operation commenced. The young doctor told me that as he cut with his knife into that beautiful white skin and saw the blood well up behind it a lump rose in his throat and he felt that he must give up the venture. His vanity, however, urged him on. His doctor friend was watching him. He must impress him with his coolness and his mastery of the position. He talked of casual things to show that he was quite at ease, but his utterances were artificial and forced.

For a time all went well. He was showing off, he felt, with some effect. But when the depths of the wound were reached a condition of things was found which puzzled him. Structures were confused and matted together, and so obscured as to be unrecognizable. He had read of nothing like this in his books. It was the tenth case. He became uneasy and, indeed, alarmed, as one who had lost his way. He ceased to chatter. He tried to retain his attitude of coolness and command. He must be bold, he kept saying to himself. He made blind efforts to find his course, became wild and finally reckless. Then a terrible thing happened. There was a tear – something gave way – something gushed forth. His heart seemed to stop. He thought he should faint. A cold sweat broke out upon his brow. He ceased to speak. His trembling fingers groped aimlessly in the depths of the wound. His friend asked: 'What has happened?' He replied with a sickly fury: 'Shut up!'

He then tried to repair the damage he had done; took up instrument after instrument and dropped them again until the patient's body was covered with soiled and discarded forceps, knives and clamps. He wiped the sweat from his brow with his hand and left a wide streak of blood across his forehead. His knees shook and he stamped to try to stop them. He cursed the doctor who was helping him, crying out: 'For God's sake do this,' or 'For God's sake don't do that'; sighed like a suffocating man; looked vacantly round the room as if for help; looked appealingly to his wife's masked face for some sign of her tender comfort, but she was more than dumb. Frenzied with despair, he told the nurse to send for Mr Heron. It was a hopeless mission, since that surgeon – even if at home – could not arrive for hours.

He tried again and again to close the awful rent, but he was now nearly dropping with terror and exhaustion. Then the anaesthetist said in a whisper: 'How much longer will you be? Her pulse is failing. She cannot stand much more.' He felt that he must finish or die. He finished in a way. He closed the wound, and then sank on a stool with his face buried in his blood-stained hands, while the nurse and the doctor applied the necessary dressing.

The patient was carried back to her bedroom, but he dared not follow. The doctor who had helped him crept away without speaking a word. He was left alone in this dreadful room with its hideous reminders of what he had done. He wandered about, looked aimlessly out of the window, but saw nothing, picked up his wife's handkerchief which was lying on the table, crunched it in his hand, and then dropped it on the floor as the red horror of it all flooded his brain. What had he done to her? She? She of all women in the world!

He caught a sight of himself in the glass. His face was smeared with blood. He looked inhuman and unrecognizable. It was not himself he saw; it was a murderer with the brand of Cain upon his brow. He looked again at her handkerchief on the ground. It was the last thing her hand had closed upon. It was a piece of her lying amid this scene of unspeakable horror. It was like some ghastly item of evidence in a murder story. He could not touch it. He could not look at it. He covered it with a towel.

In a while he washed his hands and face, put on his coat and walked into the bedroom. The blind was down; the place was almost dark; the atmosphere was laden with the smell of ether. He could see the form of his wife on the bed, but she was so still and seemed so thin. The coverlet appeared so flat, except where the points of her feet raised a little ridge. Her face was as white as marble. Although the room was very silent, he could not hear her breathe. On one side of the bed stood the nurse, and on the other side the anaesthetist. Both were motionless. They said nothing. Indeed, there was nothing to say. They did not even look up when he came in. He touched his wife's hand, but it was cold and he could feel no pulse.

In about two hours Heron, the surgeon, arrived. The young doctor saw him in an adjacent bedroom, gave him an incoherent, spasmodic account of the operation, laid emphasis on unsurmountable difficulties, gabbled something about an accident, tried to excuse himself, maintained that the fault was not his, but that circumstances were against him.

The surgeon's examination of the patient was very brief. He went into the room alone. As he came out he closed the door after him. The husband, numb with terror, was awaiting him in the lobby. The surgeon put his hand on the wretched man's shoulder, shook his head and, without uttering a single word, made his way down the stairs. He nearly stumbled over a couple of shrinking, white-faced maids who had crept up the stairs in the hope of hearing something of their young mistress.

As he passed one said: 'Is she better, doctor?' but he merely shook his head, and without a word walked out into the sunny street where some children were dancing to a barrel-organ.

The husband told me that he could not remember what he did during these portentous hours after the operation. He could not stay in the bedroom. He wandered about the house. He went into his consulting room and pulled out some half-dozen works on surgery with the idea of gaining some comfort or guidance; but he never saw a word on the printed page. He went into the dispensary and looked over the rows of bottles on the shelves to see if he could find anything, any drug, any elixir that would help. He crammed all sorts of medicines into his pocket and took them upstairs, but, as he entered the room, he forgot all about them, and when he found them in his coat a week later he wondered how they had got there. He remembered a pallid maid coming up to him and saying: 'Lunch is ready, sir.' He thought her mad.

He told me that among the horrors that haunted him during these hours of waiting not the least were the flippant and callous thoughts that would force themselves into his mind with fiendish brutality. There was, for example, a scent bottle on his wife's table – a present from her aunt. He found himself wondering why her aunt had given it to her and when, what she had paid for it, and what the aunt would say when she heard her niece was dead. Worse than that, he began composing in his mind an obituary notice for the newspapers. How should he word it? Should he say 'beloved wife', or 'dearly loved wife', and should he add all his medical qualifications? It was terrible. Terrible, too, was his constant longing to tell his wife of the trouble he was in and to be comforted by her.

Shortly after the surgeon left the anaesthetist noticed some momentary gleam of consciousness in the patient. The husband hurried in. The end had come. His wife's face was turned towards the window. The nurse lifted the blind a little so that the light fell full upon her. She opened her eyes and at once recognized her husband. She tried to move her hand towards him, but it fell listless on the sheet. A smile – radiant, grateful, adoring – illumined her face, and as he bent over her he heard her whisper: 'Wonderful boy.'

(1923)

W. E. HENLEY

William Ernest Henley (1849–1903) was one of five children of a Gloucester bookseller. At the age of twelve he was infected with skeletal tuberculosis and became a cripple (as the Victorians called the disabled). One of his feet was amputated, and his life was gloomily accepted to be sustainable only by amputation of the other leg.

In 1873, Henley was admitted to Edinburgh Royal Infirmary as a patient of Professor Lister, whose hand-cranked, carbolic-charged antiseptic apparatus was a new noise in the wards:

Over the hiss of the spray,
Comes a low cry . . .

It killed the germs in the surgeon's wound to reduce the mortality rate from 'hospital gangrene', which was higher than that of the troops at Waterloo.

Henley remained Lister's patient in the Royal Infirmary for twenty months. The leg was saved, but he continued ill, sometimes severely, understandably despondent but exemplarily resilient:

Out of the night that covers me,
Black as the pit from pole to pole,
I thank whatever gods may be
For my unconquerable soul.

In the fell clutch of circumstance
I have not winced nor cried aloud.
Under the bludgeonings of chance
My head is bloody, but unbow'd.

Hospital Verses appeared in *Cornhill Magazine* in July 1875. The previous February, Robert Louis Stevenson had visited Henley in the Royal Infirmary, 'sitting up in bed with his hair all tangled' and talking 'as cheerfully as if he has been in a King's palace'. They became friends ('A deal of Ariel, just a streak of Puck, much Antony, of Hamlet most of all' was Henley's estimation of him), they wrote four plays together, and fell out in 1901.

Henley became a busy London journalist and editor, made famous through *A Book of Verses*, published in 1888. In the spring of 1903 he wrote *A Song of Speed* on the delights of motoring, having earlier written of the (horse) *Bus Driver*:

> He's called *The General* from the brazen craft
> And dash with which he *sneaks a bit of road*,

thus displaying poetic foresight of the afflictions of mankind in the coming century.

Henley got a civil list pension of £225 in 1898. In the next year worsening health drove him to live in Worthing and in 1903 he fell from a moving train in Woking and died on 11 June.

Henley was not persistently the gloomy sufferer of these poems, but open, genial, vigorous; a humorous conversationalist. Nor was he the wasted, tubercular type, but broad-shouldered with bushy, yellow hair and blue (short-sighted) eyes, a bristling, profuse beard and moustache, as perpetuated by Rodin, whom he championed.

From In Hospital

Enter Patient

The morning mists still haunt the stony street;
The northern summer air is shrill and cold;
And lo, the Hospital, gray, quiet, old,
Where Life and Death like friendly chafferers meet.
Thro' the loud spaciousness and draughty gloom
A small, strange child – so aged yet so young! –
Her little arm besplinted and beslung,
Precedes me gravely to the waiting-room.
I limp behind, my confidence all gone.
The gray-haired soldier-porter waves me on,
And on I crawl, and still my spirits fail:
A tragic meanness seems so to environ

These corridors and stairs of stone and iron,
Cold, naked, clean – half-workhouse and half-jail.

Before

Behold me waiting – waiting for the knife.
A little while, and at a leap I storm
The thick, sweet mystery of chloroform,
The drunken dark, the little death-in-life.
The gods are good to me: I have no wife,
No innocent child, to think of as I near
The fateful minute; nothing all-too dear
Unmans me for my bout of passive strife.
Yet am I tremulous and a trifle sick,
And, face to face with chance, I shrink a little:
My hopes are strong, my will is something weak.
Here comes the basket? Thank you. I am ready.
But, gentlemen my porters, life is brittle:
You carry Caesar and his fortunes – steady!

Operation

You are carried in a basket,
  Like a carcase from the shambles,
  To the theatre, a cockpit
  Where they stretch you on a table.

Then they bid you close your eyelids,
  And they mask you with a napkin,
  And the anaesthetic reaches
  Hot and subtle through your being.

And you gasp and reel and shudder
  In a rushing, swaying rapture,

While the voices at your elbow
Fade – receding – fainter – farther.

Lights about you shower and tumble,
And your blood seems crystallising –
Edged and vibrant, yet within you
Racked and hurried back and forward.

Then the lights grow fast and furious,
And you hear a noise of waters,
And you wrestle, blind and dizzy,
In an agony of effort,

Till a sudden lull accepts you,
And you sound an utter darkness . . .
And awaken . . . with a struggle . . .
On a hushed, attentive audience.

House-Surgeon

Exceeding tall, but built so well his height
Half-disappears in flow of chest and limb;
Moustache and whisker trooper-like in trim;
Frank-faced, frank-eyed, frank-hearted; always bright
And always punctual – morning, noon, and night;
Bland as a Jesuit, sober as a hymn;
Humorous, and yet without a touch of whim;
Gentle and amiable, yet full of fight.
His piety, though fresh and true in strain,
Has not yet whitewashed up his common mood
To the dead blank of his particular Schism.
Sweet, unaggressive, tolerant, most humane,
Wild artists like his kindly elderhood,
And cultivate his mild Philistinism.

Staff-Nurse: New Style

Blue-eyed and bright of face but waning fast
Into the sere of virginal decay,
I view her as she enters, day by day,
As a sweet sunset almost overpast.
Kindly and calm, patrician to the last,
Superbly falls her gown of sober gray,
And on her chignon's elegant array
The plainest cap is somehow touched with caste.
She talks BEETHOVEN; frowns disapprobation
At BALZAC's name, sighs it at 'poor GEORGE SAND's;
Knows that she has exceeding pretty hands;
Speaks Latin with a right accentuation;
And gives at need (as one who understands)
Draught, counsel, diagnosis, exhortation.

Clinical

Hist? . . .
Through the corridor's echoes
Louder and nearer
Comes a great shuffling of feet.
Quick, every one of you,
Straight your quilts, and be decent!
Here's the Professor.

In he comes first
With the bright look we know,
From the broad, white brows the kind eyes
Soothing yet nerving you. Here at his elbow,
White-capped, white-aproned, the Nurse,
Towel on arm and her inkstand

Fretful with quills.
Here in the ruck, anyhow,

Surging along,
Louts, duffers, exquisites, students, and prigs –
Whiskers and foreheads, scarf-pins and spectacles –
Hustles the Class! And they ring themselves
Round the first bed, where the Chief
(His dressers and clerks at attention),
Bends in inspection already.

So shows the ring
Seen from behind round a conjurer
Doing his pitch in the street.
High shoulders, low shoulders, broad shoulders, narrow ones,
Round, square, and angular, serry and shove;
While from within a voice,
Gravely and weightily fluent,
Sounds; and then ceases; and suddenly
(Look at the stress of the shoulders!)
Out of a quiver of silence,
Over the hiss of the spray,
Comes a low cry, and the sound
Of breath quick intaken through teeth
Clenched in resolve. And the Master
Breaks from the crowd, and goes,
Wiping his hands,
To the next bed, with his pupils
Flocking and whispering behind him.

Now one can see.
Case Number One
Sits (rather pale) with his bedclothes
Stripped up, and showing his foot
(Alas for God's Image!)

Swaddled in wet, white lint
Brilliantly hideous with red.

Casualty

As with varnish red and glistening
Dripped his hair; his feet looked rigid;
Raised, he settled stiffly sideways:
You could see his hurts were spinal.

He had fallen from an engine,
And been dragged along the metals.
It was hopeless, and they knew it;
So they covered him, and left him.

As he lay, by fits half sentient,
Inarticulately moaning,
With his stockinged soles protruded
Stark and awkward from the blankets,

To his bed there came a woman,
Stood and looked and sighed a little,
And departed without speaking,
As himself a few hours after.

I was told it was his sweetheart.
They were on the eve of marriage.
She was quiet as a statue,
But her lip was gray and writhen.

Discharged

Carry me out
Into the wind and the sunshine,
Into the beautiful world.

O, the wonder, the spell of the streets!
The stature and strength of the horses,
The rustle and echo of footfalls,
The flat roar and rattle of wheels!
A swift tram floats huge on us . . .
It's a dream?
The smell of the mud in my nostrils
Blows brave – like a breath of the sea!

As of old,
Ambulant, undulant drapery
Vaguely and strangely provocative,
Flutters and beckons. O, yonder –
Is it? – the gleam of a stocking!
Sudden, a spire
Wedged in the mist! O, the houses,
The long lines of lofty, gray houses,
Cross-hatched with shadow and light!
These are the streets. . . .
Each is an avenue leading
Whither I will!

Free . . . !
Dizzy, hysterical, faint,
I sit, and the carriage rolls on with me
Into the wonderful world.

(1873–77)

EMILE ZOLA

The physiologist Claude Bernard (1813–78), of the Sorbonne, illuminated French medicine of the Second Empire. His glow falls upon medicine today. He clarified that we were not a skinful of jumbled and isolated organs, but that all our viscera – pancreas, stomach, liver and so on – each act chemically one upon another, to create a complex and powerful climate which influences our entire bodily function. He named this *le milieu intérieur*. Bernard was an inspired experimenter, but equally wise to the fact that research was a sternly practical activity. 'Put off your imagination, as you take off your overcoat, when you enter the laboratory; but put it on again, as you do your overcoat, when you leave,' he advised his classes.

With his overcoat hanging on its peg at home, Claude Bernard wrote, in 1865, *Introduction à l'Etude de la Médecine Expérimentale*. This expounded the Hippocratic ideal of medicine as a straightforward technique, unloaded with theory; you observed the patient, decided on his cure, and waited to see whether it worked or not. And he declared that the behaviour of man was determined broadly by both his inner and his outer *milieux*. We come to the influence of Claude Bernard upon literature. His second theory was grasped by fashionable French novelists then manifesting *le réalisme*. Being literary and not scientific they got it wrong, but they advanced joyously into *le naturalisme*, in which their characters behaved with basic awfulness. Emile Zola (1840–1902) was an enthusiast for this.

Zola so believed in *naturalisme* that he wrote twenty novels to express it – the *Rougon–Macquart* cycle, incorporating *Le Ventre de Paris*, *l'Assommoir*, *Germinal*, *La Bête Humaine* and *La Débâcle*. He judged the novelist as an observer interchangeable with the doctor. He embraced Hippolyte Taine's (1828–93) idea from the Ecole des Beaux-Arts: that the novel was a collection of human case-histories. He experimented routinely in the literary lab with Professor Taine's *naturalisme* chemistry, which held the principle that '*le vice et la vertu sont des produits comme le vitriol et le sucre*'. Zola had got over all this when he wrote *Lourdes* in 1894, but his pseudo-scientific education came in useful.

His story of the wretched sufferers aboard the ghastly Lourdes express from Paris is a prizewinning clinical description. He sees Lourdes as a doctor sees it: a grotesquerie of the sick, walking, hobbling, or helpless on stretchers, tended by the fervently sympathetic, exposed to religious glorification and self-glorification, but without any intelligently informed, purposeful or useful attention whatever. As the relief of sickness lurks behind only the taming of death in the benefits of divine dispensation, it understandably occasions a human desperation to be exploited, however virtuously, by the Catholic Church. Which made a juicy adversary for so vigorous a sabre-flourisher as Zola.

'A sudden hope, however, breaks in upon them,' Zola reflected sadly among the pilgrims. 'Supposing that after all there should be a Power greater than that of men, higher than that of science? It is the instinctive hankering after the Lie which creates human credulity.' Zola saw, correctly, that Lourdes 'cured' only those who were suffering from psychological symptoms, or whose doctors had made the wrong diagnosis, or who would get better anyway. 'Lourdes, the Grotto, the cures, the miracles, are, indeed, the creation of the need of the Lie, that necessity for credulity, which is characteristic of human nature,' he sighed later.

Lourdes was banned in Lourdes.

From Lourdes

IN THE SPEEDING train both the pilgrims and the sick, crammed on the hard benches of a third-class carriage, were just ending the Ave Maria *stella* which they had started intoning on leaving the Gare d'Orléans. Raising herself on her bed of misery, trembling with the fever of impatience, Maria glimpsed the Paris fortifications.

'Ah! The fortifications!' she exclaimed happily, despite her suffering. 'We're already out of Paris, we're on our way at last!'

In front of her, her father M. de Guersaint smiled at her joy; while the Abbé Pierre Froment, who looked on her with brotherly tenderness, so forgot himself to exclaim with a pitying uneasiness: 'Well, here we are until tomorrow morning, we won't be at Lourdes until three-forty. More than twenty-two hours on the go!'

It was half past five, the sun had just risen brightly on a clear and splendid morning. It was Friday, 19 August. But already on the horizon some heavy clouds announced a nasty day of stormy heat. And the slanting rays which pierced the compartments of the carriage had filled them with a dancing golden dust.

Reverting to her earlier misery, Marie murmured: 'Yes, twenty-two hours. *Mon Dieu!* It's a long time!'

Her father helped her to settle in the narrow box, a kind of surgical splint, in which she had lived for the past seven years. The railway had consented to make an exception, and take as baggage the two pairs of wheels which came on and off it for moving about. Tucked tight between the boards of this mobile coffin she took up three seats in the compartment; and she lay a moment with eyes shut, her face thin and sickly, still a delicate child at twenty-three, and still charming amid her lovely blonde hair, the locks of a queen that even illness had respected. Clothed in a black woollen dress, she had hanging from her neck the 'hospitalisation' card which entitled her to free treatment, marked with her name and number. She herself had insisted on such humility, not wishing to be an expense to her family, who had come down in the world. So she found herself there, in the third class, in the 'white train', the train of the most severely ill cases, the saddest of the fourteen trains which were travelling to Lourdes that day, the one packed with five hundred healthy pilgrims and nearly three hundred wretched sufferers, feeble and exhausted, twisted with pain, carted at express speed from one end of France to the other. . . .

'Monsieur l'abbé, pull down the carriage-blind. . . . Come along! We must settle in and put our house in order.'

In her black robe of a Sister of the Assumption, brightened by a white coif, a white wimple and a huge white apron, Sister Hyacinthe gave a brave smile. Her youth burnished her small, fresh mouth and the depths of her lovely blue eyes, always tender. Perhaps she was not pretty, but she was charming, delicate, tall and slim, with a boy's bosom under the bib of her apron – like a decent young man with a snowy complexion, bubbling with health, fun and innocence.

'But that sun's already burning us to a crisp! Please, madam, pull down your blind as well. . . .'

The whole carriage, the five compartments of six seats, had turned into one big room, a rattling common-room that you could take in with a single glance. Between the bare yellow wooden walls, under the white-painted panels of the roof, it was virtually a hospital ward in utter disorder, or like the rough-and-tumble of an improvised ambulance. Scattered half-hidden under the seats were chamber-pots, basins, brooms, sponges. As the train had no baggage-car, luggage had accumulated everywhere, suitcases, white wooden chests, hat-boxes, bags, a pathetic mass of poor worn-out things held together with bits of string; and the litter was repeated above, clothes, parcels, baskets hanging from the brass hooks and swinging incessantly. In the middle of this rubbish the severely ill lay on their narrow mattresses, taking up several seats, shaken by the jerky rumbling of the wheels; while those would could sit were huddled into their corners, faces pale, heads on pillows. Strictly speaking, there should have been a lady hospitaller for each compartment. At the far end could be found a second Sister of the Assumption, Sister Claire des Anges. The able-bodied pilgrims were up and about, eating and drinking. There was even a compartment entirely of women, ten pilgrims squeezed one against the other, young and old, all equally ugly, pitiful and sad. And because no one dared open the windows because of the consumptives, the heat increased and an intolerable stink arose, which seemed given off by the very shaking of the train as it thundered along.

They had told their beads at Juvisy. As six struck, they passed through the station of Brétigny at full speed, and Sister Hyacinthe stood up. It was her job to supervise the religious exercises, a programme which most of the pilgrims followed in a little book with a blue cover.

'The Angelus, my children,' she said with her smile, and the motherly air which her youth made so charming and so sweet. Once again, the Aves followed one another. When they finished, Pierre and Marie began to take notice of two women who occupied the two other corners of their compartment. The one who sat at Marie's feet was a slim blonde, of middle-class appearance aged thirty-something, faded before her time. She shrank into her place, hardly taking up any room at all, with her sombre dress, her colourless hair, her long sad face, which expressed infinite resignation and boundless sorrow. Opposite her, the other woman, who occupied the same seat as Pierre, was the same age, working-class, in a black hat, her face ravaged with misery and worry, on her knees a girl of seven, so pale, so wasted, that she could have passed for barely four. With her pinched nose, her bluish eyelids shut in a waxen face, she was unable to speak, but only to give a little moan, a soft groan, which each time tore the heart of the mother who leant over her.

'Would she like a grape?' timidly asked the other woman, silent until now. 'I have some, in my basket.'

'Thank you, madam,' replied the working-class woman. 'She only takes milk, if that. . . . I've taken care to bring a bottle.'

Succumbing to the need of confiding among the wretched, she gave her story. She was called Madame Vincent, she had lost her husband, a gilder, carried off by the consumption. Left alone with her little Rose, who filled her heart, she had worked day and night as a dressmaker to bring her up. But illness had struck. For fourteen months she had held her like that in her arms, growing more and more painful and thinner, becoming almost nothing. One day, she who never went to mass entered a church, impelled by despair, praying for the cure of her daughter; and there she had heard a voice saying, Take her to Lourdes, where the Blessed Virgin will take pity on her. Knowing no one, knowing not even how the pilgrimages were organised, she had only one idea: to work, save money for the journey, buy a ticket, and go with the thirty sous which she had left, and to take only a bottle of milk for the child, without dreaming of buying a piece of bread for herself.

'What has she got, the poor little thing?' asked the other lady.

'Oh! Madame, it's certainly the consumption of the bowels. But the doctors have names for these things. . . . To start with, she had slight pains in the stomach. Then her stomach blew up, and she suffered, oh! so much, it brought tears to your eyes. Now, her stomach's gone down; only, there's hardly anything of her, she's no longer any legs, she's so thin; and she sweats, all the time. . . .'

Then, as Rose had moaned and opened her eyes, her mother leant over her, upset and pale.

'Treasure, what's the matter? Do you want a drink?'

But already the little girl, who had stared vaguely with eyes the blue of a hazy sky, had shut them again; and she said nothing, falling back in exhaustion, white in her white dress, a stylish fancy of her mother's, who had decided on this useless expense in the hope that the Virgin would look more favourably on a little patient who was well dressed and all in white . . .

In need of distraction, Marie became interested in a motionless figure hidden under a black veil. She had no trouble in suspecting some sore to the face. Somebody had told her simply that the woman was a maid. She was from Picardy, by name Elise Rouquet, who had been forced to give up her job and lived in Paris with a sister who bullied her. No hospital would take her, because she was not otherwise ill. Deeply religious, she had been possessed for some months with an ardent wish to go to Lourdes. And Marie waited in muted fear for the fichu to be drawn aside.

'Are they small enough like that?' asked Madame de Jonquière in a motherly voice. 'Can you get them in your mouth?'

Under the black fichu a hoarse voice grunted: 'Yes, yes, madame.'

The fichu fell aside, and Marie felt a shudder of horror. It was lupus, which had invaded the nose and the mouth, spreading little by little, a slow ceaseless ulceration under the scabs, devouring the mucous membranes. Her face was drawn out like a dog's muzzle, and with her bristly hair and wide eyes she was frightening. The cartilage of the nose was almost eaten away, the mouth was awry, tugged to the left by the swollen upper lip, forming an oblique slit, filthy and formless. A sweat of blood mixed with pus ran from this enormous livid sore.

'Oh! just look at that, Pierre!' murmured Marie, trembling.

The priest shuddered in turn, watching Elise Rouquet carefully slip little pieces of bread into the bloody hole which served as a mouth. The carriage had paled before this horrible apparition. And the same thought rose in all these souls inflated with hope. Ah! Blessed Virgin, powerful Virgin, what a miracle if such an illness should be cured!

'My children, we mustn't think only of ourselves if we want to get better,' repeated Sister Hyacinthe. . . .

They had just passed Blois, already on their way for three long hours. Glancing away from Elise Rouquet, Marie's eyes fell upon a man who occupied a corner of the other compartment, to the right, the one where brother Isidore was lying helplessly. She had previously noticed him, poorly dressed in an old black frock-coat, with a thin beard, already greying. He seemed to be suffering, he was small and thin, his fleshless face was covered with sweat. He was motionless, stuck in his corner, speaking to no one, staring fixedly ahead of him with widely open eyes. And suddenly she noticed that his eyelids were drooping and that he was losing consciousness.

She caught the notice of Sister Hyacinthe.

'Sister, I think that gentleman's not very well.'

'Which one, my dear child?'

'That one, with his head fallen backwards.'

There was a stir, all the healthy pilgrims jumped up to look. And Madame de Jonquière got the idea of shouting to Martha, Brother Isidore's sister, to slap the man's hands. 'Ask him what's wrong with him,' she suggested.

Martha shook him, asked questions. But the man failed to respond, his throat gave a rattle, his eyes stayed shut.

A frightened voice was heard somewhere: 'Looks to me as if he's going to die.'

The Grotto at Lourdes has its limitations.

The great miracle was to be attempted, the exceptional divine favour ardently sought since that morning, the resurrection of a man.

Outside, the prayers continued; a furious appeal of voices which vanished into the sky of that hot summer afternoon. A covered stretcher appeared, deposited by two stretcher-bearers in the middle of the hall. It was followed by Baron Suire, President of Hospitalisation, and Berthaud, one of the administrators; the adventure had excited the entire staff, and words were exchanged in a low voice between these gentlemen and the two fathers of the Assumption. Then these two fell praying on their knees, arms flung apart like a cross, their faces lit up, transfigured by the burning desire to see manifested the omnipotence of God.

'O Lord, hear us! . . . Lord, grant us our prayer!'

They had just moved out M. Sabathier [who had been dipped, terrified, into the ice-cold spring water for his legs] and there were no other patients but little Gustave, half-dressed, forgotten on a chair. The curtains of the stretcher were drawn back, the body of the man revealed, already rigid, spare and shrunken, with wide eyes which remained obstinately open. But he was fully dressed and they had to strip him, this grisly task forcing the stretcher-bearers to hestitate a moment. Pierre noticed that the Marquis of Salmon-Roquebert – so devoted to the living without repugnance – kept out of the way, kneeling too, to avoid touching the corpse. Pierre imitated him, prostrating himself nearby, to put a good face on it.

Little by little, Father Massias was growing excited, his voice drowning that of his superior, Father Fourcade.

'Lord, give us back our brother! Lord, do so for Thy glory!'

The stretcher-bearers had now decided to pull off the man's trousers; but the legs would not give them up, and they had to lift the corpse up. The second stretcher-bearer, who was unbuttoning the old frock-coat, made the suggestion in a low voice that it would be quicker to snip everything off with a pair of scissors. Otherwise, they would be there all night.

Berthaud suddenly rushed up. He had had a quick word with Baron Suire. In his heart a politician, the baron disapproved of Father Fourcade having set out on a junket like this. Only there was now no alternative to going through with it: a crowd was waiting, praying to Heaven since morning. The wisest thing was to get it over as soon as possible, being as respectful as they could towards the dead man. And better than messing him about too much to get him in the nude, Berthaud thought it preferable to plunge him into the bath fully clad. There would be time enough for him to change, if he was resuscitated; and, if to the contrary, well, there was no harm done. *Mon Dieu!* He hastily told all this to the stretcher-bearers, and helped them to fix straps under the man's buttocks and round his shoulders.

Father Fourcade had approved of this with a nod of the head, while Father Massias redoubled his fervour.

'O Lord, breathe upon him and he shall be born anew! O Lord, give him back his soul, that he might glorify Thee!'

With an effort, the two stretcher-bearers hoisted the man by the straps, carried him over the bath and slowly lowered him into the water, tormented by the fear that he would drop off. Pierre stared horrified at the corpse being dipped, still wearing his poor old clothes, the material sticking to his bones, outlining his skeleton. He floated like a drowned man. Then – horror! – his head, despite the rigor mortis, jerked backwards; it was underwater, the stretcher-bearers struggled vainly to pull it back with the strap round his shoulders. For a moment, the man was in danger of slipping to the bottom of the bath. How could he start breathing again when he had a mouth full of water, and with his big staring eyes which seemed under that aqueous veil to have died a second time?

For the three interminable minutes that they soaked him, the two fathers of the Assumption – also the almoner – in a paroxysm of hope and faith strove after Heavenly assistance.

'O Lord, look upon him and restore him to life! O Lord, he will rise at Thy voice and convert the whole world! O Lord, Thou hast only to say the word, and the entire world will celebrate Thy name!'

As if a blood-vessel had burst in his throat, Father Massias fell upon his elbows, choking, without the strength to kiss the flagstones. And from outside came the clamour of the crowd, the cry ceaselessly repeated, kept going by the Capuchin: 'O Lord, cure our sick! O Lord, cure our sick!' It fell so oddly, that Pierre stifled a cry of rebellion. Next to him, he felt the Marquis shuddering. To general relief, Berthaud, thoroughly angry with the whole business, said curtly to the stretcher-bearers: 'Put him back!'

They retrieved the man, and put him on the stretcher with his drowned rags clinging to his limbs. Water drained from his hair and ran from his body, flooding the floor. And the dead stayed dead.

Everyone had stood up and was looking at him in a painful silence. As he was covered up and taken off, Father Fourcade followed him, taking Father Massias' shoulder and dragging his gouty leg, of which he had forgotten for the moment the painful weight. He had already recovered his powerful serenity, and could be heard informing the crowd during a silence: 'My dear brothers, my dear sisters, God did not wish to bring him back to us. That is, without doubt, because in His infinite goodness He wishes to keep him among his elect.'

(1894)
Transl. R. G.

The Franco-Prussian War ran from 19 July 1870 to 28 January 1871. It was a shattering French defeat, to be repeated even more speedily between 10 May and 25 June 1940. Both disasters pivoted on the little town of Sedan, which bridges the Meuse in the Ardennes. Both expressed French disorganisation and defeatism again the unflinching application of German efficiency.

These wars of blaring bugles, fluttering banners and ringing hoofs – or of artillery barrages, machine-guns and dive-bombers – are curious exercises in human self-destruction. European statesmen understandably enjoyed enthusiasm for the Clausewitzian principle: what lies beyond your negotiating skills to obtain, you grab. But they inflicted meanwhile on their conscripted citizens the unforgivable misery depicted with such unemotional effectiveness by Zola.

As only a fool would start a war without a reasonable chance of winning, it is lucky for mankind that science's achievement of the H-bomb has since eliminated from elaborate wars any winners at all.

From The Débâcle

'HERE, I SAY, but this one's dead.'

'Oh, Christ, so he is,' muttered the orderly. 'No point having him cluttering up the place.'

He and a comrade took up the corpse and lugged it to the mortuary which they had set up behind the laburnums. A dozen corpses were already arranged there, stiffened as they they had died, some with extended feet, as though just off the rack, others all lopsided, twisted into postures of agony. Some seemed to be sneering, with white eyes, teeth bared under crooked lips; while many, with long faces so frighteningly sad-looking, still wept huge tears. One, very young, small and thin, his head half blown away, grasped next to his heart by two convulsed hands a photograph of a girl – one of those misty cheap photographs – which was spattered with blood. And at the feet of the dead a jumble of legs and arms had piled up, everything that had been clipped away, everything that had been lopped off on the operating tables, the sweepings of a butcher's shop, the tidying into a corner of the waste flesh and bones. . . .

Next came a disarticulation of the shoulder, after the method of Lisfranc, what the surgeons called a pretty operation, something elegant and quick, hardly forty seconds to it. They had already chloroformed the patient, and an assistant seized the shoulder with two hands, four fingers in the armpit, thumbs on top. Then Bouroche [the army surgeon], armed with a big long knife, after calling: 'Sit him up!' grabbed the deltoid, transfixed the arm, sliced the muscle; then, going back to the front, he severed the joint with a single incision, and the arm dropped off, felled in three movements. The assistant had slid down his thumbs, to stop the brachial artery. 'Lay him down!' Bouroche had to laugh as he tied the ligature, because he had accomplished it in thirty-five seconds. All that remained to be done was the applying of the flap of flesh over the wound, like a smooth epaulette. He took care to make a good job of it, because of the danger of a man bleeding to death in three minutes through his brachial artery, without counting the danger of death every time you sat up an operation patient under chloroform.

Delaherche [a civilian, owner of the dye-works commandeered as a field hospital], frozen to the spot, had wanted to flee. But there was no time, the arm was already on the table. The soldier undergoing the amputation, a recruit, a stolid peasant, was coming round and he caught sight of this arm, which an orderly was carrying away to the spot behind the laburnums. He looked sharply at his shoulder and saw it cut and bleeding. He became furiously angry.

'Bloody hell! That's bloody silly, what you've just gone and done.'

Bouroche, tired out, could hardly reply. Then, with the air of a decent sort, he said: 'I did it for your own good, I didn't want you to croak, my lad. . . . And I did put it to you, and you did consent.'

'I said yes? I said yes? I didn't know what I was saying.'

His anger fell away, he began to weep hot tears.

'What am I bloody well going to do with myself now?'

He was carried back to his straw, the wax cloth of the table was briskly washed; and the pails of reddish water which they once more showered across the lawn bloodstained a flower-bed white with daisies.

(1871)
Transl. R. G.

LEO TOLSTOY

Zola depicted the surgical horrors of Napoleon III's war against Prussia without having been a soldier. Count Lev Nikolaevich Tolstoy (1828–1910) pictured those of Napoleon I's war against Russia after himself serving Tsar Nicholas I fighting Napoleon III in the Crimea. Tolstoy was on the staff of Prince Gortschakoff, marching against the Turks on the Danube, then endured the siege of Sebastopol until the French and British allies entered it, burning and empty, on 9 September 1855. How sad that no humanitarian truce allowed him to meet our spiky Miss Nightingale. What a splendid character he would have made of her.

From War and Peace

IN THE MONTH of June the battle of Friedland was fought; in this the Pavlograd Hussars bore no part; it was followed by an armistice. Rostow, feeling very deserted without his friend, and having had no news of him since his departure, was uneasy as to the possible results of his wound, and took advantage of the truce to go to the hospital, which had been established in a hamlet twice sacked by Russian and by French troops. It looked doubly dismal because the season was a fine one, and the sight of the fields gladdened the eyes, while nothing was to be seen in the ruined streets but a few natives in rags, or drunk and invalided soldiers. A stone house, with the window-panes for the most part broken, was dignified by the name of hospital. A few soldiers with limbs wrapped in bandages, pale and puffy, sat or walked up and down to warm themselves in the sun.

Rostow had hardly crossed the threshold when he felt choked and sickened by the mingled stench of drugs and decomposition that pervaded the place. On the stairs he met a Russian army-doctor with a cigar in his mouth, and with him a surgeon.

'I cannot be in two places at once,' the doctor was saying. 'I will meet you this evening at Makar Alexéïévitch's lodgings. Do the best you can. Is it not all the same in the end?'

'Whom are you wanting, highness?' said the doctor to Rostow. 'Why do you come here to take typhus fever when you have escaped the French bullets? It is a plague-stricken spot.'

'What?' said Rostow.

'The typhus is fearful; it is death to come within these walls. We have not succumbed to it, Makéïew and I,' he added, pointing to his companion, 'but five of our colleagues have been carried off. A week after a man comes in. . . . and it is all over with him. They sent us some Prussians, but it did not suit our allies at all.'

Rostow explained that he wished to see Major Denissow.

'I do not know, I do not remember him. That is not to be wondered at: I have three hospitals on my hands and four hundred sick, more or less. And we think ourselves lucky when the charitable German ladies send us two pounds of coffee and some lint every month; without it we could not hold out . . . Four hundred, think of that, without counting the fresh cases to come in.'

The surgeon's worn and weary expression betrayed his impatience of the loquacious doctor's delay.

'Major Denissow,' repeated Rostow. 'Wounded at Molliten?'

'To be sure. He is dead I think – is not he, Makéïew?' said the doctor with the utmost indifference; but the surgeon thought not.

'A red-haired man, tall?' asked the doctor; and then when Rostow described his friend, he added quite joyfully: 'To be sure; I remember. He must be dead. However, I will look through my lists. Are they in your rooms, Makéïew?'

'Makar Alexéïévitch has them. Would you take the trouble to go yourself into the officers' room?' added Makéïew, turning to Rostow.

'I strongly advise you not, my dear fellow, you run the very greatest risk,' said the doctor; but Rostow took leave of him and begged the surgeon to show him the way.

'You have no one but yourself to blame, remember, if mischief comes of it,' cried the doctor from the bottom of the stairs.

The smell in the hospital was so revolting in the narrow passage they went through, that Rostow held his nose and even staggered for a moment. A door opened on the right, and out of it came a living skeleton – pale, emaciated, and barefoot, dragging himself on crutches and looking with envious eyes at the newcomer. Our hussar glanced into the room and saw the patients lying on the floor, some on straw, some on their cloaks.

'May I go in?' he asked.

'There is nothing to see,' said the surgeon, but this reply only piqued his curiosity, and Rostow went in. The stench here was even worse and more penetrating.

In the long room, exposed to a broiling sun, lay two rows of sick and wounded, their heads towards the wall, leaving a passage down the middle; most of them were delirious, and took no notice of the intruders. The others, raising their heads as the two visitors came in, turned their wax-like faces to gaze at them with a look of expecting some providential rescue, and of involuntary jealousy of Rostow's fresh health. Rostow went forward as far as the middle of the room, and looking beyond, through half-open doors into the adjoining wards, he saw only a repetition of the same terrible sight which he stood silently contemplating. Close to his feet, almost across the passage, lay a man, a Cossack no doubt, as was easily seen by the way his hair was cut. With his arms and legs flung out, a burning face, and eyes turned up till only the whites were visible, the veins in his hands and feet swelled almost to bursting, he beat his head against the floor, saying some word again and again in a hoarse voice. Rostow bent over him to hear: 'Drink, drink!' said the poor wretch.

Rostow looked about him wondering whither he could carry the dying man to give him some water.

'Who looks after them?' he asked the surgeon.

At this moment a soldier attached to the ambulance came out of the next room, and taking Rostow for one of the hospital inspectors touched his cap as he passed.

'Carry this man away and give him some water.'

'Certainly, highness,' said the soldier, but he did not move.

'Nothing will be done,' thought Rostow, and he was about to leave the room when a gaze resolutely fixed on his face impelled him instinctively to look into one corner. An old soldier, yellow, gloomy-looking, with an unkempt grizzly beard, seemed to wish to speak to him. Rostow went up to him, and saw that one of his legs had been amputated above the knee. Next to him lay a young man quite motionless; his head thrown back, his colourless face and fixed gaze with half-shut eyelids attracted Rostow's notice. He shuddered: 'But this man, it seems to me . . .'

'Yes, highness; and we have begged and prayed,' said the old soldier, with a tremulous quiver of his jaw. 'He died at daybreak. . . . And they are men after all, and not dogs. . . .'

'He shall be removed this minute,' the surgeon hastened to throw in. 'Come, highness.'

'Yes, come, come –' said Rostow no less hurriedly; he cast down his eyes, trying to pass unobserved through the cross-fire of all these anxious eyes fixed on him with reproach and envy.

(1865–68)

ANTHELME BRILLAT-SAVARIN

Slimming is a baffling preoccupation of contemporary mankind. And big business. Weight Watchers, which eyes the waistlines of the world, is a company enjoying a $900 million a year turnover, which makes a yearly profit of some $100 million from instructing people how to eat sparingly. Weight Watchers is a subsidiary of Heinz, which makes its profits from selling food. Had such an arrangement come to the attention of Lewis Carroll, Alice would have had something else to puzzle about.

From the advice that gorges bookshops, stuffs magazines and inflates newspapers, the human race should have evolved over the past century into walking matchsticks. It has been spared this only by universal difficulty in following the overpowering instructions. A surburban case-history records:

> In the middle of the day she prepares herself a small meal of lettuce-leaf, starch-reduced crispbread, fat-free yoghurt and a cup of black coffee. She eats this alone, at the formica-topped table in the kitchen. This does not take her long, and afterwards all is washed up and tidied away diligently.
>
> About twenty minutes later, she opens the fridge door and extracts a large hunk of Irish cheddar, which she eats rapidly, standing up. A further ten minutes elapse, and she removes the lid from a circular tin to cut herself a substantial slice of dairy cream sponge sandwich. Five minutes later, she unwraps a bar of chocolate from its silver paper. The crumbs of the supplementary nutriment are gathered carefully and sprinkled down the waste-disposal unit. She may end the meal by opening the cupboard in the lounge and pouring herself a slug of vodka. This is invariably followed by a mouthwash and gargle in the bathroom upstairs.

In the seventeenth century, the 'fair round belly with good capon lin'd' was an item of normal physiology. In the eighteenth, French and Italian cooking intruded into 'the Days of good Queen

Elizabeth, when mighty Roast beef was the *Englishman's* Food; our Cookery was plain and simple as our Manners'. Bellies became rounder, to the amusement of Hogarth, Rowlandson and Gillray. Everyone who could afford to do so ate plenty. There was not much else diverting to do. 'We were very merry and no breaking up till two in morning,' recorded even the modest-living country parson James Woodforde, on 19 April 1768. 'I gave Mrs Farr a roasted Shoulder of Mutton and a plum Pudding for dinner – Veal Cutlets, Frill'd Potatoes, cold Tongue, Ham and cold roast Beef, and eggs in their shells. Punch, Wine, Beer and Cyder for drinking.' The richer needed to inflict upon themselves meatless 'banyan days' – which, according to Smollett, took 'their denomination for a sect of devotees in some parts of the East Indies who never taste flesh'. Neither did the poor, who had no option.

Slimming is of literary origin. In 1863, William Banting, a London cabinet-maker, had become so fat that he needed to walk downstairs backwards. Doctor after doctor was powerless to spare him the danger of becoming wedged in the banisters. Then a throat surgeon, William Harvey, surprised the patient with a simple instruction: cut out the milk and butter, sugar and potatoes. For breakfast, Banting got four ounces of meat, or fish, or bacon, and an ounce of toast. For his dinner, an ounce or so more meat, fruit and vegetables and another ounce of toast. At tea-time, a rusk and fruit; for supper four ounces of meat or fish. He drank milkless tea, but was happily allowed several glasses a day of sherry or claret. He lost two and a half stone in nine months. He wrote in delight *A Letter on Corpulence Addressed to the Public*, which was equally delightedly seized upon by fat men and women, who could still go up and down stairs without second thoughts. 'Banting', or 'to bant', passed into the language.

This wave of dietetic enthusiasm washed into the next century. The Directoire frock had then become fashionable – a silky sheath which concentrated the eye of the beholder and the mind of the wearer on aberrant bulges. Slimming remained steadfastly popular into the 1930s, when ladies in *Punch*, asked by their GP whether they drank at meals, were replying: 'Don't be silly, doctor, why, I don't even *eat* at meals.' A most successful and widespread dieting regime was at the end of that decade introduced by the British government.

Today's widespread dietetic obsession may possibly be the civilised replacement of mid-thirteenth-century flagellation, when the streets from Lombardy to Bohemia were interrupted day and night by processions, headed by cross-bearing priests, all conscientiously whipping themselves, and each other, bloody with leather thongs. Such elaborate masochism applied to dieting is needless. Losing weight can be as simple as losing money. It is necessary only to eat, and booze, rather less.

Anthelme Brillat-Savarin (1755–1826) was a lawyer born at Belley in the Jura, an area now spangled with Michelin stars. He became its Mayor in 1793, he was a *député* in the pre-revolutionary *Assemblé*, then fled before the Terror of 1793 to Switzerland and New York, where he played in a theatre-pit orchestra. This extract indicates that advice about losing weight has changed as little as the fatuousness of dinner-table conversations.

From The Physiology of Taste

Cogitation 21
On Obesity

Were I a qualified doctor, I should start off with a nice monograph on obesity; then I should have built my empire in that nook of the science, and I should possess the double advantage of having perfectly healthy people as my patients, and being besieged every day by the prettier half of the human race; for to have the right amount of plumpness, neither too much nor too little, is for women the study of a lifetime.

What I have not achieved, some other doctor will; and if he is at the same time clever, discreet and handsome, I predict for him a miraculous success. Exoriare aliquis nostris ex ossibus *haeres*! [Arise, you unknown heir, from my bones! (Adapted from Virgil.)] Before then I shall start my own career; for an article on obesity is indispensable in a work which has for its subject man and what he eats.

I mean by obesity that state of fatty congestion where, without the person being ill, the limbs grow little by little in volume and lose their natural shape and harmony.

There is a sort of obesity which is borne by the belly; I have never seen it in women: as they usually have softer tissues, when obesity attacks them, it spares them nowhere. I call this sort *gastrophorie*, and *gastrophores* those whom it attacks. I am of their number: but, although carrying a pretty prominent paunch, I have still a strapping leg and the untethered vigour of an Arabian steed.

I have none the less regarded my belly as a redoubtable enemy; I have conquered it majestically; but to conquer meant to fight; it was a thirty-year struggle, and I would wish it a worthwhile one for the benefit of this essay.

I will start with a snatch of more than five hundred conversations which I have had in the past with my dining companions who were threatened or attacked by obesity.

FAT MAN: I say! What delicious bread! Where do you get it from?

MYSELF: From Limet's, in the rue de Richelieu. He's baker to their Royal Highnesses the duc d'Orléans and Prince Condé. I went to him because he's next door, and I've stuck to him because he's the greatest artist in dough in the world.

FAT MAN: I'll make a note of it. I eat a lot of bread, and for *flûtes* like this I'd absolutely do without anything else.

ANOTHER FAT MAN: But what are you up to? You're drinking up your soup and leaving the lovely Carolina rice.

MYSELF: It's my diet.

FAT MAN: What a rotten diet! Rice is my delight, any sort of starch, noodles and suchlike. Nothing builds me up better, is a better buy, and is less trouble to digest.

VERY FAT MAN: Would you kindly oblige, monsieur, by passing those potatoes in front of you? There's a bit of a run on them, and I wouldn't want to be left out.

MYSELF: Monsieur, they're within your reach.

VERY FAT MAN: But aren't you going to help yourself? There's enough for the two of us, and *après nous le déluge.*

MYSELF: I don't take them. I rate the potato only as a protection against starvation; apart from that, I find nothing more eminently flavourless.

VERY FAT MAN: Gastronomical heresy! Nothing is better than potatoes. I eat them in all sorts of ways; and if there's a second helping, whether *à la Lyonnaise* or *soufflé*, I declare here and now the reservation of my rights on them.

FAT WOMAN: Would you be so good as to fetch me those Soissons beans that I see at the bottom of the table?

MYSELF: (*Executing the order while singing softly a familiar song:*)

> The *Soissonnais* are a happy lot,
> Because they've got the haricot . . .

FAT MAN: Don't make a joke of it. They're a real treasure for that part of the world. Paris forks out vast sums for them. I demand your indulgence also for the little garden beans, what we call English beans; when they're still fresh and green, they're the food of the gods.

MYSELF: A plague on beans! A plague on English beans!

FAT MAN: (*Sternly.*) I don't give a hoot for your curses. Might I say that you're alone in your opinion?

MYSELF: (*To someone else.*) Madame, may I congratulate you on your splendid health? You seem to have put on a little weight since I last had the honour of seeing you.

FAT WOMAN: That's probably my new diet.

MYSELF: How's that?

FAT WOMAN: For some time now I've had for lunch a good, thick soup; a bowl big enough for two, and what soup! You could stand you spoon up in it.

MYSELF: (*To another.*) Madame, if your eyes don't deceive me, you'll accept a piece of this charlotte? I'll slice it for you.

FAT WOMAN: Ah, monsieur! My eyes do deceive you. I have two objects of desire, and they are both to the masculine taste. That rice cake with the golden edges, and that gigantic Savoy sponge-cake. For you will know, with your way of thinking, that I dote on sweet pastries.

MYSELF: (*To another.*) While they're debating down there, would you allow me, madame, to investigate for you this frangipane tart?

FAT WOMAN: Please do. Nothing suits me better than pastry. We have a pastry-cook as a tenant; and between my daughter and myself, I really believe we consume his rent, and perhaps a bit more.

MYSELF: (*Having inspected this young person.*) This diet is doing you the world of good. Mademoiselle your daughter is very beautiful, fully armed in all directions.

FAT WOMAN: Would you believe it, her girlfriends sometimes tell her she's too fat?

MYSELF: Perhaps that's through envy.

FAT WOMAN: That may well be. Anyway, I'm marrying her off, and the first baby will put a stop to all that. . . .

You never find obesity among the savages, nor in those classes of society where they work to eat and eat to live . . .

Starch is no less fattening when borne by drinks, like beer and that sort of thing. Regular drinkers are also those with magnificent bellies, and some Parisian families who in 1817 drank beer to save money, because wine was horribly expensive, were rewarded with paunches that they did not know what to do with.

Cogitation 22
The Prevention and Cure of Obesity

Any cure for obesity must start with the basic principles: discretion in eating, moderation in sleep, exercise on foot or on horseback.

These are the premier resources that science presents us with: however, it counts for little, because I know men and their ways, and a prescription which is not executed in full has no effect.

Now:

1. It needs a strong character to leave the table still hungry; so long as the need lasts, one morsel beckons another with an irresistible attraction; and usually we eat so long as we are hungry, despite the doctors, and even following the doctors' example.

2. Suggest to the fat that they get up early, and you pierce them to the heart. They tell you that it will ruin their health; that when they get up early they are good for nothing all day long; the women complain of developing rings under the eyes; all agree to go to bed late, but they reserve the right to sleep all morning; and so goes another expedient.

3. Horse riding is an expensive cure, and not convenient for all pockets and all positions in life.

Propose to a pretty, fat woman to get on a horse, she agrees happily but under three conditions: first, that she shall have a good horse, at one and the same time lively and docile; second, that she shall have a brand-new riding-habit cut in the latest style; third, that she shall have as a riding-master an obliging and good-looking chap. It is pretty rare that all this can happen, so goodbye to riding.

Exercise on foot gives rise to plenty of other objections.

(1825)
Transl. R. G.

ALFRED, LORD TENNYSON

Lord Tennyson (1809–92) published *In the Children's Hospital* among *Ballads and Other Poems* of 1880. 'A true story told me by Mary Gladstone,' he claimed. She was the Prime Minister's vivacious third daughter, who married a clergyman. She put the tale about Emmie in one of her letters to Tennyson, after they became friendly during the summer of 1879.

The poem was 'rather distressing in [its] sentimentality', the poet's grandson later agreed with its attackers. Like the Light Brigade, Tennyson was startled into rushed retreat: 'The doctors and hospitals are unknown to me. The two children are the only characters taken from life in this little dramatic poem. The hospital nurse and not the poet is speaking throughout.' The story anyway originated not from Mary Gladstone's gossip but from *Alice's Christmas Day*, published in *St Cyprian's Banner* of December 1872, except that Emmie was not an orphan as well as a corpse. Someone had blunder'd.

Sixty-six years later, George Orwell recounted that entering hospital himself 'played the queer trick of unearthing from my memory that poem of Tennyson's. . . . I found myself remembering the whole story and atmosphere of the poem, and many of its lines complete.' It had been read to him by a childhood nurse, and they had shuddered over it together. Orwell mentions that Tennyson's outlook 'has a lot to be said for it', though he confusedly antedates the poem before the innovation of anaesthesia and antisepsis, when surgical wards were admittedly something of an animal farm.

The 'oorali' that the red-headed, booming surgeon was suspected of giving his dog is the most shiversome of the words, like woorali, wourali, woorara and urari, all meaning *curare*, the arrow-poison described by Sir Walter Ralegh on his 1595 voyage to the Orinoco. It was a syrup made from the roots of the *strychnos toxifera* creeper, which paralysed the hit animal or enemy, killing from respiratory failure without impairing consciousness. 'The wourali poison destroys life's action so gently, that the victim appears to be in no pain whatever,' wrote Charles Waterton (1782–1865) in *Wanderings in South America* of 1825.

Curare in Tennyson's time was already in medical use, for controlling the convulsions of tetanus in 1858, of epilepsy in 1860, and of rabies in 1838, when it was applied unsuccessfully to Inspector Phelps of the Nottingham police, bitten by a mad dog. Curare is innocuous if swallowed, effective only if administered either by injection or by poison-dart from a blowpipe. It was purified in 1935, and since World War Two has been in everyday use to render patients flaccid for surgery under artificial respiration, while their consciousness is evaporated in a mere whiff of anaesthetic. Odd how this unthinkingly heartless poem mentions one of this century's most beneficial drugs.

Tennyson drank a bottle of port a day for fifty years. He had the habit of pouring water into it, to make it weaker and last longer. An Oxford don once unkindly applied this notion to his poetry.

In the Children's Hospital

EMMIE

I

Our doctor had called in another, I never had seen him before,
But he sent a chill to my heart when I saw him come in at the door,
Fresh from the surgery-schools of France and of other lands –
Harsh red hair, big voice, big chest, big merciless hands!
Wonderful cures he had done, O yes, but they said too of him
He was happier using the knife than in trying to save the limb,
And that I can well believe, for he look'd so coarse and so red,
I could think he was one of those who would break their jests on the dead,
And mangle the living dog that had loved him and fawn'd at his knee –
Drench'd with the hellish oorali – that ever such things should be!

II

Here was a boy – I am sure that some of our children would die
But for the voice of Love, and the smile, and the comforting eye –
Here was a boy in the ward, every bone seem'd out of its place –

Caught in a mill and crush'd – it was all but a hopeless case:
And he handled him gently enough; but his voice and his face were not kind,
And it was but a hopeless case, he had seen it and made up his mind,
And he said to me roughly 'The lad will need little more of your care.'
'All the more need,' I told him, 'to seek the Lord Jesus in prayer;
They are all his children here, and I pray for them all as my own':
But he turn'd to me, 'Ay, good woman, can prayer set a broken bone?'
Then he mutter'd half to himself, but I know that I heard him say
'All very well – but the good Lord Jesus has had his day.'

III

Had? has it come? It has only dawn'd. It will come by and by.
O how could I serve in the wards if the hope of the world were a lie?
How could I bear with the sights and the loathsome smells of disease
But that He said 'Ye do it to me, when ye do it to these'?

IV

So he went. And we past to this ward where the younger children are laid:
Here is the cot of our orphan, our darling, our meek little maid;
Empty you see just now! We have lost her who loved her so much –
Patient of pain tho' as quick as a sensitive plant to the touch;
Hers was the prettiest prattle, it often moved me to tears,
Hers was the gratefullest heart I have found in a child of her years –
Nay you remember our Emmie; you used to send her the flowers;
How she would smile at 'em, play with 'em, talk to 'em hours after hours!
They that can wander at will where the works of the Lord are reveal'd
Little guess what joy can be got from a cowslip out of the field;
Flowers to these 'spirits in prison' are all they can know of the spring,
They freshen and sweeten the wards like the waft of an Angel's wing;

And she lay with a flower in one hand and her thin hands crost on her
breast --
Wan, but as pretty as heart can desire, and we thought her at rest,
Quietly sleeping – so quiet, our doctor said 'Poor little dear,
Nurse, I must do it to-morrow; she'll never live thro' it, I fear.'

V

I walk'd with our kindly old doctor as far as the head of the stair,
Then I return'd to the ward; the child didn't see I was there.

VI

Never since I was nurse, had I been so grieved and so vext!
Emmie had heard him. Softly she call'd from her cot to the next,
'He says I shall never live thro' it, O Annie, what shall I do?'
Annie consider'd . 'If I,' said the wise little Annie, 'was you,
I should cry to the dear Lord Jesus to help me, for, Emmie, you see,
It's all in the picture there: "Little children should come to me." '
(Meaning the print that you gave us, I find that it always can please
Our children, the dear Lord Jesus with children about his knees.)
'Yes, and I will,' said Emmie, 'but then if I call to the Lord,
How should he know that it's me? such a lot of beds in the ward!'
That was a puzzle for Annie. Again she consider'd and said:
'Emmie, you put out your arms, and you leave 'em outside on the
bed –
The Lord has so *much* to see to! but, Emmie, you tell it him plain,
It's the little girl with her arms lying out on the counterpane.'

VII

I had sat three nights by the child – I could not watch her for four –
My brain had begun to reel – I felt I could do it no more.
That was my sleeping-night, but I thought that it never would pass.
There was a thunderclap once, and a clatter of hail on the glass,
And there was a phantom cry that I heard as I tost about,

The motherless bleat of a lamb in the storm and the darkness without;
My sleep was broken besides with dreams of the dreadful knife
And fears for our delicate Emmie who scarce would escape with her
  life;
Then in the gray of the morning it seem'd she stood by me and smiled,
And the doctor came at his hour, and we went to see to the child.

VIII

He had brought his ghastly tools: we believed her asleep again –
Her dear, long, lean, little arms lying out on the counterpane;
Say that His day is done! Ah why should we care what they say?
The Lord of the children had heard her, and Emmie had past away.

(1880)

SAMUEL PEPYS

Only so exceptional a man as Samuel Pepys (1633–1703) could make the ordinariness of everyday existence enthralling. His depiction of the Great Plague, as of everything else synthesising London life, is as personal as a morning glance into his hand-mirror.

The plague cast a gloomy sky over London, day and night. Prudence urged flight. Life was intermittently dangerous and spasmodically saddening (though its casualties were officially underrated, to stiffen morale). Its news was uneasily topical. But even during a plague, someone must continue making money, the dinner, the bed. The plague became incidental to the trivial busyness, to the minor pains, empty gossip and passing pleasures which normally absorb the thoughts and energies of mankind. The plague was in all these things like London during the blitz.

Pepys applied to this frightening year the remedy of another talent, lesser but enviable – an inborn resolute cheerfulness (as assiduously encouraged among the bomb-craters by our wartime leaders). He endured the plague as a well-off worthy, living comfortably and fairly salubriously in Seething Lane in the City, a notable who knew everybody of note. And like all notables, he suffered a pressing egalitarianism: the awareness every morning that he might, like his coachman, be dead by night.

From Pepys's Diary

7 June

This morning my wife and mother rose about two o'clock; and with Mercer [Mrs Pepys's woman], Mary [chambermaid], the boy, and W. Hewer [Pepys's lifelong friend], as they had designed, took boat and down to refresh themselves on the water to Gravesend. Lay till 7 o'clock, then up and to the office upon Sir G. Carteret's [Vice-Admiral, Navy Treasurer] accounts again, where very busy; thence abroad and to the 'Change, no news of certainty being yet come from the Fleet.

Thence to the Dolphin Tavern, where Sir J. Minnes [Rear-Admiral, Comptroller of the Navy], Lord Brouncker [Navy Commissioner, President of the Royal Society], Sir Thomas Harvy and myself dined, upon Sir G. Carteret's charge, and very merry we were, Sir Thomas Harvy being very droll. . . . Thence, it being the hottest day that ever I felt in my life, and it is confessed so by all other people the hottest they ever knew in England in the beginning of June, we to the New Exchange, and there drunk whey, with much entreaty getting it for our money, and they would not be entreated to let us have one glass more. . . . And so by water home, where, weary with walking and with the mighty heat of the weather, and for my wife's not coming home, I staying walking in the garden till twelve at night, when it begun to lighten exceedingly, through the greatness of the heat. Then despairing of her coming home, I to bed. This day, much against my will, I did in Drury Lane see two or three houses marked with a red cross upon the doors, and 'Lord have mercy upon us' writ there; which was a sad sight to me, being the first of the kind that, to my remembrance, I ever saw. It put me into an ill conception of myself and my smell, so that I was forced to buy some roll-tobacco to smell and to chew, which took away the apprehension.

17 June

To the office late, and then home to bed. It struck me very deep this afternoon going with a hackney coach from my Lord Treasurer's down Holborn, the coachman I found to drive easily and easily, at last stood still, and come down hardly able to stand, and told me that he was suddenly struck very sick, and almost blind, he could not see; so I alight and went into another coach, with a sad heart for the poor man and trouble for myself, lest he should have been struck with the plague, being at the end of the town where I took him up; but God have mercy on us all!

20 June

Thanksgiving day for victory over the Dutch [Battle of Lowestoft, 3 June 1665]. Up, and to the office, where very busy alone all the morning till church time, and there heard a mean sorry sermon of Mr Mills. Then to the Dolphin Tavern, where all we officers of the Navy met with the Commissioners of the Ordinance by agreement, and dined:

where good music at my direction. Our club come to 34s. a man, nine of us. . . . This day I informed myself that there died four or five at Westminster of the plague in one alley in several houses upon Sunday last, Bell Alley, over against the Palace-gate; yet people do think that the number will be fewer in the town than it was the last week.

21 June

So homewards and to the Cross Keys at Cripplegate, where I find all the town almost going out of town, the coaches and wagons being all full of people going into the country. Here I had some of the company of the tapster's wife a while, and so home to my office, and then home to supper and to bed.

26 June

So, weary, home, and to my office a while, till almost midnight, and so to bed. The plague increases mightily, I this day seeing a house, at a bitt-maker's [ships' deck posts for securing ropes] over against St Clement's Church, in the open street, shut up; which is a sad sight.

29 June

Up and by water to Whitehall, where the court full of wagons and people ready to go out of town. Then to the Harp and Ball, and there drank and talked with Mary, she telling me in discourse that she lived lately at my neighbour's, Mr Knightly, which made me forbear further discourse. This end of the town every day grows very bad of the plague. The Mortality Bill is come to 267; which is about ninety more than the last: and of these but four in the City, which is a great blessing to us. . . . So home, calling at Somerset House, where they are all packing up too. . . .

22 July

I to Vauxhall, where to the Spring garden; but I do not see one guest there, the town being so empty of any body to come thither. Only, while I was there, a poor woman came to scold with the master of the house that a kinswoman, I think, of hers, that was newly dead of the plague, might be buried in the churchyard; for, for her part, she would not be buried in the commons [the plague death pits], as they said she should. . . . I by coach home, not meeting with but two coaches, and but two carts from Whitehall to my own house, that I could observe; and the streets mighty thin of people. I met this noon with Dr Burnett [Pepys's doctor, who died after performing a post-mortem on a plague victim], who told me, and I find in the news-book this week that he posted upon the 'Change, that whosoever did spread the report that, instead of the plague his servant was by him killed, it was forgery, and showed me the acknowledgement of the master of the pest-house, that his servant died of a bubo in his right groin, and two spots on his right thigh, which is the plague. To my office, where late writing letters, and getting myself prepared with business for Hampton Court tomorrow, and so having caused a good pullet to be got for my supper, all alone, I very late to bed.

30 August

Up betimes and to my business of settling my house and papers, and then abroad and met with Hadley, our clerk, who, upon my asking how the plague goes, he told me it increases much, and much in our parish; for, says he, there died nine this week, though I have returned but six: which is a very ill practice, and makes me think it is so in other places; and therefore the plague much greater than people take it to be. . . . So I went forth and walked towards Moorfields to see (God forbid my presumption!) whether I could see any dead corpse going to the grave; but, as God would have it, did not. But, Lord! how everybody's looks, and discourse in the street is of death, and nothing else, and few people going up and down, that the town is like a place distressed and forsaken.

6 September

Busy all the morning writing letters to several, so to dinner, to London, to pack up more things thence; and there I looked into the street and saw fires burning in the street, as it is through the whole City, by the Lord Mayor's order. Thence by water to the Duke of Albermarle's [Governor of the City, George Monk of the Restoration]: all the way fires on each side of the Thames, and strange to see in broad daylight two or three burials upon the Bankside, one at the very heels of another: doubtless all of the plague; and yet at least forty or fifty people going along with every one of them.

20 September

But, Lord! what a sad time it is to see no boats upon the River; and grass grows all up and down Whitehall court, and nobody but poor wretches in the streets! And, which is worst of all, the Duke of Albermarle showed us the number of the plague this week, brought in the last night from the Lord Mayor; that it is increased about six hundred more than the last, which is quite contrary to our hopes and expectations, from the coldness of the late season.

16 October

I walked to the Tower; but, Lord! how empty the streets are and melancholy, so many poor sick people in the streets full of sores; and so many sad stories overheard as I walk, everybody talking of this dead and that man sick, and so many in this place, and so many in that. And they tell me that, in Westminster, there is never a physician and but one apothecary left, all being dead; but that there are great hopes of a great decrease this week: God send it!

31 December

(Lord's day.) Thus ends this year, to my great joy, in this manner. I have raised my estate from £1,300 in this year to £4,400. I have got myself greater interest, I think, by my diligence, and my employments increased by that of Treasurer for Tangier, and Surveyor of the Victuals. It is true we have gone through great melancholy because of the great plague, and I put to great charges by it, by keeping my family long at Woolwich, and myself and another part of my family, my clerks, at my charge at Greenwich, and a maid at London; but I hope the King will give us some satisfaction for that. But now the plague is abated almost to nothing, and I am intending to get to London as fast as I can. . . . My whole family has been well all this while, and all my friends I know of, saving my aunt Bell, who is dead, and some children of my cousin Sarah's, of the plague. But many of such as I know very well, dead; yet, to our great joy, the town fills apace, and shops begin to be open again. Pray God continue the plague's decrease!

(1665)

DANIEL DEFOE

Daniel Defoe (?1660–1731), born Foe, the son of a Cripplegate butcher, experienced London during the Great Plague, but aged five. *A Journal of the Plague Year*, 'written by a Citizen who continued all the while in London. Never made public before', he produced in his sixties. Like *Robinson Crusoe* – which was inspired by Fifeshire's Alexander Selkirk, the sole inhabitant from 1704 to 1709 of Más a Tierra (now Juan Fernandez) in the Pacific off Chile – it is an outstandingly vivid work of 'faction'. Of Defoe: 'Nothing was too small to escape his notice, nothing was too large to fit into his comprehension. His curiosity was insatiable, and he knew how to turn the smallest detail to literary account. To write was as natural to him as to breathe, he made fiction seem like truth and truth seem like fiction.' As a further accolade, he was pilloried for satirising intolerance of the dissenters in 1703.

The plague probably inflamed Defoe's imagination from the weekly bills of mortality and the books of tragically useless cures and preventions which occupied his library. Bubonic plague, with its terrible 'tokens' of bloated lymph glands in the groin, is a disease of rats. Their fleas skip from dying rat to man, infecting him with the *Pasteurella pestis* bacilli. The sign of plague is dead rats everywhere. Odd that nobody noticed them.

From A Journal of the Plague Year

IT WAS ABOUT the beginning of September, 1664, that I, among the rest of my neighbours, heard, in ordinary discourse, that the plague was returned again in Holland; for it had been very violent there, and particularly at Amsterdam and Rotterdam, in the year 1663, whither, they say, it was brought, some said from Italy, others from the Levant, among some goods, which were brought home by their Turkey fleet; others said it was brought from Candia; others from Cyprus. It mattered not from whence it came; but all agreed it was come into Holland again. . . .

This was the beginning of May, yet the weather was temperate, variable, and cool enough, and people had still some hopes. That which encouraged them was, that the city was healthy, the whole ninety-seven parishes buried but fifty-four, and we began to hope, that as it was chiefly among the people at that end of the town, it might go no farther; and the rather, because the next week, which was from the 9th of May to the 16th, there died but three, of which not one within the whole city or liberties; and St Andrew's buried but fifteen, which was very low. 'Tis true St Giles's buried two-and-thirty, but still, as there was but one of the plague, people began to be easy. The whole bill also was very low, for the week before the bill was but 347, and the week above mentioned but 343. We continued in these hopes for a few days, but it was but for a few, for the people were no more to be deceived thus; they searched the houses, and found that the plague was really spread every way, and that many died of it every day. So that now all our extenuations abated, and it was no more to be concealed; nay, it quickly appeared that the infection had spread itself beyond all hopes of abatement; that in the parish of St Giles it was gotten into several streets, and several families lay all sick together; and, accordingly, in the weekly bill for the next week the thing began to show itself. There was indeed but fourteen set down of the plague, but this was all knavery and collusion, for in St Giles's parish they buried forty in all, whereof it was certain most of them died of the plague, though they were set down of other distempers; and though the number of all the burials were not increased above thirty-two, and the whole bill being but 385, yet there was fourteen of the spotted-fever, as well as fourteen of the plague; and we took it for granted upon the whole that there were fifty died that week of the plague.

The next bill was from the 23rd of May to the 30th, when the number of the plague was seventeen. But the burials in St Giles's were fifty-three – a frightful number! – of whom they set down but nine of the plague; but on an examination more strictly by the justices of the peace, and at the Lord Mayor's request, it was found there were twenty more who were really dead of the plague in that parish, but had been set down of the spotted-fever or other distempers, besides others concealed.

But those were trifling things to what followed immediately after; for now the weather set in hot, and from the first week in June the infection spread in a dreadful manner, and the bills rose high; the articles of the fever, spotted-fever, and teeth began to swell; for all that could conceal their distempers did it, to prevent their neighbours shunning and refusing to converse with them, and also to prevent authority shutting up their houses, which though it was not yet practised, yet was threatened, and people were extremely terrified at the thoughts of it.

The second week in June, the parish of St Giles, where still the weight of the infection lay, buried 120, whereof, though the bills said but sixty-eight of the plague, everybody said there had been 100 at least, calculating it from the usual number of funerals in that parish, as above. . . .

A watchman, it seems, had been employed to keep his post at the door of a house which was infected, or said to be infected, and was shut up. He had been there all night for two nights together, as he told his story, and the day-watchman had been there one day, and was now come to relieve him. All this while no noise had been heard in the house, no light had been seen; they called for nothing, sent him of no errands, which used to be the chief business of the watchmen; neither had they given him any disturbance, as he said, from the Monday afternoon, when he heard great crying and screaming in the house, which, as he supposed, was occasioned by some of the family dying just at that time. It seems, the night before, the dead-cart, as it was called, had been stopped there, and a servant-maid had been brought down to the door dead, and the buriers or bearers, as they were called, put her into the cart, wrapt only in a green rug, and carried her away.

The watchman had knocked at the door, it seems, when he heard that noise and crying, as above, and nobody answered a great while; but at last one looked out and said with an angry, quick tone, and yet a kind of crying voice, or a voice of one that was crying, 'What d'ye want, that ye make such a knocking?' He answered, 'I am the watchman! How do you do? What is the matter?' The person answered, 'What is that to you? Stop the dead-cart.' This, it seems, was about one o'clock. Soon after, as the fellow said, he stopped the dead-cart, and then knocked again, but nobody answered. He continued knocking, and the bellman called out several times, 'Bring out your dead;' but nobody answered, till the man that drove the cart, being called to other houses, would stay no longer, and drove away.

The watchman knew not what to make of all this, so he let them alone till the morning-man or day-watchman, as they called him, came to relieve him. Giving him an account of the particulars, they knocked at the door a great while, but nobody answered; and they observed that the window or casement at which the person had looked out who had answered before continued open, being up the two pair of stairs.

Upon this the two men, to satisfy their curiosity, got a long ladder, and one of them went up to the window and looked into the room, where he saw a woman lying dead upon the floor in a dismal manner, having no clothes on her but her shift. But though he called aloud, and putting in his long staff, knocked hard on the floor, yet nobody stirred or answered; neither could he hear any noise in the house.

He came down again upon this, and acquainted his fellow, who went up also; and finding it just so, they resolved to acquaint either the Lord Mayor or some other magistrate of it, but did not offer to go in at the window. The magistrate, it seems, upon the information of the two men, ordered the house to be broke open, a constable and other persons being appointed to be present, that nothing might be plundered; and accordingly it was so done, when nobody was found in the house but that young woman, who having been infected and past recovery, the rest had left her to die by herself, and were every one gone, having found some way to delude the watchman, and to get open the door, or get out at some back-door, or over the tops of the houses, so that he knew nothing of it; and as to those cries and shrieks which he heard, it was supposed they were the passionate cries of the family at the bitter parting, which, to be sure, it was to them all, this being the sister to the mistress of the family. The man of the house, his wife, several children, and servants, being all gone and fled, whether sick or sound, that I could never learn; nor, indeed, did I make much inquiry after it. . . .

I remember, and while I am writing this story I think I hear the very sound of it, a certain lady had an only daughter, a young maiden about nineteen years old, and who was possessed of a very considerable fortune. They were only lodgers in the house where they were. The young woman, her mother, and the maid had been abroad on some occasion, I do not remember what, for the house was not shut up; but about two hours after they came home the young lady complained she was not well; in a quarter of an hour more she vomited and had a violent pain in her head. 'Pray God,' says her mother, in a terrible fright, 'my child has not the distemper!' The pain in her head increasing, her mother ordered the bed to be warmed, and resolved to put her to bed, and prepared to give her things to sweat, which was the ordinary remedy to be taken when the first apprehensions of the distemper began.

While the bed was airing the mother undressed the young woman, and just as she was laid down in the bed, she, looking upon her body with a candle, immediately discovered the fatal tokens on the inside of her thighs. Her mother, not being able to contain herself, threw down her candle and screeched out in such a frightful manner that it was enough to place horror upon the stoutest heart in the world; nor was it one scream or one cry, but the fright having seized her spirits, she fainted first, then recovered, then ran all over the house, up the stairs and down the stairs, like one distracted, and indeed really was distracted, and continued screeching and crying out for several hours void of all sense, or, at least, government of her senses, and, as I was told, never came thoroughly to herself again. As to the young maiden, she was a dead corpse from that moment, for the gangrene which occasions the spots had spread [over] her whole body, and she died in less than two hours. But still the mother continued crying out, not knowing anything more of her child, several hours after she was dead. It is so long ago that I am not certain, but I think the mother never recovered, but died in two or three weeks after. . . .

I say they had dug several pits in another ground, when the distemper began to spread in our parish, and especially when the dead-carts began to go about, which was not, in our parish, till the beginning of August. Into these pits they had put perhaps fifty or sixty bodies each; then they made larger holes, wherein they buried all that the cart brought in a week, which, by the middle to the end of August, came to from 200 to 400 a week; and they could not well dig them larger, because of the order of the magistrates confining them to leave no bodies within six feet of the surface; and the water coming on at about seventeen or eighteen feet, they could not well, I say, put more in one pit. But now, at the beginning of September, the plague raging in a dreadful manner, and the number of burials in our parish increasing to more than was ever buried in any parish about London of no larger extent, they ordered this dreadful gulf to be dug, for such it was rather than a pit.

They had supposed this pit would have supplied them for a month or more when they dug it, and some blamed the churchwardens for suffering such a frightful thing, telling them they were making preparations to bury the whole parish, and the like; but time made it appear the churchwardens knew the condition of the parish better than they did, for the pit being finished the 4th September, I think, they began to bury in it the 6th, and by the 20th, which was just two weeks, they had thrown into it 1114 bodies, when they were obliged to fill it up, the bodies being then come to lie within six feet of the surface. . . .

This is one of the reasons why I believed then, and do believe still, that the shutting up houses thus by force, and restraining, or rather imprisoning, people in their own houses, as I said above, was of little or no service in the whole. Nay, I am of opinion it was rather hurtful, having forced those desperate people to wander abroad with the plague upon them, who would otherwise have died quietly in their beds.

I remember one citizen who, having thus broken out of his house in Aldersgate Street or thereabout, went along the road to Islington; he attempted to have gone in at the Angel Inn, and after that the White Horse, two inns known still by the same signs, but was refused; after which he came to the Pied Bull, an inn also still continuing the same sign. He asked them for lodging for one night only, pretending to be going into Lincolnshire, and assuring them of his being very sound and free from infection, which also at that time had not reached much that way.

They told him they had no lodging that they could spare but one bed up in the garret, and that they could spare that bed for one night, some drovers being expected the next day with cattle; so, if he would accept of that lodging, he might have it, which he did. So a servant was sent up with a candle with him to show him the room. He was very well dressed, and looked like a person not used to lie in a garret; and when he came to the room he fetched a deep sigh, and said to the servant, 'I have seldom lain in such a lodging as this.' However, the servant assuring him again that they had no better, 'Well,' says he, 'I must make shift; this is a dreadful time; but it is but for one night.' So he sat down upon the bedside, and bade the maid, I think it was, fetch him up a pint of warm ale. Accordingly the servant went for the ale, but some hurry in the house, which perhaps employed her other ways, put it out of her head, and she went up no more to him.

The next morning, seeing no appearance of the gentleman, somebody in the house asked the servant that had showed him upstairs what was become of him. She started. 'Alas!' says she, 'I never thought more of him. He bade me carry him some warm ale, but I forgot.' Upon which, not the maid, but some other person was sent up to see after him, who, coming into the room, found him stark dead and almost cold, stretched out across the bed. His clothes were pulled off, his jaw fallen, his eyes open in a most frightful posture, the rug of the bed being grasped hard in one of his hands, so that it was plain he died soon after the maid left him; and 'tis probable, had she gone up with the ale, she had found him dead in a few minutes after he sat down upon the bed. The alarm was great in the house, as any one may suppose, they having been free from the distemper till that disaster, which, bringing the infection to the house, spread it immediately to other houses round about it. I do not remember how many died in the house itself, but I think the maid-servant who went up first with him fell presently ill by the fright, and several others; for, whereas there died but two in Islington of the plague the week before, there died seventeen the week after, whereof fourteen were of the plague. This was in the week from the 11th of July to the 18th. . . .

We had at this time a great many frightful stories told us of nurses and watchmen who looked after the dying people; that is to say, hired nurses, who attended infected people, using them barbarously, starving them, smothering them, or by other wicked means hastening their end, that is to say, murdering of them; and watchmen, being set to guard houses that were shut up when there has been but one person left, and perhaps that one lying sick, that they have broke in and murdered that body, and immediately thrown them out into the dead-cart! and so they have gone scarce cold to the grave. . . .

It was under this John Hayward's [grave-digger] care, and within his bounds, that the story of the piper, with which people have made themselves so merry, happened, and he assured me that it was true. It is said that it was a blind piper; but, as John told me, the fellow was not blind, but an ignorant, weak, poor man, and usually walked his rounds about ten o'clock at night and went piping along from door to door, and the people usually took him in at public-houses where they knew him, and would give him drink and victuals, and sometimes farthings; and he in return would pipe and sing and talk simply, which diverted the people; and thus he lived. It was but a very bad time for this diversion while things were as I have told, yet the poor fellow went about as usual, but was almost starved; and when anybody asked how he did he would answer, the dead-cart had not taken him yet, but that they had promised to call for him next week.

It happened one night that this poor fellow, whether somebody had given him too much drink or no – John Hayward said he had not drink in his house, but that they had given him a little more victuals than ordinary at a public-house in Coleman Street – and the poor fellow, having not usually had a bellyful for perhaps not a good while, was laid all along upon the top of a bulk or stall, and fast asleep, at a door in the street near London Wall, towards Cripplegate, and that upon the same bulk or stall the people of some house, in the alley of which the house was a corner, hearing a bell, which they always rang before the cart came, had laid a body really dead of the plague just by him, thinking, too, that this poor fellow had been a dead body, as the other was, and laid there by some of the neighbours.

Accordingly, when John Hayward with his bell and the cart came along, finding two dead bodies lie upon the stall, they took them up with the instrument they used and threw them into the cart, and all this while the piper slept soundly.

From hence they passed along and took in other dead bodies, till, as honest John Hayward told me, they almost buried him alive in the cart; yet all this while he slept soundly. At length the cart came to the place where the bodies were to be thrown into the ground, which, as I do remember, was at Mount Mill; and as the cart usually stopped some time before they were ready to shoot out the melancholy load they had in it, as soon as the cart stopped the fellow awaked and struggled a little to get his head out from among the dead bodies, when, raising himself up in the cart he called out, 'Hey; where am I?' This frighted the fellow that attended about the work; but after some pause John Hayward, recovering himself, said, 'Lord, bless us! There's somebody in the cart not quite dead!' So another called to him and said, 'Who are you?' The fellow answered, 'I am the poor piper. Where am I?' 'Where are you?' says Hayward. 'Why, you are in the dead-cart, and we are going to bury you.' 'But I an't dead though, am I?' says the piper, which made them laugh a little, though, as John said, they were heartily frighted at first; so they helped the poor fellow down, and he went about his business. . . .

This running of distempered people about the streets was very dismal, and the magistrates did their utmost to prevent it; but as it was generally in the night and always sudden when such attempts were made, the officers could not be at hand to prevent it; and even when any got out in the day, the officers appointed did not care to meddle with them, because, as they were all grievously infected, to be sure, when they were come to that height, so they were more than ordinarily infectious, and it was one of the most dangerous things that could be to touch them. On the other hand, they generally ran on, not knowing what they did, till they dropped down stark dead, or till they had exhausted their spirits so as that they would fall and then die in perhaps half-an-hour or an hour; and, which was most piteous to hear, they were sure to come to themselves entirely in that half-hour or hour, and then to make most grievous and piercing cries and lamentations in the deep, afflicting sense of the condition they were in. . . .

Nothing but the immediate finger of God, nothing but omnipotent power, could have done it. The contagion despised all medicine; death raged in every corner; and had it gone on as it did then, a few weeks more would have cleared the town of all, and everything that had a soul. Men everywhere began to despair; every heart failed them for fear; people were made desperate through the anguish of their souls, and the terrors of death sat in the very faces and countenances of the people.

In that very moment, when we might very well say, 'Vain was the help of man,' – I say, in that very moment it pleased God, with a most agreeable surprise, to cause the fury of it to abate, even of itself; and the malignity declining, as I have said, though infinite numbers were sick, yet fewer died, and the very first weeks' bill decreased 1843; a vast number indeed!

It is impossible to express the change that appeared in the very countenances of the people that Thursday morning when the weekly bill came out. It might have been perceived in their countenances that a secret surprise and smile of joy sat on everybody's face. They shook one another by the hands in the streets, who would hardly go on the same side of the way with one another before. Where the streets were not too broad, they would open their windows and call from one house to another, and ask how they did, and if they had heard the good news that the plague was abated. Some would return, when they said good news, and ask, 'What good news?' and when they answered that the plague was abated and the bills decreased almost 2000, they would cry out, 'God be praised,' and would weep aloud for joy, telling them they had heard nothing of it; and such was the joy of the people that it was, as it were, life to them from the grave. I could almost set down as many extravagant things done in the excess of their joy as of their grief; but that would be to lessen the value of it.

(1722)

GEORGE ELIOT

The famous 1977 *Book of Lists* gives among 'The Fifteen Most Boring Classics' both *Silas Marner* (7) and *The Mill on the Floss* (15). George Eliot (1819–80, who was Mary Ann Evans and who became Mary Ann Cross seven months before she died) was the only author to score twice. The list needed to be little longer to include her *Middlemarch*. It is a masterpiece, of course, but a boring masterpiece, like Rembrandt's 'Night Watch' and the Pyramids.

Middlemarch, A Study of Provincial Life, nudges one thousand pages. The novel was published in 1871 but set in 1829–32, during the times of the Reform Bill and Catholic emancipation, of Tory Prime Minister the Duke of Wellington being replaced by Whig Earl Grey, a man devoted to 'peace, retrenchment and reform', of the early railways and the first legal trade unions – also of 'machine-breaking and rick-burning', trouble in the mill and on the farm.

Medical foundation stones were being laid with the BMA and the *Lancet*, but everyday medicine in the 1830s was primitive. Edward Jenner's (1749–1823) vaccination had leashed rampaging smallpox, there was colchicum for the gout, foxglove for the dropsy, and quinine for the malaria which arose mysteriously with the miasmas from the marshes. Otherwise, practice was a jumble of folk-remedies, fallacies, ignorance and luck, invigorated by the vigorous extraction of speculative bodily malevolences with leeches, blisters, bleeding-bowls and clysters.

When *Middlemarch* appeared in 1871 anaesthesia had by then removed the terror of operations and Lister's antiseptic spray had reduced their perils. In Paris, Louis Pasteur (1822–95) had the startling idea of infection being caused by living microbes, though nobody had the slightest notion what they were. Sanitation was in the fetid air. The cholera epidemics which had outraged Dickens killed ten thousand Londoners during the summer of 1847, and so concentrated minds in Westminster that a Public Health Act was passed in 1848. Doctors could become the selfless saviours of the slums during epidemics. Allan Woodcourt was in *Bleak House* (1852). In Charles Kingsley's (1819–75) *Two Years Ago* (two years previously there had been a cholera epidemic), Dr Tom Thurnall of 1857 enlightens a Cornish curate:

> 'You hate sin, you know. Well, I hate disease. Moral evil is your devil, and physical evil is mine. I hate it, little or big; I hate to see a fellow sick; I hate to see a child rickety and pale; I hate to see a speck of dirt in the street. . . . I hate neglect, incapacity, idleness, ignorance, and all the disease and misery which spring out of that.'

An admirably keen practitioner.

As valuably as flushing away the sewerage, some doctors had started thinking somewhat scientifically. *Middlemarch*'s Dr Tertius Lydgate is an 1871 doctor set in 1831, a scientist among traditionalists. He refused to give long-favoured but useless remedies. He flourished the stylish stethoscope. He diagnosed the rose-spotted typhoid fever which his colleagues missed. Lydgate's paragon was Marie François Xavier Bichat (1771–1802) of the Hôtel-Dieu in Paris, who sorted out the body's simple tissues which variously combine to construct the complex architecture of its organs. Asa Briggs in *Middlemarch and the Doctors* quotes Lydgate's ambition to: 'Pierce the obscurity of those minute processes which prepare human misery and joy, those invisible thoroughfares which are the first lurking-places of anguish, mania and crime'. Rather grand, but Lydgate saw himself extravagantly as a second Jenner. He was nevertheless an admirable bedside doctor, whom his future wife complimented: 'He cared not for "cases", but for John and Elizabeth.' Adding, 'especially Elizabeth'.

Lydgate was utterly frustrated in his ideals, his ambitions and his marriage. All of which helped to make him the first fictional medical hero, the head of an endless professional procession. (Mrs Leavis puts him second, behind the medical father of *Miss Marjoribanks* (1865), by fireside-cosy, ninety-odd-novels Margaret Oliphant (1828–97); but Dr Marjoribanks is sitcom, Dr Lydgate is heavy drama.)

George Eliot was sensitive, depressive and hypochondriacal, an absorber of medical textbooks and encyclopaedias. Such enthusiasm was infected by George Henry Lewes (1817–78), who left his wife and children to live with her for twenty-four years, and protected her from the world which is harsh even beyond book reviewers' columns. Lewes had been a medical student, but was too queasy for the operating theatre. He turned writer, a populariser of philosophy and science, like *Physiology in Common Life* (1859).

In 1879 George Eliot founded a Physiology Studentship in his memory. Then she married a New York banker.

Dr Lydgate is supposedly modelled on Sir Thomas Clifford Allbut (1836–1925), with whom she stayed in Yorkshire. He was a vicar's son who became a Leeds consulting physician – including physician to its fever hospital – rising in 1892 to be Regius Professor of Medicine at Cambridge. Sir Clifford wrote the enduring textbook *System of Medicine*, advocated fresh air for TB sufferers and reduced the clinical thermometer from greenhouse-size to its present convenient stubbiness. Middlemarch was Coventry, to be sadly immortalised sixty-nine years later.

Here is a narrow medical thread drawn out of the book.

From Middlemarch

'MARY! YOU ARE the oddest girl. But what sort of looking man is he? Describe him to me.'

'How can one describe a man? I can give you an inventory: heavy eyebrows, dark eyes, a straight nose, thick dark hair, large solid white hands – and – let me see – oh, an exquisite cambric pocket handkerchief. But you will see him. You know this is about the time of his visits.'

Rosamond blushed a little, but said, meditatively, 'I rather like a haughty manner. I cannot endure a rattling young man.'

'I did not tell you that Mr Lydgate was haughty; but *il y en a pour tous les goûts*, as little Mamselle used to say, and if any girl can choose the particular sort of conceit she would like, I should think it is you, Rosy.' . . .

'I shall be exceedingly obliged if you will look in on me here occasionally, Mr Lydgate,' the banker observed, after a brief pause. 'If, as I dare to hope, I have the privilege of finding you a valuable coadjutor in the interesting matter of hospital management, there will be many questions which we shall need to discuss in private. As to the new hospital, which is nearly finished, I shall consider what you have said about the advantages of the special destination for fevers. The decision will rest with me, for though Lord Medlicote has given the land and timber for the building, he is not disposed to give his personal attention to the object.'

'There are few things better worth the pains in a provincial town like this,' said Lydgate. 'A fine fever hospital in addition to the old infirmary might be the nucleus of a medical school here, when once we get our medical reforms; and what would do more for medical education than the spread of such schools over the country? A born provincial man who has a grain of public spirit as well as a few ideas should do what he can to resist the rush of everything that is a little better than common towards London. Any valid professional aims may often find a freer, if not a richer field, in the provinces.'

One of Lydgate's gifts was a voice habitually deep and sonorous, yet capable of becoming very low and gentle at the right moment. About his ordinary bearing there was a certain fling, a fearless expectation of success, a confidence in his own powers and integrity much fortified by contempt for petty obstacles or seductions of which he had had no experience. But this proud openness was made lovable by an expression of unaffected good-will. . . .

'The standard of that profession is low in Middlemarch, my dear sir,' said the banker. 'I mean in knowledge and skill; not in social status, for our medical men are most of them connected with respectable towns-people here. My own imperfect health has induced me to give some attention to those palliative resources which the divine mercy has placed within our reach. I have consulted eminent men in the metropolis, and I am painfully aware of the backwardness under which medical treatment labours in our provincial districts.'

'Yes; – with our present medical rules and education, one must be satisfied now and then to meet with a fair practitioner. As to all the higher questions which determine the starting-point of a diagnosis – as to the philosophy of medical evidence – any glimmering of these can only come from a scientific culture of which country practitioners have usually no more notion than the man in the moon.' . . .

There was a general impression, however, that Lydgate was not altogether a common country doctor, and in Middlemarch at that time such an impression was significant of great things being expected from him. For everybody's family doctor was remarkably clever, and was understood to have immeasurable skill in the management and training of the most skittish or vicious diseases. The evidence of his cleverness was of the higher intuitive order, lying in his lady patients' immovable conviction, and was unassailable by any objection that their intuitions were opposed by others equally strong; each lady who saw medical truth in Wrench and 'the strengthening treatment' regarding Toller and 'the lowering system' as medical perdition. For the heroic times of copious bleeding and blistering had not yet departed, still less the times of thorough-going theory, when disease in general was called by some bad name, and treated accordingly without shilly-shally – as if, for example, it were to be called insurrection, which must not be fired on with blank-cartridge, but have its blood drawn at once. The strengtheners and the lowerers were all 'clever' men in somebody's opinion, which is really as much as can be said for any living talents. Nobody's imagination had gone so far as to conjecture that Mr Lydgate could know as much as Dr Sprague and Dr Minchin, the two physicians, who alone could offer any hope when danger was extreme, and when the smallest hope was worth a guinea. Still, I repeat, there was a general impression that Lydgate was something rather more uncommon than any general practitioner in Middlemarch. And this was true. He was but seven-and-twenty, an age at which many men are not quite common – at which they are hopeful of achievement, resolute in avoidance, thinking that Mammon shall never put a bit in their mouths and get astride their backs, but rather than Mammon, if they have anything to do with him, shall draw their chariot. . . .

Lydgate was ambitious above all to contribute towards enlarging the scientific, rational basis of his profession. The more he became interested in special questions of disease, such as the nature of fever or fevers, the more keenly he felt the need for that fundamental knowledge of structure which just at the beginning of the century had been illuminated by the brief and glorious career of Bichat, who died when he was only one-and-thirty, but, like another Alexander, left a realm large enough for many heirs. . . .

'Oh, well,' said Mr Chichely, 'I blame no man for standing up in favour of his own cloth; but, coming to argument, I should like to know how a coroner is to judge of evidence if he has not had a legal training?'

'In my opinion,' said Lydgate, 'legal training only makes a man more incompetent in questions that require knowledge of another kind. People talk about evidence as if it could really be weighed in scales by a blind Justice. No man can judge what is good evidence on any particular subject, unless he knows that subject well. A lawyer is no better than an old woman at a *post-mortem* examination. How is he to know the action of a poison? You might as well say that scanning verse will teach you to scan the potato crops.'

'You are aware, I suppose, that it is not the coroner's business to conduct the *post-mortem*, but only to take the evidence of the medical witness?' said Mr Chichely, with some scorn.

'Who is often almost as ignorant as the coroner himself,' said Lydgate. 'Questions of medical jurisprudence ought not to be left to the chance of decent knowledge in a medical witness, and the coroner ought not to be a man who will believe that strychnine will destroy the coats of the stomach if an ignorant practitioner happens to tell him so.'

Lydgate had really lost sight of the fact that Mr Chichely was his Majesty's coroner, and ended innocently with the question, 'Don't you agree with me, Dr Sprague?'

'To a certain extent – with regard to populous districts, and in the metropolis,' said the Doctor. 'But I hope it will be long before this part of the country loses the services of my friend Chichely, even though it might get the best man in our profession to succeed him. I am sure Vincy will agree with me.'

'Yes, yes, give me a coroner who is a good coursing man,' said Mr Vincy, jovially. 'And in my opinion, you're safest with a lawyer. Nobody can know everything. Most things are "visitation of God". And as to poisoning, why, what you want to know is the law. Come, shall we join the ladies?' . . .

Dr Minchin was soft-handed, pale-complexioned, and of rounded outline, not to be distinguished from a mild clergyman in appearance: whereas Dr Sprague was superfluously tall; his trousers got creased at the knees, and showed an excess of boot at a time when straps seemed necessary to any dignity of bearing; you heard him go in and out, and up and down, as if he had come to see after the roofing. In short, he had weight, and might be expected to grapple with a disease and throw it; while Dr Minchin might be better able to detect it lurking and to circumvent it. They enjoyed about equally the mysterious privilege of medical reputation, and concealed with much etiquette their contempt for each other's skill. . . .

What the opposition in Middlemarch said about the New Hospital and its administration had certainly a great deal of echo in it, for heaven has taken care that everybody shall not be an originator; but there were differences which represented every social shade between the polished moderation of Dr Minchin and the trenchant assertion of Mrs Dollop, the landlady of the Tankard in Slaughter Lane.

Mrs Dollop became more and more convinced by her own asseveration, that Doctor Lydgate meant to let the people die in the Hospital, if not to poison them, for the sake of cutting them up without saying by your leave or with your leave; for it was a known 'fac' that he had wanted to cut up Mrs Goby, as respectable a woman as any in Parley Street, who had money in trust before her marriage – a poor tale for a doctor, who if he was good for anything should know what was the matter with you before you died, and not want to pry into your inside after you were gone. If that was not reason, Mrs Dollop wished to know what was; but there was a prevalent feeling in her audience that her opinion was a bulwark, and that if it were overthrown there would be no limits to the cutting-up of bodies, as had been well seen in Burke and Hare with their pitch-plaisters – such a hanging business as that was not wanted in Middlemarch!

And let it not be supposed that opinion at the Tankard in Slaughter Lane was unimportant to the medical profession: that old authentic public-house – the original Tankard known by the name of Dollop's – was the resort of a great Benefit Club, which had some months before put to the vote whether its long-standing medical man, 'Doctor Gambit', should not be cashiered in favour of 'this Doctor Lydgate', who was capable of performing the most astonishing cures, and rescuing people altogether given up by other practitioners. But the balance had been turned against Lydgate by two members, who for some private reasons held that this power of resuscitating persons as good as dead was an equivocal recommendation, and might interfere with providential favours. In the course of the year, however, there had been a change in the public sentiment of which the unanimity at Dollop's was an index.

A good deal more than a year ago, before anything was known of Lydgate's skill, the judgments on it had naturally been divided, depending on a sense of likelihood, situated perhaps in the pit of the stomach or in the pineal gland, and differing in its verdicts, but not the less valuable as a guide in the total deficit of evidence. Patients who had chronic diseases or whose lives had long been worn threadbare, like old Featherstone's, had been at once inclined to try him; also, many who did not like paying their doctor's bills thought agreeably of opening an account with a new doctor and sending for him without stint if the children's temper wanted a dose, occasions when the old practitioners were often crusty; and all persons thus inclined to employ Lydgate held it likely that he was clever. Some considered that he might do more than others 'where there was liver'; – at least there would be no harm in getting a few bottles of 'stuff' from him, since if these proved useless it would still be possible to return to the Purifying Pills, which kept you alive, if they did not remove the yellowness. But these were people of minor importance. Good Middlemarch families were of course not going to change their doctor without reason shown; and everybody who had employed Mr Peacock did not feel obliged to accept a new man merely in the character of his successor, objecting that he was 'not likely to be equal to Peacock'. . . .

Mrs Larcher having just become charitably concerned about alarming symptoms in her charwoman, when Dr Minchin called, asked him to see her then and there, and to give her a certificate for the Infirmary; whereupon after examination he wrote a statement of the case as one of tumour, and recommended the bearer Nancy Nash as an out-patient. Nancy, calling at home on her way to the Infirmary, allowed the staymaker and his wife, in whose attic she lodged, to read Dr Minchin's paper, and by this means became a subject of compassionate conversation in the neighbouring shops of Churchyard Lane as being afflicted with a tumour at first declared to be as large and hard as a duck's egg, but later in the day to be about the size of 'your fist'. Most hearers agreed that it would have to be cut out, but one had known of oil and another of 'squitchineal' as adequate to soften and reduce any lump in the body when taken enough of into the inside – the oil by gradually 'soopling', the squitchineal by eating away.

Meanwhile when Nancy presented herself at the Infirmary it happened to be one of Lydgate's days there. After questioning and examining her, Lydgate said to the house-surgeon in an undertone, 'It's not tumour: it's cramp.' He ordered her a blister and some steel mixture, and told her to go home and rest, giving her at the same time a note to Mrs Larcher, who, she said, was her best employer, to testify that she was in need of good food.

But by-and-by Nancy, in her attic, became portentously worse, the supposed tumour having indeed given way to the blister, but only wandered to another region with angrier pain. The staymaker's wife went to fetch Lydgate, and he continued for a fortnight to attend Nancy in her own home, until under his treatment she got quite well and went to work again. But the case continued to be described as one of tumour in Churchyard Lane and other streets – nay, by Mrs Larcher also; for when Lydgate's remarkable cure was mentioned to Dr Minchin, he naturally did not like to say, 'The case was not one of tumour, and I was mistaken in describing it as such,' but answered, 'Indeed! ah! I saw it was a surgical case, not of a fatal kind.' . . .

Presently Rosamond left the piano and seated herself on a chair close to the sofa and opposite her husband's face.

'Is that enough music for you, my lord?' she said, folding her hands before her and putting on a little air of meekness.

'Yes, dear, if you are tired,' said Lydgate, gently, turning his eyes and resting them on her, but not otherwise moving. Rosamond's presence at that moment was perhaps no more than a spoonful brought to the lake, and her woman's instinct in this matter was not dull.

'What is absorbing you?' she said, leaning forward and bringing her face nearer to his.

He moved his hands and placed them gently behind her shoulders.

'I am thinking of a great fellow, who was about as old as I am three hundred years ago, and had already begun a new era in anatomy.'

'I can't guess,' said Rosamond, shaking her head. 'We used to play at guessing historical characters at Mrs Lemon's, but not anatomists.'

'I'll tell you. His name was Vesalius. And the only way he could get to know anatomy as he did, was by going to snatch bodies at night, from graveyards and places of execution.'

'Oh!' said Rosamond, with a look of disgust on her pretty face, 'I am very glad you are not Vesalius. I should have thought he might find some less horrible way than that.'

'No, he couldn't,' said Lydgate, going on too earnestly to take much notice of her answer. 'He could only get a complete skeleton by snatching the whitened bones of a criminal from the gallows, and burying them, and fetching them away by bits secretly, in the dead of night.'

'I hope he is not one of your great heroes,' said Rosamond, half-playfully, half-anxiously, 'else I shall have you getting up in the night to go to St Peter's churchyard. You know how angry you told me the people were about Mrs Goby. You have enemies enough already.'

'So had Vesalius, Rosy. No wonder the medical fogies in Middlemarch are jealous, when some of the greatest doctors living were fierce upon Vesalius because they had believed in Galen, and he showed that Galen was wrong. They called him a liar and a poisonous monster. But the facts of the human frame were on his side; and so he got the better of them.'

'And what happened to him afterwards?' said Rosamond, with some interest.

'Oh, he had a good deal of fighting to the last. And they did exasperate him enough at one time to make him burn a good deal of his work. Then he got shipwrecked just as he was coming from Jerusalem to take a great chair at Padua. He died rather miserably.'

There was a moment's pause before Rosamond said, 'Do you know, Tertius, I often wish you had not been a medical man.' . . .

It was because Lydgate writhed under the idea of getting his neck beneath this vile yoke that he had fallen into a bitter moody state which was continually widening Rosamond's alienation from him. After the first disclosure about the bill of sale, he had made many efforts to draw her into sympathy with him about possible measures for narrowing their expenses, and with the threatening approach of Christmas his propositions grew more and more definite. 'We can do with only one servant, and live on very little,' he said, 'and I shall manage with one horse.' For Lydgate, as we have seen, had begun to reason, with a more distinct vision, about the expenses of living, and any share of pride he had given to appearances of that sort was meagre compared with the pride which made him revolt from exposure as a debtor, or from asking men to help him with their money.

'Of course you can dismiss the other two servants, if you like,' said Rosamond; 'but I should have thought it would be very injurious to your position for us to live in a poor way. You must expect your practice to be lowered.'

'My dear Rosamond, it is not a question of choice. We have begun too expensively. Peacock, you know, lived in a much smaller house than this. It is my fault: I ought to have known better, and I deserve a thrashing – if there were anybody who had a right to give it me – for bringing you into the necessity of living in a poorer way than you have been used to. But we married because we loved each other, I suppose. And that may help us to pull along till things get better. Come dear, put down that work and come to me.'

He was really in chill gloom about her at that moment, but he dreaded a future without affection, and was determined to resist the oncoming of division between them. Rosamund obeyed him, and he took her on his knee, but in her secret soul she was utterly aloof from him. The poor thing saw only that the world was not ordered to her liking, and Lydgate was part of that world. But he held her waist with one hand and laid the other gently on both of hers; for this rather abrupt man had much tenderness in his manners towards women, seeming to have always present in his imagination the weakness of their frames and the delicate poise of their health both in body and mind. And he began again to speak persuasively.

'I find, now I look into things a little, Rosy, that it is wonderful what an amount of money slips away in our housekeeping. I suppose the servants are careless, and we have had a great many people coming. But there must be many in our rank who manage with much less: they must do with commoner things, I suppose, and look after the scraps. It seems, money goes but a little way in these matters, for Wrench has everything as plain as possible, and he has a very large practice.'

'Oh, if you think of living as the Wrenches do!' said Rosamond, with a little turn of her neck. 'But I have heard you express your disgust at that way of living.'

'Yes, they have very bad taste in everything – they make economy look ugly. We needn't do that. I only meant that they avoid expenses, although Wrench has a capital practice.'

'Why should not you have a good practice, Tertius? Mr Peacock had. You should be more careful not to offend people, and you should send out medicines as the others do. I am sure you began well, and you got several good houses. It cannot answer to be eccentric; you should think what will be generally liked,' said Rosamond, in a decided little tone of admonition.

Lydgate's anger rose; he was prepared to be indulgent towards feminine weakness, but not towards feminine dictation. The shallowness of a waternixie's soul may have a charm until she becomes didactic. But he controlled himself, and only said, with a touch of despotic firmness –

'What I am to do in my practice, Rosy, it is for me to judge. That is not the question between us. It is enough for you to know that our income is likely to be a very narrow one – hardly four hundred, perhaps less, for a long time to come, and we must try to rearrange our lives in accordance with that fact.'

Rosamond was silent for a moment or two, looking before her, and then said, 'My uncle Bulstrode ought to allow you a salary for the time you give to the Hospital: it is not right that you should work for nothing.'

'It was understood from the beginning that my services would be gratuitous. That, again, need not enter into our discussion. I have pointed out what is the only probability,' said Lydgate, impatiently. . . .

Lydgate certainly had good reason to reflect on the service his practice did him in counteracting his personal cares. He had no longer free energy enough for spontaneous research and speculative thinking, but by the bedside of patients the direct external calls on his judgment and sympathies brought the added impulse needed to draw him out of himself. It was not simply that beneficient harness of routine which enables silly men to live respectably and unhappy men to live calmly – it was a perpetual claim on the immediate fresh application of thought, and on the consideration of another's need and trial. Many of us looking back through life would say that the kindest man we have ever known has been a medical man, or perhaps that surgeon whose fine tact, directed by deeply-informed perception, has come to us in our need with a more sublime beneficence than that of miracle-workers. Some of that twice-blessed mercy was always with Lydgate in his work at the Hospital or in private houses, serving better than any opiate to quiet and sustain him under anxieties and his sense of mental degeneracy. . . .

'I have for some time felt that I should open this subject with you in relation to our Hospital,' continued Bulstrode. 'Under the circumstances I have indicated, of course, I must cease to have any personal share in the management, and it is contrary to my views of responsibility to continue a large application of means to an institution which I cannot watch over and to some extent regulate. I shall therefore, in case of my ultimate decision to leave Middlemarch, consider that I withdraw other support to the New Hospital than that which will subsist in the fact that I chiefly supplied the expenses of building it, and have contributed further large sums to its successful working.'

Lydgate's thought, when Bulstrode paused according to his wont, was, 'He has perhaps been losing a good deal of money.' This was the most plausible explanation of a speech which had caused rather a startling change in his expectations. He said in reply –

'The loss to the Hospital can hardly be made up, I fear.'

'Hardly,' returned Bulstrode, in the same deliberate, silvery tone; 'except by some changes of plan. The only person who may be certainly counted on as willing to increase her contributions is Mrs Casaubon. I have had an interview with her on the subject, and I have pointed out to her, as I am about to do to you, that it will be desirable to win a more general support to the New Hospital by a change of system.'

Another pause, but Lydgate did not speak.

'The change I mean is an amalgamation with the Infirmary, so that the New Hospital shall be regarded as a special addition to the elder institution, having the same directing board. It will be necessary, also, that the medical management of the two shall be combined. In this way any difficulty as to the adequate maintenance of our new establishment will be removed; the benevolent interests of the town will cease to be divided.'

Mr Bulstrode had lowered his eyes from Lydgate's face to the buttons of his coat as he again paused.

'No doubt that is a good device as to ways and means,' said Lydgate, with an edge of irony in his tone. 'But I can't be expected to rejoice in it at once, since one of the first results will be that the other medical men will upset or interrupt my methods, if it were only because they are mine.'

'I myself, as you know, Mr Lydgate, highly value the opportunity of new and independent procedure which you have diligently employed: the original plan, I confess, was one which I had much at heart, under submission to the Divine Will. But since providential indications demand a renunciation from me, I renounce.' . . .

He did not know how long he had been walking uneasily backwards and forwards, but Rosamond felt that it was long, and wished that he would sit down. She too had begun to think this an opportunity for urging on Tertius what he ought to do. Whatever might be the truth about all this misery, there was one dread which asserted itself.

Lydgate at last seated himself, not in his usual chair, but in one nearer to Rosamond, leaning aside in it towards her, and looking at her gravely before he reopened the sad subject. He had conquered himself so far, and was about to speak with a sense of solemnity, as on an occasion which was not to be repeated. He had even opened his lips, when Rosamond, letting her hands fall, looked at him and said –

'Surely, Tertius –'

'Well?'

'Surely now at last you have given up the idea of staying in Middlemarch. I cannot go on living here. Let us go to London. Papa, and everyone else, says you had better go. Whatever misery I have to put up with, it will be easier away from here.' . . .

Lydgate's hair never became white. He died when he was only fifty, leaving his wife and children provided for by a heavy insurance on his life. He had gained an excellent practice, alternating, according to the season, between London and a Continental bathing-place; having written a treatise on Gout, a disease which has a good deal of wealth on its side. His skill was relied on by many paying patients, but he always regarded himself as a failure: he had not done what he once meant to do. His acquaintances thought him enviable to have so charming a wife, and nothing happened to shake their opinion. . . .

But he died prematurely of diphtheria, and Rosamond afterwards married an elderly and wealthy physician, who took kindly to her four children.

(1871)

THE BIBLE

Leprosy is caused by rod-like germs resembling those causing tuberculosis. It is spread by sneezes from infected noses. It ravaged Europe during the Middle Ages and still affects twenty million inhabitants of the Tropics. The diagnosis is made by observing small areas of numbness and red spots. This has been known a long time.

From Leviticus

WHEN A MAN shall have in the skin of his flesh a rising [a swelling], a scab, or bright spot, and it be in the skin of his flesh like the plague [the spots] of leprosy; then he shall be brought unto Aaron the priest, or unto one of his sons the priests; and the priest shall look on the plague in the skin of the flesh: and when the hair in the plague is turned white, and the plague in sight be deeper than the skin of his flesh it is a plague of leprosy: and the priest shall look on him, and pronounce him unclean. . . .

If a man also or a woman have in the skin of their flesh bright spots, even white bright spots; then the priest shall look: and, behold, if the bright spots in the skin of their flesh be darkish white; it is a freckled spot that groweth in the skin; he is clean. And the man whose hair has fallen off his head, he is bald; yet is he clean. And he that hath his hair fallen off from part of his head toward his face, he is forehead bald: yet is he clean. And if there be in the bald head, or bald forehead, a white reddish sore; it is a leprosy sprung up in his bald head, or his bald forehead.

Then the priest shall look upon it: and, behold, if the rising of the sore be white reddish in his bald head, or in his bald forehead, as the leprosy appeareth in the skin of the flesh; he is a leprous man, he is unclean: the priest shall pronounce him utterly unclean; his plague is in his head. And the leper in whom the plague is, his clothes shall be rent, and his head bare, and he shall put a covering upon his upper lip, and shall cry, Unclean, unclean.

And the days wherein the plague shall be in him he shall be defiled; he is unclean: he shall dwell alone; without the camp shall his habitation be.

13:2–3, 38–46

The inconvenience of gonorrhea has been known a long time, too.

When any man hath a running issue [a discharge] out of his flesh, because of his issue he is unclean. And this shall be his uncleanness in his issue: whether his flesh run with his issue, or his flesh be stopped from his issue, it is his uncleanness. Every bed, whereon he lieth that hath the issue, is unclean: and every thing, whereon he sitteth, shall be unclean. And whosoever toucheth his bed shall wash his clothes, and bathe himself in water, and be unclean until the even. And he that toucheth the flesh of him that hath the issue shall wash his clothes, and bathe himself in water, and be unclean until the even. And he that hath the issue spit upon him that is clean; then shall he wash his clothes, and bathe himself in water, and be unclean until the even. And what saddle soever he rideth upon that hath the issue shall be unclean.

And whosoever toucheth any thing that was under him shall be unclean until the even: and he that beareth any of those things shall wash his clothes, and bathe himself in water, and be unclean until the even. And whomsoever he toucheth that hath the issue, and hath not rinsed his hands in water, he shall wash his clothes, and bathe himself in water, and be unclean until the even. And the vessel of earth, that he toucheth that hath the issue, shall be broken: and every vessel of wood shall be rinsed in water.

And when he that hath an issue is cleansed of his issue; then he shall number to himself seven days for his cleansing, and wash his clothes, and bathe his flesh in running water, and shall be clean. And on the eighth day he shall take to him two turtledoves, or two young pigeons, and come before the Lord unto the door of the tabernacle of the congregation, and give them unto the priest: and the priest shall offer them, the one for a sin offering, and the other for a burnt offering; and the priest shall make an atonement for him before the Lord for his issue.

And if any man's seed of copulation go out from him, then he shall wash all the flesh in water, and be unclean until the even. And every garment, and every skin, whereon is the seed of copulation, shall be washed with water, and be unclean until the even.

The woman also with whom man shall lie with seed of copulation, they shall both bathe themselves in water, and be unclean until the even. And if a woman have an issue, and her issue in her flesh be blood, she shall be put apart seven days: and whosoever toucheth her shall be unclean until the even. And everything that she lieth upon in her separation shall be unclean; every thing also that she sitteth upon shall be unclean. And whosoever toucheth her bed shall wash his clothes, and bathe himself in water, and be unclean until the even. And if it be on her bed, or on any thing whereon she sitteth, when he toucheth it, he shall be unclean until the even. And if any man lie with her at all, and her flowers [menstrual discharge] be upon him, he shall be unclean seven days; and all the bed whereon he lieth shall be unclean.

15:2–24

St Augustine cautiously defined a miracle as an occurrence contrary to what is known of nature. Montaigne was more specific: that miracles arise from our ignorance of nature, not from nature itself. Miracles make scientific nonsense, but who knows? Inexorably advancing science may discover miracles of all sorts to be comfortably explainable. Jesus' human personality, and his worldly importance, would alone exert powerful effect on psychological sufferers, who today throng temporal surgeries.

Here are two of Jesus' classic cures, of a schizophrenic and a woman with persistent (and financially ruinous) gynaecological trouble. The gospels were not eyewitness accounts like tomorrow morning's papers, they were the inscription of some thirty years' oral tradition, all four of them originally anonymous. So some miracles may be pious folklore: really, the madman's shrieks frightened the Gadarene swine, causing a mass-fatal panic. The miracle of the woman with the haemorrhage is inserted into the middle of the story of another miracle, the raising of Jairus' daughter – according to some theologians, to account for Jesus' arrival, after being called to that urgent case, when the patient was already dead.

From St Mark

AND WHEN HE came out of the ship, immediately there met him out of the tombs a man with an unclean spirit, who had his dwelling among the tombs; and no man could bind him, no, not with chains: because that he had been often bound with fetters and chains, and the chains had been plucked asunder by him, and the fetters broken in pieces: neither could any man tame him. And always, night and day, he was in the mountains, and in the tombs, crying, and cutting himself with stones. But when he saw Jesus afar off, he ran and worshipped him, and cried with a loud voice, and said, What have I to do with thee, Jesus, thou son of the most high God? I adjure thee by God, that thou torment me not.

For he said unto him, Come out of the man, thou unclean spirit. And he asked him, What is thy name? And he answered, saying, My name is legion: for we are many. And he besought him much that he would not send them away out of the country. Now there was there nigh unto the mountains a great herd of swine feeding. And all the devils besought him, saying, Send us into the swine, that we may enter into them. And forthwith Jesus gave them leave. And the unclean spirits went out, and entered into the swine: and the herd ran violently down a steep place into the sea, (they were about two thousand;) and they choked in the sea.

And a certain woman, which had an issue of blood twelve years, and had suffered many things of many physicians, and had spent all that she had, and was nothing bettered, but rather grew worse, when she heard of Jesus, came in the press behind, and touched his garment. For she said, If I may touch but his clothes, I shall be whole. And straightway the fountain of her blood was dried up; and she felt in her body that she was healed of the plague.

And Jesus, immediately knowing in himself that virtue had gone out of him, turned him about in the press, and said, Who touched my clothes? And his disciples said unto him, Thou seest the multitude thronging thee, and sayest thou, Who touched me? And he looked round about to see her that had done this thing. But the woman fearing and trembling, knowing what was done in her, came and fell down before him, and told him all the truth. And he said unto her, Daughter, thy faith hath made thee whole; go in peace, and be whole of thy plague.

5:2–13, 25–34

The Pool of Bethesda may be seen in London. It was executed by Hogarth (his only mural) on the walls of the Great Hall staircase in St Bartholomew's Hospital, which was founded by the monk Rahere 1100 years afterwards.

From St John

NOW THERE IS at Jerusalem by the sheep market a pool, which is called in the Hebrew tongue Bethesda, having five porches. In these lay a great multitude of impotent folk, of blind, halt, withered, waiting for the moving of the water. For an angel went down at a certain season into the pool, and troubled the water: whosoever then first after the troubling of the water stepped in was made whole of whatsoever disease he had.

And a certain man was there, which had an infirmity thirty and eight years. When Jesus saw him lie, and knew that he had been now a long time in that case, he saith unto him, Wilt though be made whole? The impotent man answered him, Sir, I have no man, when the water is troubled, to put me into the pool: but while I am coming, another steppeth down before me. Jesus saith unto him, Rise, take up thy bed, and walk. And immediately the man was made whole, and took up his bed, and walked. . . .

5:2–9
(Authorised Version)

SPONTANEOUS COMBUSTION

The righteous, but alarming, notion of a drunkard bursting into alcoholic flames like a crêpe Suzette was already aglow in July 1681. A brandy drinker of Friesland fell insensible into bed in his clothes, ignited during the night with cries of 'Burning!', and was found with his tin buttons melted and his 'penis burnt as hard as horn and shrunk altogether'. He died five days later.

Spontaneous combustion was believed mostly to roast fat old females, though on 21 January 1825 a wholly sober seventeen-year-old broke into flames in Hamburg while sewing. The conflagration spread from her fingertip to her body and clothes; she had recovered by March, though badly blistered. The European press was illuminated on 13 June 1847 by the Countess von Görlitz going up in flames at eleven o'clock at night in Darmstadt. She was discovered by her servants with head and neck ablaze, and diagnosed by her GP Dr Graff as a fatal case of spontaneous combustion.

There was confusion of medical evidence at the inquest – the illustrious local chemist von Liebig (the father of Oxo) objecting that spontaneous bodily combustion was certainly not demonstrable in the lab. The problem of practical physics represented by the Countess was solved by a thieving manservant confessing to strangling her, banking her body with combustibles and striking a light.

A drunken, pipe-smoking Scots carrier took fire spontaneously on 29 May 1852 at the Hardmuir toll-gate, though the *Elgin Courant* the following month expressed the growing cynicism over drunkards being careless smokers, and over women wearing inflammable clothes. The *British and Foreign Medico-Chirurgical Review* pondered profoundly in 1870 'whether or not it is possible for the human body spontaneously to inflame'. Baron Dupuytren of the Hôtel Dieu in Paris (discoverer of Dupuytren's contracture of the palm) decided not. Most doctors believed otherwise, that bodily electricity sparked bodily hydrogen, while alcohol rendered more combustible the drunkard's blood, breath and belches, so men flamed like Christmas puddings. In 1938, twenty-two-year-old Phyllis Newcome burst spontaneously into flames at midnight while dancing in the Shire Hall at Romford, nineteen-year-old Maybelle Andrews having shortly before done the same in a Soho nightclub.

This notion of an everyday phoenix warmed the hands of Balzac, Washington Irving, de Quincey and Mark Twain, and fired the imagination of our next four writers. The expert deserves the last word.

CHARLES DICKENS

From Bleak House

The end of Krook, Lord Chancellor of the rag-and-bottle trade, who 'never gets beyond a certain point of either drunkenness or sobriety'.

'WHAT, IN THE Devil's name,' he says, 'is this! Look at my fingers!'

A thick, yellow liquor defiles them, which is offensive to the touch and sight and more offensive to the smell. A stagnant, sickening oil, with some natural repulsion in it that makes them both shudder.

'What have you been doing here? What have you been pouring out of window?'

'I pouring out of window! Nothing, I swear! Never, since I have been here!' cries the lodger.

And yet look here – and look here! When he brings the candle, here, from the corner of the window-sill, it slowly drips, and creeps away down the bricks; here, lies in a little thick nauseous pool.

'This is a horrible house,' says Mr Guppy, shutting down the window. 'Give me some water, or I shall cut my hand off.'

He so washes, and rubs, and scrubs, and smells and washes, that he has not long restored himself with a glass of brandy, and stood silently before the fire, when Saint Paul's bell strikes twelve, and all those other bells strike twelve from their towers of various heights in the dark air, and in their many tones. When all is quiet again, the lodger says:

'It's the appointed time at last. Shall I go?'

Mr Guppy nods, and gives him a 'lucky touch' on the back; but not with the washed hand, though it is his right hand.

He goes down-stairs; and Mr Guppy tries to compose himself, before the fire, for waiting a long time. But in no more than a minute or two the stairs creak, and Tony comes swiftly back.

'Have you got them?'

'Got them! No. The old man's not there.'

He has been so horribly frightened in the short interval, that his terror seizes the other, who makes a rush at him, and asks loudly, 'What's the matter?'

'I couldn't make him hear, and I softly opened the door and looked in. And the burning smell is there – and the soot is there, and the oil is there – and he is not there!' – Tony ends this with a groan.

Mr Guppy takes the light. They go down, more dead than alive, and holding one another, push open the door of the back shop. The cat has retreated close to it, and stands snarling – not at them; at something on the ground, before the fire. There is a very little fire left in the grate, but there is a smouldering suffocating vapour in the room, and a dark greasy coating on the walls and ceiling. The chairs and table, and the bottle so rarely absent from the table, all stand as usual. On one chair-back, hang the old man's hairy cap and coat.

'Look!' whispers the lodger, pointing his friend's attention to these objects with a trembling finger. 'I told you so. When I saw him last, he took his cap off, took out the little bundle of old letters, hung his cap on the back of the chair – his coat was there already, for he had pulled that off, before he went to put the shutters up – and I left him turning the letters over in his hand, standing just where that crumbled black thing is upon the floor.'

Is he hanging somewhere? They look up. No.

'See!' whispers Tony. 'At the foot of the same chair, there lies a dirty bit of thin red cord that they tie up pens with. That went round the letters. He undid it slowly, leering and laughing at me, before he began to turn them over, and threw it there. I saw it fall.'

'What's the matter with the cat?' says Mr Guppy. 'Look at her!'

'Mad, I think. And no wonder in this evil place.'

They advance slowly, looking at all these things. The cat remains where they found her, still snarling at the something on the ground, before the fire and between the two chairs. What is it? Hold up the light.

Here is a small burnt patch of flooring; here is the tinder from a little bundle of burnt paper, but not so light as usual, seeming to be steeped in something; and here is – is it the cinder of a small charred and broken log of wood sprinkled with white ashes, or is it coal? O Horror, he IS here! and this from which we run away, striking out the light and overturning one another into the street, is all that represents him.

Help, help, help! come into this house for Heaven's sake!

Plenty will come in, but none can help. The Lord Chancellor of that Court, true to his title in his last act, has died the death of all Lord Chancellors in all Courts, and of all authorities in all places under all names soever, where false pretences are made, and where injustice is done. Call the death by any name Your Highness will, attribute it to whom you will, or say it might have been prevented how you will, it is the same death eternally – inborn, inbred, engendered in the corrupted humours of the vicious body itself, and that only – Spontaneous Combustion, and none other of all the deaths that can be died.

(1852–3)

EMILE ZOLA

From Dr Pascal

SHE COULD SEE more and more clearly inside the room, lit by thin shafts of sunlight through the cracks in the old broken shutters. She saw her brother [eighty-four years old, sixty years drunk], dressed as always in a neat blue suit, on his head the eternal fur cap which he wore from one year's end to another. He had been putting on weight over five or six years, he was just a heap, bursting into folds of flesh. She noticed that he had dropped off to sleep while smoking, because his pipe, that short black pipe, had fallen on to his knees.

She was stuck motionless. The smouldering tobacco had spilt, his trousers had caught fire. And through the hole in the cloth, already as big as a five-franc piece, she could see his naked thigh, his red thigh, from which emerged a little blue flame.

First she thought it was his clothes – his underpants, his shirt – which had caught alight. But there was no doubt about it, she was observing his bare flesh with a little blue flame escaping from it, light and flickering, like the flame which dances across the top of a bowl of hot brandy punch. It was still hardly bigger than a night-light, soft and gentle, which the least rustle of air could put out. Then it grew bigger, it spread rapidly, his skin cracked, his fat began to melt.

A cry sprang from Félicité's throat. 'Macquart! Macquart!'

Still he did not move. He was totally insensible, drunkenness had thrown him into a coma, into total paralysis of the senses; but he was still alive, she could see his chest moving with his gentle breathing.

'Macquart! Macquart!'

Now the fat was oozing through the cracks in his skin, feeding the flame which had spread to his belly. Félicité saw that her brother was igniting like a sponge soaked in brandy – he who had been saturating himself for years in the strongest and most inflammable of spirits. Unquestionably, he would soon be on fire from head to toe.

Félicité's son, Dr Pascal, next day discovers the body.

Perhaps his uncle was asleep. But when he pushed open the kitchen door on the left a frightful stink escaped, an unbearable odour of bones and flesh fallen into a coal fire. In the room he could hardly breathe, he choked, blinded by a sort of thick vapour, a stagnant and nauseating cloud. The thin beams of light filtering through the cracks did not let him see clearly. As he made towards the fireplace, he gave up his first idea of a blaze, for there had been no fire in the grate, and all the furniture round him seemed intact. With no idea what was going on, and feeling faint in the poisoned air, he threw the shutters open violently. Light flooded in.

What the doctor could at last discern filled him with astonishment. Every object was in its place; the glass and the bottle of proof spirit [eighty-five per cent alcohol, brandy had long been water to the victim's pickled throat] stood on the table; only the chair on which his uncle must have sat showed traces of fire, its feet had become blackened, the rush half burnt. What had become of his uncle? Where had he gone? In front of the chair, on the tiles stained with a pool of grease, was a little pile of cinders, to the side of which rested the pipe, the black pipe, unbroken in its fall. All his uncle was there, in that cindery handful of dust, and he was also in the russet mist which was wafting out of the window, in the layer of soot that mantled the entire kitchen, in the horrible grease of vanished flesh which enveloped everything, slimy and stinking under the fingertips.

It was the best case of spontaneous combustion that the doctor had ever seen. He had certainly read of some surprising ones in the journals, among others that of a cobbler's wife, a drunk who fell asleep over her foot-warmer and of whom they found only a foot and a hand. He himself had until then mistrusted, without admitting it – like doctors in the past – that a body impregnated with alcohol discharged an unknown gas, capable of spontaneous combustion and of devouring flesh and bone. But he denied it no longer. Moreover, he could explain everything by re-establishing the facts: the drunken coma, the absolute insensibility, the pipe falling on the clothes which caught fire, the flesh saturated with drink which burnt and cracked, the fat which melted, one part running on the floor, the rest feeding the flames, until at last the muscles, the organs, the bones were consumed in the incineration of the whole body. All his uncle was there, with his blue suit, his fur cap that he wore from one year's end to another. Without doubt, since he had gone up like a bonfire, he had needed to perform a somersault first, to explain how the chair was hardly charred while nothing remained of him, not a bone, not a tooth, not a fingernail, nothing but that little pile of grey dust that the draught from the door threatened to sweep away.

Dr Pascal was later constrained to ask: 'But you, mother, since you were there, why didn't you put him out?'

(1893)
Transl. R. G.

FREDERICK MARRYAT

From Jacob Faithful

IT WAS AT the age of eleven years that a catastrophe took place which changed my prospects in life, and I must therefore say a little more about my father and mother, bringing up their history to that period. The propensity of my mother to ardent spirits had, as always is the case, greatly increased upon her, and her corpulence had increased in the same ratio. She was now a most unwieldy, bloated mountain of flesh, such a form as I have never since beheld, although at the time she did not appear to me to be disgusting, accustomed to witness imperceptibly her increase, and not seeing any other females except at a distance. For the last two years she had seldom quitted her bed – certainly she did not crawl out of the cabin more than five minutes during the week – indeed her obesity and habitual intoxication rendered her incapable. My father went on shore for a quarter of an hour once a month, to purchase gin, tobacco, red herrings, and decayed ship biscuit – the latter was my principal fare, except when I could catch a fish over the sides, as we lay at anchor. I was therefore a great water drinker, not altogether from choice, but from the salt nature of my food, and because my mother had still sense enough left to discern that 'Gin wasn't good for little boys'. But a great change had taken place in my father. I was now left almost altogether in charge of the deck, my father seldom coming up except to assist me in shooting the bridges, or when it required more than my exertions to steer clear of the crowds of vessels which we encountered when between them. In fact, as I grew more capable, my father became more incapable, and passed most of his time in the cabin, assisting my mother in emptying the great stone bottle. The woman had prevailed upon the man, and now both were guilty in partaking of the forbidden fruit of the Juniper Tree. Such was the state of affairs in our little kingdom, when the catastrophe occurred which I am now about to relate.

One fine summer's evening, we were floating up with the tide, deeply laden with coals, to be delivered at the proprietor's wharf, some distance above Putney Bridge; a strong breeze sprang up, and checked our progress, and we could not, as we expected, gain the wharf that night. We were about a mile and a half above the bridge when the tide turned against us, and we dropped our anchor. My father, who, expecting to arrive that evening, had very unwillingly remained sober, waited until the lighter had swung to the stream, and then saying to me, 'Remember, Jacob, we must be at the wharf early to-morrow morning, so keep alive,' he went into the cabin to indulge in his potations, leaving me in possession of the deck, and also of my supper, which I never ate below, the little cabin being so unpleasantly close. Indeed, I took all my meals alfresco, and unless the nights were intensely cold, slept on deck, in the capacious dog-kennel abaft, which had once been tenanted by the large mastiff, but he had been dead some years, was thrown overboard, and, in all probability, had been converted into Epping sausages, at 1s. per lb. Some time after his decease, I had taken possession of his apartment and had performed his duty. I had finished my supper, which I washed down with a considerable portion of Thames water, for I always drank more when above the bridges, having an idea that it tasted more pure and fresh. I had walked forward and looked at the cable to see if all was right, and then having nothing more to do, I laid down on the deck, and indulged in the profound speculations of a boy of eleven years old. I was watching the stars above me, which twinkled faintly, and appeared to me ever and anon to be extinguished and then relighted. I was wondering what they could be made of, and how they came there, when of a sudden I was interrupted in my reveries by a loud shriek, and perceived a strong smell of something burning. The shrieks were renewed again and again, and I had hardly time to get upon my legs when my father burst up from the cabin, rushed over the side of the lighter, and disappeared under the water. I caught a glimpse of his features as he passed me, and observed fright and intoxication blended together. I ran to the side where he had disappeared, but could see nothing but a few eddying circles as the tide rushed quickly past. For a few seconds I remained staggered and stupefied at his sudden disappearance and evident death, but I was recalled to recollection by the smoke which encompassed me, and the shrieks of my mother, which were now fainter and fainter, and I hastened to her assistance.

A strong empyreumatic, thick smoke ascended from the hatchway of the cabin, and, as it had now fallen calm, it mounted straight up the air in a dense column. I attempted to go in, but so soon as I encountered the smoke, I found that it was impossible; it would have suffocated me in half a minute. I did what most children would have done in such a situation of excitement and distress – I sat down and cried bitterly. In about ten minutes I removed my hands, with which I had covered up my face, and looked at the cabin hatch. The smoke had disappeared, and all was silent. I went to the hatchway, and although the smell was still overpowering, I found that I could bear it. I descended the little ladder of three steps, and called 'Mother,' but there was no answer. The lamp fixed against the after bulk-head, with a glass before it, was still alight, and I could see plainly to every corner of the cabin. Nothing was burning – not even the curtains to my mother's bed appeared to be singed. I was astonished – breathless with fear, with a trembling voice, I again called out 'Mother.' I remained more than a minute panting for breath, and then ventured to draw back the curtains of the bed – my mother was not there! but there appeared to be a black mass in the centre of the bed. I put my hand fearfully upon it – it was a sort of unctuous pitchy cinder. I screamed with horror, my little senses reeled – I staggered from the cabin, and fell down on the deck in a state amounting to almost insanity: it was followed by a sort of stupor, which lasted for many hours.

As the reader may be in some doubt as to the occasion of my mother's death, I must inform him that she perished in that very peculiar and dreadful manner, which does sometimes, although rarely, occur to those who indulge in an immoderate use of spirituous liquors. Cases of this kind do indeed present themselves but once in a century, but the occurrence of them is but too well authenticated. She perished from what is termed *spontaneous combustion*, an inflammation of the gases generated from the spirits absorbed into the system. It is to be presumed that the flames issuing from my mother's body completely frightened out of his senses my father, who had been drinking freely; and thus did I lose both my parents, one by fire and the other by water, at one and the same time.

(1834)

HERMAN MELVILLE

From Redburn

OF THE THREE newly shipped men, who in a state of intoxication had been brought on board at the dock gates, two were able to be engaged at their duties, in four or five hours after quitting the pier. But the third man yet lay in his bunk, in the self-same posture in which his limbs had been adjusted by the crimp, who had deposited him there.

His name was down on the ship's papers as Miguel Saveda, and for Miguel Saveda the chief mate at last came forward, shouting down the forecastle-scuttle, and commanding his instant presence on deck. But the sailors answered for their new comrade; giving the mate to understand that Miguel was still fast locked in his trance, and could not obey him; when, muttering his usual imprecation, the mate retired to the quarter-deck.

This was in the first dog-watch, from four to six in the evening. At about three bells, in the next watch, Max the Dutchman, who, like most old seamen, was something of a physician in cases of drunkenness, recommended that Miguel's clothing should be removed, in order that he should lie more comfortably. But Jackson, who would seldom let any thing be done in the forecastle that was not proposed by himself, capriciously forbade this proceeding.

So the sailor still lay out of sight in his bunk, which was in the extreme angle of the forecastle, behind the *bowsprit-bitts* – two stout timbers rooted in the ship's keel. An hour or two afterward, some of the men observed a strange odour in the forecastle, which was attributed to the presence of some dead rat among the hollow spaces in the side planks; for some days before, the forecastle had been smoked out, to extirpate the vermin overrunning her. At midnight, the larboard watch, to which I belonged, turned out; and instantly as every man waked, he exclaimed at the now intolerable smell, supposed to be heightened by the shaking up of the bilge-water, from the ship's rolling.

'Blast that rat!' cried the Greenlander.

'He's blasted already,' said Jackson, who in his drawers had crossed over to the bunk of Miguel. 'It's a water-rat, shipmates, that's dead; and here he is' – and with that, he dragged forth the sailor's arm, exclaiming, 'Dead as a timber-head!'

Upon this the men rushed toward the bunk, Max with the light, which he held to the man's face.

'No, he's not dead,' he cried, as the yellow flame wavered for a moment at the seaman's motionless mouth. But hardly had the words escaped, when, to the silent horror of all, two threads of greenish fire, like a forked tongue, darted out between the lips; and in a moment, the cadaverous face was crawled over by a swarm of worm-like flames.

The lamp dropped from the hand of Max, and went out; while covered all over with spires and sparkles of flame, that faintly crackled in the silence, the uncovered parts of the body burned before us, precisely like a phosphorescent shark in a midnight sea.

The eyes were open and fixed; the mouth was curled like a scroll, and every lean feature firm as in life; while the whole face, now wound in curls of soft blue flame, wore an aspect of grim defiance, and eternal death. Prometheus, blasted by fire on the rock.

One arm, its red shirt-sleeve rolled up, exposed the man's name, tattooed in vermilion, near the hollow of the middle joint; and as if there was something peculiar in the painted flesh, every vibrating letter burned so white, that you might read the flaming name in the flickering ground of blue.

'Where's that d——d Miguel?' was now shouted down among us from the scuttle by the mate, who had just come on deck, and was determined to have every man up that belonged to his watch.

'He's gone to the harbour where they never weigh anchor,' coughed Jackson. 'Come you down, sir, and look.'

Thinking that Jackson intended to beard him, the mate sprang down in a rage; but recoiled at the burning body as if he had been shot by a bullet. 'My God!' he cried, and stood holding fast to the ladder.

'Take hold of it,' said Jackson, at last, to the Greenlander; 'it must go overboard. Don't stand shaking there, like a dog; take hold of it, I say! But stop' – and smothering it all in the blankets, he pulled it partly out of the bunk.

A few minutes more, and it fell with a bubble among the phosphorescent sparkles of the damp night sea, leaving a corruscating wake as it sank.

This event thrilled me through and through with unspeakable horror; nor did the conversation of the watch during the next four hours on deck at all serve to soothe me.

But what most astonished me, and seemed most incredible, was the infernal opinion of Jackson, that the man had been actually dead when brought on board the ship; and that knowingly, and merely for the sake of the month's advance, paid into his hand upon the strength of the bill he presented, the body-snatching crimp had knowingly shipped a corpse on board of the Highlander, under the pretense of its being a live body in a drunken trance. And I heard Jackson say, that he had known of such things having been done before. But that a really dead body ever burned in that manner, I can not even yet believe. But the sailors seemed familiar with such things; or at least with the stories of such things having happened to others.

For me, who at that age had never so much as happened to hear of a case like this, of animal combustion, in the horrid mood that came over me, I almost thought the burning body was a premonition of the hell of the Calvinists, and that Miguel's earthly end was a foretaste of his eternal condemnation.

(1849)

SIR SYDNEY SMITH

From Forensic Medicine

Spontaneous Combustion

Spontaneous combustion of the human body cannot occur, and no good purpose can be served by discussing it.

(1945)

LE PETOMANE

Our ultimate conversational taboo is not death, but farting. Sex is now discussed as comfortably as cooking, but nobody mentions over dinner that other urge, equally exposed to prudery, which is universal, lifelong, irrepressible, urgent, and extinguishes itself in relieved contentment. We fart half a litre a day, partly of carbon dioxide, hydrogen sulphide, hydrogen and methane; gasses which are fermented from our dietary carbohydrate by our normal intestinal bacteria. But half of all our farts is nitrogen left from the air we swallow.

Queen Elizabeth I was less coy: 'Excommunications are the Pope's Crackfarts,' she remarked, when Pope Pius V passed one in her direction in 1570. 'I shall get a fart of a dead man as soon as a farthing of him,' was an expressive bewailment from Henry VIII's court wit and musician, John Heywood, in 1562. There is, expectedly, farting in Chaucer. In *The Miller's Tale*, Absalon, the parish clerk, who 'was somdel squaymous of fartyng', comes to steal a kiss on a coal-black night from young Alison, the carpenter's wife, who is in bed with Nicholas, the lodger, and playfully substitutes her arse through the window. Absalon returns, in vengeful response to the laughter of Nicholas, who has now risen for a piss and extrudes *his* arse through the window. 'This Nicholas anon let flee a fart', which triggered the agonising application of a red-hot coulter borrowed by Absalon from the smithy. 'I fart at thee,' is Subtle's first line to Face in Ben Jonson's *The Alchemist*.

In the mid-sixteenth century, farts were also puff-pastry balls. By the mid-eighteenth century, Voltaire was relishing the delicately flavoured pastries, *pets de nonne* (nun's farts). In the nineteenth century, the awful Frank Harris shocked the Prince of Wales by recalling a Lord Mayor of London who farted over the roast beef so richly that he forced his hostess from the table. 'There are similar instances in France, though they are treated more lightly,' Harris assured the Prince patriotically, and correctly. He recounted a lady who farted next to the Bishop of Orléans at dinner and tried as excuse to reproduce the noise innocently with her feet on the parquet. 'Oh, Madame, please don't trouble to find a rhyme,' the Bishop comforted her.

Le Pétomane was a star turn at the Moulin Rouge in the 1890s. He was the six-foot-tall, grandly moustached, handsome Joseph Pujol (1857–1945) from Marseilles. He had enjoyed an ability since boyhood of filling a normal, five-inch-long roomy rectum, its preceding three-foot-long capacious colon, even the end of his remoter small intestine, with air drawn in through his anus. He did this by grasping his knees and using his front sheet of abdominal muscles as an expanding bellows. His control of his anal sphincter – the guts' muscular nozzle – was so delicate that he could emit the air with such variations of volume and timbre that they recalled the double-bass, the trombone and violin, producing chords, arpeggios, familiar tunes and drawn-out notes lasting fifteen seconds. He could snuff a candle at twelve inches. Substituting water, he jetted a horizontal fountain five feet long. He made *La Semaine Medicale*. The Professor of Physiology at the Paris Faculty of Medicine was rightly impressed by a man using his guts as lungs and his anal sphincter as an opera singer's voice-box. M. Pujol was the only man beneficially hoist by his own petard.

A *péteux* is someone who really gets the wind up, the coward who farts, or worse, with fear. A *pétarder* is a horse which farts immoderately. A *péteuse* is a fish, the usual name for a *bouvière*, the bitterling carp. French visitors to England are confused by a widespread establishment painted 'Pet Shop'.

This appreciation is from a Parisian weekly which existed from 1880 until World War One; a journal of wit, satire and ridicule, with illustrations of elegant, tight-stayed, flowing-petticoated ladies being dressed by their maids, presumably preliminary to being undressed by the top-hatted, Toulouse-Lautrec types on the next page.

From Gil Blas Illustré, 25 September 1892

Something to Talk About

A very up-to-the-minute fellow, very *fin de siècle*, this specimen, deserving of particular study. Usually, it is a child from the provinces, the son of peasants or of *petits bourgeois*, whose vocation emerges naturally. While very young, this child becomes aware of his gifts, which worries him; he becomes shy, keeps out of the way, seeks the solitude of the woods, or, if he lives in town, of some remote closet. There he gives free range to his enthusiasm. The night resounds with his noises, he wakes up with a start. If in boarding-school, he breaks the silence of study with the sudden explosions of his zestful nature. He is haunted by the urge to become celebrated, to be someone.

As always, his parents oppose his chosen career.

'But still, I've something there!' he says, slapping his forehead.

Despite repeated refusals, he will not be beaten. He insists stubbornly that what he has in his head is not in other people's. Soon his conviction gains his parents'; they feel he has a point. Furthermore, he labours day and night, and fills the house with the turmoil of his studies.

A young man must know his way around the world, he tells them. They agree, and he leaves for Paris, his pocket empty, but his . . . heart full of hope. He is full of confidence, a faith in himself which could move mountains.

The most difficult thing is to make himself known. He presents himself at the offices of a big newspaper and gives an audition. He is on his way! Another initial difficulty is finding an acceptable name. Will he christen himself *Le Péteur*? Open the dictionary of l'Académie: '*Péteur*: Farter, one who has the habit of farting, low.' Should he call himself *Le Péteux*? 'Abusive expression: to go like *un péteux*, leave without dignity.' He must find something else. He has a brilliant inspiration: he will call himself *Le Pétomane*! The magic formula is discovered. The new title would not stir any susceptibilities and could be mentioned in any drawing-room. Words have their own nobility.

Thanks to the influence of the important newspaper, the beginner found an engagement on the Parisian stage. A *pétomane* who does not succeed first time will be done for good. His excitement is at its highest pitch. If he were going to remain silent, perhaps he would forget how to do it?

A huge crowd, eager to hear him, crammed into the theatre. All the Parisian first-nighters were there; the newcomer came downstage, turned towards the public, sweat pearling his brow. He emitted at first some timid sounds, then he plucked up courage, he abandoned himself. Note succeeded note, you felt you were listening to a tremendous fanfare. The ice was broken, the public applauded wildly. Has he become famous?

The *pétomane* enjoys a modest triumph. And what distinguishes him from his fellows at the Opera, the tenors and the basses, is that he can boast of having something inside him. An enormous number of performers could not say as much!

When his reputation is well established, he gives private shows in town. He is in keen demand in society, for soirées or for tea-parties, everyone fights to get him. The *pétomane* is always very correct, he moves in any environment with ease, he speaks only when invited. After a monologue delivered by an actor of the Comédie-Française, he takes his place on the stage; facing abut, he picks up his coat-tails and goes to it . . . resoundingly.

He has abounding tact, he knows how to strike the right note – discreet in the world of fashion, easygoing among the *bourgeoisie*, solemn among politicians. Among the common people, at a country wedding, for example, he unbuttons, he strikes a thunderous, even a vulgar, note. He knows his public.

The *pétomane* is a serious man of sound judgment. If you question him about politics, 'Who hears only one bell hears only one sound,' he says.

If you press him for an opinion, he replies simply, 'I know which way the wind's blowing.' A profound thought for all men of influence to ponder over.

He does not lack wit. Dining with a *grande dame* whom I shall not name, he was invited to demonstrate his talent over the dessert. Turning towards a captain of artillery on his right, he made this celebrated reply: 'When monsieur has fired off, I shall speak.'

The *pétomane* has success with women, his affairs make quite a noise. Between ourselves, he becomes compromised: he does not always know to contain himself in the presence of his beloved object. But who suffers not this little fault?

He tours the provinces, he is acclaimed everywhere, he is pelted with flowers; his talent moves the heart of all the old ladies. At Soissons, he is always offered a ceremonial plate of their famous haricots. He knows all the delights of fame, a businessman has launched an irrigator which bears his name.

Not everything in the garden is lovely. The *pétomane* will die without seeing the dearest desire of his life: he coverts a decoration. He does not ask for it so much as for what he does. He knows that artistes are decorated only when they quit the stage, and become its professors; it is perhaps a prejudice, but society has its prejudices; however, like his colleagues throughout France, when he is exhausted, why should he not embrace a professorial career? His art, which seems new, is very old. St Augustine talks in his *Confessions* 'of certain men who render from the bottom remarkable sounds'. Why should they not create a chair at the Conservatory of Arts? There is quite rightly a class for the trombone; an experienced *pétomane* could advantageously replace this instrument. I pass this idea for what it is worth to the Minister of Education and Arts.

The *pétomane* suffers one sadness. Up to the present, he has not been permitted to be heard at religious ceremonies; the ministers of the Church have considered his art too profane, unworthy of a holy place. Such exclusion grieves the *pétomane*; but he lives in hope. Whatever you say, the Church is not the enemy of progress; once, it refused Christian burial to actors. It went back on this decision. Who knows, if it will not ease the rules? One day, perhaps, at the wedding of a friend or at the interment of a celebrity, the *pétomane* could let forth some moving notes; at the moment of the Elevation of the Host, for instance.

The old age of the *pétomane* will be sad. Like all performers, with the years he will decline, his brilliant faculties will wither. One evening, he will appear on the stage, but out of form; despite all his efforts, his organ rebels, he stays mute. The pitiless public whistles he whom it had so lavishly adulated. The *pétomane* feels that he is finished, and with death in his soul he retires to the provinces, perhaps to his own village. Henceforth, he sees nothing but his memories; one cannot be, and have been. He slowly sinks. Sometimes, to please a friend, he consents again to perform, but it is not the same; he can hardly painfully articulate a few sounds.

One fine day he takes to his bed, and he will go out with a final . . . sigh.

Eugène Fourrier
(1892)
Transl. R. G.

MOLIERE

Molière (Jean-Baptiste Poquelin, 1622–73) was a Parisian, the son of the court upholsterer. He became an actor, in 1643 hiring a disused real tennis-court to found *L'Illustre Théâtre*, but it flopped. He was a gloomy man, who married (unhappily) the nineteen-year-old actress Amande Béjart in 1662. In 1667 he developed pulmonary tuberculosis.

Molière was a magnificent dissector of the ludicrous from mankind. He applied his skill upon doctors with gusto.

In *Le Médecin malgré lui*, Lucinde is foiled by her father Géronte in trying to marry a penniless suitor, so she pretends to be struck dumb. Géronte's search for a specialist in dumbness to effect her cure discovers Sganarelle, a woodcutter with a broad, black beard, a ruff and a yellow-and-green suit, who was once a doctor's servant and knows the jargon. Jacqueline is the family wet-nurse, Lucas her husband.

Doctors have for centuries created professional reputations as swiftly as Sganarelle, and by his methods. 'Blinding by science' is irresistible, even when the 'scientist' knows none whatever. This is from an ageless eagerness among the uninitiated to believe whatever any wiseacre tells them.

The medical profession in Molière's day barricaded itself behind towering battlements of incomprehensibility, the flowery Latin inscriptions thereon few doctors understood. These have been replaced by our sprawling scientific vocabulary, which a few more possibly can. Sganarelle's high-falutin dismissal of his anatomical bloomers: '*Oui, cela était autrefois ainsi, mais nous avons changé tout cela*,' continues to be airily brandished as an excuse for inexcusable ignorance about anything.

In his comedy-ballet *Le Malade imaginaire* of 1673, Molière returned to purging the profession which 'knows everything about disease except how to cure it'. He himself took the part of Argan (the patient), and during the fourth performance, on 17 February 1673, he suffered a massive lung haemorrhage on stage and died half an hour later.

Molière's pithy style is a superb model for comedy scriptwriters. He always knew where the laughs were. Such success rewarded his admirable working method, which was described in *The Spectator* of 1711 by Joseph Addison (1672–1719).

> Molière, as we are told by Monsieur Boileau [the poet and critic], used to read all his comedies to an old woman who was his housekeeper, as she sat with him at her work by the chimney-corner; and could foretell the success of his play in the theatre, from the reception it met at his fire-side: for he tells us that the audience always followed the old woman, and never failed to laugh in the same place.

From The Doctor in Spite of Himself

SGANARELLE: Is this the patient?

GERONTE: Yes. I have but one daughter. I should be utterly devastated if she died.

SGANARELLE: Oh, she mustn't do that. She must die only under doctor's orders.

GERONTE: Have a seat.

SGANARELLE: (*Sitting between* GERONTE *and* LUCINDE.) Here's a patient who's not at all disgusting. I'd say that a perfectly healthy man could settle down with her very nicely.

GERONTE: You've made her laugh, doctor!

SGANARELLE: So much the better. When the doctor makes the patient laugh, it's the best sign in the world. (*To* LUCINDE.) Well! What's the trouble? What have you got? Where's the pain?

LUCINDE: (*Putting her hand to her mouth, to her head, and under her chin.*) Han, hi, hon, han.

SGANARELLE: Eh? What are you saying?

LUCINDE: (*Continuing the same gestures.*) Han, hi, hon, han, han, hi, hon.

SGANARELLE: What?

LUCINDE: Han, hi, hon.

SGANARELLE: Han, hi, hon, han, ha. I don't get it. What the devil language is she talking?

GERONTE: Doctor, that's her trouble. She's been struck dumb, and up to now we haven't the first idea why. It's a bit of bad luck, which has had to put off her marriage.

SGANARELLE: Why?

GERONTE: Her intented wants to wait till she gets better, before fixing everything up.

SGANARELLE: And who is this idiot who doesn't want a dumb wife? I wish to God mine had half her trouble. I'd make damn sure not to get her cured.

GERONTE: Nevertheless, doctor, we implore you to use all your caring skills to ease her sufferings.

SGANARELLE: Don't worry. Tell me something. This illness, it lies on her heavily?

GERONTE: Yes, doctor.

SGANARELLE: So much the better. Does she get terrible pain?

GERONTE: Terrible!

SGANARELLE: Better still. Does she go to the you-know-what?

GERONTE: Yes.

SGANARELLE: Copiously?

GERONTE: No idea.

SGANARELLE: What she produces is commendable?

GERONTE: I wouldn't know about these things.

SGANARELLE: (*To* LUCINDE.) Let me have your arm. (*To* GERONTE.) Her pulse tells me that your daughter is dumb.

GERONTE: Yes, doctor, that's exactly her trouble. You've got it first time.

SGANARELLE: Ha, ha!

JACQUELINE: Just look! How he's divined her illness!

SGANARELLE: We great doctors, we know things at a glance. An ignoramus would have been embarrassed, and would have said to you: Oh, it's this and that. But me, I hit the target first shot. I reveal to you that your daughter is dumb.

GERONTE: Yes, but I very much wish you could tell me why.

SGANARELLE: Nothing easier. It comes from her having lost the power of speech.

GERONTE: Fair enough. But the reason, if you please, for her losing the power of speech?

SGANARELLE: All the best authorities will tell you that it's an impediment in the action of the tongue.

GERONTE: Yes, but still, what's your opinion on this impediment in the action of her tongue?

SGANARELLE: Aristotle, on that subject, said . . . some wonderful things.

GERONTE: I know.

SGANARELLE: He was a great man.

GERONTE: Without doubt.

SGANARELLE: An altogether great men. (*Jerking up his arm from the elbow.*) A man who was greater than me by that much. To return to our line of argument. I believe that this impediment in the action of the tongue is caused by certain humours, what we learned experts call morbid humours, that's to say . . . morbid humours. Especially the humours formed by the exhalations of influences which arise at the site of illnesses coming . . . so to say . . . from . . . Do you know Latin?

GERONTE: Afraid not.

SGANARELLE: (*Standing suddenly.*) You don't know even a bit of Latin?

GERONTE: Not a bit.

SGANARELLE: (*Enthusiastically.*) *Cabricias arci thuram, catalamus, singulariter, nominativo, haec musa* – the muse – *bonus, bona, bonum. Deus sanctus, est-ne oratio latinas? Etiam*, yes. *Quare*, why? *Quia substantivo, et adjectivum, concordat in generi, numerum, et casus.*

GERONTE: Ah! If only I'd studied it!

JACQUELINE: What a clever man he is!

LUCAS: It's so lovely, I can't understand a syllable.

SGANARELLE: Now these vapours which I'm telling you about, they pass from the left side where the liver is, to the right side where the heart is. It so happens that the lung, that we call in Latin *armyan*, communicates with the brain, which we call in Greek *nasmus*, by means of the vena cava, which we call in Hebrew *cubile*. They stand in the path of the aforesaid vapours, which replenish the ventricles of the scapula. And because these aforesaid vapours . . . follow my argument closely, I beg you . . . and because these aforesaid vapours possess a certain malignancy . . . listen to this carefully, I do beseech you.

GERONTE: Yes.

SGANARELLE: Possess a certain malignancy which is caused . . . pay attention, if you please.

GERONTE: I'm following you.

SGANARELLE: Which is caused by the acidity of the humours produced in the concavity of the diaphragm. It happens that these vapours . . . *Ossabandus, nequeis, nequer, potarinum, quipsa milus*. That's exactly what's making your daughter dumb.

JACQUELINE: Ah! How well it's all put by our doctor.

LUCAS: If only I had his gift of the gab.

GERONTE: You certainly can't reason better than that. There's one little thing that strikes me. It's the location of the liver and the heart. It seems to me that you've got them the wrong way round. Isn't the heart on the left side, and the liver on the right side?

SGANARELLE: Yes, that was once the case. But we have changed all that. We now practise medicine by an entirely new method.

GERONTE: That's something I didn't know, and I beg pardon for my ignorance.

SGANARELLE: No harm in that. You're not obliged to be just as clever as we are.

GERONTE: Of course not. But doctor, what do you think needs doing for this illness?

SGANARELLE: What do I think needs doing?

GERONTE: Yes.

SGANARELLE: My advice is that you put her back to bed, and make her take as medicine a quantity of bread soaked in wine.

GERONTE: Why so, doctor?

SGANARELLE: Because there exists in wine and bread, mixed together, a sympathetic force which makes you speak. Didn't you know, you give nothing but to parrots, and they learn to speak through eating it?

GERONTE: Yes, that's true! What a great man! Quick, lots of bread and wine.

SGANARELLE: I'll be back this evening to see how she's getting along.

(1666)
Transl. R. G.

THE LAZARUS SYNDROME

Jesus' apparent misdiagnosis is compensated amply, if malodorously.

THE BIBLE

From St John

NOW A CERTAIN man was sick, named Lazarus, of Bethany, the town of Mary and her sister Martha. (It was that Mary which anointed the Lord with ointment, and wiped his feet with her hair, whose brother Lazarus was sick.) Therefore his sisters sent unto him, saying, Lord, behold, he whom thou lovest is sick. When Jesus heard that, he said, This sickness is not unto death, but for the glory of God, that the Son of God might be glorified thereby. Now Jesus loved Martha, and her sister, and Lazarus. When he had heard therefore that he was sick, he abode two days still in the same place where he was. Then after that saith he to his disciples, Let us go into Judea again. . . .

These things said he: and after that he saith unto them, Our friend Lazarus sleepeth; but I go, that I may awake him out of sleep. Then said his disciples, Lord, if he sleep, he shall do well. Howbeit Jesus spake of his death: but they thought that he had spoken of taking a rest in sleep. Then said Jesus unto them plainly, Lazarus is dead. And I am glad for your sakes that I was not there, to the intent ye may believe; nevertheless let us go unto him. . . .

Then when Jesus came, he found that he had lain in the grave four days already. . . . Then said Martha unto Jesus, Lord, if thou hadst been here, my brother had not died. But I know, that even now, whatsoever thou will ask of God, God will give it thee. Jesus saith unto her, Thy brother shall rise again. Martha saith unto him, I know that he shall rise again in the resurrection at the last day. Jesus said unto her, I am the resurrection and the life: he that believeth in me, though he were dead, yet shall he live. . . . And said, Where have ye laid him? They said unto him, Lord, come and see. Jesus wept. . . .

Jesus therefore again groaning in himself cometh to the grave. It was a cave, and a stone lay upon it. Jesus said, Take away the stone. Martha, the sister of him that was dead, saith unto him, Lord, by this time he stinketh: for he hath been dead four days. Jesus said unto her, Said I not unto thee, that, if thou wouldest believe, thou shouldest see the glory of God? And they took away the stone from the place where the dead was laid. And Jesus lifted up his eyes, and said, Father, I thank thee that thou hast heard me. And I knew that thou hearest me always: But because of the people which stand by I said it, that they may believe that thou hast sent me. And when he thus had spoken, he cried in a loud voice, Lazarus, come forth. And he that was dead came forth, bound hand and foot with graveclothes: and his face was bound about with a napkin. Jesus saith unto them, Loose him, and let him go.

11: 1–44
(Authorised Version)

The miracle of Lazarus is not always welcome.

EDGAR ALLAN POE (1809–49)

From The Premature Burial

TO BE BURIED while alive is, beyond question, the most terrific of those extremes which has ever fallen to the lot of mere mortality. That it has frequently, very frequently, so fallen, will scarcely be denied by those who think. The boundaries which divide life and death are at best shadowy and vague. Who shall say where the one ends, and where the other begins? We know that there are diseases in which occur total cessations of all apparent functions of vitality, and yet in which these cessations are merely suspensions, properly so called. They are only temporary pauses in the incomprehensible mechanism. A certain period elapses, and some unseen mysterious principle again sets in motion the magic pinions and the wizard wheels. The silver cord was not forever loosed, nor the golden bowl irreparably broken. But where, meantime, was the soul . . .?

For several years I had been subject to attacks of the singular disorder which physicians have agreed to term catalepsy, in default of a more definitive title. Although both the immediate and the predisposing causes, and even the actual diagnosis of this disease, are still mysterious, its obvious and apparent character is sufficiently well understood. Its variations seem to be chiefly of degree. Sometimes the patient lies, for a day only, or even for a shorter period, in a species of exaggerated lethargy. He is senseless and externally motionless; but the pulsation of the heart is still faintly perceptible; some traces of warmth remain; a slight colour lingers within the centre of the cheek; and, upon application of a mirror to the lips, we can detect a torpid, unequal, and vacillating action of the lungs. Then again the duration of the trance is for weeks – even for months; while the closest scrutiny and the most rigorous medical tests fail to establish any material distinction between the state of the sufferer and what we conceive of absolute death. Very usually, he is saved from premature interment solely by the knowledge of his friends that he has been previously subject to catalepsy, by the consequent suspicion excited, and, above all, by the non-appearance of decay. The advances of the malady are, luckily, gradual. The first manifestations, although marked, are unequivocal. The fits grow successively more and more distinctive, and endure each for a longer term than the preceding. In this lies the principal security from inhumation. The unfortunate whose *first* attack should be of the extreme character which is occasionally seen would almost inevitably be consigned alive to the tomb.

My own case differed in no important particular than those mentioned in medical books. Sometimes, without any apparent cause, I sank, little by little, into a condition of semi-syncope, or half swoon; and, in this condition, without pain, without ability to stir, or, strictly speaking, to think, but with a dull lethargic consciousness of life and of the presence of those who surrounded my bed, I remained, until the crisis of the disease restored me, suddenly, to perfect sensation. At other times I was quickly and impetuously smitten. I grew sick, and numb, and chilly, and dizzy, and so fell prostrate at once. Then, for weeks, all was void, and black, and silent, and Nothing became the universe. Total annihilation could be no more. From these latter attacks I awoke, however, with a gradation slow in proportion to the suddenness of the seizure. . . .

Fantasies such as these, presenting themselves at night, extended their terrific influence far into my waking hours. My nerves became thoroughly unstrung, and I fell a prey to perpetual horror. I hesitated to ride, or to walk, or to indulge in any exercise that would carry me from home. In fact, I no longer dared trust myself out of the immediate presence of those who were aware of my proneness to catalepsy, lest, falling into one of my usual fits, I should be buried before my real condition could be ascertained. I doubted the care, the fidelity, of my dearest friends. I dreaded that, in some trance of more than customary duration, they might be prevailed upon to regard me as irrecoverable. I even went so far as to fear that, as I occasioned much trouble, they might be glad to consider any very protracted attack as sufficient excuse for getting rid of me altogether. It was in vain they endeavoured to reassure me by the most solemn promises. I exacted the most sacred oaths, that under no circumstances they would bury me until decomposition had so materially advanced as to render farther preservation impossible. And, even then, my mortal terrors would listen to no reason – would accept no consolation. I entered into a series of elaborate precautions. Among other things, I had the family vault so remodelled as to admit of being readily opened from within. The slightest pressure upon a long lever that extended far into the tomb would cause the iron portals to fly back. There were arrangements also for the free admission of air and light, and convenient receptacles for food and water, within immediate reach of the coffin intended for my reception. This coffin was warmly and softly padded, and was provided with a lid, fashioned upon the principle of the vault-door, with the addition of springs so contrived that the feeblest movement of the body would be sufficient to set it at liberty. Besides all this, there was suspended from the roof of the tomb, a large bell, the rope of which, it was designed, should extend through a hole in the coffin, and so be fastened to one of the hands of the corpse. But, alas! what avails the vigilance against the Destiny of man? Not even these well-contrived securities sufficed to save from the uttermost agonies of living inhumation a wretch to these agonies foredoomed!

There arrived an epoch – as often before there had arrived – in which I found myself emerging from total unconsciousness into the first feeble and indefinite sense of existence. Slowly – with a tortoise gradation – approached the faint grey dawn of the psychal day. A torpid uneasiness. An apathetic endurance of dull pain. No care – no hope – no effort. Then, after a long interval, a ringing in the ears; then, after a lapse still longer, a pricking or tingling sensation in the extremities; then a seemingly eternal period of pleasurable quiescence, during which the awakening feelings are struggling into thought; then a brief resinking into nonentity; then a sudden recovery. At length the slight quivering of an eyelid, and immediately thereupon, an electric shock of terror, deadly and indefinite, which sends the blood in torrents from the temples to the heart. And now the first positive effort to think. And now the first endeavour to remember. And now a partial and evanescent success. And now the memory has so far regained its dominion, that, in some measure, I am cognizant of my state. I feel that I am not awaking from ordinary sleep. I recollect that I have been subject to catalepsy. And now, at last, as if by the rush of an ocean, my shuddering spirit is overwhelmed by the one grim Danger – by the one spectral and ever-prevalent Idea.

For some minutes after this fancy possessed me, I remained without motion. And why? I could not summon courage to move. I dared not make the effort which was to satisfy me of my fate – and yet there was something at my heart which whispered me *it was sure*. Despair – such as no other species of wretchedness ever calls into being – despair alone urged me, after long irresolution, to uplift the heavy lids of my eyes. I uplifted them. It was dark – all dark. I knew that the fit was over. I knew that the crisis of my disorder had long passed. I knew that I had now fully recovered the use of my visual faculties; and yet it was dark – all dark – the intense and utter raylessness of the Night that endureth for evermore.

I endeavoured to shriek; and my lips and my parched tongue moved convulsively together in the attempt – but no voice issued from the cavernous lungs, which, oppressed as if by the weight of some incumbent mountain, gasped and palpitated, with the heart, at every elaborate and struggling inspiration.

The movement of the jaws, in this effort to cry aloud, showed me that they were bound up, as is usual with the dead. I felt, too, that I lay upon some hard substance; and by something similar my sides were, also, closely compressed. So far, I had not ventured to stir any of my limbs – but now I violently threw up my arms, which had been lying at length, with the wrists crossed. They struck a solid wooden substance, which extended above my person at an elevation of not more than six inches from my face. I could no longer doubt that I reposed within a coffin at last.

And now, amid all my infinite miseries, came sweetly the cherub Hope – for I thought of my precautions. I writhed, and made spasmodic exertions to force open the lid: it would not move. I felt my wrists for the bell-rope: it was not to be found. And now the Comforter fled forever, and a still sterner Despair reigned triumphant; for I could not help perceiving the absence of the paddings which I had so carefully prepared – and then, too, there came suddenly to my nostrils the strong peculiar odour of moist earth. The conclusion was irresistible. I was *not* within the vault. I had fallen into a trance whilst absent from home – while among strangers – when or how I could not remember – and it was they who had buried me as a dog – nailed up in some common coffin – and thrust, deep, deep, and forever, into some ordinary and nameless *grave*.

As this awful conviction forced itself, thus, into the innermost chambers of my soul, I once again struggled to cry aloud. And in this second endeavour I succeeded. A long, wild, and continuous shriek, or yell, of agony, resounded through the realms of the subterrene Night.

'Hillo! hillo, there!' said a gruff voice, in reply.

'What the devil's the matter now?' said a second.

'Get out o' that!' said a third.

'What do you mean by yowling in that ere kind of style, like a cattymount?' said a fourth; and hereupon I was seized and shaken without ceremony, for several minutes, by a junto of very rough-looking individuals. They did not arouse me from my slumber – for I was wide awake when I screamed – but they restored me to the full possession of my memory.

This adventure occurred near Richmond, in Virginia. Accompanied by a friend, I had proceeded, upon a gunning expedition, some miles down the banks of James River. Night approached, and we were overtaken by a storm. The cabin of a small sloop lying at anchor in the stream, and laden with garden mould, afforded us the only available shelter. We made the best of it, and passed the night on board. I slept in one of the only two berths in the vessel – and the berths of a sloop of sixty or seventy tons need scarcely be described. That which I occupied had no bedding of any kind. Its extreme width was eighteen inches. The distance of its bottom from the deck overhead was precisely the same. I found it a matter of exceeding difficulty to squeeze myself in. Nevertheless, I slept soundly; and the whole of my vision – for it was no dream, and no nightmare – arose naturally from the circumstances of my position – from my ordinary bias of thought – and from the difficulty, to which I have alluded, of collecting my senses, and especially of regaining my memory, for a long time after awaking from slumber. The men who shook me were the crew of the sloop, and some labourers engaged to unload it. From the load itself came the earthy smell. The bandage about the jaws was a silk handkerchief in which I had bound up my head, in default of my customary night-cap.

(1844)

The resurrection is not always the resumption of life. Before the Anatomy Act of 1832 regulated so vital an activity, the gruesome trade of the 'resurrectionists' furnished 'the table' of utterly reputable anatomy lecturers.

I have itemised their technique:

1. Wait till dark.
2. Post a couple of lookouts against rival resurrectionists and excitable relatives.
3. Dig a hole in the loose earth *at the head* of the grave. Use a flat daggerlike spade of *wood*, to avoid noise with the stones. Spread canvas sheet for soil, keeping grass uncontaminated.
4. Apply two hooks to coffin lid, pull with rope, splinter lid (pack hole with sacks to muffle cracking noise).
5. Take body *by both ears*, extract.
6. Replace shroud. That would be stealing. A body belongs to nobody.
7. Sack up body.
8. Make good, remove tools from site, decamp.

It should take an hour.

During the 1820s, the legendary sack-'em-up men Burke and Hare provided the pickings for five hundred medical students at Dr Robert Knox's private anatomy school, No. 10 Surgeons' Square, Edinburgh. Burke and Hare had enterprisingly speeded up their deliveries by plying living bodies with whisky, and then suffocating them. One such was eighteen-year-old Mary Patterson, a Canongate tart, whose appearance naked the next morning brought distraught recognition to many dissectors – including Knox's assistant, the future Queen's surgeon Sir William Fergusson.

In 1881, at Kinneard Cottage in Pitlochry, sixty-five miles away up in the Grampians, Robert Louis Stevenson (1850–94) mixed these ingredients for *The Body-Snatchers*. But he laid the story aside as 'being horrid'. On 13 November 1884, Stevenson's thirty-fourth birthday, the *Pall Mall Gazette* wanted a sensational Christmas piece from him at £5 per thousand words. Stevenson sighed that the morphine necessitated by his chronic cough made him too sleepy – it 'moderates the hay' but 'sews up the donkey'. He sent instead the filed tale, its title reduced to the singular. He rather grandly refused the full £40, protesting it not worth so much. The story was a huge success, advertised by the *Pall Mall Gazette* with such effective grotesquerie that the police marched up to strip the sandwich-men of their boards.

Robert Louis Stevenson is a medical riddle. Was he a sad but glorious victim of the 'white plague' – tuberculosis – like Keats, Chopin, Katherine Mansfield and George Orwell? He was diagnosed aged twenty-two by Sir Andrew Clark of the London Hospital (who diagnosed also Keats and Chopin) as suffering 'pthisis and nervous exhaustion', and prescribed the Riviera. This advice dispatched him to Menton, then Davos, California, Bournemouth, and finally to Valima in Samoa, where he died, but not of tuberculosis. On 3 December 1894 he was getting up a bottle of his best Burgundy for dinner when he cried 'What's that?', held his head, and died at 8.10 p.m. from a subarachnoid haemorrhage round the brain. Dr Livingstone Trudeau, another tuberculosis expert with whom Stevenson resided at Saranac Lake in upstate New York, declared that despite his lung haemorrhages Stevenson did not have pulmonary tuberculosis: he never found any tubercle bacilli in his spit. So perhaps all his journeys were not really necessary.

ROBERT LOUIS STEVENSON

The Body-Snatcher

EVERY NIGHT IN the year, four of us sat in the small parlour of the George at Debenham – the undertaker, and the landlord, and Fettes, and myself. Sometimes there would be more; but blow high, blow low, come rain or snow or frost, we four would be each planted in his own particular armchair. Fettes was an old drunken Scotchman, a man of education obviously, and a man of some property, since he lived in idleness. He had come to Debenham years ago, while still young, and by a mere continuance of living had grown to be an adopted townsman. His blue camlet cloak was a local antiquity, like the church-spire. His place in the parlour at the George, his absence from church, his old, crapulous, disreputable vices, were all things of course in

Debenham. He had some vague Radical opinions and some fleeting infidelities, which he would now and again set forth and emphasise with tottering slaps upon the table. He drank rum – five glasses regularly every evening; and for the greater portion of his nightly visit to the George sat, with his glass in his right hand, in a state of melancholy alcoholic saturation. We called him the Doctor, for he was supposed to have some special knowledge of medicine, and had been known, upon a pinch, to set a fracture or reduce a dislocation; but beyond these slight particulars, we had no knowledge of his character and antecedents.

One dark winter night – it had struck nine some time before the landlord joined us – there was a sick man in the George, a great neighbouring proprietor suddenly struck down with the apoplexy on his way to Parliament; and the great man's still greater London doctor had been telegraphed to his bedside. It was the first time that such a thing had happened in Debenham, for the railway was but newly open, and we were all proportionately moved by the occurrence.

'He's come,' said the landlord, after he had filled and lighted his pipe.

'He?' said I. 'Who? – not the doctor?'

'Himself,' replied our host.

'What is his name?'

'Doctor Macfarlane,' said the landlord.

Fettes was far through his third tumbler, stupidly fuddled, now nodding over, now staring mazily around him; but at the last word he seemed to awaken, and repeated the name 'Macfarlane' twice, quietly enough the first time, but with sudden emotion at the second.

'Yes,' said the landlord, 'that's his name, Doctor Wolfe Macfarlane.'

Fettes became instantly sober; his eyes awoke, his voice became clear, loud, and steady, his language forcible and earnest. We were all startled by the transformation, as if a man had risen from the dead.

'I beg your pardon,' he said, 'I am afraid I have not been paying much attention to your talk. Who is this Wolfe Macfarlane?' And then, when he had heard the landlord out, 'It cannot be, it cannot be,' he added; 'and yet I would like well to see him face to face.'

'Do you know him, Doctor?' asked the undertaker, with a gasp.

'God forbid!' was the reply. 'And yet the name is a strange one; it were too much to fancy two. Tell me, landlord, is he old?'

'Well,' said the host, 'he's not a young man, to be sure, and his hair is white; but he looks younger than you.'

'He is older, though; years older. But,' with a slap upon the table, 'it's the rum you see in my face – rum and sin. This man, perhaps, may have an easy conscience and a good digestion. Conscience! Hear me speak. You would think I was some good, old, decent Christian, would you not? But no, not I; I never canted. Voltaire might have canted if he'd stood in my shoes; but the brains' – with a rattling fillip on his bald head – 'the brains were clear and active, and I saw and made no deductions.'

'If you know this doctor,' I ventured to remark, after a somewhat awful pause, 'I should gather that you do not share the landlord's good opinion.'

Fettes paid no regard to me.

'Yes,' he said, with sudden decision, 'I must see him face to face.'

There was another pause, and then a door was closed rather sharply on the first floor, and a step was heard upon the stair.

'That's the doctor,' cried the landlord. 'Look sharp, and you can catch him.'

It was but two steps from the small parlour to the door of the old George Inn; the wide oak staircase landed almost in the street; there was room for a Turkey rug and nothing more between the threshold and the last round of the descent; but this little space was every evening brilliantly lit up, not only by the light upon the stair and the great signal lamp below the sign, but by the warm radiance of the bar-room window. The George thus brightly advertised itself to passers-by in the cold street. Fettes walked steadily to the spot, and we, who were hanging behind, beheld the two men meet, as one of them had phrased it, face to face. Dr Macfarlane was alert and vigorous. His white hair set off his pale and placid, although energetic, countenance. He was richly dressed in the finest of broadcloth and the whitest of linen, with a great gold watch-chain, and studs and spectacles of the same precious material. He wore a broad-folded tie, white and speckled with lilac, and he carried on his arm a comfortable driving-coat of fur. There was no doubt but he became his years, breathing as he did, of wealth and consideration; and it was a surprising contrast to see our parlour sot – bald, dirty, pimpled, and robed in his old camlet cloak – confront him at the bottom of the stairs.

'Macfarlane!' he said somewhat loudly, more like a herald than a friend.

The great doctor pulled up short on the fourth step, as though the familiarity of the address surprised and somewhat shocked his dignity.

'Toddy Macfarlane!' repeated Fettes.

The London man almost staggered. He stared for the swiftest of seconds at the man before him, glanced behind him with a sort of scare, and then in a startled whisper, 'Fettes!' he said, 'you!'

'Ay,' said the other, 'me! Did you think I was dead too? We are not so easy shut of our acquaintance.'

'Hush, hush!' exclaimed the doctor. 'Hush, hush! this meeting is so unexpected – I can see you are unmanned. I hardly knew you, I confess, at first; but I am overjoyed – overjoyed to have this opportunity. For the present it must be how-d'ye-do and goodbye in one, for my fly is waiting, and I must not fail the train; but you shall – let me see – yes – you shall give me your address, and you can count on early news of me. We must do something for you, Fettes. I fear you are out at elbows; but we must see to that for auld lang syne, as once we sang at suppers.'

'Money!' cried Fettes; 'money from you! The money that I had from you is lying where I cast it in the rain.'

Dr Macfarlane had talked himself into some measure of superiority and confidence, but the uncommon energy of this refusal cast him back into his first confusion.

A horrible, ugly look came and went across his almost venerable countenance. 'My dear fellow,' he said, 'be it as you please; my last thought is to offend you. I would intrude on none. I will leave you my address, however –'

'I do not wish it – I do not wish to know the roof that shelters you,' interrupted the other. 'I heard your name; I feared it might be you; I wished to know if, after all, there were a God; I know now that there is none. Begone!'

He still stood in the middle of the rug, between the stair and doorway; and the great London physician, in order to escape, would be forced to step to one side. It was plain that he hesitated before the thought of this humiliation. White as he was, there was a dangerous glitter in his spectacles; but while he still paused uncertain, he became aware that the driver of his fly was peering in from the street at this unusual scene and caught a glimpse at the same time of our little body from the parlour, huddled by the corner of the bar. The presence of so many witnesses decided him at once to flee. He crouched together, brushing on the wainscot, and made a dart like a serpent, striking for the door. But his tribulation was not entirely at an end, for even as he was passing Fettes clutched him by the arm and these words came in a whisper, and yet painfully distinct, 'Have you seen it again?'

The great rich London doctor cried out aloud with a sharp, throttling cry; he dashed his questioner across the open space, and, with his hands over his head, fled out of the door like a detected thief. Before it had occurred to one of us to make a movement the fly was already rattling toward the station. The scene was over like a dream, but the dream had left proofs and traces of its passage. Next day the servant found the fine gold spectacles broken on the threshold, and that very night we were all standing breathless by the bar-room window, and Fettes at our side, sober, pale, and resolute in look.

'God protect us, Mr Fettes!' said the landlord, coming first into possession of his customary senses. 'What in the universe is all this? These are strange things you have been saying.'

Fettes turned toward us; he looked us each in succession in the face. 'See if you can hold your tongues,' said he. 'That man Macfarlane is not safe to cross; those that have done so already have repented it too late.'

And then, without so much as finishing his third glass, far less waiting for the other two, he bade us goodbye and went forth, under the lamp of the hotel, into the black night.

We three turned to our places in the parlour, with the big red fire and four clear candles; and as we recapitulated what had passed, the first chill of our surprise soon changed into a glow of curiosity. We sat late; it was the latest session I have known in the old George. Each man, before we parted, had his theory that he was bound to prove; and none of us had any nearer business in this world than to track out the past of our condemned companion, and surprise the secret that he shared with the great London doctor. It is no great boast, but I believe I was a better hand at worming out a story than either of my fellows at the George; and perhaps there is now no other man alive who could narrate to you the following foul and unnatural events.

In his young days Fettes studied medicine in the schools of Edinburgh. He had talent of a kind, the talent that picks up swiftly what it hears and readily retails it for its own. He worked little at home; but he was civil, attentive, and intelligent in the presence of his masters. They soon picked him out as a lad who listened closely and remembered well; nay, strange as it seemed to me when I first heard it, he was in those days well favoured, and pleased by his exterior. There was, at that period, a certain extramural teacher of anatomy, whom I shall here designate by the letter K. His name was subsequently too well known. The man who bore it skulked through the streets of Edinburgh in disguise, while the mob that applauded at the execution of Burke called loudly for the blood of his employer. But Mr K— was then at the top of his vogue; he enjoyed a popularity due partly to his own talent and address, partly to the incapacity of his rival, the university professor. The students, at least, swore by his name, and Fettes believed himself, and was believed by others, to have laid the foundations of success when he acquired the favour of this meteorically famous man. Mr K— was a bon vivant as well as an accomplished teacher; he liked a sly illusion no less than a careful preparation. In both capacities Fettes enjoyed and deserved his notice, and by the second year of his attendance he held the half-regular position of second demonstrator, or sub-assistant in his class.

In this capacity the charge of the theatre and lecture-room devolved in particular upon his shoulders. He had to answer for the cleanliness of the premises and the conduct of the other students, and it was a part of his duty to supply, receive, and divide the various subjects. It was with a view to this last – at that time very delicate – affair that he was lodged by Mr K— in the same wynd, and at last in the same building, with the dissecting-rooms. Here, after a night of turbulent pleasures, his hand still tottering, his sight still misty and confused, he would be called out of bed in the black hours before the winter dawn by the unclean and desperate interlopers who supplied the table. He would open the door to these men, since infamous throughout the land. He would help them with their tragic burden, pay them their sordid price, and remain alone, when they were gone, with the unfriendly relics of humanity. From such a scene he would return to snatch another hour or two of slumber, to repair the abuses of the night, and refresh himself for the labours of the day.

Few lads could have been more insensible to the impressions of a life thus passed among the ensigns of mortality. His mind was closed against all general considerations. He was incapable of interest in the fate and fortunes of another, the slave of his own desires and low ambitions. Cold, light, and selfish in the last resort, he had that modicum of prudence, miscalled morality, which keeps a man from inconvenient drunkenness or punishable theft. He coveted, besides, a measure of consideration from his masters and his fellow-pupils, and he had no desire to fail conspicuously in the external parts of life. Thus he made it his pleasure to gain some distinction in his studies, and day after day rendered unimpeachable eye-service to his employer, Mr K—. For his day of work he indemnified himself by nights of roaring, blackguardly enjoyment; and when that balance had been struck, the organ that he called his conscience declared itself content.

The supply of subjects was a continual trouble to him as well as to his master. In that large and busy class, the raw material of the anatomist kept perpetually running out; and the business thus rendered necessary was not only unpleasant in itself, but threatened dangerous consequences to all who were concerned. It was the policy of Mr K— to ask no questions in his dealings with the trade. 'They bring the body, and we pay the price,' he used to say, dwelling on the alliteration – '*quid pro quo*.' And, again, and somewhat profanely, 'Ask no questions,' he would tell his assistants, 'for conscience' sake.' There was no understanding that the subjects were provided by the crime of murder. Had that idea been broached to him in words, he would have recoiled in horror; but the lightness of his speech upon so grave a matter was, in itself, an offence against good manners, and a temptation to the men with whom he dealt. Fettes, for instance, had often remarked to himself upon the singular freshness of the bodies. He had been struck again and again by the hangdog, abominable looks of the ruffians who came to him before the dawn; and putting things together clearly in his private thoughts, he perhaps attributed a meaning too immoral and too categorical to the unguarded counsels of his master. He understood his duty, in short, to have three branches: to take what was brought, to pay the price, and to avert the eye from any evidence of crime.

One November morning this policy of silence was put sharply to the test. He had been awake all night with a racking toothache – pacing his room like a caged beast or throwing himself in fury on his bed – and had fallen at last into that profound, uneasy slumber that so often follows on a night of pain, when he was awakened by the third or fourth angry repetition of the concerted signal. There was a thin, bright moonshine; it was bitter cold, windy, and frosty; the town had not yet awakened, but an indefinable stir already preluded the noise and business of the day. The ghouls had come later than usual, and they seemed more than usually eager to be gone. Fettes, sick with sleep, lighted them upstairs. He heard their grumbling Irish voices through a dream; and as they stripped the sack from their sad merchandise he leaned dozing, with his shoulder propped against the wall; he had to shake himself to find the men their money. As he did so his eyes lighted on the dead face. He started; he took two steps nearer, with the candle raised.

'God Almighty!' he cried. 'That is Jane Galbraith!'

The men answered nothing, but they shuffled nearer the door.

'I know her, I tell you,' he continued. 'She was alive and hearty yesterday. It's impossible she can be dead; it's impossible you should have got this body fairly.'

'Sure, sir, you're mistaken entirely,' said one of the men.

But the other looked Fettes darkly in the eyes, and demanded the money on the spot.

It was impossible to misconceive the threat or to exaggerate the danger. The lad's heart failed him. He stammered some excuses, counted out the sum, and saw his hateful visitors depart. No sooner were they gone than he hastened to confirm his doubts. By a dozen unquestionable marks he identified the girl he had jested with the day before. He saw, with horror, marks upon her body that might well betoken violence. A panic seized him, and he took refuge in his room. There he reflected at length over the discovery that he had made; considered soberly the bearing of Mr K—'s instructions and the danger to himself of interference in so serious a business, and at last, in sore perplexity, determined to wait for the advice of his immediate superior, the class assistant.

This was a young doctor, Wolfe Macfarlane, a high favourite among all the reckless students, clever, dissipated, and unscrupulous to the last degree. He had travelled and studied abroad. His manners were agreeable and a little forward. He was an authority on the stage, skilful on the ice or the links with skate or golf-club; he dressed with nice audacity, and, to put the finishing touch upon his glory, he kept a gig and a strong trotting-horse. With Fettes he was on terms of intimacy; indeed, their relative positions called for some community of life; and when subjects were scarce the pair would drive far into the country in Macfarlane's gig, visit and desecrate some lonely graveyard, and return before dawn with their booty to the door of the dissecting-room.

On that particular morning Macfarlane arrived somewhat earlier than his wont. Fettes heard him, and met him on the stirs, told him his story, and showed him the cause of his alarm. Macfarlane examined the marks on her body.

'Yes,' he said, with a nod, 'it looks fishy.'

'Well, what should I do?' asked Fettes.

'Do?' repeated the other. 'Do you want to do anything? Least said soonest mended, I should say.'

'Someone else might recognise her,' objected Fettes 'She was as well known as the Castle Rock.'

'We'll hope not,' said Macfarlane, 'and if anybody does – well, you didn't, don't you see, and there's an end. The fact is, this has been going on too long. Stir up the mud, and you'll get K— into the most unholy trouble; you'll be in a shocking box yourself. So will I, if you come to that. I should like to know how any one of us would look, or what the devil we should have to say for ourselves, in any Christian witness-box. For me, you know there's one thing certain – that, practically speaking, all our subjects have been murdered.'

'Macfarlane!' cried Fettes.

'Come now!' sneered the other. 'As if you hadn't suspected it yourself!'

'Suspecting is one thing –'

'And proof another. Yes, I know; and I'm as sorry as you are this should have come here,' tapping the body with his cane. 'The next best thing for me is not to recognise it; and,' he added coolly, 'I don't. You may, if you please. I don't dictate, but I think a man of the world would do as I do; and I may add, I fancy that is what K— would look for at our hands. The question is, Why did he choose us two for his assistants? And I answer, Because he didn't want old wives.'

This was the tone of all others to affect the mind of a lad like Fettes. He agreed to imitate Macfarlane. The body of the unfortunate girl was duly dissected, and no one remarked or appeared to recognise her.

One afternoon, when his day's work was over, Fettes dropped into a popular tavern and found Macfarlane sitting with a stranger. This was a small man, very pale and dark, with coal-black eyes. The cut of his features gave a promise of intellect and refinement which was but feebly realised in his manners, for he proved, upon a nearer acquaintance, coarse, vulgar, and stupid. He exercised, however, a very remarkable control over Macfarlane; issued orders like the Great Bashaw; became inflamed at the least discussion or delay, and commented rudely on the servility with which he was obeyed. This most offensive person took a fancy to Fettes on the spot, plied him with drinks, and honoured him with unusual confidences on his past career. If a tenth part of what he confessed were true, he was a very loathsome rogue; and the lad's vanity was tickled by the attention of so experienced a man.

'I'm a pretty bad fellow myself,' the stranger remarked, 'but Macfarlane is the boy – Toddy Macfarlane I call him. Toddy, order your friend another glass.' Or it might be, 'Toddy, you jump up and shut the door.' 'Toddy hates me,' he said again. 'Oh, yes, Toddy, you do!'

'Don't you call me that confounded name,' growled Macfarlane.

'Hear him! Did you ever see the lads play knife? He would like to do that all over my body,' remarked the stranger.

'We medicals have a better way than that,' said Fettes. 'When we dislike a dead friend of ours, we dissect him.'

Macfarlane looked up sharply, as though this jest were scarcely to his mind.

The afternoon passed. Gray, for that was the stranger's name, invited Fettes to join them at dinner, ordered a feast so sumptuous that the tavern was thrown into commotion, and when all was done commanded Macfarlane to settle the bill. It was late before they separated; the man Gray was incapably drunk. Macfarlane, sobered by his fury, chewed the cud of the money he had been forced to squander and the slights he had been obliged to swallow. Fettes, with various liquors singing in his head, returned home with devious footsteps and a mind entirely in abeyance. Next day Macfarlane was absent from the class, and Fettes smiled to himself as he imagined him still squiring the intolerable Gray from tavern to tavern. As soon as the hour of liberty had struck he posted from place to place in quest of his last night's companions. He could find them, however, nowhere; so returned early to his rooms, went early to bed, and slept the sleep of the just.

At four in the morning he was awakened by the well-known signal. Descending to the door, he was filled with astonishment to find Macfarlane with his gig, and in the gig one of those long and ghastly packages with which he was so well acquainted.

'What?' he cried. 'Have you been out alone? How did you manage?'

But Macfarlane silenced him roughly, bidding him turn to business. When they had got the body upstairs and laid it on the table, Macfarlane made at first as if he were going away. Then he paused and seemed to hesitate; and then, 'You had better look at the face,' said he, in tones of some constraint. 'You had better,' he repeated, as Fettes only stared at him in wonder.

'But where, and how, and when did you come by it?' cried the other.

'Look at the face,' was the only answer.

Fettes was staggered; strange doubts assailed him. He looked from the young doctor to the body, and then back again. At last, with a start, he did as he was bidden. He had almost expected the sight that met his eyes, and yet the shock was cruel. To see, fixed in the rigidity of death and naked on that coarse layer of sackcloth, the man whom he had left well clad and full of meat and sin upon the threshold of a tavern, awoke, even in the thoughtless Fettes, some of the terrors of the conscience. It was a *cras tibi* which re-echoed in his soul, that two whom he had known should have come to lie upon these icy tables. Yet these were only secondary thoughts. His first concern regarded Wolfe. Unprepared for a challenge so momentous, he knew not how to look his comrade in the face. He durst not meet his eye, and he had neither words nor voice at his command.

It was Macfarlane himself who made the first advance. He came up quietly behind and laid his hand gently but firmly on the other's shoulder.

'Richardson,' said he, 'may have the head.'

Now Richardson was a student who had long been anxious for that portion of the human subject to dissect. There was no answer, and the murderer resumed: 'Talking of business, you must pay me; your accounts, you see, must tally.'

Fettes found a voice, the ghost of his own: 'Pay you!' he cried. 'Pay you for that?'

'Why, yes, of course you must. By all means and on every possible account, you must,' returned the other. 'I dare not give it for nothing, you dare not take it for nothing; it would compromise us both. This is another case like Jane Galbraith's. The more things are wrong the more we must act as if all were right. Where does old K— keep his money?'

'There,' answered Fettes hoarsely, pointing to a cupboard in the corner.

'Give me the key, then,' said the other calmly, holding out his hand.

There was an instant's hesitation, and the die was cast. Macfarlane could not suppress a nervous twitch, the infinitesimal mark of an immense relief, as he felt the key between his fingers. He opened the cupboard, brought out pen and ink and a paper-book that stood in one compartment, and separated from the funds in a drawer a sum suitable to the occasion.

'Now, look here,' he said, 'there is the payment made – first proof of your good faith: first step to your security. You have now to clinch it by a second. Enter the payment in your book, and then you for your part may defy the devil.'

The next few seconds were for Fettes an agony of thought; but in balancing his terrors it was the most immediate that triumphed. Any future difficulty seemed almost welcome if he could avoid a present quarrel with Macfarlane. He set down the candle which he had been carrying all this time, and with a steady hand entered the date, the nature, and the amount of the transaction.

'And now,' said Macfarlane, 'it's only fair that you should pocket the lucre. I've had my share already. By-the-bye, when a man of the world falls into a bit of luck, has a few shillings extra in his pocket – I'm ashamed to speak of it, but there's a rule of conduct in the case. No treating, no purchase of expensive class-books, no squaring of old debts; borrow, don't lend.'

'Macfarlane,' began Fettes, still somewhat hoarsely, 'I have put my neck in a halter to oblige you.'

'To oblige me?' cried Wolfe. 'Oh, come! You did, as near as I can see the matter, what you downright had to do in self-defence. Suppose I got into trouble, where would you be? This second little matter flows clearly from the first. Mr Gray is the continuation of Miss Galbraith. You can't begin and then stop. If you begin, you must keep on beginning; that's the truth. No rest for the wicked.'

A horrible sense of blackness and the treachery of fate seized hold upon the soul of the unhappy student.

'My God!' he cried, 'but what have I done? and when did I begin? To be made a class assistant – in the name of reason, where's the harm in that? Service wanted the position; Service might have got it. Would *he* have been where *I* am now!'

'My dear fellow,' said Macfarlane, 'what a boy you are! What harm *has* come to you? What harm *can* come to you if you hold your tongue? Why, man, do you know what this life is? There are two squads of us – the lions and the lambs. If you're a lamb, you'll come to lie upon these tables like Gray or Jane Galbraith; if you're a lion, you'll live and drive a horse like me, like K—, like all the world with any wit or courage. You're staggered at the first. But look at K—! My dear fellow, you're clever, you have pluck. I like you, and K— likes you. You were born to lead the hunt; and I tell you, on my honour and my experience of life, three days from now you'll laugh at all these scarecrows like a High School boy at a farce.'

And with that Macfarlane took his departure and drove off up the wynd in his gig to get under cover before daylight. Fettes was thus left alone with his regrets. He saw the miserable peril in which he stood involved. He saw, with inexpressible dismay, that there was no limit to his weakness, and that, from concession to concession, he had fallen from the arbiter of Macfarlane's destiny to his paid and helpless accomplice. He would have given the world to have been a little braver at the time, but it did not occur to him that he might still be brave. The secret of Jane Galbraith and the cursed entry in the day-book closed his mouth.

Hours passed; the class began to arrive; the members of the unhappy Gray were dealt out to one and to another, and received without remark. Richardson was made happy with the head; and before the hour of freedom rang Fettes trembled with exultation to perceive how far they had already gone toward safety.

For two days he continued to watch, with increasing joy, the dreadful process of disguise.

On the third day Macfarlane made his appearance. He had been ill, he said; but he made up for lost time by the energy with which he directed the students. To Richardson in particular he extended the most valuable assistance and advice, and that student, encouraged by the praise of the demonstrator, burned high with ambitious hopes, and saw the medal already in his grasp.

Before the week was out Macfarlane's prophecy had been fulfilled. Fettes had outlived his terrors and had forgotten his baseness. He began to plume himself upon his courage, and had so arranged the story in his mind that he could look back on these events with an unhealthy pride. Of his accomplice he saw but little. They met, of course, in the business of the class; they received their orders together from Mr K—. At times they had a word or two in private, and Macfarlane was from first to last particularly kind and jovial. But it was plain that he avoided any reference to their common secret; and even when Fettes whispered to him that he had cast in his lot with the lions and forsworn the lambs, he only signed to him smilingly to hold his peace.

At length an occasion arose which threw the pair once more into a closer union. Mr K— was again short of subjects; pupils were eager, and it was a part of this teacher's pretensions to be always well supplied. At the same time there came the news of a burial in the rustic graveyard at Glencorse. Time has little changed the place in question. It stood then, as now, upon a cross road, out of call of human habitations, and buried fathom deep in the foliage of six cedar trees. The cries of the sheep upon the neighbouring hills, the streamlets upon either hand, one loudly singing among pebbles, the other dripping furtively from pond to pond, the stir of the wind in mountainous old flowering chestnuts, and once in seven days the voice of the bell and the old tunes of the precentor, were the only sounds that disturbed the silence around the rural church. The Resurrection Man – to use a by-name of the period – was not to be deterred by any of the sanctities of customary piety. It was part of his trade to despise and desecrate the scrolls and trumpets of old tombs, the paths worn by the feet of worshippers and mourners, and the offerings and the inscriptions of bereaved affection. To rustic neighbourhoods, where love is more than commonly tenacious, and where some bonds of blood or fellowship unite the entire society of a parish, the body-snatcher, far from being repelled by natural respect, was attracted by the ease and safety of the task. To bodies that had been laid in earth, in joyful expectation of a far different awakening, there came that hasty, lamp-lit, terror-haunted resurrection of the spade and mattock. The coffin was forced, the cerements torn, and the melancholy relics, clad in sackcloth, after being rattled for hours on moonless byways, were at length exposed to uttermost indignities before a class of gaping boys.

Somewhat as two vultures may swoop upon a dying lamb, Fettes and Macfarlane were to be let loose upon a grave in that green and quiet resting-place. The wife of a farmer, a woman who had lived for sixty years and been known for nothing but good butter and a godly conversation, was to be rooted from her grave at midnight and carried, dead and naked, to that far-away city that she had always honoured with her Sunday's best; the place beside her family was to be empty till the crack of doom; her innocent and almost venerable members to be exposed to that last curiosity of the anatomist.

Late one afternoon the pair set forth, well wrapped in cloaks and furnished with a formidable bottle. It rained without remission – a cold, dense, lashing rain. Now and again there blew a puff of wind, but these sheets of falling water kept it down. Bottle and all, it was a sad and silent drive as far as Penicuik, where they were to spend the evening. They stopped once, to hide their implements in a thick bush not far from the churchyard, and once again at the Fisher's Tryst, to have a toast before the kitchen fire and vary their nips of whisky with a glass of ale. When they reached their journey's end the gig was housed, the horse was fed and comforted, and the two young doctors in a private room sat down to the best dinner and the best wine the house afforded. The lights, the fire, the beating rain upon the window, the cold, incongruous work that lay before them, added zest to their enjoyment of the meal. With every glass their cordiality increased. Soon Macfarlane handed a little pile of gold to his companion.

'A compliment,' he said. 'Between friends these little d—d accommodations ought to fly like pipe-lights.'

Fettes pocketed the money, and applauded the sentiment to the echo. 'You are a philosopher,' he cried. 'I was an ass till I knew you. You and K— between you, by the Lord Harry! but you'll make a man of me.'

'Of course we shall,' applauded Macfarlane. 'A man? I tell you, it required a man to back me up the other morning. There are some big, brawling, forty-year-old cowards who would have turned sick at the look of the d—d thing; but not you – you kept your head. I watched you.'

'Well, and why not?' Fettes thus vaunted himself. 'It was no affair of mine. There was nothing to gain on the one side but disturbance, and on the other I could count on your gratitude, don't you see?' And he slapped his pocket till the gold pieces rang.

Macfarlane somehow felt a certain touch of alarm at these unpleasant words. He may have regretted that he had taught his young companion so successfully, but he had no time to interfere, for the other noisily continued in this boastful strain:

'The great thing is not to be afraid. Now, between you and me, I don't want to hang – that's practical; but for all cant, Macfarlane, I was born with a contempt. Hell, God, Devil, right, wrong, sin, crime, and all the old gallery of curiosities – they may frighten boys, but men of the world, like you and me, despise them. Here's to the memory of Gray!'

It was by this time growing somewhat late. The gig, according to order, was brought round to the door with both lamps brightly shining, and the young men had to pay their bill and take the road. They announced that they were bound for Peebles, and drove in that direction till they were clear of the last houses of the town; then, extinguishing the lamps, returned upon their course, and followed a by-road toward Glencorse. There was no sound but that of their own passage, and the incessant, strident pouring of the rain. It was pitch dark; here and there a white gate or a white stone in the wall guided them for a short space across the night; but for the most part if was at a foot pace, and almost groping, that they picked their way through that resonant blackness to their solemn and isolated destination. In the sunken woods that traverse the neighbourhood of the burying-ground the last glimmer failed them, and it became necessary to kindle a match and re-illumine one of the lanterns of the gig. Thus, under the dripping trees, and environed by huge and moving shadows, they reached the scene of their unhallowed labours.

The were both experienced in such affairs, and powerful with the spade; and they had scarce been twenty minutes at their task before they were rewarded by a dull rattle on the coffin lid. At the same moment, Macfarlane, having hurt his hand upon a stone, flung it carelessly above his head. The grave, in which they now stood almost to the shoulders, was close to the edge of the plateau of the graveyard; and the gig lamp had been propped, the better to illuminate their labours, against a tree, and on the immediate verge of the steep bank descending to the stream. Chance had taken a sure aim with the stone. Then came a clang of broken glass; night fell upon them; sounds alternately dull and ringing announced the bounding of the lantern down the bank, and its occasional collision with the trees. A stone or two, which it had dislodged in its descent, rattled behind it into the profundities of the glen; and then silence, like night, resumed its sway; and they might bend their hearing to its utmost pitch, but naught was to be heard except the rain, now marching to the wind, now steadily falling over miles of open country.

They were so nearly at an end of their abhorred task that they judged it wisest to complete it in the dark. The coffin was exhumed and broken open; the body inserted in the dripping sack and carried between them to the gig; one mounted to keep it in its place, and the other, taking the horse by the mouth, groped along by wall and bush until they reached the wider road by the Fisher's Tryst. Here was a faint, diffused radiancy, which they hailed like daylight; by that they pushed the horse to a good pace and began to rattle along merrily in the direction of the town.

They had both been wetted to the skin during their operations, and now, as the gig jumped among the deep ruts, the thing that stood propped between them fell now upon one and now upon the other. At every repetition of the horrid contact each instinctively repelled it with the greater haste; and the process, natural although it was, began to tell upon the nerves of the companions. Macfarlane made some ill-favoured jest about the farmer's wife, but it came hollowly from his lips, and was allowed to drop in silence. Still their unnatural burden bumped from side to side; and now the head would be laid, as if in confidence, upon their shoulders, and now the drenching sackcloth would flap icily about their faces. A creeping chill began to possess the soul of Fettes. He peered at the bundle, and it seemed somehow larger than at first. All over the country-side, and from every degree of distance, the farm dogs accompanied their passage with tragic ululations; and it grew and grew upon his mind that some unnatural miracle had been accomplished, that some nameless change had befallen the dead body, and that it was in fear of their unholy burden that the dogs were howling.

'For God's sake,' said he, making a great effort to arrive at speech, 'for God's sake, let's have a light!'

Seemingly Macfarlane was affected in the same direction; for, though he made no reply, he stopped the horse, passed the reins to his companion, got down, and proceeded to kindle the remaining lamp. They had by that time got no farther than the cross-road down to Auchenclinny. The rain still poured as though the deluge were returning, and it was no easy matter to make a light in such a world of wet and darkness. When at last the flickering blue flame had been transferred to the wick and began to expand and clarify, and shed a wide circle of misty brightness round the gig, it became possible for the two young men to see each other and the thing they had along with them. The rain had moulded the rough sacking to the outlines of the body underneath; the head was distinct from the trunk, the shoulders plainly modelled; something at once spectral and human riveted their eyes upon the ghastly comrade of their drive.

For some time Macfarlane stood motionless, holding up the lamp. A nameless dread was swathed, like a wet sheet, about the body, and tightened the white skin upon the face of Fettes; a fear that was meaningless, a horror of what could not be, kept mounting to his brain. Another beat of the watch, and he had spoken. But his comrade forestalled him.

'That is not a woman,' said Macfarlane, in a hushed voice.

'It was a woman when we put her in,' whispered Fettes.

'Hold that lamp,' said the other. 'I must see her face.'

And as Fettes took the lamp his companion untied the fastenings of the sack and drew down the cover from the head. The light fell very clear upon the dark, well-moulded features and smooth-shaven cheeks of a too familiar countenance, often beheld in dreams of both of these young men. A wild yell rang up into the night; each leaped from his own side into the roadway: the lamp fell, broke, and was extinguished; and the horse, terrified by this unusual commotion, bounded and went off toward Edinburgh at a gallop, bearing along with it, sole occupant of the gig, the body of the dead and long-dissected Gray.

(1884)

TOBIAS SMOLLETT

In the War of Jenkins's Ear (1739–42), surgeon's mate aboard HMS *Cumberland* in Rear-Admiral Sir Chaloner Ogle's West India squadron – which was besieging the galleons of Cartagena (disastrously) – was Tobias George Smollett (1721–71), from Dumbartonshire. He recorded that this assault upon the continent of New Spain was 'marked by folly and irresolution, the troops abandoned by sickness and despair, and the enterprise was abandoned as impractical'. He stayed on in Jamaica and married an heiress.

Smollet had been to Glasgow University, where he started writing verses, was then apprenticed to a Glasgow surgeon, but at eighteen took Johnson's noblest prospect which a Scotchman ever sees, the high road that leads him to London. He was going to make a fortune on the stage with his tragedy *The Regicide*.

The play followed George Buchanan's (1506–82) story in Latin of the 'horrid assassination' of James I of Scotland, on 20 February 1437, while supping with the Queen in a monastery near Perth, despite a gallant maid of honour using her arm as a door-bolt. The conspirators later publicly suffered 'lingering and exquisite torments'. James's uncle the Earl of Athol's first day of this was occupied by being hoisted and lowered on a rope until all his bones were disjointed, on the second he was 'crowned with a diadem of red-hot iron', on the third he was executed as a traitor, the other conspirators meanwhile being tortured 'with diabolical ingenuity'. Smollett's play was five acts in blank verse, like *Macbeth*. This fell flat in London.

Smollett's script had been 'taken into the protection of one of those little fellows who are sometimes called great men [theatre managers], and, like other orphans, neglected accordingly'. As hopeful playwrights who similarly suffer today, Smollett was 'stung with resentment', so he went to sea instead.

Smollett became MD Aberdeen in 1750, practised in London in Downing Street, then at Bath, but with lack of success – or of popularity, after his *Essay on the External Use of Water* proved that the water at Bath was much like the water everywhere else. After

Peregrine Pickle in 1751, he abandoned medicine and settled in Chelsea, became a busy editor of journals and books, a translator, playwright and pamphleteer. He sparked fiery quarrels, doing three months for libel in 1759 after discrediting an admiral's courage in his *Critical Review*. In the Marshalsea he found he could work harder than ever, between receiving visitors like Goldsmith and Garrick. In 1766 he published the exemplary realistic *Travels in France and Italy*, winning Sterne's nickname 'Smelfungus'. He abandoned England in 1769, ill and poor, wrote *Humphrey Clinker* and died at Monte Nero, near Leghorn. Like Molière, Smollett had a crackshot eye for the ludicrous in people and their doings. If he was fundamentally coarse, so is life.

To become a naval surgeon necessitated for Smollett an examination. Roderick Random's viva voce at Surgeons' Hall is split between the insults of a bullying examiner, the laughs round the table scored by a waggish one, and a hot argument between all dozen on a surgical point, which leaves the candidate ignored, fills up the time, and obliges them to pass him by default. These three experiences persist in medical folklore today.

From The Adventures of Roderick Random

AT THAT INSTANT, a young fellow came out from the place of examination, with a pale countenance, his lip quivering, and his looks as wild as if he had seen a ghost. He no sooner appeared, than all flocked about him with the utmost eagerness, to know what reception he had met with; which, after some pause, he described, recounting all the questions they had asked, with the answers he made. In this manner we obliged no less than twelve to recapitulate, which, now the danger was past, they did with much pleasure, before it fell to my lot. At length the beadle called my name, with a voice that made me tremble as much as if it had been the sound of the last trumpet: however, there was no remedy. I was conducted into a large hall, where I saw about a dozen of grim faces sitting at a long table; one of whom bade me come forward in such an imperious tone, that I was actually for a minute or two bereft of my senses. The first question he put to me was – 'Where was you born?' To which I answered – 'In Scotland.' – 'In Scotland,' said he, 'I know that very well; we have scarce any other countrymen to examine here; you Scotchmen have overspread us of late, as the locusts did Egypt: I ask you in what part of Scotland you was born?' I named the place of my nativity, which he had never before heard of. He then proceeded to interrogate me about my age, the town where I served my time, with the term of my apprenticeship; and when I informed him that I served three years only, he fell into a violent passion; swore it was a shame and a scandal to send such raw boys into the world as surgeons; that it was a great presumption in me, and an affront upon the English, to pretend to sufficient skill in my business, having served so short a time, when every apprentice in England was bound seven years at least; that my friends would have done better if they had made me a weaver or shoemaker, but their pride would have me a gentleman, he supposed, at any rate, and their poverty could not afford the necessary education. This exordium did not at all contribute to the recovery of my spirits, but on the contrary reduced me to such a situation that I was scarce able to stand; which being perceived by a plump gentleman who sat opposite to me, with a skull before him, he said Mr Snarler was too severe upon the young man; and turning towards me, told me, I need not be afraid, for nobody would do me any harm; then bidding me take time to recollect myself, he examined me touching the operation of the trepan, and was very well satisfied with my answers. The next person who questioned me was a wag, who began by asking if I had ever seen amputation performed; and I replying in the affirmative, he shook his head, and said – 'What! upon a dead subject, I suppose? If,' continued he, 'during an engagement at sea, a man should be brought to you with his head shot off, how would you behave?' After some hesitation, I owned such a case had never come under my observation; neither did I remember to have seen any method of cure proposed for such an accident, in any of the systems of surgery I had perused. Whether it was owing to the simplicity of my answer or the archness of the question, I know not, but every member at the board deigned to smile, except Mr Snarler, who seemed to have very little of the *animal risibile* in his constitution. The facetious member, encouraged by the success of his last joke, went on thus – 'Suppose you was called to a patient of a plethoric habit, who had been bruised by a fall, what would you do?' I answered, I would bleed him immediately. 'What,' said he, 'before you had tied up his arm?' But this stroke of wit not answering his expectation, he desired me to advance to the gentleman who sat next him, and who, with a pert air, asked what method of cure I would follow in wounds of the intestines. I repeated the method of cure as it is prescribed by the best chirurgical writers; which he heard to an end, and then said with a supercilious smile – 'So you think by such treatment the patient might recover?' I told him, I saw nothing to make me think otherwise. 'That may be,' resumed he. 'I won't answer for your foresight; but did you ever know a case of this kind succeed?' I acknowledged I did not, and was about to tell him I had never seen a wounded intestine; but he stopped me, by saying with some precipitation – 'Nor never will. I affirm that all wounds of the intestines, whether great or small, are mortal.' – 'Pardon me, brother,' says the fat gentleman, 'there is very good authority –' Here he was interrupted by the other, with 'Sir, excuse me, I despise all authority. *Nullius in verba.* I stand upon my own bottom.' – 'But, Sir, Sir,' replied his antagonist, 'the reason of the thing shews.' – 'A fig for reason,' cried this sufficient member, 'I laugh at reason, give me ocular demonstration.' The corpulent gentleman began to wax warm, and observed that no man acquainted with the anatomy of the parts would advance such an extravagant assertion. This *inuendo* enraged the other so much, that he started up, and in a furious tone exclaimed – 'What, Sir! do you question my knowledge in anatomy?' By this time all the examiners had espoused the opinion of one or other of the disputants, and raised their voices all together, when the chairman commanded silence, and ordered me to withdraw. In less than a quarter of an hour, I was called in again, received my qualifications sealed up, and was ordered to pay five shillings. I laid down my half-guinea upon the table, and stood some time, until one of them bade me be gone; to this I replied – 'I will, when I have got my change': upon which another threw me five shillings and sixpence, saying, I should not be a true Scotchman if I went away without my change. I was afterwards obliged to give three shillings and sixpence to the beadles, and a shilling to an old woman who swept the hall. This disbursement sunk my finances to thirteenpence halfpenny.

(1748)

GUSTAVE FLAUBERT

Gustave Flaubert (1821–80) was the son of a Rouen surgeon. Family upbringing certainly sharpened the realism of this wide-ranging satire on an operation which went disastrously septic. Such was the dolefully common sequel to surgery when *Madame Bovary* appeared in 1857, and until Lord Lister invented the disinfectant operating technique in 1865. Nor did the popularity of chloroform, which emerged from Edinburgh in 1847, seem then to have penetrated rural France.

Flaubert had himself considered studying medicine, but instead read law in Paris, and failed his exams. He was at the time afflicted with the *petit mal* type of youthful epilepsy. In 1846 he went home to his widowed mother at Croisset, and settled down to write *Madame Bovary*. Like George Eliot's *Middlemarch*, it is subtitled *A Study of Provincial Life*. But Flaubert's dissertation is more cheerfully entertaining, and its sexual conflict delightfully livelier.

Everyone forgets about *Doctor* Bovary. He met Madame when he was called to see her father, a farmer who had incurred a fractured leg while coming home from his Twelfth Night celebrations. Charles Bovary married Emma as a fresh widower, after encouragement from the patient when he called to pay his bill (he gave the doctor a turkey, as well). Charles's newly-married life at Yonville in Normandy sounds delightful.

From Madame Bovary

IN SNOW, IN rain, Charles went on horseback, taking all the short cuts. He ate omelettes on farmhouse tables, shoved his arms into damp beds, got the warm squirt of freshly-let blood in his face, listened to noises in chests, examined slop-basins, rolled up a lot of dirty linen. But at night he found a roaring fire, the table laid, a comfortable room, and a charmingly turned-out wife, who smelt lovely; he had no idea where this scent came from, or if it was not her skin perfuming her undies.

Later on in his marriage, Dr Bovary decides to improve his local reputation with a spectacular operation.

Homais, the local chemist, had recently read a panegyric about a novel method of curing club-foot. And as he was keen on progress, he got the patriotic notion that Yonville, to keep up with the world, should offer club-foot operations.

'After all,' he said to Emma, 'what's the risk? Look –' He counted on his fingers the advantages of the experiment. 'Success is almost certain. Relief and beautification of the patient, celebrity quickly acquired by the operator. Now then, why shouldn't your husband help our poor Hippolyte, across at the Lion d'Or? You can bet the fellow wouldn't fail to chatter about his cure to all the travellers, and then –'

Homais lowered his voice and looked round him. 'What's to stop me sending the papers a little report about it? Eh? Good Lord! An article gets around . . . people talk . . . everything snowballs. And then what? Who knows?'

In short, Bovary would be a success. Nothing warned Emma that he was not up to the job. And what satisfaction it would give her, to have put him on the way to inflating his reputation and his fortune. She did so want to lean on something more solid than love.

Pushed by her and the chemist, Charles allowed himself to be convinced. He got Dr Duval's book from Rouen, and every evening, head in hands, buried himself in the pages.

While he was studying the deformity equino-varus and equino-valgus, that is to say the *stréphocatopdie*, the *stréphendopodie* and the *stréphexopodie* (or, to put it better, the different deviations of the foot, downwards, inwards or outwards), also the *stréphypopodie* and the *stréphanopodie* (otherwise, torsion downwards and inversion upwards), M. Homais was finding all sorts of reasons to exhort the employee of the Inn to let himself be operated upon.

'You'll hardly feel a thing! Well, perhaps a bit of discomfort, just a little prick, like when you're bled a little. Why, it's even less bother than cutting a nasty corn.'

Hippolyte considered the matter, rolling his stupid eyes.

'To tell the truth,' continued the chemist, 'this is really none of my business. You're the only one I'm thinking of. From pure humanity! I want to see you, my friend, freed from your hideous limp, also this displacement of the lumbar region, which – however much you try and pretend otherwise – must hurt awfully while doing your job.'

Then Homais pointed out how much stronger and nimbler he would be afterwards, adding the hint that he would also be better equipped to please the ladies, to which the ostler gave a dim-witted smile. Then he attacked his vanity. 'Aren't you a man, damn it? What would happen if you were called up, to go and fight for your country? Eh, Hippolyte?'

Homais departed, declaring that he could not understand this obstinacy, this blindness which refused to see the benefits of science.

The unfortunate fellow gave in, because it all became a conspiracy. Binet, who of course never stuck his nose into other people's business, Madame Lefrançois, Artémise, the neighbours, even the mayor himself M. Tuvache, absolutely everybody buttonholed him, sermonised him, quite shamed him. But what cast the die was that *it would cost him nothing*. Bovary would even pay for the instruments. Emma had the idea of this generosity, and Charles agreed, telling himself from the bottom of his heart that his wife was an angel.

Taking the advice of the chemist, and after a couple of false starts, he got the local joiner, helped by the locksmith, to construct a clumsy box weighing about eight pounds, not sparing the iron, the wood, steel-plating, leather, nuts and bolts.

But to know which of Hippolyte's tendons to incise, he had first to diagnose what variety of club-foot he had.

The foot was almost in a straight line with the leg, which did not stop it being turned inwards. It was a variety of club-foot with a slight equino-varus, or perhaps a slight equino-varus severely complicated with a club-foot. But upon this club-foot, as large as a horse's hoof, with its rough skin, hardened tendons, grossly deformed toes, and nails as black as the nails of a horseshoe, the patient pranced about from morning to night like a deer. You could always see him out in the Place, jumping round the carts while thrusting ahead of him his deformed limb. The leg seemed even more vigorous than the other one. By dint of being used, it had developed the moral attributes of patience and energy. When it was overworked, it seemed rather to like it.

In any event, as it was a case of club-foot it necessitated incising the tendon Achilles, leaving for subsequent treatment the anterior tibialis muscle to free the varus. The doctor did not dare risk two operations at one fell swoop. He was already trembling with the fear of straying into some important anatomical region of which he knew nothing.

Neither Ambroise Paré [(1509–90) 'the father of French surgery'], when applying for the first time since Celsus [Roman physician *fl.* 50 AD], after an interval of fifteen centuries, the direct ligature of an artery; neither Dupuytren [Baron, French surgeon (1778–1835)] about to incise an abscess through a thick bed of brain; neither Gensoul [French surgeon (1797–1858)] performing the first removal of the maxilla, certainly did not have so palpitating a heart, so quivering a hand, so tense a mind, as M. Bovary approaching Hippolyte with a tenotomy scalpel in his fingers.

Exactly as in hospital, on a side-table stood a pile of lint, waxed threads and plenty of bandages – a pyramid of bandages, every bandage in the chemist's shop. M. Homais had been organising it all since daybreak, to impress everybody and to impress himself.

Charles incised the skin. A brisk crack was heard. The tendon was incised, the operation was over. Hippolyte was astounded. He fell upon Bovary's hands and covered them with kisses.

'Now calm down,' said the chemist. 'You can express grateful recognition of your benefactor later.'

He went downstairs to announce the outcome to the five or six curious onlookers assembled in the Inn courtyard, and who imagined that Hippolyte was going to reappear walking straight. Then Charles went home – having buckled the patient into the joiner's mechanical boot – where Emma was waiting nervously at the door. She fell upon him; they shifted to the dinner-table; he ate heartily, and even demanded a cup of coffee with the dessert, a debauch that he permitted himself only on Sundays when they had company.

The evening was all charm, chat and shared dreams. He spoke of their coming fortune, of future improvements to the home. He envisaged his reputation spreading, his prosperity flourishing, his wife loving him for ever and a day. And she was delighted to refresh her soul with new feelings, feelings which were healthier and better, to feel at last a little tenderness for the poor boy who cherished her. The idea of Rudolph, for a moment, passed through her mind. But her eyes went back to Charles. She even noticed, with some surprise, that he had not got at all bad teeth.

They were in bed the next morning when M. Homais, brushing aside the cook, burst into their bedroom holding a freshly written sheet of paper. It was the publicity which he intended for the *Final de Rouen*. He had brought it for them to read.

'You read it,' said Bovary.

He read: '"Despite the prejudices which still cover part of the face of Europe like a net, light has begun to gleam upon the fields of our countryside. This is so because, last Tuesday, our little town of Yonville was the seat of a surgical procedure which was at the same moment an act of superb philanthropy. M. Bovary, one of our most distinguished practitioners –"'

'That's too much! Too much!' said Charles, strangled with emotion.

'No, no, not at all! Not a bit of it. "Operated on a club-foot –" I haven't put the scientific term, because, you know, in a newspaper, nobody would understand it. It's important that the masses –'

'Of course,' said Bovary. 'Carry on.'

'Right you are,' said the chemist. '"M. Bovary, one of our most distinguished practitioners, operated on a club-foot called Hippolyte Tautain, ostler for the last twenty-five years at the hotel Lion d'Or, which is kept by the widow Madame Lefrançois in the Place d'Armes. The novelty of the experiment, and the interest occasioned by the subject, had attracted such a crowd of our townsmen that it actually blocked the entrance to the Inn. The operation worked like a charm. Hardly any drops of blood appeared on the skin, only to show that the rebellious tendon had at last to succumb to the practice of the surgical art. The patient, oddly enough (we affirm this *de visu*) barely professed any pain. His condition, up to now, leaves nothing to desire. Everything points to the belief that his convalescence will be short. And who knows if, at the next village fête, we shall not even see our good Hippolyte joining the revels amid a chorus of merrymakers, thus proving to every eye, by his zest and his *entrechats*, his complete cure? All honour therefore to our learned benefactors! Honour to the untiring spirits who burn the midnight oil for the betterment, or better still the cure, of their fellow men! Honour! Three times honour! Is it not an occasion for crying out that the blind shall see, the deaf hear and the lame walk? But what was once a fanatical promise to the chosen few, science now accomplishes for everyone! We will keep our readers up to date with the progress of this remarkable cure."'

Which did not prevent, five days later, mother Lefrançois appearing in a state and crying: 'Help! He's dying! What shall I do?'

Charles hurried across to the Lion d'Or. The chemist, observing him cross the Place hatless, abandoned his shop. He appeared himself breathless, flushed, worried, and asking everyone going upstairs, 'What's up with our interesting case of club-foot?'

The club-foot was writhing in frightful convulsions, so violent that the mechanical boot in which his leg was imprisoned banged against the wall, threatening to knock a hole in it.

With considerable care, to avoid shifting the position of the limb, Charles removed the box. He met a frightful spectacle. The outline of the foot had disappeared in a huge swelling, the entire skin seemed about to burst, and was covered with bruises occasioned by the famous machine. Hippolyte had been complaining of pain, but nobody took any notice. It had now to be admitted that he had not been entirely wrong, so the foot was left exposed for some hours. But the oedema was barely reduced before the two wise men judged it right to replace the limb in the apparatus, screwing it up the tighter to speed things along. Three days later, Hippolyte could stand it no longer. They again ripped off the contraption, to be even more astonished at their results. A bluish swelling encased the leg, with a patchy red cellulitis from which exuded a black fluid. The patient had taken a serious turn for the worse.

Hippolyte began to worry. Old mother Lefrançois installed him in a little room by the kitchen, so that at least he had some distraction. But the tax inspector who dined every day complained bitterly about such neighbourliness. So they shifted Hippolyte to the billiard-room.

He lay there writhing under his bulky bed-covers, pale, unshaven, hollow-eyed, from time to time turning his sweaty head on a dirty pillow buzzing with flies. Madame Bovary came to see him. She brought him cloths for his linseed poultices, she consoled him, she encouraged him. He did not otherwise lack company, on market-days in particular, when the countryfolk all round him banged away at the billiard-balls, sparred with the cues, smoked, drank, sang, bawled.

'How are you getting along?' they said, slapping him on the shoulder. 'Ah! You're not glorying in it, that's pretty obvious. But it's all your own fault, isn't it?' Adding, 'You ought to do this . . . do that . . .'

They told stories of people who had all been cured by different treatment from his. By way of consolation, they added, 'Aren't you coddling yourself a bit? Why don't you get up? You're lying about like a king! Oh, it doesn't really matter, you old fraud. But you don't smell very nice, I must say.'

The gangrene rose higher and higher. It made Bovary feel ill himself. He was there every hour, every minute. Hippolyte gazed at him with terrified eyes and stammered and sobbed: 'When will I be made better? Save me! Oh, how miserable I am! How miserable I am!'

The doctor left, always advising him to stick to his diet.

'Don't hear a word of it,' old mother Lefrançois went on. 'Haven't they made a big enough martyr of you already? You'll just get feebler and feebler. Come on, drink up!'

She brought him such delicious soup, such slices of mutton, such chunks of bacon, and sometimes little glasses of eau-de-vie which he had not the energy to raise to his lips.

The *abbé* Bournisien, hearing that he was worse, demanded to see him. He started by expressing pity for his illness, meanwhile declaring that he should rejoice in it, because it was God's will, and he should speedily profit from the occasion to make his peace with the Lord.

'For you neglect your duties a bit,' said the ecclesiastic paternally. 'I never see you in church. How many years is it since you went near an altar? I know you've got work to do, that the rough-and-tumble of the world might brush aside reflections upon your eternal salvation. But now's the moment to think about it. Don't despair, mind you. I've known the greatest sinners, about to appear before the judgment of God (though you've hardly reached that stage yet, I know perfectly well), who have implored His mercy, and who certainly died in the most favourable circumstances. Let's hope that, exactly like them, you'll set us such a good example. However, as a precaution, I beseech you to recite morning and night a Hail, Mary! and an Our Father Who Art in Heaven. Yes, do that. Do it for me. I should be most obliged. It isn't going to cost you anything, is it? Promise?'

The poor devil promised. The *curé* came back during the following days. He chatted to the innkeeper, and even told her stories salted with little jokes and puns which were beyond Hippolyte, returning to religious matters as circumstances demanded, and assuming a befitting face.

His zeal seemed to work, because soon the case of club-foot was expressing a wish to make the pilgrimage to Bon-Secours if he got better. To which M. Bournisien replied that he couldn't see any objection, two heads are better than one, as it were. And he wasn't risking anything, was he?

The chemist was indignant about what he called *these priestly manoeuvres*. He asserted that they interfered with Hippolyte's convalescence, and he repeated to Madame Lefrançois: 'Let him alone! Let him alone! You're messing about with his mental state, with all your mysticism.'

But the good woman did not want to know. As far as the chemist went, the whole business was *entirely his fault*. Out of contrariness, she hooked over the patient's bed-head a stoop of holy water, full to the brim, with a twig of box-wood for good measure.

But religion seemed no more helpful than surgery, and the unstoppable rot continued rising from the legs towards the belly. However much they varied the medicines and changed the poultices the muscles became more and more flaccid, and at last Charles responded with an affirmative nod when old mother Lefrançois asked him if she could not, as a desperate measure, summon M. Canivet of Neufchâtel, who was a big noise.

Doctor of medicine, fifty years old, enjoying high standing and pleased with himself, this fellow practitioner could hardly prevent himself sniggering when he discovered the leg gangrenous to the knee. Having declared briefly that he must amputate, he crossed to the chemist's shop to hurl abuse at the asses who had managed to reduce the unfortunate man to such a state. Grabbing M. Homais by the coat-button, he shouted throughout the shop: 'This was one of those inventions from Paris! Look at the ideas of those gentlemen in the capital! It's the same as squints, chloroform and crushing bladder stones, a load of old nonsense that the government wants to keep going. They're a lot of smart alecs, stuffing you with treatments without worrying about the consequences. The rest of us aren't as high-falutin. We're not a bunch of intellectuals, pretty boys or sweethearts. We're doctors, healers, and we wouldn't think for a moment of operating on anyone who was in splendid health. Correcting club-feet! *Can* you straighten club-feet? It's as if you'd rather like – for example – to straighten out a hunchback or two.'

Homais squirmed under this dissertation, hiding his unease behind a diplomatic smile. He needed to keep in with M. Canivet, whose prescriptions sometimes reached Yonville. Nor did he spring to Bovary's defence, nor offer a single observation of his own. Jettisoning his principles, he submitted his dignity to the more serious matter of keeping his business.

A mid-thigh amputation by the surgeon Canivet made a considerable event in the village. All the inhabitants rose early, and the Grande-Rue, crammed with people, had something of the lugubrious air as if about to accomplish an execution. Everyone in the grocer's was talking about Hippolyte's illness. The shops sold nothing, and Madame Tuvache, the mayor's wife, did not budge from the window, in her keenness to see the arrival of the operator.

He appeared in his gig, driving himself. The springs on the right-hand side had for so long groaned under the burden of his corpulence, it made the carriage lean rather as it went along, and you could see on the cushion next to him a vast box, covered with a red sheepskin, of which the three brass locks glittered fearsomely.

Entering the porch of the Lion d'Or like a whirlwind, the surgeon ordered in an enormous voice the unharnessing of his horse. Then he went into the stables to see if it was eating its oats. Arriving at his patients' houses, he occupied himself first with his mare and his carriage. People were always saying about this: 'Ah! M. Canivet, he's a one!' And they rated him all the higher for this unshakeable aplomb. The universe could burst apart, annihilating the last man, but that would be of secondary importance to the perseverance of his usual habits.

Homais presented himself.

'I'm counting on you,' said the surgeon. 'Are we ready? Let's go!'

But the chemist confessed, blushing, that he was too sensitive to behold such an operation. 'When you're just a looker-on,' he said, 'the imagination, you know, hits you. Then I've a nervous system so delicate –'

'Balls,' interrupted Canivet. 'On the contrary, you strike me as a case of incipient apoplexy. Which doesn't surprise me in the least, all you pharmacists are continually lurking in the kitchen, which ends up by ruining your health. Look at me! Every morning, up at four, shave in cold water – I never feel the cold – I never wear flannel, I never catch a chill, I'm absolutely sound in wind and limb. I live sometimes this way, sometimes that, like a philosopher, I eat what's put before me. That's why I'm not delicate like you, and it doesn't make the slightest difference if I cut up a Christian or the first chicken that comes along. It's all a matter of habit, wouldn't you say? Of habit . . . of habit . . .'

Without taking the slightest notice of Hippolyte, who was sweating anxiously between the sheets, the pair started a conversation in which the chemist compared the sang-froid of a surgeon with that of a general, a comparison agreeable to Canivet, who became effusive about the demands of his art. He regarded it as a holy calling, though one disgraced by the local medical officers. Returning to the patient at last, he examined the bandages brought by Homais, the same ones as had embellished the club-foot operation, and asked for someone to hold the leg. They sent out for Lestiboudois, and M. Canivet, having rolled up his sleeves, went into the billiard-room, while the chemist stayed with

Artémise and the innkeeper, both whiter than their aprons, ears cocked towards the door.

Bovary meanwhile had not dared to shift from his house. He remained downstairs in the parlour, sitting in the chimney-corner without a fire, chin on chest, hands clasped, eyes staring. What a cock-up! he thought. What a disappointment! He had taken every imaginable precaution. The hand of fate was meddling with him. Could he hope that it really mattered? If Hippolyte died afterwards, it was he who had killed him. What reason could he give on his rounds, when people asked about it? Perhaps he *had* slipped up somewhere? He thought deeply, but he could not see how.

But surely the most famous surgeons often made mistakes. But people would not believe it. On the contrary, they would laugh and gossip nastily. It would get around as far as Forges! As far as Neufchâtel! To Rouen! Everywhere! Who knew if his colleagues might not write things against him? A row would blow up, he would have to reply in the newpapers. Hippolyte could even sue him! He saw himself dishonoured, ruined, lost. His imagination, swamped by fancies, bobbed in the middle of them like an empty barrel tossed into the sea and wallowing upon the waves.

Emma, sitting opposite, looked at him. She did not share his humiliation. She suffered one of her own: to have imagined that such a man was not completely worthless, though she had twenty times already starkly seen him as a nonentity.

Charles walked up and down the room. His boots squeaked on the floorboards.

'Sit down,' she said. 'You're getting on my nerves.'

He sat.

What was she up to (she who was so intelligent!), again to make a mistake? What deplorable mania had ruined her existence by continual sacrifices? She recalled her desires for luxury, all the privations of her soul, the meanness of her marriage, her dreams falling into the mud like wounded swallows, everything that she had wanted, everything that she had refused herself, everything that she might have had. Why? Why?

Amid the silence that shrouded the village, an ear-splitting scream rang through the air. Bovary went pale and appeared about to faint. She nervously twitched her eyebrows, then went on with her thoughts. It was all for him, for this human being, this man who understood nothing, who felt nothing! There he was, sitting calmly, without any suspicion of the ridicule with which her name was henceforth going to be tarnished along with his. She had made an effort to love him, and it had quite made her cry when she repented having given herself to another.

'But perhaps it *was* a valgus?' Bovary exclaimed suddenly, pondering.

The unexpected shock of this phrase fell on her own reflections like a ball of lead on a silver plate. Emma gave a start, and raised her head searching for something to say. They stared at each other in silence, as though astounded to see each other, so distant were they in thought from one another. Charles looked at her with the glazed eye of a drunk, listening, motionless, to the last cries of the amputee – long, drawn-out moans broken in fits and starts by jerky screams, like the distant howls of some beast getting its throat cut.

Emma bit her livid lips, and, rolling between her fingers some fragments of coral which she had broken, fixed Charles with the sharp end of her pupils, like two fiery arrows ready to shoot. Everything about him irritated her now. His face, his clothes, all the things he never said, his whole being, his very existence. She repented, as if of a crime, her past virtue, and what was left of it collapsed under the furious blows of her pride. She delighted in all the wicked ironies of adultery triumphant. Memories of her lover returned with dizzying attraction, she threw herself heart and soul upon them, worshipping the image with a new enthusiasm. Charles himself seemed totally detached from her life, gone for ever, utterly impossible and reduced to nothingness, as if he were on the point of perishing and suffering his death agonies under her eyes.

They heard footsteps in the street. Charles peered out. Through the lowered Venetian blind he saw beside the covered market in the bright sunlight the surgeon Canivet, mopping his brow with his silk scarf. Homais was behind him, in his hands a big red box. The two of them crossed towards the chemist's shop.

Through sudden tenderness and despondency, he turned towards his wife and said: 'Kiss me, love.'

'Leave me alone,' she snapped back, red with rage.

'What's up? What's the matter with you?' he replied, shattered. 'Calm down, pull yourself together! You know perfectly well how I love you . . . come to me . . .'

'Enough!' she shouted, with a ghastly look on her face.

Escaping from the room, Emma slammed the door so hard that the barometer jumped from the wall and crashed to the floor.

Charles fell back into his chair, confused, wondering what had got into her, speculating about a nervous affliction, starting to cry, and vaguely feeling swirling round him something which was deadly and beyond understanding.

When Rudolph arrived in the garden that evening, he found his mistress waiting for him at the bottom of the steps. They hugged each other, and all their pique melted like snow in the heat of their kisses.

(1857)
Transl. R. G.

Dr Bovary's marriage ended as disastrously as his surgery.

THOMAS MALTHUS

The bleak bedfellow of Fanny Hill and Lady Chatterley and Lolita is Thomas Robert Malthus (1766–1834). His *Essay on the Principle of Population*, published anonymously in 1789, is the most dampening book about sex ever written. Expectedly from a Cambridge wrangler, he forebodes with mathematical severity that man and woman cannot go on both eating and copulating as if there were no tomorrow. This had not occurred to anyone before.

Malthus came from a family of eight at 'The Rookery', Dorking; his father was one of Jean Jacques Rousseau's executors. He was schooled at Warrington Dissenting Academy, and later became a fellow of Jesus College, until ritually expelled by marriage in 1804. He was the curate at Albury, near Guildford, and in 1805 the first British Professor of History and Political Economy at Haileybury College, recently founded to educate the servants of the East India Company. Malthus was cheerful, benevolent, sociable, at ease in Latin, Greek, French and Italian; a cricketer in summer and a skater in winter, he raised three children, had a cleft palate, and is buried in Bath Abbey.

Malthus's ideas were greeted with abuse and have been lodged with muddleheaded perversity. He was not the conceiver of contraception. Hogarth's Rake was progressing amid sheep's-gut condoms fifty years earlier; Boswell was bucking on his linen 'armour' before Malthus himself was born. But these amorous devices were ensheathed to exclude syphilis and gonorrhea, only incidentally to avoid the issue of 'a promiscuous concubinage'. You never tried them in the wife.

Malthus's suggested 'checks to population' were: moral restraint, late marriage, no irregular gratifications, no promiscuous intercourse nor violations of the marriage bed, and no unnatural passions. Only vaguely he mentions 'positive checks' and 'improper acts to conceal the consequences of irregular connections' – contraception and abortion. His fundamental argument against joyfully unhampered conception was that the population increases by geometrical progression, but food supplies by arithmetical – a mathematical item unlikely to be in the forefront of the mind in the heat of the moment.

From An Essay on the Principle of Population *and* A Summary View

THE GREAT AND unlooked-for discoveries that have taken place of late years in natural philosophy, the increasing diffusion of general knowledge from the extension of the art of printing, the ardent and unshackled spirit of inquiry that prevails throughout the lettered and even unlettered world, the new and extraordinary lights that have been thrown on political subjects which dazzle and astonish the understanding, and particularly that tremendous phenomenon in the political horizon, the French Revolution, which, like a blazing comet, seems destined either to inspire with fresh life and vigour, or to scorch up and destroy the shrinking inhabitants of the earth, have all concurred to lead many able men into the opinion that we were touching on a period big with the most important changes, changes that would in some measure be decisive of the future fate of mankind.

It has been said that the great question is now at issue, whether man shall henceforth start forwards with accelerated velocity towards illimitable, and hitherto unconceived, improvement, or be condemned to a perpetual oscillation between happiness and misery, and after every effort remain still at an immeasurable distance from the wished-for goal. . . .

I think I may fairly make two postulata.

First, That food is necessary to the existence of man.

Secondly, That the passion between the sexes is necessary and will remain nearly in its present state.

These two laws, ever since we have had any knowledge of mankind, appear to have been fixed laws of our nature, and, as we have not hitherto seen any alteration in them, we have no right to conclude that they will ever cease to be what they now are, without an immediate act of power in that Being who first arranged the system of the universe, and for the advantage of his creatures, still executes, according to fixed laws, all its various operations.

I do not know that any writer has supposed that on this earth man will ultimately be able to live without food. But Mr Godwin [philosopher, publicist, Shelley's father-in-law] has conjectured that the passion between the sexes may in time be extinguished. As, however, he calls this part of his work a deviation into the land of conjecture, I will not dwell longer upon it at present than to say that the best arguments for the perfectibility of man are drawn from a contemplation of the great progress that he has already made from the savage state and the difficulty of saying where he is to stop. But towards the extinction of the passion between the sexes, no progress whatever has hitherto been made. It appears to exist in as much force at present as it did two thousand or four thousand years ago. . . .

I think it will be allowed, that no state has hitherto existed (at least that we have any account of) where the manners were so pure and simple, and the means of subsistence so abundant, that no check whatever has existed to early marriages, among the lower classes, from a fear of not providing well for their families, or among the higher classes, from a fear of lowering their condition in life. Consequently in no state that we have yet known has the power of population been left to exert itself with perfect freedom.

Whether the law of marriage be instituted or not, the dictate of nature and virtue seems to be an early attachment to one woman. Supposing a liberty of changing in the case of an unfortunate choice, this liberty would not affect population till it arose to a height greatly vicious; and we are now supposing the existence of a society where vice is scarcely known.

In a state therefore of great equality and virtue, where pure and simple manners prevailed, and where the means of subsistence were so abundant that no part of the society could have any fears about providing amply for a family, the power of population being left to exert itself unchecked, the increase of the human species would evidently be much greater than any increase that has been hitherto known.

In the United States of America, where the means of subsistence have been more ample, the manners of the people more pure, and consequently the checks to early marriages fewer, than in any of the modern states of Europe, the population has been found to double itself in twenty-five years. . . .

When we are assured that China is the most fertile country in the world, that almost all the land is in tillage, and that a great part of it bears two crops every year, and further, that the people live very frugally, we may infer with certainty that the population must be immense, without busying ourselves in inquiries into the manners and habits of the lower classes and the encouragements to early marriages. But these inquiries are of the utmost importance, and a minute history of the customs of the lower Chinese would be of the greatest use in ascertaining in what manner the checks to a further population operate; what are the vices, and what are the distresses that prevent an increase of numbers beyond the ability of the country to support. . . .

England, as one of the most flourishing states of Europe, may be fairly taken for an example, and the observations made will apply with but little variation to any other country where the population increases slowly.

The preventive check appears to operate in some degree through all the ranks of society in England. There are some men, even in the highest rank, who are prevented from marrying by the idea of the expenses that they must retrench, and the fancied pleasures that they must deprive themselves of, on the supposition of having a family. These considerations are certainly trivial, but a preventive foresight of this kind has objects of much greater weight for its contemplation as we go lower.

A man of liberal education, but with an income only just sufficient to enable him to associate in the rank of gentlemen, must feel absolutely certain that if he marries and has a family he shall be obliged, if he mixes at all in society, to rank himself with moderate farmers and the lower class of tradesmen. The woman that a man of education would naturally make the object of his choice would be one brought up in the same tastes and sentiments with himself and used to the familiar intercourse of a society totally different from that to which she must be reduced by marriage. Can a man consent to place the object of his affection in a situation so discordant, probably, to her tastes and inclinations? Two or three steps of descent in society, particularly at this round of the ladder, where education ends and ignorance begins, will not be considered by the generality of people as a fancied and chimerical, but a real and essential, evil. If society be held desirable, it surely must be free, equal, and reciprocal society, where benefits are conferred as well as received, and not such as the dependant finds with his patron or the poor with the rich.

These considerations undoubtedly prevent a great number in this rank of life from following the bent of their inclinations in an early attachment. Others, guided either by a stronger passion, or a weaker judgement, break through these restraints, and it would be hard indeed, if the gratification of so delightful a passion as virtuous love, did not, sometimes, more than counterbalance all its attendant evils. But I fear it must be owned that the more general consequences of such marriages are rather calculated to justify than to repress the forebodings of the prudent....

The servants who live in gentlemen's families have restraints that are yet stronger to break through in venturing upon marriage. They possess the necessaries, and even the comforts of life, almost in as great plenty as their masters. Their work is easy and their food luxurious compared with the class of labourers. And their sense of dependence is weakened by the conscious power of changing their masters, if they feel themselves offended. Thus comfortably situated at present, what are their prospects in marrying? Without knowledge or capital, either for business, or farming, and unused and therefore unable, to earn a subsistence by daily labour, their only refuge seems to be a miserable alehouse, which certainly offers no very enchanting prospect of a happy evening to their lives. By much the greater part, therefore, deterred by this uninviting view of their future situation, content themselves with remaining single where they are....

Notwithstanding, then, the institution of the poor laws in England, I think it will be allowed that considering the state of the lower classes altogether, both in the towns and in the country, the distresses which they suffer from the want of proper and sufficient food, from hard labour and unwholesome habitations, must operate as a constant check to incipient population.

To these two great checks to population, in all long-occupied countries, which I have called the preventive and the positive checks, may be added vicious customs with respect to women, great cities, unwholesome manufactures, luxury, pestilence, and war....

The institution of marriage, or at least, of some express or implied obligation on every man to support his own children, seems to be the natural result of these reasonings in a community under the difficulties that we have supposed.

The view of these difficulties presents us with a very natural origin of the superior disgrace which attends a breach of chastity in the woman than in the man. It could not be expected that women should have resources sufficient to support their own children. When therefore a woman was connected with a man, who had entered into no compact to maintain her children, and, aware of the inconveniences that he might bring upon himself, had deserted her, these children must necessarily fall for support upon the society, or starve. And to prevent the frequent recurrence of such an inconvenience, as it would be highly unjust to punish so natural a fault by personal restraint or infliction, the men might agree to punish it with disgrace. The offence is besides more obvious and conspicuous in the woman, and less liable to any mistake. The father of a child may not always be known, but the same uncertainty cannot easily exist with regard to the mother. . . .

Yet, even here, it must be allowed, that the power of government is rather indirect than direct, as the object to be attained depends mainly upon such a conduct on the part of individuals as can seldom be directly enforced by laws, though it may be powerfully influenced by them.

This will appear, if we consider more particularly the nature of those checks which have been classed under the general heads of preventive and positive.

It will be found that they are all resolvable into *moral restraint, vice,* and *misery*. And if, from the laws of nature, some check to the increase of population be absolutely inevitable, and human institutions have any influence upon the extent to which each of these checks operates, a heavy responsibility will be incurred, if all that influence, whether direct or indirect, be not exerted to diminish the amount of vice and misery.

Moral restraint, in application to the present subject, may be defined to be, abstinence from marriage, either for a time or permanently, from prudential considerations, with a strictly moral conduct towards the sex in the interval. And this is the only mode of keeping population on a level with the means of subsistence which is perfectly consistent with virtue and happiness. All other checks, whether of the preventive or the positive kind, though they may greatly vary in degree, resolve themselves into some form of vice or misery.

The remaining checks of the preventive kind are: the sort of intercourse which renders some of the women of large towns unprolific; a general corruption of morals with regard to the sex, which has a similar effect; unnatural passions and improper arts to prevent the consequences of irregular connections. These evidently come under the head of vice. . . .

In a review of the checks to population in the different states of modern Europe, it appears that the positive checks to population have prevailed less, and the preventive checks more, than in ancient times, and in the more uncultivated parts of the world. The destruction occasioned by war has unquestionably abated, both on account of its occurring, on the whole, less frequently, and its ravages not being so fatal, either to man or the means of his support, as they were formerly. And although, in the earlier periods of the history of modern Europe, plagues, famines, and mortal epidemics were not infrequent, yet, as civilization and improvement have advanced, both their frequency and their mortality have been greatly reduced, and in some countries they are now almost unknown. This diminution of the positive checks to population, as it has been certainly much greater in proportion than the actual increase of food and population, must necessarily have been accompanied by an increasing operation of the preventive checks; and probably it may be said with truth, that, in almost all the more improved countries of modern Europe, the principal check which at present keeps the population down to the level of the actual means of subsistence is the prudential restraint on marriage.

(1798 and 1830)

OLIVER WENDELL HOLMES

We must have something from Dr Oliver Wendell Holmes (1809–94). 'The world's great men have not commonly been great scholars, nor its great scholars great men,' he remarked in *The Autocrat of the Breakfast-Table* of 1858. Holmes was not quite either. He was a gentlemanly academic, in a Boston which was overwhelmingly both. With charming self-effacement, he expounded daily in his literary boarding-house before an audience which included the schoolmistress, the divinity student, and the young fellow whom they call John, over the assumed flapjacks, sunnyside-up eggs, waffles and maple syrup, coffee and maybe Boston baked beans, even hominy grits. Holmes was Professor of Anatomy at Harvard for thirty-five years, and he bestowed the name 'anaesthesia' a month after its birth (in Boston).

From The Autocrat of the Breakfast-Table

MY FRIEND, THE Professor, began talking with me one day in a dreamy sort of way. I couldn't get at the difficulty for a good while, but at last it turned out that somebody had been calling him an old man. – He didn't mind his students calling him *the* old man, he said. That was a technical expression, and he thought that he remembered hearing it applied to himself when he was about twenty-five. It may be considered as a familiar and sometimes endearing appellation. An Irishwoman calls her husband 'the old man', and he returns the caressing expression by speaking of her as 'the old woman'. But now, said he, just suppose a case like one of these. A young stranger is overheard talking of you as a very nice old gentleman. A friendly and genial critic speaks of your green old age as illustrating the truth of some axiom you had uttered with reference to that period of life. What *I* call an old man is a person with a smooth, shining crown and a fringe of scattered white hairs, seen in the streets on sunshiny days, stooping as he walks, bearing a cane, moving cautiously and slowly; telling old stories, smiling at present follies, living in a narrow world of dry habits; one that remains waking when others have dropped asleep, and keeps a little night-lamp flame of life burning year after year, if the lamp is not upset, and there is only a careful hand held round it to prevent the puffs of wind from blowing the flame out. That's what I call an old man.

Now, said the Professor, you don't mean to tell me that I have got to that yet? Why, bless you, I am several years short of the time when – [I knew what was coming, and could hardly keep from laughing; twenty years ago he used to quote it as one of those absurd speeches men of genius will make, and now he is going to argue from it] – several years short of the time when Balzac says that men are – most – you know – dangerous to – the hearts of – in short, most to be dreaded by duennas that have charge of susceptible females. – What age is that? said I, statistically. – Fifty-two years, answered the Professor. – Balzac ought to know, said I, if it is true that Goethe said of him that each of his stories must have been dug out of a woman's heart. But fifty-two is a high figure.

Stand in the light of the window, Professor, said I. – The Professor took up the desired position. – You have white hairs, I said. – Had 'em any time these twenty years, said the Professor. – And the crow's-foot, – *pes anserinus*, rather. The Professor smiled, as I wanted him to, and the folds radiated like the ridges of a half-opened fan, from the outer corner of the eyes to the temples. – And the calipers, said I. – What are the *calipers*? he asked, curiously. – Why, the parenthesis, said I. – *Parenthesis*? said the Professor; what's that? – Why, look in the glass when you are disposed to laugh, and see if your mouth isn't framed in a couple of crescent lines, – so, my boy ( ). – It's all nonsense, said the Professor; just look at my *biceps*; – and he began pulling off his coat to show me his arm. Be careful, said I; you can't bear exposure to the air, at your time of life, as you could once. – I will box with you, said the Professor, row with you, walk with you, ride with you, swim with you, or sit at table with you, for fifty dollars a side. – Pluck survives stamina, I answered.

The Professor went off a little out of humour. A few weeks afterwards he came in, looking very good-natured, and brought me a paper, which I have here, and from which I shall read you some portions, if you don't object. He had been thinking the matter over, he said, – had read Cicero 'De Senectute', and made up his mind to meet old age half way. These were some of his reflections that he had written down: so here you have:

THE PROFESSOR'S PAPER

There is no doubt when old age begins. The human body is a furnace which keeps in blast three score years and ten, more or less. It burns about three hundred pounds of carbon a year (besides other fuel), when in fair working order, according to a great chemist's estimate. When the fire slackens, life declines; when it goes out, we are dead.

It has been shown by some noted French experimenters, that the amount of combustion increases up to about the thirtieth year, remains stationary to about forty-five, and then diminishes. This last is the point where old age starts from. The great fact of physical life is the perpetual commerce with the elements, and the fire is the measure of it.

About this time of life, if food is plenty where you live, – for that, you know, regulates matrimony, – you may be expecting to find yourself a grandfather some fine morning; a kind of domestic felicity that gives one a cool shiver of delight to think of, as among the not remotely possible events.

I don't mind much those slipshod lines Dr Johnson wrote to Thrale, telling her about life's declining from *thirty-five*; the furnace is in full blast for ten years longer, as I have said. The Romans came very near the mark; their age of enlistment reached from seventeen to forty-six years.

What is the use of fighting against the seasons, or the tides, or the movements of the planetary bodies, or this ebb in the wave of life that flows through us? We are old fellows from the moment the fire begins to go out. Let us always behave like gentlemen when we are introduced to new acquaintance.

Incipit Allegoria Senectutis

Old age, this is Mr Professor; Mr Professor, this is Old Age.

Old Age. – Mr Professor, I hope to see you well. I have known you for some time, though I think you did not know me. Shall we walk down the street together?

Professor (drawing back a little). – We can talk more quietly, perhaps, in my study. Will you tell me how it is you seem to be acquainted with everybody you are introduced to, though he evidently considers you an entire stranger?

Old Age. – I make it a rule never to force myself upon a person's recognition until I have known him at least *five years*.

Professor. – Do you mean to say that you have known me so long as that?

Old Age. – I do. I left my card on you longer ago than that, but I am afraid you never read it; yet I see you have it with you.

Professor. – Where?

Old Age. – There, between your eyebrows, – three straight lines running up and down; all the probate courts know that token, – 'Old Age, his mark'. Put your forefinger on the inner end of one eyebrow, and your middle finger on the inner end of the other eyebrow; now separate the fingers, and you will smooth out my sign-manual; that's the way you used to look before I left my card on you.

Professor. – What message do people generally send back when you first call on them?

Old Age. – *Not at home*. Then I leave a card and go. Next year I call; get the same answer; leave another card. So for five or six, – sometimes ten years or more. At last, if they don't let me in, I break in through the front door or the windows.

We talked together in this way some time. Then Old Age said again, – Come, let us walk down the street together, – and offered me a cane, an eye-glass, a tippet, and a pair of over-shoes. – No, much obliged to you, said I. I don't want those things, and I had a little rather talk with you here, privately, in my study. So I dressed myself up in a jaunty way and walked out alone; – got a fall, caught a cold, was laid up with a lumbago, and had time to think over this whole matter.

Explicit Allegoria Senectutis

We have settled when old age begins. Like all Nature's processes, it is gentle and gradual in its approaches, strewed with illusions, and all its little griefs soothed by natural sedatives. But the iron hand is not less irresistible because it wears the velvet glove. The button-wood throws off its bark in large flakes, which one may find lying at its foot, pushed out, and at last pushed off, by that tranquil movement from beneath, which is too slow to be seen, but too powerful to be arrested. One finds them always, but one rarely sees them fall. So it is our youth drops from us, – scales off, sapless and lifeless, and lays bare the tender and immature fresh growth of old age. Looked at collectively, the changes of old age appear as a series of personal insults and indignities, terminating at last in death, which Sir Thomas Browne has called 'the very disgrace and ignominy of our natures'.

My lady's cheek can boast no more
The cranberry white and pink it wore;
And where her shining locks divide,
The parting line is all too wide –

No, no, – this will never do. Talk about men, if you will, but spare the poor women. . . .

That all spasmodic cerebral action is an evil is not perfectly clear. Men get fairly intoxicated with music, with poetry, with religious excitement, – oftenest with love. Ninon de l'Enclos said she was so easily excited that her soup intoxicated her, and convalescents have been made tipsy by a beef-steak.

There are forms and stages of alcoholic exaltation which, in themselves, and without regard to their consequences, might be considered as positive improvements of the persons affected. When the sluggish intellect is roused, the slow speech quickened, the cold nature warmed, the latent sympathy developed, the flagging spirit kindled, – before the trains of thought become confused, or the will perverted, or the muscles relaxed, – just at the moment when the whole human zoöphyte flowers out like a full-blown rose, and is ripe for the subscription-paper or the contribution-box, – it would be hard to say that a man was, at that very time, worse, or less to be loved, than when driving a hard bargain with all his meaner wits about him. The difficulty is, that the alcoholic virtues don't wash; but until the water takes their colours out, the tints are very much like those of the true celestial stuff.

(Here I was interrupted by a question which I am very unwilling to report, but have confidence enough in those friends who examine these records to commit to their candour.

A *person* at table asked me whether I 'went in for rum as a steady drink?' – His manner made the question highly offensive, but I restrained myself, and answered thus: –)

Rum I take to be the name which unwashed moralists apply alike to the product distilled from molasses and the noblest juices of the vineyard. Burgundy 'in all its sunset glow' is rum. Champagne, 'the foaming wine of Eastern France', is rum. Hock, which our friend, the Poet, speaks of as:

'The Rhine's breastmilk, gushing cold and bright,
Pale as the moon, and maddening as her light,'

is rum. Sir, I repudiate the loathsome vulgarism as an insult to the first miracle wrought by the Founder of our religion! I address myself to the company. I believe in temperance, nay, almost in abstinence, as a rule for healthy people. I trust that I practise both. But let me tell you, there are companies of men of genius into which I sometimes go, where the atmosphere of intellect and sentiment is so much more stimulating than alcohol, that, if I thought fit to take wine, it would be to keep me sober.

Among the gentlemen that I have known, few, if any, were ruined by drinking. My few drunken acquaintances were generally ruined before they became drunkards. The habit of drinking is often a vice, no doubt, – sometimes a misfortune, – as when an almost irresistible hereditary propensity exists to indulge in it, – but oftenest of all a *punishment*. . . .

The soul of a man has a series of concentric envelopes round it, like the core of an onion, or the innermost of a nest of boxes. First, he has his natural garment of flesh and blood. Then, his artificial integuments, with their true skin of solid stuffs, their cuticle of lighter tissues, and their variously-tinted pigments. Thirdly, his domicile, be it a single chamber or a stately mansion. And then, the whole visible world, in which Time buttons him up as in a loose outside wrapper.

You shall observe, – the Professor said, – for, like Mr John Hunter [London surgeon, 1728–93] and other great men, he brings in that *shall* with great effect sometimes, – you shall observe that a man's clothing or series of envelopes does after a certain time mould itself upon his individual nature. We know this of our hats, and are always reminded of it when we happen to put them on wrong side foremost. We soon find that the beaver is a hollow cast of the skull, with all its irregular bumps and depressions. Just so all that clothes a man, even to the blue sky which caps his head, – a little loosely, – shapes itself to fit each particular being beneath it. Farmers, sailors, astronomers, poets, lovers, condemned criminals, all find it different, according to the eyes with which they severally look.

But our houses shape themselves palpably on our inner and outer natures. See a householder breaking up and you will be sure of it. There is a shell-fish which builds all manner of smaller shells into the walls of its own. A house is never a home until we have crusted it with the spoils of a hundred lives besides those of our own past. See what these are and you can tell what the occupant is.

(1858)

TAKING THE CURE

'All too often the doctor's advice to travel is but advising his patient to go and die far from home in a foreign land,' said Christopher Home Douglas bleakly in 1874. He was an Edinburgh accountant, whose wife suffered 'severe and almost incessant coughing and breathlessness; and these again, by their severity and continuance, gave rise to debility, which as time went on continued to grow greater'. (It was probably asthma.)

But to follow the sun was an undisputable prescription, when there was no other treatment to follow at all. It was also a splendid way for doctors to get rid of difficult patients.

Douglas himself travelled abroad with a pocketful of thermometers, which he hung out of his hotel windows to compile their readings with enthusiastic accountancy. At 2 p.m. on 15 December 1870 the temperature at Gibraltar was 68 °F. Over Easter 1871 it was 67.9 °F in Seville, where: 'There is a piece of Good Friday observance practised here which, were it only transferred to Sunday, might give Sabbatarians some hope of the ultimate conversion of Spain. Domestic bells are not rung on Good Friday. Even in the hotels the dinner bell is not rung. The waiters have to climb the stairs and knock at each door to announce the advent of dinner.'

CHRISTOPHER HOME DOUGLAS

From Searches for Summer

IT MAY BE held presumptuous on the part of a non-medical man to speak on questions of health, but this fact just leads me to the consideration of what I think the commonest and greatest error of all. It lies in supposing that for the cure or mitigation of disease you are to look mainly to medical science, instead of to your own observation, self-candour, and self-control [so foreseeing today's fashionable 'alternative medicine'].

Invalids may fairly be divided into three classes. Those who are organically and hopelessly diseased; those who are functionally diseased; and those who, having no disease at all, have come abroad to relieve the ennui of country residence with a little fun and flirtation, most legitimate objects in my opinion; and there can be no doubt that if climate is often falsely accused, so does it often receive credit to which it is not entitled, and the improvement effected by amusement and relaxation is generally attributed to 'change of air'.

And while the doctor is supposed to be able to absolve men from the consequences of their sins, these consequences are, I find among invalids in general abroad, always set down to the fault of the climate. It is quite astounding to hear the wonderful, inexhaustible variety of detractive adjectives and epithets applied to this scapegoat, such as, too bracing, too stringent, relaxing, too elastic, not elastic enough, too heavy, a tightness in the air, a hardness in the air, too subject to electric influences, etc.

I remember an invalid lady who had been to morning church one Sunday, and – I fear it may be impolite to say so – had taken a very *un*invalid *déjeuner* thereafter, come home from afternoon church with a headache, and no appetite for dinner; which two facts she accounted for, quite to her own satisfaction, by the presence of 'an intoxicating lightness in the air of this place'.

He gives a ghoulish warning:

To plunge out of burning sunshine into an ice-cold cathedral is enough to give a strong man cold; to an invalid it may be, and often is, fatal.

St Peter's has much to answer for.

'The season' at Menton, and along the Riviera generally, comes abruptly to an end on the 25th of April. On or before this date, therefore, you must depart; unless, that is to say, you are gifted with quite an extraordinary strength of mind – as much, perhaps, as it might require to remain in town in August.

But even in Edinburgh folk were peculiar about the seasons:

Whence comes it that the female housekeeper of well-regulated mind in Scotland commonly rebels against domestic fires in the month of June? Call on your friend Mrs Smith during the first week of May, and, though it chance to be warm as ordinarily in July, you will find a cheerful fire in the drawing-room grate. But call on the same lady any day in June, the temperature being possibly 20° below that which prevailed during your former visit, and you will find Mrs Smith's drawing-room fireless, cold as an ice-house, the polished steel bars of the grate glittering like so many ribs of ice, Mrs Smith herself looking blue and pinched, with a tendency to redness in the end of her nose. But June is June; and if it is not summer, it ought to be – why *ought* to be, it is hard to say. Why we go on believing, in spite of all the evidence to the contrary, that summer weather usually reached Great Britain before mid-summer, it is difficult to understand.

By 1872:

My wife had now made so great progress that we were encouraged to believe that another winter in the south might effect a complete cure.

There are some energetic spirits who, having a definite end in view, have no peace of mind except in working so as to arrive at it in the shortest time possible. Men so endowed, having Nice or Menton as their goal, travel from London to Paris in one day, and from Paris to Nice in little more than another; and without the necessity which formerly existed of changing carriages at Marseilles. Loiterers on the way mostly halt at Dijon, an interesting old town, in a pretty country, and with an excellet hotel – the Hotel de Jura. Here, therefore, if so minded, you may advantageously station yourself as it were on a little island, and watch the human torrent as it flows past you. The Paris train is due at half-past three, at which hour, therefore, you place yourself at your window, to enjoy the daily excitement of observing the new arrivals – ambulance loads, as you may figure them to be, of the wounded in life's fight: pale Oxford men who have broken down on the threshold of their way to the woolsack; young ladies who have sickened in their first winter campaign, and to whose wan cheeks the roses of an English summer have declined to lend their hues; gouty papas with florid faces, fondly hoping that the effects of a quarter of a century of over-feeding will disappear in the mellow air of the Riviera. A mixture there is of healthful blood come to help its ailing kindred – brothers and husbands wrenched for a while from business, whose souls, regardless of Alpine crag and avalanche, are still on 'Change in Manchester or Glasgow, with buxom matrons who come down to dinner in costly silks, and flash their diamond rings in each other's eyes across the table. Then there is the inevitable couple fresh from their country town – husband and wife, or brother and sister, who are all in all to each other, who never speak to strangers, and converse innocently aloud in the reading-room about their domestic concerns: wonder if Bobby will have cut his first tooth by the time they return, and if the new clock will have been put up in their village town-hall by that date.

You meet at *table d'hôte*, talk about coughs and bronchial affections, climates, Nice, Menton, Algiers, and so on. Next day at 2 p.m. comes the exodus, and for a couple of hours all is still. At four, more ambulance loads arrive, with new styles of coughs and rheumatisms. Now and again someone halts for a day or two like yourself. You are possibly pleased with each other, and at parting exchange cards and hope to meet again – waifs of humanity, borne on the crests of passing waves, you are grateful to each other for having beguiled that dreary gulf of time in hotel life which begins after dinner and commonly only ends at bedtime. Having leisure for the purpose, one speculates curiously over this flow of maimed existence. Some folks must work or starve; but a short life or a prolonged vegetation – say five years of active life or twenty-five of aimless dawdle – is the alternative offered to many. One might imagine that somewhere there exists a grim power which amuses itself with mortals as they amuse themselves with fish. Some tinselled lure is temptingly played before your eyes. You seize it greedily. Then comes a wholly undreamt-of twinge, and you find a hook in your flesh, in the shape of a lung or heart disease. After allowing you more or less line, the unseen hand winds you up, and with an unceremonious knock on the head deposits you in its sombre creel. The first frenzied appeal on finding oneself, so to speak, 'hooked', is, of course, to the doctor, who, with a faith on the part of the public which must to him be quite touching, is called on and expected to perform a miracle, – to enable overworked brain and stomach to continue to overwork themselves, and to restore and maintain health under conditions of disease.

(1874)

Jane Austen (1775–1817) took everyone to Bath.

JANE AUSTEN

From Northanger Abbey

EVERY MORNING NOW brought its regular duties; – shops were to be visited; some new part of the town to be looked at; and the Pump-room to be attended, where they paraded up and down for an hour, looking at everybody and speaking to no one. The wish of a numerous acquaintance in Bath was still uppermost with Mrs Allen, and she repeated it after every fresh proof, which every morning brought, of her knowing nobody at all.

They made their appearance in the Lower Rooms; and here fortune was more favourable to our heroine. The master of the ceremonies introduced to her a very gentlemanlike young man as a partner; – his name was Tilney. He seemed to be about four or five and twenty, was rather tall, had a pleasing countenance, a very intelligent and lively eye, and, if not quite handsome, was very near it. His address was good, and Catherine felt herself in high luck. There was little leisure for speaking while they danced; but when they were seated at tea, she found him as agreeable as she had already given him credit for being. He talked with fluency and spirit – and there was an archness and pleasantry in his manner which interested, though it was hardly understood by her. After chatting some time on such matters as naturally arose from the objects around them, he suddenly addressed her with – 'I have hitherto been very remiss, madam, in the proper attentions of a partner here; I have not yet asked you how long you have been in Bath; whether you were ever here before; whether you have been at the Upper Rooms, the theatre, and the concert; and how you like the place altogether. I have been very negligent – but are you now at leisure to satisfy me in these particulars? If you are I will begin directly.'

'You need not give yourself that trouble, sir.'

'No trouble, I assure you, madam.' Then forming his features into a set smile, and affectedly softening his voice, he added, with a simpering air, 'Have you been long in Bath, madam?'

'About a week, sir,' replied Catherine, trying not to laugh.

'Really!' with affected astonishment.

'Why should you be surprised, sir?'

'Why, indeed?' said he, in his natural tone – 'but some emotion must appear to be raised by your reply, and surprise is more easily assumed, and not less reasonable than any other. – Now let us go on. Were you never here before, madam?'

'Never, sir.'

'Indeed! Have you yet honoured the Upper Rooms?'

'Yes, sir, I was there last Monday.'

'Have you been to the theatre?'

'Yes, sir, I was at the play on Tuesday.'

'To the concert?'

'Yes, sir, on Wednesday.'

'And are you altogether pleased with Bath?'

'Yes – I like it very well.'

'Now I must give one smirk, and then we may be rational again.'

Catherine turned away her head, not knowing whether she might venture to laugh.

'I see what you think of me,' said he gravely – 'I shall make but a poor figure in your journal to-morrow.'

'My journal!'

'Yes, I know exactly what you will say: Friday, went to the Lower Rooms; wore my sprigged muslin robe with blue trimmings – plain black shoes – appeared to much advantage; but was strangely harassed by a queer, half-witted man, who would make me dance with him, and distressed me by his nonsense.'

'Indeed I shall say no such thing.'

'Shall I tell you what you ought to say?'

'If you please.'

'I danced with a very agreeable young man, introduced by Mr King; had a great deal of conversation with him – seems a most extraordinary genius – hope I may know more of him. *That*, madam, is what I *wish* you to say.'

'But, perhaps, I keep no journal.'

'Perhaps you are not sitting in this room, and I am not sitting by you. These are points in which a doubt is equally possible. Not keep a journal!

How are your absent cousins to understand the tenor of your life in Bath without one? How are the civilities and compliments of every day to be related as they ought to be, unless noted down every evening in a journal? How are your various dresses to be remembered, and the particular state of your complexion, and curl of your hair to be described in all their diversities, without having constant recourse to a journal? – My dear madam, I am not so ignorant of young ladies' ways as you wish to believe me; it is this delightful habit of journalizing which largely contributes to form the easy style of writing for which ladies are so generally celebrated. Everybody allows that the talent of writing agreeable letters is peculiarly female. Nature may have done something, but I am sure it must be essentially assisted by the practice of keeping a journal.'

'I have sometimes thought,' said Catherine, doubtingly, 'whether ladies do write so much better letters than gentlemen! That is, I should not think the superiority was always on our side.'

'As far as I have had opportunity of judging, it appears to me that the usual style of letter-writing among women is faultless, except in three particulars.'

'And what are they?'

'A general deficiency of subject, a total inattention to stops, and a very frequent ignorance of grammar.'

'Upon my word! I need not have been afraid of disclaiming the compliment. You do not think too highly of us in that way.'

'I should no more lay it down as a general rule that women write better letters than men, than that they sing better duets, or draw better landscapes. In every power, of which taste is the foundation, excellence is pretty fairly divided between the sexes.'

They were interrupted by Mrs Allen: – 'My dear Catherine,' said she, 'do take this pin out of my sleeve; I am afraid it has torn a hole already; I shall be quite sorry if it has, for this is a favourite gown, though it cost but nine shillings a yard.'

'That is exactly what I should have guessed it, madam,' said Mr Tilney, looking at the muslin.

'Do you understand muslins, sir?'

'Particularly well; I always buy my own cravats, and am allowed to be an excellent judge; and my sister has often trusted me in the choice of a gown. I bought one for her the other day, and it was pronounced to be a prodigious bargain by every lady who saw it. I gave but five shillings a yard for it, and a true Indian muslin.'

Mrs Allen was quite struck by his genius. 'Men commonly take so little notice of those things,' said she. 'I can never get Mr Allen to know one of my gowns from another. You must be a great comfort to your sister, sir.'

'I hope I am, madam.'

'And pray, sir, what do you think of Miss Morland's gown?'

'It is very pretty, madam,' said he, gravely examining it, 'but I do not think it will wash well; I am afraid it will fray.'

'How can you,' said Catherine, laughing, 'be so –' she had almost said, strange.

'I am quite of your opinion, sir,' replied Mrs Allen; 'and so I told Miss Morland when she bought it.'

'But then you know, madam, muslin always turns to some account or other; Miss Morland will get enough out of it for a handkerchief, or a cap, or a cloak. – Muslin can never be said to be wasted. I have heard my sister say so forty times, when she has been extravagant in buying more than she wanted, or careless in cutting it to pieces.'

'Bath is a charming place, sir; there are so many good shops here. We are sadly off in the country; not but what we have very good shops in Salisbury, but it is so far to go; – eight miles is a long way; Mr Allen says it is nine, measured nine; but I am sure it cannot be more than eight; and it is such a fag – I come back tired to death. Now here one can step out of doors and get a thing in five minutes.'

Mr Tilney was polite enough to seem interested in what she said; and she kept him on the subject of muslins till the dancing recommenced. Catherine feared, as she listened to their discourse, that he indulged himself a little too much with the foibles of others. – 'What are you thinking of so earnestly?' said he, as they walked back to the ball-room; – 'not of your partner, I hope, for, by that shake of the head, your meditations are not satisfactory.'

Catherine coloured, and said, 'I was not thinking of anything.'

'That is artful and deep, to be sure; but I had rather be told at once that you will not tell me.'

'Well, then, I will not.'

'Thank you; for now we shall soon be acquainted, as I am authorized to tease you on this subject whenever we meet, and nothing in the world advances intimacy so much.'

They danced again; and, when the assembly closed, parted, on the lady's side at least, with a strong inclination for continuing the acquaintance. Whether she thought of him so much, while she drank her warm wine and water, and prepared herself for bed, as to dream of him when there, cannot be ascertained; but I hope it was no more than in a slight slumber, or a morning doze at most; for if it be true, as a celebrated writer has maintained, that no young lady can be justified in falling in love before the gentleman's love is declared, it must be very improper that a young lady should dream of a gentleman before the gentleman is first known to have dreamt of her. How proper Mr Tilney might be as a dreamer or a lover, had not yet perhaps entered Mr Allen's head, but that he was not objectionable as a common acquaintance for his young charge he was on inquiry satisfied; for he had early in the evening taken pains to know who her partner was, and had been assured of Mr Tilney's being a clergyman, and of a very respectable family in Gloucestershire.

(1818)

It is better to travel hopefully than to arrive at the conclusion that you are going to die at home. This sombre impulse was strengthened a century ago by the sanatoria which sprang from the mountain-tops of Switzerland. They roofed the only treatment for sufferers from pulmonary tuberculosis, 'the white plague' which slew Europe's young as indiscriminately as did its wars.

Those who could afford to took their holed, bleeding, sputum-rattling lungs, within their fevered and wasting bodies, to the cold, clean, thin air and the unimpeded sunshine and snow, to languish under a regimen of well-nourished outdoor rest until they healed, or died, or gave up hope. By the 1920s, a scientific gloss was applied to the cleanly walls of sanatoria: the slower bodily metabolism and the shallower breathing enforced by chilly immobility possibly calmed the inflamed lung and contracted its cavities. Perhaps the Alps were ever a therapeutic mirage. Clinical debate about this was happily ended in 1944 by the discovery in the United States of the antibiotic streptomycin, which killed the tuberculosis bacillus and allowed the Swiss sanatoria to reopen as excellently sited hotels.

The poor sanatorium inmates, preoccupied with health, death and each other, provided, like the transient occupants of desert islands, isolated country houses or ocean liners, a convenient concentration of novelists' characters. Thomas Mann's (1875–1955) *The Magic Mountain* won the Nobel Prize for Literature in 1929. This extract from its beginning depicts sanatorium life with sickly reality.

THOMAS MANN

From The Magic Mountain

IT WAS ABOUT eight o' clock, and still daylight. A lake was visible in the distant landscape, its waters grey, is shores covered with black fir-forests that climbed the surrounding heights, thinned out, and gave place to bare, mist-wreathed rock. They stopped at a small station. Hans Castorp heard the name called out: it was 'Davos-Dorf'. Soon he would be at his journey's end. And suddenly, close to him, he heard a voice, the comfortable Hamburg voice of his cousin, Joachim Ziemssen, saying: 'Hullo, there you are! Here's where you get out!' and peering through the window saw his cousin himself, standing below on the platform, in a brown ulster, bare-headed, and looking more robust than ever in his life before. He laughed and said again: 'Come along out, it's all right!'

'But I'm not there yet!' said Hans Castorp, taken aback, and still seated.

'Oh, yes, you are. This is the village. It is nearer to the sanatorium from here. I have a carriage. Just give us your things.'

And laughing, confused, in the excitement of arrival and meeting, Hans Castorp reached bag, overcoat, the roll with stick and umbrella, and finally *Ocean Steamships* out of the window. Then he ran down the narrow corridor and sprang out upon the platform to greet his cousin properly. The meeting took place without exuberance, as between people of traditional coolness and reserve. Strange to say, the cousins had always avoided calling each other by their first names, simply because they were afraid of showing too much feeling. And, as they could not well address each other by their last names, they confined themselves, by established custom, to the thou.

A man in livery with a braided cap looked on while they shook hands, quickly, not without embarrassment, young Ziemssen in military position, heels together. Then he came forward to ask for Hans Castorp's luggage ticket; he was the concierge of the International Sanatorium Berghof, and would fetch the guest's large trunk from the other station while the gentlemen drove directly up to supper. This man limped noticeably; and so, curiously enough, the first thing Hans Castorp said to his cousin was: 'Is that a war veteran? What makes him limp like that?'

'War veteran! No fear!' said Joachim, with some bitterness. 'He's got it in his knee – or, rather, he had it – the knee-pan has been removed.'

Hans Castorp bethought himself hastily.

'So that's it?' he said, and as he walked on turned his head and gave a quick glance back. 'But you can't make me believe you've still got anything like that the matter with you! Why, you look as if you had just come from manoeuvres!' And he looked sidelong at his cousin.

Joachim was taller and broader than he, a picture of youthful vigour, and made for a uniform. He was of the very dark type which his blond-peopled country not seldom produces, and his already nut-brown skin was tanned almost to bronze. With his large, black eyes and small, dark moustache over the full, well-shaped mouth, he would have been distinctly handsome if his ears had not stood out. Up to a certain period they had been his only trouble in life. Now, however, he had others.

Hans Castorp went on: 'You're coming back down with me, aren't you? I see no reason why not.'

'Back down with you?' asked his cousin, and turned his large eyes full upon him. They had always been gentle, but in these five months they had taken on a tired, almost sad expression. 'When?'

'Why, in three weeks.'

'Oh, yes, you are already on the way back home, in your thoughts,' answered Joachim. 'Wait a bit. You've only just come. Three weeks are nothing at all, to us up here – they look like a lot of time to you, because you are only up here on a visit, and three weeks is all you have. Get acclimatized first – it isn't so easy, you'll see. And the climate isn't the only queer thing about us. You're going to see some things you've never dreamed of – just wait. About me – it isn't such smooth sailing as you think, you with your "going home in three weeks". That's the class of ideas you have down below. Yes, I am brown, I know, but it is mostly snow-burning. It doesn't mean much, as Behrens always says; he told me at the last regular examination it would take another half year, pretty certainly.'

'Half a year? Are you crazy?' shouted Hans Castorp. They had climbed into the yellow cabriolet that stood in the stone-paved square in front of the shed-like station, and as the pair of brown horses started up, he flounced indignantly on the hard cushions. 'Half a year! You've been up here half a year already! Who's got so much time to spend –'

'Oh, time – !' said Joachim, and nodded repeatedly, straight in front of him, paying his cousin's honest indignation no heed. 'They make pretty free with a human being's idea of time, up here. You wouldn't believe it. Three weeks are just like a day to them. You'll learn all about it,' he said, and added: 'One's ideas get changed.'

Hans Castorp regarded him earnestly as they drove. 'But seems to me you've made a splendid recovery,' he said, shaking his head.

'You really think so, don't you?' answered Joachim; 'I think I have too.' He drew himself up straighter against the cushions, but immediately relaxed again. 'Yes, I am better,' he explained, 'but I am not cured yet. In the left lobe, where there were rales, it only sounds harsh now, and that is not so bad; but lower down it is still *very* harsh, and there are rhonchi in the second intercostal space.'

'How learned you've got,' said Hans Castorp.

'Fine sort of learning! God knows I wish I'd had it sweated out of my system in the service,' responded Joachim. 'But I still have sputum,' he said, with a shoulder-shrug that was somehow indifferent and vehement both at once, and became him but ill. He half pulled out and showed to his cousin something he carried in the side pocket of his overcoat, next to Hans Castorp. It was a flat, curving bottle of bluish glass, with a metal cap.

'Most of us up here carry it,' he said, shoving it back. 'It even has a nickname; they make quite a joke of it. You are looking at the landscape?'

Hans Castorp was. 'Magnificent!' he said.

'Think so?' asked Joachim.

They had driven for a space straight up the axis of the valley, along an irregularly built street that followed the line of the railway; then, turning to the left, they crossed the narrow tracks and a watercourse, and now trotted up a high-road that mounted gently toward the wooded slopes. Before them rose a low, projecting, meadow-like plateau, on which, facing south-west, stood a long building, with a cupola and so many balconies that from a distance it looked porous, like a sponge. In this building lights were beginning to show. It was rapidly growing dusk. The faint rose-colour that had briefly enlivened the overcast heavens was faded now, and there reigned the colourless, soulless, melancholy transition-period that comes just before the onset of night. The populous valley, extended and rather winding, now began to show lights everywhere, not only in the middle, but here and there on the slopes at either hand, particularly on the projecting right side, upon which buildings mounted in terrace formation. Paths ran up the sloping meadows to the left and lost themselves in the vague blackness of the pine forest. Behind them, where the valley narrowed to its entrance, the more distant ranges showed a cold, slaty blue. A wind had sprung up, and made perceptible the chill of evening.

'No, to speak frankly, I don't find it so overpowering,' said Hans Castorp. 'Where are the glaciers, and the snow peaks, and the gigantic heights you hear about? These things aren't very high, it seems to me.'

'Oh, yes, they are,' answered Joachim. 'You can see the tree line almost everywhere, it is very sharply defined; the fir-trees leave off, and after that there is absolutely nothing but bare rock. And up there to the right of the Schwarzhorn, that tooth-shaped peak, there is a glacier – can't you see the blue? It is not very large, but it is a glacier right enough, the Skaletta. Piz Michel and Tinzenhorn, in the notch – you can't see them from here – have snow all the year round.'

'External snow,' said Hans Castorp.

'External snow, if you like. Yes, that's all very high. But we are frightfully high ourselves: sixteen hundred metres above sea-level. That's why the peaks don't seem any higher.'

'Yes, what a climb that was! I was scared to death, I can tell you. Sixteen hundred metres – that is over five thousand feet, as I reckon it. I've never been so high up in my life.' And Hans Castorp took in a deep, experimental breath of the strange air. It was fresh, and that was all. It had no perfume, no content, no humidity; it breathed in easily; and held for him no associations.

'Wonderful air,' he remarked, politely.

'Yes, the atmosphere is famous. But the place doesn't look its best to-night. Sometimes it makes a much better impression – especially when there is snow. But you can get sick of looking at it. All of us up here are frightfully fed up, you can imagine,' said Joachim, and twisted his mouth into an expression of disgust that was as unlike him as the shoulder-shrug. It looked irritable, disproportionate.

'You have such a queer way of talking,' said Hans Castorp.

'Have I?' said Joachim, concerned, and turned to look at his cousin.

'Oh, no, of course I don't mean you really have – I suppose it just seemed so to me for the moment,' Hans Castorp hastened to assure him. It was the expression 'all of us up here', which Joachim had used several times, that had somehow struck him as strange and given him an uneasy feeling.

'Our sanatorium is higher up than the village, as you see,' went on Joachim. 'Fifty metres higher. In the prospectus it says a hundred, but it is really only fifty. The highest of the sanatoriums is the Schatzalp –

you can't see it from here. They have to bring their bodies down on bob-sleds in the winter, because the roads are blocked.'

'Their bodies? Oh, I see. Imagine!' said Hans Castorp. And suddenly he burst out laughing, a violent, irrepressible laugh, which shook him all over and distorted his face, that was stiff with the cold wind, until it almost hurt. 'On bob-sleds! And you can tell me it just like that, in cold blood! You've certainly got pretty cynical in these five months.'

'Not at all,' answered Joachim, shrugging again. 'Why not? It's all the same to them, isn't it? But maybe we do get cynical up here. Behrens is a cynic himself – but he's a great old bird after all, an old corps-student. He is a brilliant operator, they say. You will like him. Krokowski is the assistant – devilishly clever article. They mention his activities specially, in the prospectus. He psycho-analyses the patients.'

'He what? Psycho-analyses – how disgusting!' cried Hans Castorp; and now his hilarity altogether got the better of him. He could not stop. The psycho-analysis had been the finishing touch. He laughed so hard that the tears ran down his cheeks; he put up his hands to his face and rocked with laughter. Joachim laughed just as heartily – it seemed to do him good; and thus, in great good spirits, the young people climbed out of the wagon, which had slowly mounted the steep, winding drive and deposited them before the portal of the International Sanatorium Berghof.

On their right as they entered, between the main door and the inner one, was the porter's lodge. An official of the French type, in the grey livery of the man at the station, was sitting at the telephone, reading the newspaper. He came out and led them through the well-lighted halls, on the left of which lay the reception-rooms. Hans Castorp peered in as he passed, but they were empty. Where, then, were the guests, he asked, and his cousin answered: 'In the rest-cure. I had leave to-night to go out and meet you. Otherwise I am always up in my balcony, after supper."

Hans Castorp came near bursting out again. 'What! You lie out on your balcony at night, in the damp?' he asked, his voice shaking.

'Yes, that is the rule. From eight to ten. But come and see your room now, and get a wash.'

They entered the lift – it was an electric one, worked by the Frenchman. As they went up, Hans Castorp wiped his eyes.

'I'm perfectly worn out with laughing,' he said, and breathed through his mouth. 'You've told me such a lot of crazy stuff – that about the psycho-analysis was the last straw. I suppose I am a bit relaxed from the journey. And my feet are cold – are yours? But my face burns so, it is really unpleasant. Do we eat now? I feel hungry. Is the food decent up here?'

They went noiselessly along the coco matting of the narrow corridor, which was lighted by electric lights in white glass shades set in the ceiling. The walls gleamed with hard white enamel paint. They had a glimpse of a nursing sister in a white cap, and eyeglasses on a cord that ran behind her ear. She had the look of a Protestant sister – that is to say, one working without a real vocation and burdened with restlessness and ennui. As they went along the corridor, Hans Castorp saw, beside two of the white-enamelled, numbered doors, certain curious, swollen-looking, balloon-shaped vessels with short necks. He did not think, at the moment, to ask what they were.

'Here you are,' said Joachim. 'I am next you on the right. The other side you have a Russian couple, rather loud and offensive, but it couldn't be helped. Well, how do you like it?'

There were two doors, an outer and an inner, with clothes-hooks in the space between. Joachim had turned on the ceiling light, and in its vibrating brilliance the room looked restful and cheery, with practical white furniture, white washable walls, clean linoleum, and white linen curtains gaily embroidered in modern taste. The door stood open; one saw the lights of the valley and heard distant dance-music. The good Joachim had put a vase of flowers on the chest of drawers – a few bluebells and some yarrow, which he had found himself among the second crop of grass on the slopes.

'Awfully decent of you,' said Hans Castorp. 'What a nice room! I can spend a couple of weeks here with pleasure.'

'An American woman died here day before yesterday,' said Joachim. 'Behrens told me directly that she would be out before you came, and you might have the room. Her fiancé was with her, an English officer of marines, but he didn't behave very well. He kept coming out in the corridor to cry, just like a little boy. He rubbed cold cream on his cheeks, because he was close-shaven and the tears smarted. Night before last she had two first-class haemorrhages, and that was the finish. But she has been gone since yesterday morning, and after they took her away of course they fumigated the room thoroughly with formalin, which is the proper thing to use in such cases.'

Hans Castorp took in this information with a sprightly, yet half-distraught air. He was standing with his sleeves pushed back before the roomy wash-hand-basin, the taps of which shone in the electric light, and gave hardly a glance at the white metal bed with its fresh coverlet.

'Fumigated it, eh? That's ripping,' he said loquaciously and rather absurdly, as he washed and dried his hands. 'Methyl aldehyde; yes, that's too much for the bacteria, no matter how strong they are. H_2CO. But it's a powerful stench. Of course, perfect sanitation is absolutely essential.' He spoke with more of a Hamburg accent than his cousin, who had broken himself of it since his student days. Hans Castorp continued volubly. 'But what I was about to say was, probably the officer of marines used a safety-razor; one makes oneself sore with those things easier than with a well-sharpened blade – at least, that is my experience, and I use them both by turns. Well, and salt water would naturally make a tender skin smart, so he got in the way, in the service, of rubbing in cold cream. I don't see anything strange about that . . .' He rattled on: said that he had two hundred Maria Mancinis (his cigar) in his trunk, the customs officers had been very courteous; and gave his cousin greetings from various people at home. 'Don't they heat the room here?' he broke off to inquire, and ran to put his hands on the radiator.

'No, they keep us pretty cool,' answered Joachim. 'The weather would have to be different from this before they put on the heat in August.'

'August, August!' said Hans Castorp. 'But I am cold, abominably cold; I mean in my body, for my face burns shockingly – just feel it!'

This demand was entirely foreign to the young man's nature – so much so that he himself was disagreeably impressed as he heard himself make it. Joachim did not take up the offer, but merely said: 'That is the air – it doesn't mean anything; Behrens himself is purple in the face all day long. Some people never get used to it. Come along now, do, or we shan't get anything to eat.'

Outside they saw the nursing sister again, peering short-sightedly and inquisitively after them. But in the first storey Hans Castorp suddenly stopped, rooted to the spot by a perfectly ghastly sound coming from a little distance off round a bend in the corridor. It was not a loud sound, but so distinctly horrible that Hans Castorp made a wry face and looked wide-eyed at his cousin. It was coughing, obviously, a man coughing; but coughing like to no other Hans Castorp had ever heard, and compared with which any other had been a magnificent and healthy manifestation of life: a coughing that had no conviction and gave no relief, that did not even come out in paroxysms, but was just a feeble, dreadful welling-up of the juices of organic dissolution.

'Yes,' said Joachim. 'That's a bad case. An Austrian aristocrat, you know, very elegant. He's a born horseman – a gentleman rider. And now he's come to this. But he still gets about.'

As they went, Hans Castorp discoursed earnestly upon the gentleman rider's cough.

'You must realize,' he said, 'that I've never heard anything like it before. It is entirely new to me, and naturally it makes a great impression. There are different kinds of cough, dry and loose, and people always say the loose one is better than the other, the barking kind. When I had croup, in my youth' (he actually said 'in my youth'!), 'I bayed like a wolf, and I can still remember how glad everybody was when it got looser. But a cough like this – I didn't know there was such a cough! It isn't a human cough at all. It isn't dry and yet isn't loose either – that is very far from being the right word for it. It is just as if one could look right into him when he coughs, and see what it looks like: all slime and mucous –'

'Oh,' said Joachim, 'I hear it every day, you don't need to describe it to me.'

But Hans Castorp could not get over the coughing he had heard. He kept repeating that he could see right into the gentleman rider's vitals; when they reached the restaurant his travel-weary eyes had an excited glitter.

In the Restaurant

It was charming in the restaurant, elegantly appointed and well lighted. The room lay to the right of the hall, opposite the salons, and was, Joachim explained, used chiefly by new arrivals, and by guests eating out of the usual meal hours or entertaining company. But it also served for birthday feasts, farewell parties, even to celebrate a favourable report after a general examination. There were lively times here in the restaurant on occasion, Joachim said, and champagne flowed freely. Now, no one was here but a solitary lady of some thirty years, reading a book and humming; she kept tapping the table-cloth lightly with the middle finger of her left hand. After the young people had taken their places, she changed hers, in order to sit with her back to them. Joachim explained in a low voice that she suffered from shyness as from a disease, and ate all her meals in the restaurant, with a book. It was said that she had entered her first tuberculosis sanatorium as a young girl, and had never lived in the world since.

'So compared with her, you are only a novice, with your five months; and still will be when you have a year on your back,' said Hans Castorp to his cousin; whereat Joachim, with his newly acquired shoulder-shrug, took up the menu.

They had sat down at the raised table in the window, the pleasantest spot in the room, facing each other against the cream-coloured hangings, their faces lighted by the red-shaded table-lamp. Hans Castorp clasped his freshly washed hands and rubbed them together in agreeable anticipation – a habit of his when he sat down to table, perhaps because his ancestors had said grace before meat. They were served by a friendly maid in black frock and white apron. She had a pleasant, throaty voice, and her broad face was indisputably healthy-coloured. To his great amusement, Hans Castorp learned that the waitresses here were called 'dining-room girls'. They ordered a bottle of Gruaud Larose, and Hans Castorp sent it back to have it warmed. The food was excellent: asparagus soup, stuffed tomatoes, a roast with vegetables, an exceedingly well-prepared sweet, cheese, and fruit. Hans Castorp ate heartily, though his appetite did not turn out quite so stout as he had thought. But he always ate a good deal, out of pure self-respect, even when he was not hungry.

Joachim paid scant honour to the meal. He was tired of the cooking, he said; they all were, up here, and it was customary to grumble at the food. If one had to sit up here for ever and a day – ! But, on the other hand, he partook of the wine with gusto, not to say abandon; and repeatedly, though with careful avoidance of emotional language, expressed his joy at having somebody here with whom one could have a little rational conversation.

'Yes, it's first-rate you've come,' he said, and his gentle voice betrayed some feeling. 'I must say it is really an event for me – it is certainly a change, anyhow, a break in the everlasting monotony.'

'But time must go fast, living up here,' was Hans Castorp's view.

'Fast and slow, as you take it,' answered Joachim. 'It doesn't go at all, I tell you. You can't call it time – and you can't call it living either!' he said with a shake of the head, and fell to his glass again.

Hans Castorp drank too, though his face was like fire. Yet he was still cold, and felt a curious restlessness in his limbs, at once pleasurable and troubling. His words fell over each other, he often mis-spoke and passed it over with a deprecating wave. Joachim too was in a lively humour, and their conversation continued in a still freer and more convivial vein after the humming, tapping lady had got up suddenly and left the room. They gesticulated with their forks as they ate, nodded, shrugged their shoulders, talked with their mouths full. Joachim wanted to hear about Hamburg, and brought the conversation round to the proposed regulation of the Elbe.

'Epoch-making,' said Hans Castorp. 'Epoch-making for the development of our shipping. Can't be over-estimated. We've budgeted fifty millions for immediate expenditure and you may be sure we know what we're about.'

But notwithstanding all the importance he attached to the projected improvement, he jumped away from the theme and demanded that Joachim tell him more about life 'up here' and about the guests – which the latter straightaway did, being only too pleased to be able to unbosom himself. He had to repeat the story of the corpses sent down by bobsleigh, and vouch for its truth. Hans Castorp being taken by another fit of laughing, his cousin laughed too, with hearty enjoyment, and told other funny things to add fuel to their merriment. There was a lady sitting at his table, named Frau Stöhr, the wife of a Cannstadt musician; a rather serious case, she was, and the most ignorant creature he had ever seen. She said diseased for deceased, quite seriously, and she called Krokowski the Asst. And you had to take it all in without cracking a smile. She was a regular gossip – most people were, up here – and published it broadcast that another lady, a certain Frau Iltis, carried a 'steriletto' on her person. 'That is exactly what she called it, isn't that priceless?' They lolled in their chairs, they flung themselves back and laughed so hard that they shook; and they began to hiccup at nearly the same time.

Now and then Joachim's face would cloud over and he would remember his lot.

'Yet, we sit here and laugh,' he said, with a long face, his words interrupted by the heaving of his diaphragm, 'we sit here and laugh, but there's no telling when I shall get away. When Behrens says half a year, you can make up your mind it will be more. It *is* hard, isn't it? – you just tell me if you don't think it is pretty hard on me. I had already been accepted, I could have taken my exams next month. And now I have to drool about with a thermometer stuck in my mouth, and count the howlers of this ignorant Frau Stöhr, and watch the time slipping away. A year is so important at our age. Down below, one goes through so many changes, and makes so much progress, in a single year of life. And I have to stagnate up here – yes, just stagnate like a filthy puddle; it isn't too crass a comparison.'

Strange to say, Hans Castorp's only reply to all this was a query as to whether it was possible to get porter up here; when Joachim looked at him, in some astonishment, he perceived that his cousin was overcome with sleep, that in fact he was actually nodding.

'But you are going to sleep!' said Joachim. 'Come along, it is time we both went to bed.'

'"You can't call it time,"' quoth Hans Castorp, thick-tongued. He went with his cousin, rather bent and stiff in the knees, like a man bowed to the earth with fatigue. However, in the dimly lighted corridor he pulled himself sharply together on hearing his cousin say: 'There's Krokowski sitting there. I think I'll just have to present you, as briefly as possible.'

Dr Krokowski sat in the bright light at the fire-place of one of the reception rooms, close to the folding doors. He was reading a paper, and got up as the young people approached.

Joachim, in military position, heels together, said: 'Herr Doctor, may I present my cousin Castorp from Hamburg? He has just arrived.'

Dr Krokowski greeted the new inmate with a jovial and robust heartiness, as who should say that with him all formality was superfluous, and only jocund mutual confidence in place. He was about thirty-five years old, broad-shouldered and fleshy, much shorter than either of the youths before him, so that he had to tip back his head to look them in the face. He was unusually pale, of a translucent, yes, phosphorescent pallor, that was further accentuated by the dark ardour of his eyes, the blackness of his brows, and his rather long, full whisker, which ended in two points and already showed some white threads. He had on a black double-breasted, somewhat worn sack suit; black, open-worked sandal-like shoes over grey woollen socks, and a soft turn-down collar, such as Hans Castorp had previously seen worn only by a photographer in Danzig, which did, in fact, lend a certain stamp of the studio to Dr Krokowski's appearance. Smiling warmly and showing his yellow teeth in his beard, he shook the young man by the hand, and said in a baritone voice, with rather a foreign drawl: 'Wel-come to our midst, Herr Castorp! May you get quickly acclimatized and feel yourself at home among us! Do you come as a patient, may I ask?'

It was touching to see Hans Castorp labour to master his drowsiness and be polite. It annoyed him to be in such bad form, and with the self-consciousness of youth he read signs of indulgent amusement in the warmth of the Assistant's manner. He replied, mentioning his examinations and his three weeks' visit, and ended by saying he was, thank God, perfectly healthy.

'Really?' asked Krokowski, putting his head teasingly on one side. His smile grew broader. 'Then you are a phenomenon worthy of study. I, for one, have never in my life come across a perfectly healthy human being. . . .'

(1924)

Hans Castorp was discovered to have a tuberculosis focus in his upper left lung. He stayed there seven years.

SIR THOMAS BROWNE

Sir Thomas Browne (1605–82) is a scholarly sun shining upon the medical literary scene, if obscured for everyday strollers by the opacity of his style. To fill the idle hours of 1635 at Shibden Hall, Yorkshire, he wrote *Religio Medici*, a paradoxical confession of Christian faith from a medical sceptic. It made the papal *Index Expurgatorius* with flattering promptitude. Browne was a Wykehamist who went to Pembroke College, Oxford, and then to Montpellier, Padua and Leyden, all three fashionable centres of medical learning. In 1637 he settled for life as a GP in Norwich, tranquil amid the East Anglian barley during the Civil Wars of 1642–49, writing *Urn Burial* on mortality and immortality (1658), *Pseudodoxia Epidemica* on the vulgar errors of mankind (1646), and *Christian Morals*, which was published in 1716 and edited by Dr Johnson in 1756. Here is Sir Thomas on body and soul.

From Religio Medici

IN OUR STUDY of Anatomy there is a mass of mysterious Philosophy, and such as reduced the very Heathens to Divinity: yet, amongst all those rare discoveries and curious pieces I find in the Fabrick of Man, I do not so much content myself, as in that I find not, there is no Organ or Instrument for the rational Soul; for in the brain, which we term the seat of Reason, there is not any thing of moment more than I can discover in the crany of a beast: and this is a sensible and no inconsiderable argument of the inorganity of the Soul, at least in that sense we usually so receive it. Thus we are men, and we know not how: there is something in us that can be without us, and will be after us; though it is strange that it hath no history what it was before us, nor cannot tell how it entred in us.

Now, for these walls of flesh, wherein the Soul doth seem to be immured before the Resurrection, it is nothing but an elemental composition, and a Fabrick that must fall to ashes. *All flesh is grass*, is not onely metaphorically, but litterally, true; for all those creatures we behold are but the herbs of the field, digested into flesh in them, or more remotely carnified in our selves. Nay further, we are what we all abhor, *Anthropophagi* and Cannibals, devourers not onely of men, but of our selves; and that not in an allegory, but a positive truth; for all this mass of flesh which we behold, came in at our mouths; this frame we look upon, hath been upon our trenchers; in brief, we have devour'd our selves. I cannot believe the wisdom of Pythagoras did ever positively, and in a literal sense, affirm his Metempsychosis, or impossible transmigration of the Souls of men into beasts. Of all Metamorphoses or transmigrations, I believe only one, that is of Lots wife; for that of Nebuchodonosor proceeded not so far: in all others I conceive there is no further verity than is contained in their implicite sense and morality. I believe that the whole frame of a beast doth perish, and is left in the same state after death as before it was materialled unto life: that the Souls of men know neither contrary nor corruption; that they subsist beyond the body, and outlive death by the priviledge of their proper natures, and without a Miracle; that the Souls of the faithful, as they leave Earth, take possession of Heaven: that those apparitions and ghosts of departed persons are not the wandring souls of men, but the unquiet walks of Devils, prompting and suggesting us unto mischief, blood, and villainy: instilling and stealing into our hearts that the blessed Spirits are not at rest in their graves, but wander sollicitous of the affairs of the World. But that those phantasms appear often, and do frequent Coemeteries, Charnel-houses, and Churches, it is because those are the dormitories of the dead, where the Devil, like an insolent Champion, beholds with pride the spoils and Trophies of his Victory over Adam.

This is that dismal conquest we all deplore, that makes us so often cry, *O Adam, quid fecisti?* I thank God I have not those strait ligaments, or narrow obligations to the World, as to dote on life, or be convulst and tremble at the name of death. Not that I am insensible of the dread and horrour thereof; or by raking into the bowels of the deceased, continual sight of Anatomies, Skeletons, or Cadaverous reliques, like Vespilloes, or Grave-makers, I am become stupid, or have forgot the apprehension of Mortality; but that, marshalling all the horrours, and contemplating the extremities thereof, I find not anything therein able to daunt the courage of a man, much less a well-resolved Christian; and therefore am not angry at the errour of our first Parents, or unwilling to bear a part of this common fate, and like the best of them to dye, that is, to cease to breathe, to take a farewel of the elements, to be a kind of nothing for a moment, to be within one instant of a Spirit. When I take a full view and circle of my self without this reasonable moderator, and equal piece of Justice, Death, I do conceive my self the miserablest person extant. Were there not another life that I hope for, all the vanities of this World should not intreat a moment's breath from me: could the Devil work my belief to imagine I could never dye, I would not outlive that very thought. I have so abject a conceit of this common way of existence, this retaining to the Sun and Elements, I cannot think this is to be a Man, or to live according to the dignity of humanity. In exspectation of a better, I can with patience embrace this life, yet in my best meditations do often defie death; I honour any man that contemns it, nor can I highly love any that is afraid of it: this makes me naturally love a Souldier, and honour those tattered and contemptible Regiments that will die at the command of a Sergeant. For a Pagan there may be some motives to be in love with life; but for a Christian to be amazed at death, I see not how he can escape this Dilemma, that he is too sensible of this life, or hopeless of the life to come.

(1642)

And on death and burial:

From Urn Burial

WHEN THE FUNERALL pyre was out, and the last valediction over, men took a lasting adieu of their interred Friends, little expecting the curiosity of future ages should comment upon their ashes, and, having no old experience of the duration of their Reliques, held no opinion of such after-considerations.

But who knows the fate of his bones, or how often he is to be buried? who hath the Oracle of his ashes, or whither they are to be scattered? . . .

Beside, to preserve the living, and make the dead to live, to keep men out of their Urnes, and discourse of humane fragments in them, is not impertinent unto our profession; whose study is life and death, who daily behold examples of mortality, and of all men least need artificial *mementos*, or coffins by our bedside, to minde us of our graves. . . .

The Solemnities, Ceremonies, Rites of their Cremation or enterrment, so solemnly delivered by Authours, we shall not disparage our Reader to repeat. Only the last and lasting part in their Urns, collected bones and Ashes, we cannot wholly omit or decline that Subject, which occasion lately presented, in some discovered among us.

In a Field of old *Walsingham*, not many moneths past, were digged up between fourty and fifty Urnes, deposited in a dry and sandy soil, not a yard deep, nor farre from one another: Not all strictly of one figure, but most answering these described: some containing two pounds of bones, distinguishable in skulls, ribs, jawes, thigh-bones, and teeth, with fresh impressions of their combustion. Besides the extraneous substances, like peeces of small boxes, or combes handsomely wrought, handles of small brasse instruments, brazen nippers, and in one some kinde of Opale.

Near the same plot of ground, for about six yards compasse, were digged up coals and incinerated substances, which begat conjecture that this was the *Ustrina* or place of burning their bodies, or some sacrificing place unto the *Manes*, which was properly below the surface of the ground, as the *Arae* and Altars unto the gods and *Heroes* above it.

That these were the urnes of *Romanes* from the common custome and place where they were found, is no obscure conjecture, not farre from a *Romane* Garrison, and but five Miles from *Brancaster*, set down by ancient Record under the name of *Brannodunum*. And where the adjoyning Towne, containing seven Parishes, in no very different sound, but Saxon Termination, still retains the name of *Burnham*, which being an early station, it is not improbable the neighbour parts were filled with habitations, either of *Romanes* themselves, or *Brittains Romanised*, which observed the *Romane* customs. . . .

How the bulk of a man should sink into so few pounds of bones and ashes, may seem strange unto any who considers not its constitution, and how slender a masse will remain upon an open and urging fire of the carnall composition. Even bones themselves reduced into ashes, do abate a notable proportion. And consisting much of a volatile salt, when that is fired out, make a light kind of cinders. Although their bulk be disproportionable to their weight, when the heavy principle of Salt is fired out, and the Earth almost only remaineth; Observable in sallow, which makes more Ashes than Oake; and discovers the common fraud of selling Ashes by measure, and not by ponderation.

Some bones make best Skeletons, some bodies quick and speediest ashes. . . .

Christians dispute how their bodies should lye in the grave. In urnall interrment they clearly escaped this controversie; though we decline the Religious consideration, yet in cemiteriall and narrower burying-places, to avoid confusion and crosse position, a certain posture were to be admitted; which even Pagan civility observed. The *Persians* lay North and South, the *Megarians* and *Phoenicians* placed their heads to the East; The *Athenians*, some think, towards the West, which Christians still retain. And *Beda* will have it to be the posture of our Saviour. That he was crucified with his face toward the West, we will not contend with tradition and probable account; But we applaud not the hand of the Painter, in exalting his Crosse so high above those on either side; since hereof we finde no authentick account in history, and even the crosses found by *Helena*, pretend no such distinction from longitude or dimension.

To be knav'd out of our graves, to have our sculs made drinking-bowls, and our bones turned into Pipes, to delight and sport our Enemies, are Tragicall abominations escaped in burning Burials.

Urnall interrments and burnt Reliques lye not in fear of worms, or to be an heritage for Serpents; In carnall sepulture, corruptions seem peculiar unto parts, and some speak of snakes out of the spinall marrow. But while we suppose common wormes in graves, 'tis not easie to finde any there; few in Churchyards above a foot deep, fewer or none in Churches, though in fresh decayed bodies. Teeth, bones, and hair, give the most lasting defiance to corruption. In an Hydropicall body, ten years buried in the Church-yard, we met with a fat concretion, where the nitre of the Earth, and the salt and lixivious liquor of the body, had coagulated large lumps of fat, into the consistence of the hardest castle-soap; whereof part remaineth with us. After a battle with the *Persians*, the *Roman* Corps decayed in few dayes, while the *Persian* bodies remained dry and uncorrupted. Bodies in the same ground do not uniformly dissolve, nor bones equally moulder; whereof in the opprobrious disease we expect no long duration. The body of the Marquesse of *Dorset* seemed sound and handsomely cereclothed, that after seventy-eight years was found uncorrupted. . . .

But the iniquity of oblivion blindely scattereth her poppy, and deals with the memory of men without distinction to merit of perpetuity. Who can but pity the founder of the Pyramids?

(1658)

O. Henry

North Carolina doctor's son O. Henry – who was William Sydney Porter (1862–1910) – like Oscar Wilde went to jail. He did three years and three months in the State Penitentiary at Columbus, Ohio, for embezzling $1,150 while working as a teller in the First National Bank at Austin, Texas. He had run off to South America, but returned on hearing that the wife who had eloped with him aged seventeen was ill with pulmonary tuberculosis. He was arrested in 1897. O. Henry was reputedly one of his guards.

He had himself contacted tuberculosis in his twenties, which obliged him to abandon the job as his uncle's drug-store clerk, and to pass two years living on the ranch of Texas ranger 'Red' Hall, an acclaimed scourge of rustlers, outlaws and Red Indians. There he learned the cowboy arts.

Before his overshadowing embarrassment, O. Henry had bought in 1894 the satirical weekly *Iconoclast*, which he enlivened, illustrated and renamed the *Rolling Stone*, but it flopped. He became instead a daily columinst on the Houston *Post*. In prison, he was given the jobs of medical assistant and bookkeeper, and there started writing – indeed, publishing – short stories. His wife had died of tuberculosis six months after his return to her, and he had a daughter kept in ignorance of the reason for his further absence. After release, O. Henry lived in New York on a bottle of whisky a day, and in 1907 he remarried, to a childhood sweetheart. In the end, the tuberculosis got him, too.

O. Henry invented the ten-minute story. Maupassant, Chekhov, Robert Louis Stevenson and Henry James all had their shorter stories, but O. Henry's could be leafed through in a magazine. This demands economy in characterisation, plotting and action of Shakespearian admonition. He wrote some six hundred, often about the New York inhabitants who became *The Four Million* in 1906. Damon Runyon (1880–1946) of *Guys and Dolls* owes him more than somewhat.

This story is a masterly exploitation of implication. It suffers an irrelevant technical fault: aphasia is loss of speech, loss of memory is amnesia.

A Ramble in Aphasia

My wife and I parted on that morning in precisely our usual manner. She left her second cup of tea to follow me to the front door. There she plucked from my lapel the invisible strand of lint (the universal act of woman to proclaim ownership) and bade me take care of my cold. I had no cold. Next came her kiss of parting – the level kiss of domesticity flavoured with Young Hyson. There was no fear of the extemporaneous, of variety spicing her infinite custom. With the deft touch of long malpractice, she dabbed awry my well-set scarf-pin; and then, as I closed the door, I heard her morning slippers pattering back to her cooling tea.

When I set out I had no thought or premonition of what was to occur. The attack came suddenly.

For many weeks I had been toiling, almost night and day, at a famous railroad law case that I won triumphantly but a few days previously. In fact, I had been digging away at the law almost without cessation for many years. Once or twice good Doctor Volney, my friend and physician, had warned me.

'If you don't slacken up, Bellford,' he said, 'you'll go suddenly to pieces. Either your nerves or brain will give way. Tell me, does a week pass in which you do not read in the papers of a case of aphasia – of some man lost, wandering nameless, with his past and his identity blotted out – and all from that little brain-clot made by overwork or worry?'

'I always thought,' said I, 'that the clot in those instances was really to be found on the brains of the newspaper reporters.'

Dr Volney shook his head.

'The disease exists,' he said. 'You need a change or a rest. Court-room, office and home – there is the only route you travel. For recreation you – read law books. Better take warning in time.'

'On Thursday nights,' I said defensively, 'my wife and I play cribbage. On Sundays she reads to me the weekly letter from her mother. That law books are not a recreation remains yet to be established.'

That morning as I walked I was thinking of Doctor Volney's words. I was feeling as well as I usually did – possibly in better spirits than usual.

I awoke with stiff and cramped muscles from having slept long on the incommodious seat of a day coach. I leaned my head against the seat and tried to think. After a long time I said to myself: 'I must have a name of some sort.' I searched my pockets. Not a card; not a letter; not a paper or monogram could I find. But I found in my coat pocket nearly $3,000 in bills of large denomination. 'I must be someone, of course,' I repeated to myself, and began again to consider.

The car was well crowded with men, among whom I told myself, there must have been some common interest, for they intermingled freely, and seemed in the best good-humour and spirits. One of them – a stout, spectacled gentleman enveloped in a decided odour of cinnamon and aloes – took the vacant half of my seat with a friendly nod, and unfolded a newspaper. In the intervals between his periods of reading, we conversed, as travellers will, on current affairs. I found myself able to sustain the conversation on such subjects with credit, at least to my memory. By and by my companion said:

'You are one of us, of course. Fine lot of men the West sends in this time. I'm glad they held the convention in New York; I've never been East before. My name's R. P. Bolder – Bolder & Son, of Hickory Grove, Missouri.'

Though unprepared, I rose to the emergency, as men will when put to it. Now must I hold a christening, and be at once babe, parson, and parent. My senses came to the rescue of my slower brain. The insistent odour of drugs from my companion supplied one idea; a glance at his newspaper, where my eye met a conspicuous advertisement, assisted me further.

'My name,' said I glibly, 'is Edward Pinkhammer. I am a druggist, and my home is in Cornopolis, Kansas.'

'I knew you were a druggist,' said my fellow-traveller affably. 'I saw the callous spot on your right forefinger where the handle of the pestle rubs. Of course, you are a delegate to our National Convention.'

'Are all these men druggists?' I asked wonderingly.

'They are. This car came through from the West. And they're your old-time druggists, too – none of your patent tablet-and-granule pharmashootists that use slot machines instead of a prescription desk. We percolate our own paregoric and roll our own pills, and we ain't above handling a few garden seeds in the spring, and carrying a sideline of confectionery and shoes. I tell you, Hampinker, I've got an idea to spring on this convention – new ideas is what they want. Now, you know the shelf bottles of tartar emetic and Rochelle salt Ant. et Pot. Tart. and Sod. et Pot. Tart. – one's poison, you know, and the other's harmless. It's easy to mistake one label for the other. Where do druggists mostly keep 'em? Why, as far apart as possible, on different shelves. That's wrong. I say keep 'em side by side so when you want one you can always compare it with the other and avoid mistakes. Do you catch the idea?'

'It seems to me a very good one,' I said.

'All right! When I spring it on the convention you back it up. We'll make some of these Eastern orange-phosphate-and-massage-cream professors that think they're the only lozenges in the market look like hypodermic tablets.'

'If I can be of any aid,' I said, warming, 'the two bottles of – er –'

'Tartrate of antimony and potash, and tartrate of soda and potash.'

'Shall henceforth sit side by side,' I concluded firmly.

'Now, there's another thing,' said Mr Bolder. 'For an excipient in manipulating a pill mass which do you prefer – the magnesia carbonate or the pulverized glycerrhiza radix?'

'The – er – magnesia,' I said. It was easier to say than the other word.

Mr Bolder glanced at me distrustfully through his spectacles.

'Give me the glycerrhiza,' said he. 'Magnesia cakes.'

'Here's another one of these fake aphasia cases,' he said, presently, handing me his newspaper, and laying his finger upon an article. 'I don't believe in 'em. I put nine out of ten of 'em down as frauds. A man gets sick of his business and his folks and wants to have a good time. He skips out somewhere, and when they find him he pretends to have lost his memory – don't know his own name, and won't even recognize the strawberry mark on his wife's left shoulder. Aphasia! Tut! Why can't they stay at home and forget?'

I took the paper and read, after the pungent headlines, the following:

> 'Denver, June 12 – Elwyn C. Bellford, a prominent laywer, is mysteriously missing from his home since three days ago, and all efforts to locate him have been in vain. Mr Bellford is a well-known citizen of the highest standing, and has enjoyed a large and lucrative law practice. He is married and owns a fine home and the most extensive private library in the State. On the day of his disappearance, he drew quite a large sum of money from his bank. No one can be found who saw him after he left the bank. Mr Bellford was a man of singularly quiet and domestic tastes, and seemed to find his happiness in his home and profession. If any clue at all exists to his strange disappearance, it may be found in

the fact that for some months he had been deeply absorbed in an important law case in connection with the Q. Y. and Z. Railroad Company. It is feared that overwork may have affected his mind. Every effort is being made to discover the whereabouts of the missing man.'

'It seems to me you are not altogether uncynical, Mr Bolder,' I said, after I had read the despatch. 'This has the sound, to me, of a genuine case. Why should this man, prosperous, happily married and respected, choose suddenly to abandon everything? I know that these lapses of memory do occur, and that men do find themselves adrift without a name, a history or a home.'

'Oh, gammon and jalap!' said Mr Bolder. 'It's larks they're after. There's too much education nowadays. Men know about aphasia, and they use it for an excuse. The women are wise, too. When it's all over they look you in the eye, as scientific as you please, and say: "He hypnotized me."'

Thus Mr Bolder diverted, but did not aid me with his comments and philosophy.

We arrived in New York about ten at night. I rode in a cab to an hotel, and I wrote my name 'Edward Pinkhammer' in the register. As I did so I felt pervade me a splendid, wild, intoxicating buoyancy – a sense of unlimited freedom, of newly attained possibilities. I was just born into the world. The old fetters – whatever they had been – were stricken from my hands and feet. The future lay before me a clear road such as an infant enters, and I could set out upon it equipped with a man's learning and experience.

I thought the hotel clerk looked at me five seconds too long. I had no baggage.

'The Druggists' Convention,' I said. 'My trunk has somehow failed to arrive.' I drew out a roll of money.

'Ah!' said he, showing an auriferous tooth, 'we have quite a number of the Western delegates stopping here.' He struck a bell for the boy.

I endeavoured to give colour to my rôle.

'There is an important movement on foot among us Westerners,' I said, 'in regard to a recommendation to the convention that the bottles containing the tartrate of antimony and potash, and the tartrate of sodium and potash, be kept in a contiguous position on the shelf.'

'Gentleman to three-fourteen,' said the clerk hastily. I was whisked away to my room.

The next day I bought a trunk and clothing, and began to live the life of Edward Pinkhammer. I did not tax my brain with endeavours to solve problems of the past.

It was a piquant and sparkling cup that the great island city held up to my lips. I drank of it gratefully. The keys of Manhattan belong to him who is able to bear them. You must be either the city's guest or its victim.

The following few days were as gold and silver. Edward Pinkhammer, yet counting back to his birth by hours only, knew the rare joy of having come upon so diverting a world full-fledged and unrestrained. I sat entranced on the magic carpets provided in theatres and roof-gardens, that transported one into strange and delightful lands full of frolicsome music, pretty girls and grotesque, drolly extravagant parodies upon humankind. I went here and there at my own dear will, bound by no limits of space, time or comportment. I dined in weird cabarets, at weirder tables d'hôte to the sound of Hungarian music and the wild shouts of mercurial artists and sculptors. Or, again, where the night life quivers in the electric glare like a kinetoscopic picture, and the millinery of the world, and its jewels, and the ones whom they adorn, and the men who make all three possible are met for good cheer and the spectacular effect. And among all these scenes that I have mentioned I learned one thing that I never knew before. And that is that the key to liberty is not in the hands of Licence, but Convention holds it. Comity has a toll-gate at which you must pay, or you may not enter the land of Freedom. In all the glitter, the seeming disorder, the parade, the abandon, I saw this law, unobtrusive, yet like iron, prevail. Therefore, in Manhattan you must obey these unwritten laws, and then you will be freest of the free. If you decline to be bound by them, you put on shackles.

Sometimes, as my mood urged me, I would seek the stately murmuring palm-rooms, redolent with high-born life and delicate restraint, in which to dine. Again I would go down to the waterways in steamers packed with vociferous, bedecked, unchecked, love-making clerks and shop-girls to their crude pleasures on the island shores. And there was always Broadway – glistening, opulent, wily, varying, desirable Broadway – growing upon one like an opium habit.

One afternoon as I entered my hotel a stout man with a big nose and a black moustache blocked my way in the corridor. When I would have passed around him, he greeted me with offensive familiarity.

'Hallo, Bellford!' he cried loudly. 'What the deuce are you doing in

New York? Didn't know anything could drag you away from that old book den of yours. Is Mrs B. alone or is this a little business run alone, eh?'

'You have made a mistake, sir,' I said coldly, releasing my hand from his grasp. 'My name is Pinkhammer. You will excuse me.'

The man dropped to one side, apparently astonished. As I walked to the clerk's desk I heard him call to a bell-boy and say something about telegraph blanks.

'You will give me my bill,' I said to the clerk, 'and have my baggage brought down in half an hour. I do not care to remain where I am annoyed by confidence men.'

I moved that afternoon to another hotel, a sedate, old-fashioned one on lower Fifth Avenue.

There was a restaurant a little way off Broadway where one could be served almost al fresco in a tropic array of screening flora. Quiet and luxury and a perfect service made it an ideal place in which to take luncheon or refreshment. One afternoon I was there picking my way to a table among the ferns when I felt my sleeve caught.

'Mr Bellford!' exclaimed an amazingly sweet voice.

I turned quickly to see a lady seated alone – a lady of about thirty, with exceedingly handsome eyes, who looked at me as though I had been her very dear friend.

'You were about to pass me,' she said accusingly. 'Don't tell me you did not know me. Why should we not shake hands – at least once in fifteen years?'

I shook hands with her at once. I took a chair opposite her at the table. I summoned with my eyebrows a hovering waiter. The lady was philandering with an orange ice. I ordered a *crème de menthe*. Her hair was reddish bronze. You could not look at it, because you could not look away from her eyes. But you were conscious of it as you are conscious of sunset while you look into the profundities of a wood at twilight.

'Are you sure you know me?' I asked.

'No,' she said, smiling, 'I was never sure of that.'

'What would you think,' I said, a little anxiously, 'if I were to tell you that my name is Edward Pinkhammer, from Cornopolis, Kansas.'

'What would I think?' she repeated, with a merry glance. 'Why, that you had not brought Mrs Bellford to New York with you, of course. I do wish you had. I would have liked to see Marian.' Her voice lowered slightly – 'You haven't changed much, Elwyn.'

I felt her wonderful eyes searching mine and my face more closely.

'Yes, you have,' she amended, and there was a soft, exultant note in her latest tones; 'I see it now. You haven't forgotten. You haven't forgotten for a year or a day or an hour. I told you you never could.'

I poked my straw anxiously in the *crème de menthe.*

'I'm sure I beg your pardon,' I said, a little uneasy at her gaze. 'But that is just the trouble. I have forgotten. I've forgotten everything.'

She flouted my denial. She laughed deliciously at something she seemed to see in my face.

'I've heard of you at times,' she went on. 'You're quite a big lawyer out West – Denver, isn't it, or Los Angeles? Marian must be very proud of you. You knew, I suppose, that I married six months after you did. You may have seen it in the papers. The flowers alone cost two thousand dollars.'

She had mentioned fifteen years. Fifteen years is a long time.

'Would it be too late,' I asked somewhat timorously, 'to offer you congratulations?'

'Not if you dare do it,' she answered, with such fine intrepidity that I was silent, and began to crease patterns on the cloth with my thumbnail.

'Tell me one thing,' she said, leaning towards me rather eagerly – 'a thing I have wanted to know for many years – just from a woman's curiosity, of course – have you ever dared since that night to touch, smell or look at white roses – at white roses wet with rain and dew?'

I took a sip of *crème de menthe.*

'It would be useless, I suppose,' I said, with a sigh, 'for me to repeat that I have no recollection at all about these things. My memory is completely at fault. I need not say how much I regret it.'

The lady rested her arms upon the table, and again her eyes disdained my words and went travelling by their own route direct to my soul. She laughed softly, with a strange quality in the sound – it was a laugh of happiness – yes, and of content – and of misery. I tried to look away from her.

'You lie, Elwyn Bellford,' she breathed blissfully. 'Oh, I know you lie!'

I gazed dully into the ferns.

'My name is Edward Pinkhammer,' I said. 'I came with the delegates to the Druggists' National Convention. There is a movement on foot for arranging a new position for the bottles of tartrate of antimony and tartrate of potash, in which, very likely, you would take little interest.'

A shining landau stopped before the entrance. The lady rose. I took her hand, and bowed.

'I am deeply sorry,' I said to her, 'that I cannot remember. I could explain, but fear you would not understand. You will not concede Pinkhammer; and I really cannot at all conceive of the – the roses and other things.'

'Good-bye, Mr Bellford,' she said, with her happy, sorrowful smile, as she stepped into her carriage.

I attended the theatre that night. When I returned to my hotel, a quiet man in dark clothes, who seemed interested in rubbing his finger-nails with a silk handkerchief, appeared, magically, at my side.

'Mr Pinkhammer,' he said casually, giving the bulk of his attention to his forefinger, 'may I request you to step aside with me for a little conversation? There is a room here.'

'Certainly,' I answered.

He conducted me into a small, private parlour. A lady and a gentleman were there. The lady, I surmised, would have been unusually good-looking had her features not been clouded by an expression of keen worry and fatigue. She was of a style of figure and possessed colouring and features that were agreeable to my fancy. She was in a travelling-dress; she fixed upon me an earnest look of extreme anxiety, and pressed an unsteady hand to her bosom. I think she would have started forward, but the gentleman arrested her movement with an authoritative motion of his hand. He then came, himself, to meet me. He was a man of forty, a little grey about the temples, and with a strong, thoughtful face.

'Bellford, old man,' he said cordially, 'I'm glad to see you again. Of course we know everything is all right. I warned you, you know, that you were overdoing it. Now, you'll go back with us, and be yourself again in no time.'

I smiled ironically.

'I have been "Bellforded" so often,' I said, 'that it has lost its edge. Still, in the end, it may grow wearisome. Would you be willing at all to entertain the hypothesis that my name is Edward Pinkhammer, and that I never saw you before in my life?'

Before the man could reply a wailing cry came from the woman. She sprang past his detaining arm. 'Elwyn!' she sobbed, and cast herself upon me, and clung tight. 'Elwyn,' she cried again, 'don't break my heart. I am your wife – call my name once – just once! I could see you dead rather than this way.'

I unwound her arms respectfully, but firmly.

'Madam,' I said severely, 'pardon me if I suggest that you accept a resemblance too precipitately. It is a pity,' I went on, with an amused laugh, as the thought occurred to me, 'that this Bellford and I could not be kept side by side upon the same shelf like tartrates of sodium and antimony for purposes of identification. In order to understand the allusion,' I concluded airily, 'it may be necessary for you to keep an eye on the proceedings of the Druggists' National Convention.'

The lady turned to her companion, and grasped his arm.

'What is it, Doctor Volney? Oh, what is it?' she moaned.

He led her to the door.

'Go to your room for a while,' I heard him say. 'I will remain and talk with him. His mind? No, I think not – only a portion of the brain. Yes, I am sure he will recover. Go to your room and leave me with him.'

The lady disappeared. The man in dark clothes also went outside, still manicuring himself in a thoughtful way. I think he waited in the hall.

'I would like to talk with you a while, Mr Pinkhammer, if I may,' said the gentleman who remained.

'Very well, if you care to,' I replied, 'and will excuse me if I take it comfortably; I am rather tired.' I stretched myself upon a couch by a window and lit a cigar. He drew a chair near by.

'Let us speak to the point,' he said soothingly. 'Your name is not Pinkhammer.'

'I know that as well as you do,' I said coolly. 'But a man must have a name of some sort. I can assure you that I do not extravagantly admire the name of Pinkhammer. But when one christens one's self, suddenly the fine names do not seem to suggest themselves. But suppose it had been Scheringhausen or Scroggins! I think I did very well with Pinkhammer.'

'Your name,' said the other man seriously, 'is Elwyn C. Bellford. You are one of the first lawyers in Denver. You are suffering from an attack of aphasia, which has caused you to forget your identity. The cause of it was over-application to your profession, and, perhaps, a life too bare of natural recreation and pleasures. The lady who has just left the room is your wife.'

'She is what I would call a fine-looking woman,' I said, after a judicial pause. 'I particularly admire the shade of brown in her hair.'

'She is a wife to be proud of. Since your disappearance, nearly two weeks ago, she has scarcely closed her eyes. We learned that you were in New York through a telegram sent by Isidore Newman, a travelling man from Denver. He said that he had met you in an hotel here, and that you did not recognize him.'

'I think I remember the occasion,' I said. 'The fellow called me "Bellford", if I am not mistaken. But don't you think it about time, now, for you to introduce yourself?'

'I am Robert Volney – Doctor Volney. I have been your close friend for twenty years, and your physician for fifteen. I came with Mrs Bellford to trace you as soon as we got the telegram. Try, Elwyn, old man – try to remember!'

'What's the use to try!' I asked, with a little frown. 'You say you are a physician. Is aphasia curable? When a man loses his memory, does it return slowly, or suddenly?'

'Sometimes gradually and imperfectly; sometimes as suddenly as it went.'

'Will you undertake the treatment of my case, Doctor Volney?' I asked.

'Old friend,' said he, 'I'll do everything in my power, and will have done everything that science can do to cure you.'

'Very well,' said I. 'Then you will consider that I am your patient. Everything is in confidence now – professional confidence.'

'Of course,' said Doctor Volney.

I got up from the couch. Someone had set a vase of white roses on the centre table – a cluster of white roses freshly sprinkled and fragrant. I threw them far out of the window, and then I laid myself upon the couch again.

'It will be best, Bobby,' I said, 'to have this cure happen suddenly. I'm rather tired of it all, anyway. You may go now and bring Marian in. But, oh, Doc,' I said, with a sigh, as I kicked him on the shin – 'good old Doc – it was glorious!'

(*c.* 1900)

FRIGYES KARINTHY

Frigyes Karinthy (1888–1938) was the Hungarian humorous writer who in 1916 produced a sequel to *Gulliver's Travels*, which made a more cheerful traveller's tale than Swift's. At ten past seven on the evening of 10 March 1935, Karinthy was taking tea at the Café Central on the Egyetemtér in Budapest, at his usual table by the window facing the University Library, when he heard the rumbling, reverberating, rising and fading din of a passing train. He stared out, puzzled. There were no trains anywhere around in Budapest. Four times the noise was repeated. Perhaps it was some new means of locomotion in the streets? Sitting in the same seat the next day, he heard another train pass. 'This time I did not turn towards the window, for I knew that my own tympanum was to blame.' It was the first symptom of the cerebral tumour which brought him, a month later, into the care of neurosurgeon Professor Olivecrona in Stockholm. This account of the operation on his skull under local anaesthetic has the enviable detachment of an intelligent martyr.

From A Journey Round My Skull

AFTER THIS ANNOUNCEMENT I appear to have sunk into a deep sleep, for I can remember nothing more about that evening, nor did I wake up during the night. I slept for ten hours on end and awoke next morning to find that I was being wheeled along the corridor. I was not at all drowsy, in fact my mind was abnormally clear and rational. I had not the slightest sensation of fear or any other emotion. It was the typical early morning mood when one has shaken off the night and its mysteries, and looks at the world with an almost ironical detachment. A day or two ago I had a glimpse from outside of the operating theatre to which I was now being taken. There was so large a No. 13 on the door that, half blind as I was, I could see it distinctly. I lay on my back, looking at the ceiling and waiting in the midst of a whiteness that was almost painful. People were walking close to me. I heard them speaking to one another in low tones, and their whispering struck me as distinctly comical. What could it be they were whispering about, and why had they to be so discreet about it? They had not brought me here to be discreet with me. . . . I could see a white coat approaching, but I watched it only out of the corner of my eye, as I felt no curiosity about the face. They were wheeling me into the theatre now. Four hands laid hold of me by the feet and head and placed me on a narrow table like an ironing-board. They proceeded to turn me over on to my stomach, and fitted my head into an oval hollow, so as to allow of my breathing. I knew that I was to remain for hours in the same attitude, and I tried to find a comfortable position for my face and nose. Before settling down I spied out the land. To right and left of me I could just make out a corner of the sheet. Hardly anything else was visible. I stretched out my arms beside me.

They had begun to whisper once more above my head, but in a more decided tone. This was followed by another silence. I felt a cold touch of metal on the nape of my neck. A muffled whirring sound told me that they were shaving my head. This time the clippers did not stop short at the back, as when the barber uses them to smarten one up behind. They ran the whole length of my skull, removing the hair in long swathes. Afterwards, I felt them soaping my head, but by the time the razor came into play I was already bald.

For some minutes I could hear only the sound of footsteps. Then I felt a slight prick on the top of my head. No doubt they were giving me an injection. I wondered if the Professor had arrived. He probably had, because out of the corner of my eye I now saw two white coats moving. I felt them place some sort of blunt instrument against my head. This looked like the real thing. . . .

There was an infernal scream as the steel plunged into my skull. It sank more and more rapidly through the bone, and the pitch of its scream became louder and more piercing every second. I had just time to say to myself that it must be the electric trephine. They needn't have bothered to be so discreet about their whispering . . . ! My head throbbed and roared like a thousand-horse-power engine suddenly starting up. It thundered as if the infernal regions had opened or the earth were quaking. I never had a chance to think whether it was hurting me or not. Suddenly, there was a violent jerk, and the noise stopped. Having penetrated the skull the point was revolving freely in a space that offered no resistance. I felt a warm, silent rush of liquid inside my head, as if the blood were flowing *inwards* from the hole which had been made.

The silence lasted only a moment. An inch or so further on, the trephine struck into the skull and began again. I observed this second perforation more coldly, for it no longer came as a surprise. Again the trephine shot through the skull, and again the noise stopped. Once more, the blood seemed to rush inwards. Then I had the sensation that they were fumbling about with tubes. I wondered what was happening. Were there to be no more perforations? I heard people hurrying backwards and forwards. The two white coats had disappeared. Suddenly, the operating table began to move.

I was being gently wheeled through open doors and along passages. We went into two lifts, one of which took us up and the other down. I saw the carpet sliding past under my face, and wondered where I was being taken. An iron door closed. The freshness of the air suggested that it must be a large room.

More whispers and footsteps. Someone turned me on to my side and fixed my head. Photographic plates were lowered from the ceiling in front of my face. A violet light shone, followed by darkness and then by the light again. They turned me on to my back and fixed my head in another position. I was in the X-ray room. There were so many curtains, hangings and transverse beams attached to the ceiling that it looked like the back stage of a theatre. Everything was neatly and elegantly lowered from the ceiling as required. On the floor there was no trace of instruments or of the appliances used by this modern Inquisition. I was back once more in the taciturn, smiling Dr Lysholm's department. The perforations in my skull had therefore been made so that fresh photographs could be taken. They had drained the fluid from my brain cavities, and had filled them with air. That explained all the fumbling I had been conscious of. The actual opening of my skull had still to come. For a long time they kept turning me over, placing me in new positions and photographing me afresh. I began to wonder how long it was all going to last. Occasionally I caught sight of whole figures as they passed, but I saw nothing of Lysholm. One quarter of an hour went by after another.

At last I heard the table creak as they began to wheel me back to the operating theatre. Corridors, lifts, and corridors again. . . . They closed the door of the theatre, and I felt them wheel me under the lamp.

Several minutes passed. No doubt they were examining the photographs. When they came up to me I was lying on my stomach again with my face in the hollow. Someone made my head firm by fixing broad plaster bands over my temples. He pulled them tight and attached them to the edge of the table, so that my head should be perfectly rigid, as if bound to the guillotine. Looking down, I saw a basin under my head, and I could see that as yet there was nothing in it. I felt them tightening the straps by which my hands and feet were to be secured. I tried to move the extremities of my limbs, but they refused to give a millimetre. I could not make the slightest movement of any kind. It was going to be hard work to stand it. I began breathing regularly, to a calm, even rhythm.

There was a fumbling movement about my neck and down my back. This time I knew what was happening, for I had seen it done myself. The nurses were arranging cloths around the area to be operated on. The Professor must be washing his hands, but I could not hear the splashing of water. Perhaps he was talking meanwhile to the other doctors. While I was being photographed he had surely lighted a cigarette in the next room and had laid the stub prudently on the edge of the ash-tray as soon as I was brought back. Afterwards, they would hand him his rubber gloves, put the sterilized gauze over his mouth, and attach the little electric lamp to his forehead.

Dead silence. I felt a succession of little pricks in a circle. Get on – that's enough now! My skin isn't so sensitive as all that. It didn't hurt me, but I distinctly felt the sharp point describe a wide circle on my head. It went over the same path a second time. Then, I felt one long horizontal incision at the back of my neck, though this did not hurt me, either. I heard the tinkle of forceps being jumbled up together and then being handled separately. This went on for a long while. I tried to see what was going on, and managed to make out an area as large as a handkerchief at the bottom of the white coat moving in front of me. It was bespattered with black spots like a speckled handkerchief. Of course, blood spouted from the arteries in jerks, instead of flowing evenly as from the veins. . . . I felt soft gestures, as if my flesh were being opened and folded back. The skull was certainly exposed by now, and the aponeurosis had contracted on to the nape of my neck. For the third time I heard the trephine strike my skull.

'Well, bye-bye, Frici!' I said aloud, and it did not surprise me that no one answered.

The noise was now more infernal and continuous than ever. I began to wonder if they couldn't get through the skull, and, in my anxiety, I stiffened my neck, as if I ought to be co-operating with them and holding myself rigid under the impact of the trephine. Otherwise, I felt that the skull might split down the whole of its length. . . . The roar of the trephine completely deafened me. After a while the noise seemed to become a little less strident, as if they were enlarging the aperture already made. At last, it stopped altogether.

Yes, it had actually stopped at last. And high time, too! Don't you think that's enough, Professor? What I mean is. . . . It was more than enough for me, I can tell you! I was in an arrogant, almost bellicose mood and completely conscious. A violent contempt for myself swept over me.

There was a sudden jerk, as if he had seized the opening with a pair of forceps. It was followed by a straining sensation, a feeling of pressure, a cracking sound, and a terrific wrench. . . . Something broke with a dull noise. After a moment it began all over again. A straining sensation, a feeling of pressure, a cracking sound, and a terrific wrench. . . . This process was repeated many times. Each cracking sound reminded me of taking the lid off a jam-jar, while the process as a whole was like splitting open a wooden packing-case, plank by plank. The Professor seemed to be working downwards towards the back of my head, breaking off great pieces of bone as he went. The last one of all seemed so far down my neck that it felt like the topmost vertebra. For a long time it obstinately refused to give way, but at last he managed to wrench it out.

The brutality of the operation had begun to work me up into a frenzy. I abandoned myself to it with a savage voluptuousness, and longed to help him in his task. Gasping for breath, I urged him on with secret exhortations. A veritable fury of destruction seized hold of me. Give it socks! I wanted to shout. Break it up! Smash away! Bust it to bits! Now go for the vertebra! That's it! And again! Catch hold of it harder, man! Twist it round, can't you? You've got to break it! That's the way – it's coming! It's come! Now the next one! Smash into it, butchers! . . . I was struggling for my breath. Everything had gone red in front of my eyes. If I had had an axe or a lump of iron in my hand I should have hit out with it and smashed up myself and everyone else, with the wild recklessness of a maniac.

In the midst of my rage I heard a gentle, comforting human voice. Its effect on me was like that of a cool hand on a madman's forehead, or like the calmly lifted sword of a Crusader quelling some African pagan.

'*Wie fühlen Sie sich jetzt?*'

Could it be Olivecrona's voice? It must have been, although I did not recognize him, for never before or since has it seemed to me so gentle and encouraging – so full of wise sympathy and kindliness. Was *this* his real nature, or was it just because the gauze softened his voice? I felt profoundly ashamed of myself. At the same moment my open head began to hurt. I was surprised to hear my lips form a polite, embarrassed answer, instead of swearing at the pain.

'*Danke, Herr Professor, . . . es geht gut!*'

After this my mood underwent a change. Once the trephining of the skull was over there ensued a relative silence. But I did not find this silence reassuring. A feeling of weakness came over me, and at the same instant a sudden fear. Good God – I mustn't lose consciousness! What had the Professor said to my wife? 'I don't administer a general anaesthetic to Europeans, for the risk is twenty-five per cent less if a patient remains conscious.' So there *was* something in it after all – we were really co-operating. I had to look after my side of the business, as he was looking after his. It might all depend on thousandths of a millimetre. The moment I lost consciousness I should probably lose my life.

I had to be careful what I was doing. I must concentrate my attention and mechanically produce thoughts which were coherent and sensible. Whatever happened, I had to remain conscious. Let me see, what was the position? I was awake, I knew where I was, and that I was being operated on. At that very moment, in all probability, they were opening the cerebral membrane. That was quite a straightforward job – just a little slit and an application of forceps here and there, like a dressmaker fitting clips on her material. By a logical, yet unexpected process, I thought of Cushing's operation in the amateur film. Yes, that had been a nice, clean piece of work. I remembered saying, 'It looks like the kitchen of a luxury hotel, with the chef in his white coat cleaning a sheep's brains to make croquettes of them.' No, that was an absurd idea. . . . Something better, quickly! What could I think about? Ah yes, that would be an idea. If I could remember where I put my fountain-pen in the drawer of my bed table, I should know I was still conscious. No, that wasn't any good, either. I'd rather try . . . I'd try repeating . . .

that Hungarian ballad. Yes, if I tried the ballad, it would help me to measure time as well, for it lasted a quarter of an hour from beginning to end. Anyhow, that would be something gained. I accordingly began: 'The Knight Pázmány strode up and down, In his gloomy castle hall . . .'

'Wie fühlen Sie sich jetzt?'
'Danke, Herr Professor . . . es geht . . .'

This time it was not my voice at all. I heard someone answer in a high-pitched, quavering tone that came from far away in the distance. What was the use of speaking like that? I'd rather not answer at all. It wasn't worth frightening myself for nothing.

Besides, we ought to be nearing the end now. However long had I been lying strapped on the table? My hands and feet had gone completely numb. Why didn't they loosen the straps a little? Just a shade would be enough, but that shade would make all the difference. Did they think I'd throw myself about or upset the table? It was all a lot of rot! If they didn't undo them my arms and legs would be bursting soon. They'd die of suffocation. . . .

Once more there was a sound of pumping and draining, and I could hear the drip, drip of a liquid. How much longer were these gentlemen going to fumble about in my skull? They saw how quiet and well-behaved I was keeping. How long, then, did they propose to go on with their scratching and manipulating? Couldn't they do me the honour now and again of telling me what they were doing with my head? After all, I had been invited to this party, too. . . . I should be most interested to know how much longer they thought of using my brain for their soft, woolly fumblings.

Yes, *I* should be interested to know. *I* . . .

The fellow lying here on the table. . . . After all, those gentlemen and I had never been and would never again be on such confidential terms with one another as we were at that moment, for I knew that they had their fingers in my brain. They had been draining off some more fluid to get at their objective, and now they were making my brain ready for the assault. Yes, it was my brain. I fancied it must be throbbing now. . . .

Pain? No, I had no pain.

Although my brain didn't hurt at all, it did hurt me when one of the instruments fell on to the glass slab with a sharp, metallic sound. A certain idea passing through my mind hurt me, too. It had nothing to do with my present situation, but I could not get rid of the idea. It kept forcing itself on my notice, and the attempt to thrust it back was painful.

No, my brain did not hurt. Perhaps it was more exasperating this way than if it had. I would have preferred it to hurt me. More terrifying than any actual pain was the fact that my position seemed *impossible*. It was impossible for a man to be lying here with his skull open and his brain exposed to the outer world – impossible for him to lie here and live. It was impossible, incredible, indecent, for him to remain alive – and not merely alive, but conscious and in his right mind. It wasn't decent or natural – just as it wasn't natural . . . when at an altitude . . . of fifteen thousand feet . . . you had a very heavy object . . . very heavy . . . and it didn't fall . . . as it ought to do. . . . No, not that. . . . What was it, gentlemen, that the duckling said . . . in its quiet, apologetic way . . . when they came . . . to wring its neck . . . ? 'Don't carve me with that knife. . . . It might bring you . . . bad luck . . . !'

Stop that whispering, gentlemen! I could hear everything you say, if I weren't ashamed to listen. . . . They were whispering continually, faster and faster. Faster and faster they kept whispering – and more and more obstinately. They were getting quite shameless about it. Don't whisper like that . . . ! It isn't done, I tell you. It's not my fault. I feel ashamed of the whole thing. Get on, get on, can't you! It's time you covered up my naked brain. . . .

This must have happened at the moment when they removed the band from Olivecrona's forehead, and when, thrusting a micro-lamp into the cavity, he was able to see, and even to touch, the tumour. There it was, growing on the slightly inflamed right side of the cerebellum, under the second lobe of the *pia mater*. It was now eleven o'clock, and the operation had so far been going on for two hours.

(1937)

JAMES BRIDIE

James Bridie (Osborne Henry Mavor, 1888–1951) of Glasgow savoured regular West End success from 1930 with *The Anatomist* – which was about Dr Robert Knox in Edinburgh and the sack-'em-up men Burke and Hare – until *Mr Bolfry* with Alastair Sim in 1943 and *Daphne Laureola* with Dame Edith Evans in 1949. Bridie wrote forty plays of wisdom, charm, gaiety and wit, but perceiving the financial fragility of the theatre remained Professor of Medicine in Glasgow.

The Umbilicus was a lecture addressed in 1939 to the Glasgow Southern Medical Society. Bridie submitted it afterwards to the *British Medical Journal*, whose Editor suffered from a widespread myopia of seeing the serious only in the solemn, and only the frivolous in the comic. Bridie demurred that the *BMJ* had printed it 'in that part of the journal devoted principally to discussion of mileage, branch meetings, the deaths and marriages of doctors, and the birth of their offspring, and learned discussions on the filling-up of forms. Mr Bridie was rather hurt at this location of his essay. He intended it as a scientific contribution.'

The intelligent reader will recognise it as such, and will be aided in its appreciation by reading it while contemplating his or her own.

From The Umbilicus

A VALUED COLLEAGUE of mine was accustomed, when the stream of his learning from time to time grew fitful, to entertain his students by drawing round the umbilicus of a patient a little blue circle and to question them and expatiate upon that remarkable structure. He confined himself, I think, to its 'surgical' aspects; that is to say, to the view of the umbilicus as a possible object of mutilation; for that is what I conceive to be the difference between the 'medical' and the 'surgical' aspects of any condition or structure whatever. At the very threshold of our discussion, then, the umbilicus teaches us something of value. We must have pondered many a time as students of medicine why the part should be considered equal to the whole; why a branch of therapeutics should be dignified by a chair and a department and an equal number of lectures to those delivered on the art of medicine itself.

My definition of the 'surgical' aspect is a neat and compact answer to these questionings; for, indeed, everything in this world varies according to the spirit in which we approach it. To the householder, the door of his safe is a protection to his property; to the burglar, an obstacle. To the poet, the dreamer, and the painter a landscape may have one meaning; to the prospector for minerals and precious metals, another. To the sculptor, the umbilicus is a graceful and exact focal point from which structure radiates; to the surgeon it is a target.

To us, as physicists, chemists, biologists, anatomists, physiologists, pathologists, physicians, and philosophers – for we are trained in all these arts – the umbilicus has wider aspects. The approaches of biophysics and metaphysics, of eschatology and skatology are equally familiar and open to us. It is with some of these aspects I wish to detain you to-night.

The umbilicus is a cicatricial structure situated – in classical sculpture – four-tenths of the way between the xiphisternum and the os pubis. On the modern abdomen this measurement and the depression or prominence of the object vary between wide limits. Its general appearance varies with the individual and with the sex of the individual. That of the heroine of the *Song of Songs* was described as resembling 'a round goblet which wanted not liquor'. Others, on the other hand, as all of us have had the opportunity of observing for ourselves, are no such matter.

It contains, possibly, the vestiges of the umbilical vessels and of that remarkable structure, the urachus. And that is all *Gray's Anatomy* has to say about the umbilicus from the strictly anatomical point of view, except that it is the largest hole in the linea alba, but that, in the adult, it is obliterated, bunged up, stopped, no longer so much as an aperture.

In anatomy, then, it is little better than a mere landmark. When we assume the spectacles of the embryologist, however, it takes on great importance. If one may be allowed a poetical image, it is all that remains of the stem that bound us to the parental stalk. It is a reminder that we have been plucked and must sooner or later die. It might be said that when the stem is severed we cease to live in any true sense. We may be ornamental like roses or useful like cabbages, but only for a little. Our dissolution has begun. . . .

If you wish me to be more precise, practical and professional on the subject of the umbilicus, I remind you that it is the site of a large series of pathological conditions. These, in the adult, include:

1. Hernia.
2. Warts.
3. Naevi.
4. Polypi.
5. Epitheliomata.
6. Calculi.
7. Eczema.
8. Fistulae, urinary, biliary, and faecal, congenital and acquired. . . .

As you have seen from the daily press, a monster compaign is about to be started to raise funds for a Hospital for Diseases of the Umbilicus. With it is to be associated a university lectureship, which, it is hoped, may one day be raised to the dignity of a chair and a voice in the deliberations of the Senate.

Funds for the hospital will be raised by borrowing from the bank; by collecting pennies from the working-classes; by inducing the dying rich to make wills in favour of the hospital; by organising balls and fancy-dress processions; by blackmailing industrialists; by appointing wealthy persons to the board of management; by engaging an actress to weep into the microphone; and by another thousand or so traditionally dignified methods. The balance sheet will, I fear, be faked. Nurses will be persuaded to work for nothing by intimidating them with examination papers on physiology, anatomy, pathology, and omphalology into believing that they are being trained for their profession. After a ridiculously short time, however, it will be possible to pay them as much as one pound per week. Omphalologists will, of course, tumble over one another for the privilege of serving their masters, the board of governors, and, indirectly, the general public. The status, you see, will be valuable.

The status will be further improved when the Royal College of Omphalology gets under way. The omphalologists who get in on the ground floor will become Fellows of the Royal College of Umbilical and Urachal Surgeons (FRUUS), and membership will be open to specialists who submit themselves for examination and pay a considerable fee. . . .

Medicine nowadays is so enormously complicated that it is only possible to master one department of it thoroughly. This truth has, unfortunately, percolated out to the general public. They – or such of them as can afford to pay a fee in guineas – quite reasonably demand the best skill available for the curing of whatever disorder afflicts whatever part of their cubic content. 'The Drama's laws the

Drama's patrons give. And those who live to please must please to live,' if I may borrow a figure from a profession of which I have also some knowledge. 'Medicine's laws, Medicine's patrons give.' It is almost impossible to reach the top of one's profession – that is to say, to have a butler, a Rolls-Royce, and a shooting – if one forgets this cardinal rule. . . .

I have used the phrase – 'the study of the umbilicus'. As you know, a cult of Yogis on the Himalayas devotes a considerable period of its life to contemplating its own navels, repeating at the same time 'Om mane padme hum', or some such helpful phrase. We may take this dignified occupation as symbolic of the attitude of the Thinker in all ages and climates. To persist in this exercise produces certain obvious clinical effects. The body becomes bent and crumpled, the forehead protrudes, and the feet and hands tend to become superimposed one upon the other. In short, we get that well-recognised foetal attitude so characteristic of the professional speculative philosopher. The desire to return to the maternal cavern, to foetal life, is sublimated into physical fact. The philosopher becomes a foetus. And who shall say that he is wrong? The foetal state is a reposeful state, and if there is one thing for which the human anatomy was specially constructed it was for repose.

The phrase 'erect posture' has blinded research to this admirable instance of adaptation. Given a flat surface, man can oppose to it the three flat surfaces of his temporal bone, his scapula, and his iliac bone, with the springing cushions of serratus magnus, his vastas externus, and his peroneal muscles. Or he can lie on his back, a posture long sustained by no other uncarapaced animal except in death. It is little wonder that his sleep is the amazement of the animal kingdom. It is superior to the long unconsciousness of hibernating animals. They curl their vegetative organs into the smallest bulk and lie in an uncomfortable tight knot in a condition near to death. How different is man! Man's great lungs heave and blow, his noble heart thuds merrily, and his marvellous bowels continue in gentle peristalsis, his brain is the house of a thousand lovely fancies, his liver, his blood, his glands, transform the dead cells of his food into the living elements of his body and slay his myriad of airy foes. He is badly constructed for locomotion by road or by tree. The slowest fish swims faster. He is adapted primarily for rest.

This and much more to the same purpose we can learn from the contemplation of the umbilicus or navel.

The word 'navel' is itself of absorbing interest. It means the hub of a wheel. Round the umbilicus we rotate. We are both centripetal and centrifugal. At moments we are drawn towards our natural centre and at moments we fly away from it. It may have occurred to you that the centrifugal element has seriously influenced this address. Let us concentrate on the centre of things.

Undoubtedly the most impressive name for the umbilicus is the Greek word *omphalos*. Professor Popochik, the etymologist, tells us that omphalos means the drawing together of the band of the helmet that held the crest or plume. The pleasant picture of a spray of feathers springing from the umbilicus of each of us need not detain us. I wish to draw your attention to the sonority of the word 'omphalos', and to regret, in passing, that Celsus thought fit to change the noble-sounding name of a noble organ to the pedestrian word 'umbilicus'. . . .

I do not suggest that the gravity of the doctor ought to be or is pure artistry and play-acting. You all know that beautiful picture by Luke Fildes which shows a middle-aged man scratching his beard and wondering what the devil is the matter with a sick child he is expected to cure. That is the master-condition of all honest men who live by the practice of medicine – 'What the devil is the matter?' they ask themselves continually from the lobby to the bedside; from the bedside to the post-mortem room and after that. When that questioning of the soul is answered or ignored, we know that the devil himself has taken the wicked doctor into his keeping.

We unfortunate quacks are confronted with a concatenation of living, dying, and functioning cells so complicated that it is impossible to understand the simplest of the processes concerned. To make matters worse, these concatenations are influenced arbitrarily by indefinable things called the will and the mind. Every single one of the pretensions by which we make a living is unfounded. Even our plain men of their hands, the surgeons, pretend to a manual skill few of them possess. How many of them could make a chest of drawers or a pair of trousers? We must face the fact that our way of living is infiltrated with lies and false pretences. Our only defence, and it is a good one, is that we do not spare ourselves in bringing some sort of shabby comfort to the sick and dying; and that most of us are animated in greater or less degree by altruism. Altruism is a very rare quality indeed, and can be claimed as an integral part of its regulations by no other close corporation. This goodness slightly tips the scale in our favour. It outweighs our lies and our thefts; our false prophecies and our witchcraft.

It is small wonder that, in this welter of bewilderment and deceit, we strive from time to time to grasp some shred of exact knowledge. We are empirics and know it, but we like to think that in some respects we are better than the bone-setter. This is what leads us to focus our earnest attention on some such organ as the thyroid or the umbilicus. This is what leads us to become, as it were, Masters of the Umbilicus. This is what leads us to listen with close regard to such a lecture as I am delivering to-night on that specialised and apparently insignificant structure.

There are degrees, as you know, of ignorance. You and I are now almost in a position to smile gently at the poor artisan who had recently moved into a Corporation house and decided to indulge himself in a bath. While he was voluptuously sensing for the first time the sting of the hot water on his body surface, he noticed his umbilicus. After a period of consideration he got out of the bath, fetched a screwdriver, and unscrewed his umbilicus, with the most catastrophic results. Yet we are wrong to despise him. We are accustomed to pride ourselves on our courageous feats of surgery. I have an uneasy feeling that the courage is on the side of the patient. Our artisan showed courage and embarked on his experiment with only a relatively smaller armament of understanding than many of our own pioneers. . . .

Here, too, the umbilicus can help us. That tight and tidy little knot may serve to remind us that we are neatly tied up parcels delivered in millions from the Universal Store. We must avoid claiming undue importance for any individual parcel, even if that parcel happens to be ourself. There is a temptation for any creature who seems obviously to be doing the work of the Almighty to imagine himself a god. This is particularly so in medicine, and an almost unavoidable error in the hospital physician or surgeon. He is surrounded by respectful and even adoring acolytes, and he holds the power of life and death over helpless persons. It is small wonder if he becomes, like the superintendent's dog, an orgulous animal. If he is to avoid madness he must stand aside from the business from time to time and deride himself and his colleagues.

(1939)

JOHN KEATS

John Keats (1795–1821) graces our anthology because he was a doctor. He was the son of a West Countryman, who became ostler of the Swan and Hoop at Moorgate in the City of London. Keats was born (prematurely) in Finsbury, and was schooled by the Revd John Clarke out in the country at Enfield. When he was eight, his father fell off a horse and killed himself. His mother swiftly remarried, separated, and went to live in Edmonton, another village to the north of London. She died in March 1810 of pulmonary tuberculosis, leaving John Keats in the care of a pair of guardians, who apprenticed him aged fifteen to the local surgeon, Mr Thomas Hammond. Four years later, his indentures were cancelled after a quarrel. On 1 October 1815 Keats became a student at Guy's Hospital, living like young Dickens in Borough, south of London Bridge. He qualified on 26 July 1816 as a Licenciate of the Society of Apothecaries (with credit).

Keats had then already a sonnet printed by Leigh Hunt in the *Examiner*. The December after achieving his LSA he published *On First Looking into Chapman's Homer*, after which medicine became an irrelevance. He had nursed his mother and his brother Tom, who in 1818 also died of tuberculosis. On 3 February 1820 Keats himself coughed up blood, making the wretched prognosis: 'I know the colour of that blood! It is arterial blood. I cannot be deceived in that colour. That drop of blood is my death warrant. I must die.' Which proved sadly correct beside the Spanish Steps in Rome a year later.

The magnificence of Keats's poems needs no mirroring. But here is one which he pencilled on the paper cover of a friend's *Syllabus of Chemistry Lectures* at Guy's.

Women, Wine, and Snuff

Give me women, wine and snuff
Until I cry out 'hold, enough!'
You may do so sans objection
Till the day of resurrection;
For bless my beard they aye shall be
My beloved Trinity.

(1815–16)

JOHANN SCHILLER

Johann Christoph Friedrich (*Ode to Joy*) von Schiller (1795–1805) was born in Württemberg, the son of an army surgeon. He suffered an unsettled childhood during the Seven Years War, and afterwards from the unreliability of his father's pay, contemplated the Church, was conscripted by his father's commander Duke Eugen into his new military academy at Ludwigsburg, was ordered to study law, which he hated. He escaped into medicine at Stuttgart, where he qualified in 1780, but, like Keats, was aware of functioning literary wings. Schiller was a regimental surgeon in Stuttgart when his revolutionary drama *Die Räuber* became a hit in Mannheim, whereupon he was commanded by the Duke to stop writing, fled, wrote the history of the Netherlands' liberation from the Spanish and in 1788 became a professor at Jena. In 1799 he moved to Weimar, where his friend Goethe was manager of the local theatre, and where he died aged forty-five from pulmonary tuberculosis. His lyrics for Beethoven have become familiar as the EC theme song. This verse, as casual as Keats's pencilled on a Guy's chemistry syllabus, is about physiognomists, who erroneously read character from the face. The 'science' started with Aristotle, and Charles Darwin was writing *The Expression of the Emotions in Man and Animals* even in 1872. The poem's argument is soundly applicable to many exhibitions of genuine learning.

Epitaph on a Certain Physiognomist

On ev'ry nose he rightly read
What intellects were in the head:
And yet – that he was not the one
By whom God meant it to be done,
This on his *own* he never read.

(Date unknown)

ROBERT BRIDGES

Robert Seymour Bridges OM (1844–1930) was the only doctor to become Poet Laureate. He was appointed in 1913, between Alfred Austin (who was a lawyer, and did not get into *The Oxford Book of English Verse*) and John Masefield OM (who was a sailor, and really did go butting through the Channel in the mad March days). Bridges went to Eton and Oxford and qualified at St Bartholomew's Hospital in the City of London. He became casualty physician to Bart's, then assistant physician at Great Ormond Street Children's Hospital and physician at the Great Northern Hospital near Holloway Gaol. He abandoned medicine aged thirty-eight and settled in Oxford to compose poetry, found the Society for Pure English, and keep Oxford University Press up to the mark over spelling, typefaces and printing. He is a poet too subtle and austere for the unfastidious reader (me), who finds him colourless and trite. He is best at Nature, befitting his training in a complex manifestation of it.

Anniversary

What is sweeter than new-mown hay,
Fresher than winds o'er-sea that blow,
Innocent above children's play.
Fairer and purer than winter snow,
Frolic as are the morns of May?
– If it should be what best I know!

What is richer than thoughts that stray
From reading of poems that smoothly flow . . . ?

'The summer trees are tempest-torn'

The summer trees are tempest-torn,
The hills are wrapped in a mantle wide
Of folding rain by the mad wind borne
Across the country side.

His scourge of fury is lashing down
The delicate-rankèd golden corn,
That never more shall rear its crown
And curtsey to the morn.

There shews no care in heaven to save
Man's pitiful patience, or provide
A season for the season's slave,
Whose trust hath toiled and died.

So my proud spirit in me is sad,
A wreck of fairer fields to mourn,
The ruin of golden hopes she had,
My delicate-rankèd corn.

(1890)

London Snow

When men were all asleep the snow came flying,
In large white flakes falling on the city brown,
Stealthily and perpetually settling and loosely lying,
Hushing the latest traffic of the drowsy town;
Deadening, muffling, stifling its murmurs failing;
Lazily and incessantly floating down and down:
Silently sifting and veiling road, roof and railing;
Hiding difference, making unevenness even,
Into angles and crevices softly drifting and sailing.

All night it fell, and when full inches seven
It lay in the depth of its uncompacted lightness,
The clouds blew off from a high and frosty heaven;
And all woke earlier for the unaccustomed brightness
Of the winter dawning, the strange unheavenly glare:
The eye marvelled – marvelled at the dazzling whiteness;
The ear hearkened to the stillness of the solemn air;
No sound of wheel rumbling nor of foot falling,
And the busy morning cries came thin and spare.
Then boys I heard, as they went to school, calling,
They gathered up the crystal manna to freeze
Their tongues with tasting, their hands with snowballing;
Or rioted in a drift, plunging up to the knees;
Or peering up from under the white-mossed wonder,
'O look at the trees!' they cried, 'O look at the trees!'
With lessened load a few carts creak and blunder,
Following along the white deserted way,
A country company long dispersed asunder:
When now already the sun, in pale display
Standing by Paul's high dome, spread forth below
His sparkling beams, and awoke the stir of the day.
For now doors open, and war is waged with the snow;
And trains of sombre men, past tale of number,
Tread long brown paths, as toward their toil they go:
But even for them awhile no cares encumber
Their minds diverted; the daily word is unspoken,
The daily thoughts of labour and sorrow slumber
At the sight of the beauty that greets them, for the charm they
Have broken.

(1880)

The Sleeping Mansion

As our car rustled swiftly
  along the village lane,
we caught sight for a moment
  of the old house again,

Which once I made my home in –
  ev'n as a soul may dwell
enamouring the body
  that she loveth so well:

But I long since had left it;
  what fortune now befals
finds me on other meadows
  by other trees and walls.

The place look'd blank and empty,
  a sleeper's witless face
which to his mind's enchantment
  is numb, and gives no trace.

And to that slumbering mansion
  was I come as a dream,
to cheer her in her stupor
  and loneliness extreme.

I knew what sudden wonder
  I brought her in my flight;
what rapturous joy possess'd her,
  what peace and soft delight.

(1921)

Dr Punch

Punch named the only clinical technique to have persisted since 1884:

FIRST LADY: What sort of doctor is he?
SECOND LADY: Oh, well, I don't know very much about his ability; but he's got a very good *bedside manner*!

Punch enjoyed an enduring professional relationship with doctors. They displayed each of Dicky Doyle's trademark covers – which, if you look, has Mr Punch at the bottom riding an ass, garlanded by and clutching at muslined girls, while contemplating concernedly his enormous erection – for month after month upon their waiting-room tables; while Punch amicably applied its ulnar process to their thoracic cages (as *Punch* would have put it).

LOCAL PRACTITIONER [to pretty wife, as he goes through his day-book and ledger]: Old Smith hasn't called me lately about his indigestion. You'd better ask him to dinner.
AMERICAN PHYSICIAN [in tails, to English ditto]: Now in Vienna they're first-rate at diagnosis; but, then, you see, they always make a point of confirming it by a post-mortem!
THE LADY KEROSINE DE COLZA [progressing, fan-waving, downstairs amid footmen]: I cannot tell you how pleased I am to meet you here, Dr Blenkinsop, and especially to go down to dinner with you.
DR BLENKINSOP [an eminent physician, much pleased]: You flatter me, I'm sure, Lady Kerosine!
LADY KEROSINE: Oh no! It's so nice to sit by somebody who can tell you what to eat, drink and avoid, you know!

Another stout party needing resuscitation.

Punch started on 17 July 1841. Later it invited favoured contributors to carve their initials on its vast dining-table, an honour cherished by those who grinned at honours. Only Mark Twain refused: two-thirds of Thackeray would suffice for him. *Punch* was the Nelson's Column of English humour, withstanding 150 years of intensifying erosion by the humour of newspapers, the wireless and television before it collapsed. Possibly the new proprietor, on passing the traditional Friday lunch party round the table, and hearing a sound of revelry not by night but by extremely late afternoon, rightly decided that its feeble circulation was incapable of further nourishment.

Punch had two Victorian doctors.

PERCIVAL LEIGH

Percival Leigh (1813–89), who signed as 'Fusbos', qualified in 1834 at St Bartholomew's Hospital, round the corner from the *Punch* office in Bouverie Street. A fellow-student at Bart's was John Leech (1817–64), son of a coffee-house owner, who studied medicine at his father's wish but abandoned it, unqualified, at his father's misfortunes. Leech drew for *Punch*'s issue No. 3, and soon for everything: who needs other memorial than Scrooge, forever crouched in night-cap in his bare room with his gruel over a meagre fire with a single candle, confronting pigtailed Marley's Ghost? Leech made £40,000 out of *Punch*. He was a close friend of Thackeray – they were at Charterhouse together and are now close together at Kensal Green.

Another fellow-student of Dr Leigh's was Sir James Paget, Serjeant Surgeon to Queen Victoria with two diseases named after him, who recorded Leigh as an admirable diagnostician. This was confirmed when Leigh – 'The Professor' at the *Punch* table – ordered a dramatist guest who complained laughingly of a sprained leg instantly to summon a cab, take to his bed and call his doctor, and within a month the man was gratifyingly dead. When Leigh was run over aged seventy, he thundered to the two house-surgeons in the accident ward, who were engrossed in his tibia, 'Drop that leg, you confounded blockheads!' and indicated the correct fracture. When his stuff grew senile, *Punch* still bought it and sent him proofs which were never published. He stayed at the table unbrokenly until his end.

> With what a shock it comes of yearning pain,
> The thought that we that presence ne'er again
> At the old board may see!

Punch wrote the next week. They don't sell magazines like that any more.

Leigh's big literary success was *Ye Manners and Customs of Ye Englyshe & Mr Pips Hys Diary*, illustrations by Dicky Doyle.

From Mr Pips Hys Diary

A DRAWYNGE ROOM DAY. SAYNTE IAMES HYS STREETE.

TO FEE THE Nobility and Gentry, and other great Company, go to the QUEEN'S Drawing-Room, with a Friend to St. James's Street, where did ftand in front of BOODLE'S Club-Houfe in the Rain, which was heavy, and fpoiled my Paris Hat, coft me twelve Shillings. But the Sight of the Show was almoft worth the Damage; for the Red and Blue Uniforms of the Army and Navy Officers, with their Orders on their Breafts, and their Cocked Hats and Plumes in their Laps, and the Ladies of Quality in their Silks and Satins of all Manner of Colours, and their Hair crowned with Oftrich Feathers, and fparkling with Pearls and Diamonds, did much delight me to behold. I do not remember that, when I was a Boy, I was ever more taken with a Pageant at Bartholomew Fair. Though I wifh I could have had as good a View of the Gentlefolks within the Carriages as I had of the Lackeys outfide, who, with their fupercilious Airs, and their Jackanapes Garb, did divert me more than ever. I do continually marvel at the enormous Calves of thofe Varlets, for which one might almoft think they were reared, like a fort of Cattle. Indeed, I fhould have believed that their Stockings were ftuffed, if I had not feen one of them wince when a Horfe chanced to lay hold of his leg.

(1849)

Everyday Victorian humour has survived less robustly than everyday Victorian cooking.

ALBERT SMITH

Pushy, bumptious, vulgar Albert Richard Smith (1816–60) was disliked round the *Punch* table, particularly by wit Douglas Jerrold, whom Smith threatened to horsewhip (it was only a toy whip). A Surrey doctor's son, Smith qualified at the Middlesex Hospital, shared digs with artist John Leech, and became a surgeon-dentist in Tottenham Court Road. In 1852 he turned his ascent of Mont Blanc into an 'Entertainment' at the Egyptian Hall, which 'made of Smith one of the lions of the day, and of his St Bernard, which had accompanied him, the most petted beast in the metropolis'. He produced popular novels in the Dickens genre. *The Adventures of Mr Ledbury* (1844) was followed by an equally rambling story containing this depiction of life before British Rail.

From The Struggles and Adventures of Christopher Tadpole

'MRS PEARCE IS better to-day, Sir,' observed Mr Mole [the doctor's assistant], looking at a list of patients. 'It was only a fright.'

'Let me see,' said the Doctor: 'the wind blew the cowl down the chimney into her room – did it not.'

'Yes, sir: and all her fear was that the baby would be born with a tin head that turned round, and a pointer dog on the top of it. But she's quite pacified now.'

'Well; that's a comfort,' said Dr Aston. 'Hush! what's the bell tolling for?'

'Not one of ours,' said Mr Mole: 'Kidge's I think.' (Mr Kidge was the opposition practitioner). 'He's killed Stevens' child at last, and they are going to bury it. I saw the coffin in Mr Tack's window last night. It's all blue and silver: so handsome that it's to be wrapped up in brown paper when it's buried.'

'Anything new at the Union House to-day, Mr Mole?'

'Nothing, Sir, but a tipsy tramp who broke the windows. I had his hair cut short, gave him some pills, and put him in a warm bath; and that frightened him so, that he ran away an hour afterwards, quite sober.'

The Doctor wrote his directions in the day-book; the medicines were made up: and then he sat down to tea with Mr Mole, at which meal they usually sought relaxation in pinning out butterflies, polishing pebbles, and such light work. And unless their services were again required, this lasted until supper. But, on this evening, soon after the candles were lighted, there was a bustle in the quiet street before the Doctor's house, unwonted at such an hour. A rude cart was driven up to the door, followed by some boys and workmen, and the surgery bell was rung somewhat hurriedly.

'Here's an accident, Sir,' said Mr Mole, as he answered the bell, and returned. 'They say a man's hurt on the railway at the cutting; and want you to come directly. They've sent a cart for you.'

Dr Aston went to the messenger: but finding from the locality that he could get to it across the fields upon foot, much sooner than by going round the road, he dismissed the man, and telling Mr Mole to look out his case of instruments and bring it with him, prepared to start.

'Ah!' said Mrs Grittles [the housekeeper], as she gave him his lantern: 'more of your instution scrapes. There'd never have been steam if it hadn't been for the littery lecturers.'

The Doctor could not help smiling at his housekeeper's noted aversion to science, as he took the light and set off with Mr Mole across the field contiguous to the town.

It was a dark night in the country: and when they got near the spot where the accident had occurred, it was as much as the Doctor could do to make out the way, for the railway in progress had entirely altered the face of the country. All the old landmarks – the trees, and rails, and gates – had been swept away: hills of loose earth, in which carriage wheels sank inches deep, rose where all had been a plain but a few months before: and entire headlands had disappeared, or formed the portals of yawning subterranean caverns, piercing the strata that had reposed above each other since the deluge, from which the fossil bones and shells belonging to the monsters of former oceans were once more brought to light, and the gaze of human eyes fell on them, possibly for the first time.

'Down here, Sir: this is the way; mind how you come,' said a man, who appeared to have been looking out for them and held up some burning fir-cones, which blazed and sputtered at the end of a branch, to light them.

They crossed a bank of earth, and then saw the intended line in a deep cutting, far below them; its direction marked by the glare of the coal fires, which were burning for the men to work by almost as far as the eye could reach, and throwing their gigantic shadows upon the walls of the mighty trench. The men were shouting to each other constantly: and this noise, coupled with the roaring of the masses of gravel that occasionally fell in, the clattering of the trams constantly passing on the rails now loosely laid down, and the rattling of the horses' harness, had a demoniacal effect, the more so that merely the outlines of the navigators in their rude dresses – and some with scarcely any at all – could be made out.

Dr Aston and his assistant followed their guide with some difficulty down the slope of the cutting, and then went along the rails to a small hovel, built at the side, of turf and boards, in which Rockey was lying; in fact, he had lived, or rather slept in it, during the time he had been working there. Some of the labourers were standing round; and they had brought one of the fire-cages to the door, which alone lighted the interior; beyond the comparatively feeble rays from the Doctor's lantern. As he came up they drew away and allowed him to enter.

The man was on the floor, kept there by the efforts of four of his comrades, beneath whose united grasp he was kicking and plunging to be released, swearing at the same time frightfully. There was a terrible gash across his temple, from which the blood had been flowing down his face, and his left hand was almost crushed. But in spite of this, his strength was marvellous, as he heaved up, every half-minute, notwithstanding all the power that bore against him; and as Dr Aston came in he fixed his glaring eyes upon him, but evidently without any consciousness.

'Wut!' he shouted in his convulsions. 'Wut! Smi*ler*! Hold hard! or I'll cut the liver out of you. Let him have his head; d— your stupid eyes, let him go! Hi!'

And he again poured out a string of oaths.

'Is he in liquor?' asked the Doctor.

'Well – you see we don't know, sir,' replied one of the men. 'He'd been adrinking with some of the navvies at the beer-shop before he went off with the trams; and when he got to the inclined plane they forgot to put the breaks on.'

'Then he was run over.'

'No – not exactly. The trams came upon the horse's legs and frightened him, and he knocked Rockey down. His pardner there knows about it, but he's raything gone.'

He pointed to a fellow who was leaning against the wall gazing heavily at the scene, and evidently intoxicated.

'Well, what do you know about this, my man,' asked Dr Aston.

'It's all right,' answered the fellow in thickened imperfect accents; it's all as right as a trivut. Who says it ain't?'

'Oh – I don't, I'm sure,' answered the Doctor, somewhat alarmed at the fierce manner in which the 'navvy' asked the last question.

'You're a gen'leman,' continued the man, 'Dr Aston – you know me, and I've know'd you long, and what I says is that a man's a man and who says he isn't? Ooray! Three cheers for Dr Aston. Three – cheers – for –'

And whilst he was speaking he settled down quietly upon the ground, and appeared to go off into a stertorous sleep immediately. The Doctor seeing there was no information to be got from that quarter, turned to the sufferer.

'Now stand aside, my good men,' he said. 'A little more light and a little air. Take his neckcloth off.'

One of the men untied the steaming crimson rag that was round his throat, and threw it on the ground.

'Mind, Bill,' said another: 'perhaps there's money in it. Now, only one of you look, and then we shall know who's got it, if there is. Suppose the Doctor takes it.'

Dr Aston undid the folds, and a small parcel fell from them. After untwisting several envelopes of paper, he turned out a small diamond buckle, of antique form.

'Precious stones,' observed one of the men. 'Lor! who'd a thought of Rockey having they about him.'

The Doctor placed the ornament in his pocket and turned to the wounded man; who was again struggling furiously, until every muscle appeared contracted into an iron cord.

'This is more than drunkenness,' he said: 'it is delirium. Stop: do not hold him so tight: he is getting quieter.'

The men relaxed their grasp; and the sufferer ceased swearing at the same minute, as a heavy stifling breathing, more like a snore, took the place of his imprecations.

'That was just like he was when we brought him in first,' said one of the men, 'until Bill Howard got the gin down his throat.'

'Why, you didn't do that, surely?' remarked the Doctor.

'We'd got nothink else,' answered the man.

'And how much did you give him?'

'Oh – not a pint; because there's the bottle; and I'd had a sup from it; and some was spilt. But we revived him at once.'

'Too much – didn't us, Bill?'

'I never see such a one to kick as he was,' replied the other. 'Look out: he's off again.'

'We must get him away from here before we can do anything,' said the Doctor. 'Have you a hurdle, or a shutter, or the tail-board of a cart, or anything you can carry him on?'

But whilst he was yet speaking, the wounded man, with extraordinary force, heaved up his body, almost in an arch – his head and feet alone resting on the ground, again entirely overcoming the power of the others to keep him down. His eyes glared at the bystanders until they appeared to be starting from his head: and with open mouth and protruding tongue he seemed about to break out into another volley of delirious blasphemy, when suddenly every muscle relaxed; a deep expiration, like that of a person who has held his breath for a long time, followed; and he lay still upon the ground.

'He is gone,' said Dr Aston, lifting up the hand, which, when he had felt for the pulse, fell passively back again. 'Now, you cannot leave the body here,' he added after a short pause. 'What will you do with it?'

(1848)

George Bernard Shaw

From 1902 to 1946, Professor Sir Almroth Wright headed the Inoculation Department at St Mary's Hospital, beside the soot-speckled glass arches of puffing Paddington Station in London. George Bernard Shaw (1856–1950) often came to tea at the Department library, with its wooden chairs, single settee, kitchen table and gas-ring for the kettle. The two Irishmen had known, respected and misunderstood each other since the start of the century, and Shaw always enjoyed sharing the language and unguarded confidences of medical men.

'The cure for disease, the elimination of human disease altogether, lies in the intelligent application of vaccine therapy,' Sir Almroth believed. He had no option. The infinitely more effective antibiotics lay half a century in the future. Wright had been Professor at the Army Medical College in Hampshire during the Boer War, where he discovered how to prevent typhoid fever, by injecting killed typhoid germs which stimulated the body to kill the live ones. The idea caught on with the Army in time for the next war. He was similarly an enthusiast for the the human white blood corpuscle, the phagocyte, the diligent, struggling devourer of invasive germs. Sir Almroth demonstrated the phagocyte to act more efficiently with a blood constituent, opsonin (Greek for 'to prepare food for'). 'Opsonin is what you butter the disease germs with to make your white blood corpuscles eat them,' Shaw put it, while bestowing the inoculators' rallying cry of 'Stimulate the phagocytes!'

Sir Almroth's mind had frostily budded philosophy, in *The Unexpurgated Case Against Woman Suffrage*. Shaw's flowered luxuriantly in medicine, its petals blowing in the prevailing Shavian wind:

> But, after all, what is operating? Only manual labor . . . as I always tell people, the operation will do them no harm: indeed, I've known the nervous shake-up and the fortnight in bed do people a lot of good after a hard London season.

All professions are conspiracies against the laity.

When you know as much as I do of the ignorance and superstition of the patients, youll wonder that we're half as good as we are.

The most tragic thing in the world is a sick doctor.

Shaw kept it up when he was dying, after fracturing his hip while lopping trees at Ayot St Lawrence. Told proudly by his doctor, after treatment of his long-standing kidney condition, 'Now your urine's normal,' he replied, 'Normal for whom?'

The doctor's dilemma was suggested to Shaw by one of Wright's assistants over tea, who was complaining proudly that the Inoculation Department had more work than it could handle. So which lives should be saved? A bleak question the more often uttered, now the infinite demands upon medicine overstretch medicine's finite financial resources. Sir Almroth himself walked out of the first night of *The Doctor's Dilemma* at the Court Theatre on 20 November 1906. Not because he objected to his caricature as Sir Colenso Ridgeon, but because of the thought that Shaw had solved the dilemma by killing off the wrong patient, the feckless artist Dubedat instead of the worthy Doctor Blenkinsop.

From The Doctor's Dilemma

ACT I

Newly knighted SIR COLENSO RIDGEON*'s consulting-room in Queen Anne Street on 15 June 1903. The senior practitioner (*SIR PATRICK CULLEN*) is paying a call.*

RIDGEON: You keep up your interest in science, do you?

SIR PATRICK: Lord! yes. Modern science is a wonderful thing. Look at your great discovery! Look at all the great discoveries! Where are they leading to? Why, right back to my poor dear old father's ideas and discoveries. He's been dead now over forty years. Oh, it's very interesting.

RIDGEON: Well, theres nothing like progress, is there?

SIR PATRICK: Dont misunderstand me, my boy. I'm not belittling your discovery. Most discoveries are made regularly every fifteen years; and it's fully a hundred and fifty since yours was made last. Thats something to be proud of. But your discovery's not new. It's only inoculation. My father practised inoculation until it was made criminal in eighteen-forty. That broke the poor old man's heart, Colly: he died of it. Youve brought us back to inoculation.

Riskily pricking a smallpox patient's pus into a healthy arm became illegal after Jenner's discovery of safe vaccination with cowpox.

RIDGEON: I know nothing about smallpox. My line is tuberculosis and typhoid and plague. But of course the principle of all vaccines is the same.

SIR PATRICK: Tuberculosis? Mmmm! Youve found out how to cure consumption, eh?

RIDGEON: I believe so.

SIR PATRICK: Ah yes. It's very interesting. What is it the old cardinal says in Browning's play? 'I have known four and twenty leaders of revolt.' Well, Ive known over thirty men that found out how to cure consumption. Why do people go on dying of it, Colly? Devilment, I suppose. There was my father's old friend George Boddington of Sutton Coldfield. He discovered the open-air cure in eighteen-forty. He was ruined and driven out of his practice for only opening the windows; and now we wont let a consumptive patient have as much as a roof over his head. Oh, it's very very interesting to an old man.

RIDGEON: You old cynic, you dont believe a bit in my discovery.

SIR PATRICK: No, no: I dont go quite so far as that, Colly. But still, you remember Jane Marsh?

RIDGEON: Jane Marsh? No.

SIR PATRICK: You dont!

RIDGEON: No.

SIR PATRICK: You mean to tell me that you dont remember the woman with the tuberculous ulcer on her arm?

RIDGEON: (*Enlightened*) Oh, your washerwoman's daughter. Was her name Jane Marsh? I forgot.

SIR PATRICK: Perhaps youve forgotten also that you undertook to cure her with Koch's tuberculin.

RIDGEON: And instead of curing her, it rotted her arm right off. Yes: I remember. Poor Jane! However, she makes a good living out of that arm now by shewing it at medical lectures.

Another of Sir Colenso's visitors that felicitatory morning is Mr Cutler Walpole, the surgeon.

SIR PATRICK: Oh, have him up. (RIDGEON *rings.*) He's a clever operator, is Walpole, though he's only one of your chloroform surgeons. In my early days, you made your man drunk; and the porters and students held him down; and you had to set your teeth and finish the job fast. Nowadays you work at your ease; and the pain doesnt come until afterwards, when you've taken your cheque and rolled up your bag and left the house. I tell you, Colly, chloroform has done a lot of mischief. It's enabled every fool to be a surgeon.

RIDGEON: (*To Emmy, who answers the bell.*) Shew Mr Walpole up.

EMMY: He's talking to the lady.

The lady is the wife – well, one of two – of the young, tubercular artist Louis Dubedat, who so engagingly borrows money from all his doctors.

RIDGEON: (*Exasperated*) Did I not tell you –

(*Emmy goes out without heeding him. He gives it up, with a shrug, and plants himself with his back to the console, leaning resignedly against it.*)

SIR PATRICK: I know your Cutler Walpoles and their like. Theyve found out that a man's body's full of bits and scraps of old organs he has no mortal use for. Thanks to chloroform, you can cut half a dozen of them out without leaving him any worse, except for the illness and the guineas it costs him. I knew the Walpoles well fifteen years ago. The father used to snip off the ends of people's uvulas [you can see it dangling at the back of your throat] for fifty guineas, and paint throats with caustic every day for a year at two guineas a time. His brother-in-law extirpated tonsils for two hundred guineas until he took up women's cases at double the fees. Cutler himself worked hard at anatomy to find something fresh to operate on; and at last he got hold of something he calls the nuciform sac, which he's made quite the fashion. People pay him five hundred guineas to cut it out. They might as well get their hair cut for all the difference it makes; but I suppose they feel important after it. You can't go out to dinner now without your neighbour bragging to you of some useless operation or other.

Sir Arbuthnot Lane of Guy's was at the time removing the entire colon for everything from migraine and rheumatism to marital disharmony. The nuciform sac is not in Gray's *Anatomy*.

EMMY: (*Announcing.*) Mr Cutler Walpole. (*She goes out.*)

(CUTLER WALPOLE *is an energetic, unhesitating man of forty with a cleanly modelled face. . . . In comparison with* RIDGEON*'s delicate broken lines, and* SIR PATRICK*'s softly rugged aged ones, his face looks machine-made and beeswaxed; but his scrutinizing, daring eyes give it life and force. He never seems at a loss, never in doubt: one feels that if he made a mistake he would make it thoroughly and firmly. . . . He goes straight across to* RIDGEON *and shakes hands with him.)*

WALPOLE: Me dear Ridgeon, best wishes! heartiest congratulations! You deserve it.

RIDGEON: Thank you.

WALPOLE: As a man, mind you. You deserve it as a man. The opsonin is simple rot, as any capable surgeon can tell you; but we're all delighted to see your personal qualities officially recognized. Sir Patrick: how are you? I sent you a paper lately about a little thing I invented: a new saw. For shoulder blades.

SIR PATRICK: (*Meditatively.*) Yes: I got it. It's a good saw: a useful, handy instrument.

WALPOLE: (*Confidently.*) I knew youd see its points.

SIR PATRICK: Yes: I remember that saw sixty-five years ago.

WALPOLE: What!

SIR PATRICK: It was called a cabinetmaker's jimmy then.

WALPOLE: Get out! Nonsense! Cabinetmaker be ——

RIDGEON: Never mind him, Walpole. He's jealous.

WALPOLE: By the way, I hope I'm not disturbing you two in anything private.

RIDGEON: No, no. Sit down. I was only consulting him. I'm rather out of sorts. Overwork, I suppose.

WALPOLE: (*Swiftly.*) I know whats the matter with you. I can see it in your complexion. I can feel it in the grip of your hand.

RIDGEON: What is it?

WALPOLE: Blood-poisoning.

RIDGEON: Blood-poisoning! Impossible.

WALPOLE: I tell you, blood-poisoning. Ninety-five per cent of the human race suffer from chronic blood-poisoning, and die of it. It's as simple as ABC. Your nuciform sac is full of decaying matter – undigested food and waste products – rank ptomaines. Now you take my advice, Ridgeon. Let me cut it out for you. Youll be another man afterwards.

SIR PATRICK: Dont you like him as he is?

WALPOLE: No I dont. I dont like any man who hasnt a healthy circulation. I tell you this: in an intelligently governed country people wouldnt be allowed to go about with nuciform sacs, making themselves centres of infection. The operation ought to be compulsory: it's ten times more important than vaccination.

SIR PATRICK: Have you had your own sac removed, may I ask?

WALPOLE: (*Triumphantly.*) I havnt got one. Look at me! Ive no symptoms. I'm as sound as a bell. About five per cent of the population havnt got any; and I'm one of the five per cent. I'll give you an instance. You know Mrs Jack Foljambe: the smart Mrs Foljambe? I operated at Easter on her sister-in-law, Lady Gorran, and found she had the biggest sac I ever saw: it held two ounces. Well, Mrs Foljambe had the right spirit – the genuine hygienic instinct. She couldn't stand her sister-in-law being a clean, sound woman, and she simply a whited sepulchre. So she insisted on my operating on her, too. And by George, sir, she hadnt any sac at all. Not a trace! Not a rudiment! I was so taken aback – so interested, that I forgot to take the sponges out, and was stitching them up inside her when the nurse missed them. Somehow, I'd made sure she'd have an exceptionally large one. (*He sits down on the couch, squaring his shoulders and shooting his hands out of his cuffs as he sets his knuckles akimbo.*)

EMMY: (*Looking in.*) Sir Ralph Bloomfield Bonington . . .

(*He is a tall man, with a head like a tall and slender egg. . . . Even broken bones, it is said, have been known to unite at the sound of his voice.*)

B.B.: Aha! Sir Colenso, Sir Colenso, eh? Welcome to the order of knighthood.

RIDGEON: (*Shaking hands.*) Thank you, B.B.

B.B.: What! Sir Patrick! And how are we today? a little chilly? a little stiff? but hale and still the cleverest of us all. (SIR PATRICK *grunts.*) What! Walpole! the absent-minded beggar: eh?

WALPOLE: What does that mean?

B.B.: Have you forgotten the lovely opera singer I sent you to have that growth taken off her vocal chords?

WALPOLE: (*Springing to his feet.*) Great heavens, man, you dont mean to say you sent her for a throat operation!

B.B.: (*Archly.*) Aha! Ha ha! Aha! (*trilling like a lark as he shakes his finger at* WALPOLE). You removed her nuciform sac. Well, well! force of habit! Never mind, ne-e-e-ver mind. She got back her voice after it, and thinks you the greatest surgeon alive; and so you are, so you are, so you are.

(1906)

STEPHEN LEACOCK

Members of other academic faculties – such as lawyers, who reduce humans to paragraphs of print – have no conception of medicine, even when they write books attacking it. The incomparable Stephen Butler Leacock (1869–1944), who was Professor of Economics at McGill University in Montreal, clearly understood medicine and doctors only too damn well.

How to be a Doctor

CERTAINLY THE PROGRESS of science is a wonderful thing. One can't help feeling proud of it. I must admit that I do. Whenever I get talking to anyone – that is, to anyone who knows even less about it than I do – about the marvellous development of electricity, for instance, I feel as if I had been personally responsible for it. As for the linotype and the aeroplane and the vacuum house-cleaner, well, I am not sure that I didn't invent them myself. I believe that all generous-hearted men feel just the same way about it.

However, that is not the point I am intending to discuss. What I want to speak about is the progress of medicine. There, if you like, is something wonderful. Any lover of humanity (or of either sex of it) who looks back on the achievements of medical science must feel his heart glow and his right ventricle expand with the pericardiac stimulus of a permissible pride.

Just think of it. A hundred years ago there were no bacilli, no ptomaine poisoning, no diphtheria, and no appendicitis. Rabies was but little known, and only imperfectly developed. All of these we owe to medical science. Even such things as psoriasis and parotitis and trypanosomiasis, which are now household names, were known only to the few, and were quite beyond the reach of the great mass of the people.

Or consider the advance of the science on its practical side. A hundred years ago it used to be supposed that fever could be cured by the letting of blood; now we know positively that it cannot. Even seventy years ago it was thought that fever was curable by the administration of sedative drugs; now we know that it isn't. For the matter of that, as recently as thirty years ago, doctors thought that they could heal a fever by means of low diet and the application of ice; now they are absolutely certain that they cannot. This instance shows the steady progress made in the treatment of fever. But there has been the same cheering advance all along the line. Take rheumatism. A few generations ago people with rheumatism used to have to carry round potatoes in their pockets as a means of cure. Now the doctors allow them to carry absolutely anything they like. They may go round with their pockets full of water-melons if they wish to. It makes no difference. Or take the treatment of epilepsy. It used to be supposed that the first thing to do in sudden attacks of this kind was to unfasten the patient's collar and let him breathe; at present, on the contrary, many doctors consider it better to button up the patient's collar and let him choke.

In only one respect has there been a decided lack of progress in the domain of medicine, that is in the time it takes to become a qualified practitioner. In the good old days a man was turned out thoroughly equipped after putting in two winter sessions at a college and spending his summers in running logs for a sawmill. Some of the students were turned out even sooner. Nowadays it takes anywhere from five to eight years to become a doctor. Of course, one is willing to grant that our young men are growing stupider and lazier every year. This fact will be corroborated at once by any man over fifty years of age. But even when this is said it seems odd that a man should study eight years now to learn what he used to acquire in eight months.

However, let that go. The point I want to develop is that the modern doctor's business is an extremely simple one, which could be acquired in about two weeks. This is the way it is done.

The patient enters the consulting-room. 'Doctor,' he says, 'I have a bad pain.' 'Where is it?' 'Here.' 'Stand up,' says the doctor, 'and put your arms up above your head.' Then the doctor goes behind the patient and strikes him a powerful blow in the back. 'Do you feel that,' he says. 'I do,' says the patient. Then the doctor turns suddenly and lets him have a left hook under the heart. 'Can you feel that,' he says viciously, as the patient falls over on the sofa in a heap. 'Get up,' says the doctor, and counts ten. The patient rises. The doctor looks him over very carefully without speaking, and then suddenly fetches him a blow in the stomach that doubles him up speechless. The doctor walks over to the window and reads the morning paper for a while. Presently he turns and begins to mutter more to himself than the patient. 'Hum!' he says, 'there's a slight anaesthesia of the tympanum.' 'Is that so?' says the patient, in an agony of fear. 'What can I do about it, doctor?' 'Well,' says the doctor, 'I want you to keep very quiet; you'll have to go to bed and stay there and keep quiet.' In reality, of course, the doctor hasn't the least idea what is wrong with the man; but he *does* know that if he will go to bed and keep quiet, awfully quiet, he'll either get quietly well again or else die a quiet death. Meantime, if the doctor calls every morning and thumps and beats him, he can keep the patient submissive and perhaps force him to confess what is wrong with him.

'What about diet, doctor?' says the patient, completely cowed.

The answer to this question varies very much. It depends on how the doctor is feeling and whether it is long since he had a meal himself. If it is late in the morning and the doctor is ravenously hungry, he says: 'Oh, eat plenty, don't be afraid of it; eat meat, vegetables, starch, glue, cement, anything you like.' But if the doctor has just had lunch and if his breathing is short-circuited with huckleberry pie, he says very firmly: 'No, I don't want you to eat anything at all: absolutely not a bite; it won't hurt you, a little self-denial in the matter of eating is the best thing in the world.'

'And what about drinking?' Again the doctor's answer varies. He may say: 'Oh, yes, you might drink a glass of lager now and then, or, if you prefer it, a gin and soda or a whisky and Apollinaris, and I think before going to bed I'd take a hot Scotch with a couple of lumps of white sugar and a bit of lemon-peel in it and a good grating of nutmeg on the top.' The doctor says this with real feeling, and his eye glistens with the pure love of his profession. But if, on the other hand, the doctor has spent the night before at a little gathering of medical friends, he is very apt to forbid the patient to touch alcohol in any shape, and to dismiss the subject with great severity.

Of course, this treatment in and of itself would appear too transparent, and would fail to inspire the patient with a proper confidence. But nowadays this element is supplied by the work of the analytical laboratory. Whatever is wrong with the patient, the doctor insists on snipping off parts and pieces and extracts of him and sending them mysteriously away to be analysed. He cuts off a lock of the patient's hair, marks it, 'Mr Smith's Hair, October, 1910.' Then he clips off the lower part of the ear, and wraps it in paper, and labels it, 'Part of Mr

Smith's Ear, October, 1910.' Then he looks the patient up and down, with the scissors in his hand, and if he sees any likely part of him he clips it off and wraps it up. Now this, oddly enough, is the very thing that fills the patient up with that sense of personal importance which is worth paying for. 'Yes,' says the bandaged patient, later in the day to a group of friends much impressed, 'the doctor thinks there may be a slight anaesthesia of the prognosis, but he's sent my ear to New York and my appendix to Baltimore and a lock of my hair to the editors of all the medical journals, and meantime I am to keep very quiet and not exert myself beyond drinking a hot Scotch with lemon and nutmeg every half-hour.' With that he sinks back faintly on his cushions, luxuriously happy.

And yet, isn't it funny?

You and I and the rest of us – even if we know all this – as soon as we have a pain within us, rush for a doctor as fast as a hack can take us. Yes, personally, I even prefer an ambulance with a bell on it. It's more soothing.

(1910)

Sir Walter Scott

I am fond of Scotch, haggis, Forfar bridies, Loch Ness, baps, bagpipes, cullen skink, tattie drottle and Scots terriers, but I cannot stand the novels of Walter Scott (1771–1832). His characters in my ears enjoy the monstrous smugness of a cosy tea-party – buttered scones, petticoat-tail shortbread and Dundee cake – around a roaring midwinter fire in Morningside following a victory at Murrayfield. I apologise to Scottish readers for my quirk: the English are as full of quirks as the Mad Hatter.

If Scott wrote *The Surgeon's Daughter*, the surgeon's daughter must nevertheless be entertained. The surgeon himself was Gideon Gray of Middlemas, one of the 'village doctors, from whom Scotland reaps more benefit, and to whom she is perhaps more ungrateful, than to any other class of men, excepting her school-masters'. He was sketched from Sir Walter's own doctor, Ebenezer Clarkson, who lived in the market-place, Selkirk. The gist of the story was furnished over breakfast by Scott's friend and researcher Joseph Train, antiquary, labourer's son and militiaman. The preface holds a remark about the publisher: 'He understands his business too well, and follows it too closely, to desire to enter into literary discussions, wisely considering that he who has to sell books has seldom leisure to read them.' A persistent wisdom.

From The Surgeon's Daughter

For late and dangerous journeys through an inaccessible country for services of the most essential kind, rendered at the expense, or risk at least, of his own health and life, the Scottish village doctor receives at best a very moderate recompense, often one which is totally inadequate, and very frequently none whatsoever. He has none of the ample resources proper to the brothers of the profession in an English town. The burgesses of a Scottish borough are rendered, by their limited means of luxury, inaccessible to gout, surfeits, and all the comfortable chronic diseases, which are attendant on wealth and indolence. . . .

Like the ghostly lover of Bürger's Leonora, he mounts at midnight, and traverses in darkness paths which, to those less accustomed to them, seem formidable in daylight, through straits where the slightest aberration would plunge him into a morass, or throw him over a precipice, on to cabins which his horse might ride over without knowing they lay in his way, unless he happened to fall through the roofs. When he arrives at such a stately termination of his journey, where his services are required, either to bring a wretch into the world, or prevent one from leaving it, the scene of misery is often such, that far from touching the hard-saved shillings which are gratefully offered to him, he bestows his medicines as well as his attendance – for charity. . . .

In short, there is no creature in Scotland that works harder and is more poorly requited than the country doctor, unless perhaps it may be his horse. Yet the horse is, and indeed must be, hardy, active, and indefatigable, in spite of a rough coat and indifferent condition; and so you will often find in his master, under an unpromising and blunt exterior, professional skill and enthusiasm, intelligence, humanity, courage, and science.

Mr Gideon Gray, surgeon in the village of Middlemas, situated in one of the midland counties of Scotland, led the rough, active, and ill-rewarded course of life which we have endeavoured to describe. He was a man between forty and fifty, devoted to his profession, and of such reputation in the medical world, that he had been more than once, as opportunities occurred, advised to exchange Middlemas, and its meagre circle of practice, for some of the larger towns in Scotland, or for Edinburgh itself. This advice he had always declined. He was a plain blunt man, who did not love restraint, and was unwilling to subject himself to that which was exacted in polite society. He had not himself found out, nor had any friend hinted to him, that a slight touch of the cynic, in manner and habits, gives the physician, to the common eye, an air of authority which greatly tends to enlarge his reputation. . . .

One autumn night, a four-horse carriage appears at the doctor's door. A gentleman in riding-dress leaves a woman in labour, with a fee of twenty guineas.

'She is of rank,' he said, 'and a foreigner; let no expense be spared. We designed to have reached Edinburgh, but were forced to turn off the road by an accident.' Once more he said, 'Let no expense be spared, and manage that she may travel as soon as possible.'

'That,' said the Doctor, 'is past my control. Nature must not be hurried, and she avenges herself of every attempt to do so.'

'But art,' said the stranger, 'can do much,' and he proffered a second purse, which seemed as heavy as the first.

'Art,' said the Doctor, 'may be recompensed, but cannot be purchased. . . .'

> The child is baptised Richard Middlemas and the father disappears, leaving the doctor £100. In her fourth puerperal week, the mother's own father arrives with a king's messenger, who arrests her. The doctor is left holding the baby, and the mother's father leaves him £1,000. Four years later the doctor's own wife has a daughter, Menie, but dies in labour. At fourteen, Richard meets Tom Hillary.

He was a lad about twenty, as smart as small, but distinguished for the accuracy with which he dressed his hair, and the splendour of a laced hat and embroidered waistcoat, with which he graced the church of Middlemas on Sundays. Tom Hillary had been bred an attorney's clerk in Newcastle-upon-Tyne, but, for some reason or other, had found it more convenient of late years to reside in Scotland, and was recommended to the Town-clerk of Middlemas, by the accuracy and beauty with which he transcribed the records of the burgh. It is not improbable that the reports concerning the singular circumstances of Richard Middlemas's birth, and the knowledge that he was actually possessed of a considerable sum of money, induced Hillary, though so much his senior, to admit the lad to his company, and enrich his youthful mind with some branches of information, which, in that retired corner, his pupil might otherwise have been some time in attaining. Amongst these were certain games at cards and dice, in which the pupil paid, as was reasonable, the price of initiation by his losses to his instructors. . . .

> Richard determines to study medicine, and his father sends the doctor £100.

At the same period when Dr Gray took under his charge his youthful lodger Richard Middlemas, he received proposals from the friends of one Adam Hartley to receive him also as an apprentice. The lad was the son of a respectable farmer on the English side of the Border, who, educating his eldest son to his own occupation, desired to make his second a medical man, in order to avail himself of the friendship of a great man, his landlord, who had offered to assist his views in life, and represented a doctor or surgeon as the sort of person to whose advantage his interest could be most readily applied. Middlemas and Hartley were therefore associated in their studies. In winter they were boarded in Edinburgh, for attending the medical classes which were necessary for taking their degree. Three or four years thus passed on, and, from being mere boys, the two medical aspirants shot up into young men, who, being both very good-looking, well dressed, well bred, and having money in their pockets, became personages of some importance in the little town of Middlemas, where there was scarce anything that could be termed an aristocracy, and in which beaux were scarce and belles were plenty. . . .

In their persons there was a still more strongly marked distinction. Adam Hartley was full middle size, stout, and well limbed; and an open English countenance, of the genuine Saxon mould, showed itself among chestnut locks, until the hairdresser destroyed them. He loved the rough exercises of wrestling, boxing, leaping, and quarterstaff, and frequented, when he could obtain leisure, the bull-baitings and football matches by which the burgh was sometimes enlivened.

Richard, on the contrary, was dark, like his father and mother, with high features, beautifully formed, but exhibiting something of a foreign character; and his person was tall and slim, though muscular and active. His address and manners must have been natural to him, for they were, in elegance and ease, far beyond any example which he could have found in his native burgh. He learned the use of the small-sword while in Edinburgh, and took lessons from a performer at the theatre, with the purpose of refining his mode of speaking. He became also an amateur of the drama, regularly attending the playhouse, and assuming the tone of a critic in that and other lighter departments of literature. To fill up the contrast, so far as taste was concerned, Richard was a dexterous and successful angler – Adam, a bold and unerring shot. Their efforts to surpass each other in supplying Dr Gray's table rendered his housekeeping much preferable to what it had been on former occasions; and, besides, small presents of fish and game are always agreeable amongst the inhabitants of a country town, and contributed to increase the popularity of the young sportsmen. . . .

> Richard Middlemas and Adam Hartley develop rivalry over Menie to the point of duelling. But the doctor will not have it. 'A fine story it would be of my apprentices shooting each other with my own pistols! Let me see either of you fit to treat a gunshot wound, before you think of inflicting one . . .' The lucky Englishman wins bloodlessly.

'Dr Gray was pleased to say something to me very civil about my proficiency in the duties of our profession; and, to my great astonishment, asked me, whether, as he was now becoming old, I had any particular objection to continue in my present situation, but with some pecuniary advantages, for two years longer; at the end of which he promised to me that I should enter into partnership with him. . . . But,' continued Hartley, 'that is not all. The Doctor says – he proposes – in short, if I can render myself agreeable, in the course of these two years, to Miss Menie Gray, he proposes that when they terminate I should become his son as well as his partner.'

As he spoke, he kept his eye fixed on Richard's face, which was for a moment strongly agitated; but instantly recovering, he answered, in a tone where pique and offended pride vainly endeavoured to disguise themselves under an affectation of indifference, 'Well, Master Adam, I cannot but wish you joy of the patriarchal arrangement. . . .'

> Unfortunately, 'Mr Middlemas . . . had the inestimable advantage of possessing Miss Gray's affections,' so Adam Hartley decides to sail to India as a surgeon's mate. Richard Middlemas re-encounters Tom Hillary.

He was now called Captain; his dress was regimental, and his language martial. . . . Dr Gray, who was an enemy to everything that approached to fanfaronade, and knew enough of the world to lay it down as a sort of general rule, that he who talks a great deal of fighting is seldom a brave soldier, and he who always speaks about wealth is seldom a rich man at bottom.

The Captain tempts Richard.

'If you, my dear fellow,' continued he, extending his hand to Middlemas, 'would think of changing sheephead broth and haggis for mulligatawny and curry, I can only say, that though it is indispensable that you should enter the service at first simply as a cadet, yet by ——, you should live like a brother on the passage with me; and no sooner were we through the surf at Madras, than I would put you in the way of acquiring both wealth and glory. You have, I think, some trifle of money – a couple of thousands or so?'

'About a thousand or twelve hundred,' said Richard, affecting the indifference of his companion, but feeling privately humbled by the scantiness of his resources.

'It is quite as much as you will find necessary for the outfit and passage,' said his adviser; 'and, indeed, if you had not a farthing, it would be the same thing; for if I once say to a friend, I'll help you, Tom Hillary is not the man to start for fear of the cowries. However, it is as well you have something of a capital of your own to begin upon.' . . .

But what about Menie?

'What, Miss Green, the old pottercarrier's daughter? – a likely girl enough, I think.'

'My master is a surgeon,' said Richard, 'not an apothecary, and his name is Gray.'

'Ay, ay, Green or Grey – what does it signify? He sells his own drugs, I think, which we in the south call being a pottercarrier. The girl is a likely girl enough for a Scottish ball-room. But is she up to anything? Has she any *nous*?'

'Why, she is a sensible girl, save in loving me,' answered Richard; 'and that, as Benedick says, is no proof of her wisdom, and no great argument of her folly.'

'But has she spirit – spunk – dash – a spice of the devil about her?'

'Not a penny-weight – the kindest, simplest, and most manageable of human beings,' answered the lover.

'She won't do then,' said the monitor, in a decisive tone. 'I am sorry for it, Dick; but she will never do. There are some women in the world that can bear their share in the bustling life we live in India – ay, and I have known some of them drag forward husbands that would otherwise have stuck fast in the mud till the day of judgment. Heavens knows how they paid the turnpikes they pushed them through! But these were none of your simple Susans, that think their eyes are good for nothing but to look at their husbands, or their fingers but to sew baby-clothes. Depend on it, you must give up your matrimony, or your views of preferment. If you wilfully tie a clog round your throat, never think of running a race; but do not suppose that your breaking off with the lass will make any very terrible catastrophe. A scene there may be at parting; but you will soon forget her among the native girls, and she will fall in love with Mr Tapeitout, the minister's assistant and successor. She is not goods for the Indian market, I assure you.' . . .

Richard Middlemas gets as far as the Isle of Wight. There he gets drunk, and ends up in the military hospital.

Agony softened her shriek, Insanity hushed its senseless clamours, and even Death seemed desirous to stifle his parting groan in the presence of Captain Seelencooper. This official was the superintendent, or, as the miserable inhabitants termed him, the Governor of the Hospital. He had all the air of having been originally a turnkey in some ill-regulated jail – a stout, short, bandy-legged man, with one eye, and a double portion of ferocity in that which remained. He wore an old-fashioned tarnished uniform, which did not seem to have been made for him; and the voice in which this minister of humanity addressed the sick was that of a boatswain shouting in the midst of a storm. He had pistols and a cutlass in his belt; for his mode of administration being such as provoked even hospital patients to revolt, his life had been more than once in danger amongst them. He was followed by two assistants, who carried handcuffs and strait-jackets.

As Seelencooper made his rounds, complaint and pain were hushed, and the flourish of the bamboo, which he bore in his hand, seemed powerful as the wand of a magician to silence all complaint and remonstrance.

'I tell you the meat is as sweet as a nosegay – and for the bread, it's good enough, and too good, for a set of lubbers, that lie shamming Abraham, and consuming the Right Honourable Company's victuals – I don't speak to them that are really sick, for God knows I am always for humanity.'

'If that be the case, sir,' said Richard Middlemas, whose lair the Captain had approached, while he was thus answering the low and humble complaints of those by whose bed-side he passed – 'if that be the case, sir, I hope your humanity will make you attend to what I say.'

'And who the devil are you?' said the Governor, turning on him his single eye of fire, while a sneer gathered on his harsh features, which were so well qualified to express it.

'My name is Middlemas – I come from Scotland, and have been sent here by some strange mistake. I am neither a private soldier, nor am I indisposed, more than by the heat of this cursed place.'

'Why then, friend, all I have to ask you is, whether you are an attested recruit or not?'

'I was attested at Edinburgh,' said Middlemas, 'but –'

'But what the devil would you have, then? – you are enlisted – the Captain and the Doctor sent you here – surely they know best whether you are private or officer, sick or well.'

'But I was promised,' said Middlemas – 'promised by Tom Hillary –'

'Promised, were you? Why, there is not a man here that has not been promised something by somebody or another, or perhaps has promised something to himself. This is the land of promise, my smart fellow, but you know it is India that must be the land of performance. So good morning to you. The Doctor will come his rounds presently, and put you all to rights.'

'Stay but one moment – one moment only – I have been robbed.'

'Robbed! look you there now,' said the Governor – 'everybody that comes here has been robbed. – Egad, I am the luckiest fellow in Europe – other people in my line have only thieves and blackguards upon their hands; but none come to my ken but honest, decent, unfortunate gentlemen, that have been robbed!'

'Take care how you treat this so lightly, sir,' said Middlemas; 'I have been robbed of a thousand pounds.'

Here Governor Seelencooper's gravity was totally overcome, and his laugh was echoed by several of the patients, either because they wished to curry favour with the superintendent, or from the feeling which influences evil spirits to rejoice in the tortures of those who are sent to share their agony.

'A thousand pounds!' exclaimed Captain Seelencooper, as he recovered his breath – 'Come, that's a good one – I like a fellow that does not make two bites of a cherry – why, there is not a cull in the ken that pretends to have lost more than a few hoggs, and here is a servant to the Honourable Company that has been robbed of a thousand pounds! Well done, Mr Tom of Ten Thousand – you're a credit to the house, and to the service, and so good morning to you.' . . .

But wait!

To enforce the discipline of their soldiers, the Court committed full power to one of their own body, General Witherington. The General was an officer who had distinguished himself highly in their service. He had returned from India five or six years before, with a large fortune, which he had rendered much greater by an advantageous marriage with a rich heiress. The General and his lady went little into society, but seemed to live entirely for their infant family, those in number being three, two boys and a girl. Although he had retired from the service, he willingly undertook the temporary charge committed to him, and, taking a house at a considerable distance from the town of Ryde, he proceeded to enrol the troops into separate bodies, appoint officers of capacity to each, and, by regular training and discipline, gradually to bring them into something resembling good order. He heard their complaints of ill usage in the articles of provisions and appointments, and did them upon all occasions the strictest justice, save that he was never known to restore one recruit to his freedom from the service, however unfairly or even illegally his attestation might have been obtained.

'It is none of my business,' said General Witherington, 'how you became soldiers, – soldiers I found you, and soldiers I will leave you. But I will take especial care that as soldiers you shall have everything, to a penny or a pin's head, that you are justly entitled to.' He went to work without fear or favour, reported many abuses to the Board of Directors, had several officers, commissaries, &c., removed from the service, and made his name as great a terror to the peculators at home as it had been to the enemies of Britian in Hindostan.

Captain Seelencooper, and his associates in the hospital department, heard and trembled, fearing that their turn should come next; but the General, who elsewhere examined all with his own eyes, showed a reluctance to visit the hospital in person. Public report industriously imputed this to fear of infection. Such was certainly the motive; though it was not fear for his own safety that influenced General Witherington, but he dreaded lest he should carry the infection home to the nursery, on which he doted. The alarm of his lady was yet more unreasonably sensitive; she would scarcely suffer the children to walk abroad, if the wind but blew from the quarter where the hospital was situated.

But Providence baffles the precautions of mortals. In a walk across the fields, chosen as the most sheltered and sequestered, the children, with their train of Eastern and European attendants, met a woman who carried a child that was recovering from the small-pox. The anxiety of the father, joined to some religious scruples on the mother's part, had postponed inoculation, which was then scarcely come into general use. The infection caught like a quick-match, and ran like wildfire through all those in the family who had not previously had the disease. One of the General's children, the second boy, died, and two of the ayahs, or black female servants, had the same fate. The hearts of the father and mother would have been broken for the child they had lost, had not their grief been suspended by anxiety for the fate of those who lived, and who were confessed to be in imminent danger. They were like persons distracted, as the symptoms of the poor patients seemed gradually to resemble more nearly that of the child already lost.

While the parents were in this agony of apprehension, the General's principal servant, a native of Northumberland like himself, informed him one morning that there was a young man from the same county among the hospital doctors, who had publicly blamed the mode of treatment observed towards the patients, and spoken of another which he had seen practised with eminent success.

'Some impudent quack,' said the General, 'who would force himself into business by bold assertions. Dr Tourniquet and Dr Lancelot are men of high reputation.'

'Do not mention their reputation,' said the mother, with a mother's impatience. 'Did they not let my sweet Reuben die? What avails the reputation of the physician, when the patient perisheth?'

'If his honour would but see Dr Hartley,' said Winter, turning half towards the lady, and then turning back again to his master. 'He is a very decent young man, who, I am sure, never expected what he said to reach your honour's ears; – and he is a native of Northumberland.'

'Send a servant with a led horse,' said the General; 'let the young man come hither instantly.'

It is well known that the ancient mode of treating the small-pox was to refuse to the patient everything which Nature urged him to desire, and, in particular, to confine him to heated rooms, beds loaded with blankets, and spiced wine, when nature called for cold water and fresh air. A different mode of treatment had of late been adventured upon by some practitioners, who preferred reason to authority, and Gideon Gray had followed it for several years with extraordinary success.

When General Witherington saw Hartley, he was startled at his youth; but when he heard him modestly, but with confidence, state the difference of the two modes of treatment, and the rationale of his practice, he listened with the most serious attention. So did his lady, her streaming eyes turning from Hartley to her husband, as if to watch what impression the arguments of the former were making upon the latter. General Witherington was silent for a few minutes after Hartley had finished his exposition, and seemed buried in profound reflection. 'To treat a fever,' he said, 'in a manner which tends to produce one, seems indeed to be adding fuel to fire.'

'It is – it is,' said the lady. 'Let us trust this young man, General Witherington. We shall at least give our darlings the comforts of the fresh air and cold water, for which they are pining.'

But the General remained undecided. 'Your reasoning,' he said to Hartley, 'seems plausible; but still it is only hypothesis. What can you show to support your theory, in opposition to the general practice?'

'My own observation,' replied the young man. 'Here is a memorandum-book of medical cases which I have witnessed. It contains twenty cases of small-pox, of which eighteen were recoveries.'

'And the two others?' said the General.

'Terminated fatally,' replied Hartley; 'we can as yet but partially disarm this scourge of the human race.'

'Young man,' continued the General, 'were I to say that a thousand gold mohurs were yours in case my children live under your treatment, what have you to peril in exchange?'

'My reputation,' answered Hartley, firmly.

'And you could warrant on your reputation the recovery of your patients?'

'God forbid I should be so presumptuous! But I think I could warrant my using those means which, with God's blessing, afford the fairest chance of a favourable result.'

'Enough – you are modest and sensible, as well as bold, and I will trust you.'

The lady, on whom Hartley's words and manner had made a great impression, and who was eager to discontinue a mode of treatment which subjected the patients to the greatest pain and privation, and had already proved unfortunate, eagerly acquiesced, and Hartley was placed in full authority in the sick-room.

Windows were thrown open, fires reduced or discontinued, loads of bed-clothes removed, cooling drinks superseded mulled wine and spices. The sick-nurses cried out murder. Drs Tourniquet and Lancelot retired in disgust, menacing something like a general pestilence, in vengeance of what they termed rebellion against the neglect of the aphorisms of Hippocrates. Hartley proceeded quietly and steadily, and the patients got into a fair road of recovery. . . .

Now well in with General Witherington, Dr Adam Hartley decently draws his attention to the plight of Richard Middlemas.

'The youth must indeed have had strangely hard-hearted, or careless parents,' said Mrs Witherington, in accents of pity.

'He never knew them, madam,' said Hartley; 'there was a mystery on the score of his birth. A cold, unwilling, and almost unknown hand dealt him out his portion when he came of lawful age, and he was pushed into the world like a bark forced from shore, without rudder, compass, or pilot.'

Here General Witherington involuntarily looked to his lady, while, guided by a similar impulse, her looks were turned upon him. They exchanged a momentary glance of deep and peculiar meaning, and then the eyes of both were fixed on the ground.

'Were you brought up in Scotland?' said the lady, addressing herself, in a faltering voice, to Hartley. 'And what was your master's name?'

'I served my apprenticeship with Mr Gideon Gray, of the town of Middlemas,' said Hartley.

'Middlemas! Gray!' repeated the lady, and fainted away.

Hartley offered the succours of his profession; the husband flew to support her head, and the instant that Mrs Witherington began to recover, he whispered to her, in a tone betwixt entreaty and warning, 'Zilia, beware – beware!'

Some imperfect sounds which she had begun to frame died away upon her tongue.

'Let me assist you to your dressing-room, my love,' said her obviously anxious husband. . . .

Richard Middlemas, now a Lieutenant, is recieved by General Witherington and his wife Zilia.

'Mr Hartley was not particularly communicative about your affairs,' said the General; 'nor do I wish to give you the pain of entering into them. What I desire to know is, if you are pleased with your destination to Madras?'

'Perfectly, please your Excellency – anywhere, so that there is no chance of meeting the villain Hillary.'

'Oh! Hillary's services are too necessary in the purlieus of St Giles's, the Lowlights of Newcastle, and such like places, where human carrion can be picked up, to be permitted to go to India. However, to show you the knave has some grace, there are the notes of which you were robbed. You will find them the very same paper which you lost, except a small sum which the rogue had spent, but which a friend has made up, in compassion for your sufferings.' Richard Middlemas sank on one knee, and kissed the hand which restored him to independence.

'Pshaw!' said the General, 'you are a silly young man;' but he withdrew not his hand from his caresses. This was one of the occasions on which Dick Middlemas could be oratorical.

'Oh, my more than father,' he said, 'how much greater a debt do I owe to you than to the unnatural parents, who brought me into this world by their sin, and deserted me through their cruelty!'

Zilia, as she heard these cutting words, flung back her veil, raising it on both hands till it floated behind her like a mist, and then, giving a faint groan, sank down in a swoon. Pushing Middlemas from him with a hasty movement, General Witherington flew to his lady's assistance, and carried her in his arms, as if she had been a child, into the anteroom, where an old servant waited with the means of restoring suspended animation, which the unhappy husband too truly anticipated might be useful. These were hastily employed, and succeeded in calling the sufferer to life, but in a state of mental emotion that was terrible.

Her mind was obviously impressed by the last words which her son had uttered – 'Did you hear him, Richard?' she exclaimed, in accents terribly loud, considering the exhausted state of her strength. 'Did you hear the words? It was Heaven speaking our condemnation by the voice of our own child. But do not fear, my Richard, do not weep! I will answer the thunder of Heaven with its own music.'

She flew to a harpsichord which stood in the room, and, while the servant and master gazed on each other, as if doubting whether her senses were about to leave her entirely, she wandered over the keys, producing a wilderness of harmony, composed of passages recalled by memory, or combined by her own musical talent, until at length her voice and instrument united in one of those magnificent hymns in which her youth had praised her Maker, with voice and harp, like the Royal Hebrew who composed it. The tear ebbed insensibly from the eyes which she turned upwards – her vocal tones, combining with those of the instrument, rose to a pitch of brilliancy seldom attained by the most distinguished performers, and then sank into a dying cadence, which fell, never again to rise – for the songstress had died with her strain. . . .

The rest is inescapably an anticlimax. Richard Middlemas goes to India, shoots his Commanding Officer, disguises himself as a black servant and becomes the Bukshee (General) of an Amazonian Begum, Mrs Montreville, a Swiss widow. She had sailed from England with a lady's companion, who is Menie Gray, whom she plots to sell to the tyrant Prince Tippoo of Seringapatam, which Menie secretly pleads Adam Hartley to hurry from Madras and prevent. All ends happily at the Durbar, where Prince Tippoo's father arrives disguised as a fakir to shame him out of it, Menie is compensated in gold, and Richard Middlemas, the new Governor of Bangalore, is run over by his own elephant.

The surgeon's daughter unromantically does not marry Dr Hartley, who two years later succumbs to the widespread contagious distemper he is treating and leaves her his money. In his memory, she spurns 'many advantageous offers of a matrimonial character' and – what seldom occurs – 'unmarried though wealthy' returns to perform good works in her native village of Middlemas. Sir Walter is more comfortable in the Cheviots than the Himalayas.

(1827)

FRANÇOIS RABELAIS

Doctors *ipso facto* have a Rabelaisian sense of humour.

Doctors professionally conduct Pope's proper study of mankind, man. Who is:

> In doubt to deem himself a god, or beast;
> In doubt his mind or body to prefer;
> Born but to die, and reas'ning but to err.

The anthropological monarch, crowned flashingly with artistic and philosophical diadems, forgets that he – or she – is but an organism who salivates, urinates, defecates, copulates, ambulates, articulates and cerebrates and who is terribly ashamed that he or she inescapably farts, belches, smells in the feet and armpits, gluttonises, swigs, vomits, brags, lies, fattens, itches, picks its nose, scratches its arse and fondles its own genitals. This is obviously a funny situation.

François Rabelais (?1495–1553), like Hippocrates, whose Greek *Aphorisms* he edited, was intrigued by the coarse functioning and behaviour of man, rather than the theories that had been earnestly constructed to explain both. Rabelais was a lawyer's son from Chinon, which lies near the confluence of the Vienne and the Loire. He became a Franciscan monk, transferring in 1524 to the less austere Benedictines. In 1530 he abandoned the cowl for the leech at Montpellier, acquiring its MD in 1537. He lectured on Hippocrates and Galen and in 1532 became physician and demonstrator in anatomy to the Lyons municipal hospital. He earned forty livres a year, but was sacked for taking unauthorised trips to Rome, as personal doctor to his friend Cardinal Jean du Bellay. Rabelais then had a mistress and two children. An esteemed physician, in 1546 he was appointed town doctor to Metz, on 120 livres a year. In 1550 Rabelais was bestowed ecclesiastical livings near Paris and Le Mans, but avoided them. He died in Paris, perhaps at Saint-Maur Abbey, where he was an honorary canon.

In 1532 Rabelais published *Pantagruel* under his anagram 'Alcofribas Nasier', and in 1534 *Gargantua.* It caused a fuss. On 23 October 1533 *Pantagruel* was condemned by the Sorbonne as obscene, and Rabelais faced prosecution for heresy (which is the self-righteous, but self-evidently alarmed, suppression of thought). Luckily, he had Cardinal du Bellay behind him and King François I on his side. Rabelais was a jovial satirist, a scorner of asceticism, a scoffer of dogmas and despiser of hypocrisy, a master neologist, a surrealist and a fantastic jester, who rightly saw that the mockery of man's little failings was the agreeable alternative to affording them unthinking contempt, or solemn condemnation, or shamed concealment. What a splendid chap to have in the hospital mess.

Pantagruel becomes ill, as he does everything else, in the grand manner.

From Pantagruel

A WHILE AFTER this the good Pantagruel fell sick, and had such an illness in his stomach, that he could neither eat nor drink; and because one mischief seldom comes alone, he had got also the hot piss, which tormented him more than you would believe. His physicians, nevertheless, helped him very well, and, with store of lenitives and diuretic drugs, made him piss away his pain. His urine was so hot, that since that time it is not yet cold, and you have of it in divers places of France, according to the course that it took, and they are called the hot baths; as at Coderets; at Limous; at Dast; at Ballervie; at Nerie; at Bourbonensy, and elsewhere. In Italy, at Mongros; at Appone; at Sancto Petro de Padua; at St Helen; at Casa Nuova; at St Bartolomee in the county of Bologna; at the Loretta; and a thousand other places.

And I wonder much at a rabble of foolish philosophers and physicians, who spend their time in disputing, whence the heat of the said waters cometh, whether it be by reason of borax, or sulphur, or allum, or saltpetre, that is within the mine: for they do nothing but dote, and better were it for them to rub their arse against a thistle, than to waste away their time thus in disputing of that whereof they know not the original; for the resolution is easy, neither need we to inquire any further, than that the said baths came by a hot piss of the good Pantagruel.

Now to tell you after what manner he was cured of his principal disease, I let pass how for a minorative he took four hundred pound weight of colophoniac scammony; sixscore and eighteen cart-loads of cassia; eleven thousand and nine hundred pounds weight of rhubarb; besides other confused jumblings of sundry drugs. You must understand, that, by the advice of the physicians, it was ordered, that what did offend his stomach should be taken away; and therefore they made seventeen great balls of copper, each whereof was bigger than that which is to be seen on the top of St Peter's needle at Rome, and in such sort, that they did open in the midst, and shut with a spring. Into one of them entered one of his men, carrying a lantern and a torch lighted, and so Pantagruel swallowed him down like a little pill: into seven others went seven country fellows, having every one of them a shovel on his neck: into nine others entered nine wood-carriers, having each of them a basket hung at his neck: and so were they swallowed down like pills. When they were in his stomach, every one undid his spring, and came out of their cabins; the first whereof was he that carried the lantern: and so they fell more than half a league into a most horrible gulph, more stinking and infectious than ever was Mephitis, or the marishes of Camerina, or the abominably unsavoury lake of Sorbona, whereof Strabo maketh mention. And had it not been that they had very well antidoted their stomach, heart, and wine-pot, which is called the noddle, they had been altogether suffocated and choked with these detestable vapours. O what a perfume! O what an evaporation, wherewith to bewray the masks or mufflers of young mangy queans! After that, with groping and smelling, they came near to the fecal matter, and the corrupted humours. Finally, they found a montjoy or heap of ordure and filth: then fell the pioneers to work to dig it up, and the rest with their shovels filled the baskets; and, when all was cleansed, every one retired himself into his ball.

This done, Pantagruel, enforcing himself to a vomit, very easily brought them out, and they made no more show in his mouth than a fart in yours; but when they came merrily out of their pills, I thought upon the Grecians coming out of the Trojan horse. By this means was he healed, and brought unto his former state and convalescence. And of these brazen pills you have one at Orleans, upon the steeple of the holy cross church.

(1532)

GIOVANNI BOCCACCIO

'How many valiant men, how many fair ladies, breakfasted with their kinsfolk and that night supped with their ancestors in the other world,' was Giovanni Boccaccio's (1313–75) cogent assessment of the Black Death of 1348. Bubonic plague was inflicted by the rat-flea upon the Middle Ages with more deadly certainty than war. Boccaccio was the illegitimate son of a Florentine merchant who died of it. Between March and July 1348, 100,000 perished within the walls of Florence – in the streets, or discovered by the stink of their decomposing bodies at home, the dead hooked out by the *becchini* corpse-carriers, their biers perforce shared, their burial services anxiously gabbled. Like in young Chaucer's London, their grave was 'a huge trench, in which they laid the corpses as they arrived by hundreds at a time, piling them up as merchandise is stowed in the hold of a ship . . . a dead man was then of no more account that a dead goat would be today,' Boccaccio reflected ten years afterwards.

The *Decameron* was among the first books to be printed, at Venice in 1471. Without it, we should have had no *Canterbury Tales*. Its hundred stories were exchanged over ten days in the garden of a remote Florentine villa, by refugees from the slaughter. This pleasant tale underlines the dangers besetting seduction of a doctor's wife.

From The Decameron

Fourth Day, Story Ten

YOU MUST UNDERSTAND, then, that not long since lived at Salerno a famous doctor in surgery, called Master Mazzeo della Montagna, who in his old age had married a young and beautiful wife, of the same city. There being such a disproportion in their years, he spared no cost of clothes and jewels, and gratified her in everything of that kind she could wish for, so that she appeared far beyond any other lady in the city. Truly, indeed, she lacked other gratifications (her case resembling that of the wife of Ricciardo di Chinzica, of whose calendar you have already heard), for her husband's ability was not commensurate with his will or her desires; therefore she wisely sought to relieve him as much as possible; and, looking out amongst the young gentlemen abroad, she at last fixed upon one, on whom she settled her entire hope and affection, and he, being made sensible of it, showed the same regard for her. He was named Ruggieri da Jeroli, and of a noble family, but had been always of a rakish disposition, on which account he had disobliged all his friends so far that none of them would see him, and he was now branded all over Salerno for everything that was vile and wicked. This had no weight with her, who admired him for a different reason, and by her maid's assistance they were brought together. After they had given each other proofs of their mutual fondness, she reproved him for his past conduct, and desired that, for her sake, he would leave off those wicked courses; and, to take away all temptation, supplied him from time to time with money. The affair being carried on in this manner between them with a good deal of caution, it happened that the doctor had a patient in the meantime, who had a bad leg; this he told the person's friends was owing to a decayed bone, which he was obliged to take out to make a cure; otherwise he must either lose his leg or his life; but yet he looked upon it as a very doubtful case. They therefore bade him do as he thought most proper.

Now the doctor, supposing that the patient would never be able to endure the pain without an opiate, deferred the operation till the evening; and in the meantime ordered a water to be distilled from a certain composition, which, being drunk, would throw a person asleep as long as he judged it necessary in this particular case, and which, being brought home, he set in his chamber window, without saying what it was. Now when the evening came on which he was to perform this operation, a messenger arrived from some very considerable persons at Malfi, who were his friends, charging him to come away instantly, for that there had been a great fray among them, in which many people were wounded. The doctor then put off the operation upon the man's leg till morning, and went in a boat directly to Malfi; whilst the lady, knowing that he would be out all night, had her gallant brought privately into her chamber, where she locked him in, till certain persons of her family were gone to bed.

Ruggieri, waiting thus in the chamber, expecting his mistress, and being extremely thirsty, whether from some fatigue, or salt meat that he had eaten, or rather from a bad habit which he had of drinking, happened to cast his eye upon the bottle of water which the doctor had ordered for his patient, and, imagining it was something pleasant to drink, took it all off at a draught; when, in a little time, he fell into a profound lethargy. The lady made what haste she could to her chamber, and, finding him fast asleep, began with a low voice to try to wake him; but he making no reply, nor even stirring, she was much disturbed, and shook him roughly, saying, 'Get up, sluggard! If thou art disposed to sleep, thou shouldst have stayed at home, and not come to sleep here.'

He being pushed in that manner, fell down from a chest, on which he was sitting, upon the ground, and showed no more sense or feeling than if he had been really dead. She was now under greater concern, and began to pull him by the nose, as well as twinge him by the beard, but it was all of no service, for he had tethered his ass too securely. On this she really suspected him to be dead, and pinched and burnt his flesh with the candle, till, finding all to no purpose, and being no doctress, although her husband was a doctor, she took it for granted he was so.

You may easily suppose what her grief now must be, as she loved him beyond all the world; and, not daring to make any noise, she for some time continued silently deploring her calamity, till fearing at last lest dishonour should follow, she thought some means must be contrived to convey him out of the house. Not knowing how to order it herself, she called her maid, and advised with her about it. The girl was under great surprise, and, trying all means to rouse him to no purpose, agreed with her mistress that he was certainly dead, and that it was best to get him away. The lady then said, 'But whither can we carry him, that it may never be suspected tomorrow, when he shall be found, that he was brought from hence?' 'Madam,' she replied, 'I saw late this evening, before a joiner's shop in our neighbourhood, a good large chest; if it be not taken into the house again, we may put him in there well enough, giving him two or three slashes with a penknife. Whoever finds him will scarcely imagine that we should put him there rather than anywhere else; on the contrary, it will rather be supposed that he has been upon some bad exploit, because he has a general ill character, and that he was killed by his adversary, and so shut up in the chest.' She approved of her maid's advice in everything save the wounding him, saying that for all the world she would never consent to that. Accordingly she sent the maid to see if the chest were still there, who brought her back word that it was. And, being stout and lusty, she took him on her shoulders, whilst the lady went first to see that nobody was in the way, and coming to the chest they threw him in, and, shutting the lid, left him there.

The same day two young men, who lent money upon interest, chanced to take a house a little farther on in the same street. These, being willing to gain much and spend but little, and having need of household goods, had taken notice of that chest the day before, and were resolved, if it should be left there all night, to steal it away. At midnight, then, they went and carried it off, without examining at all into it, though it seemed to be very heavy, and set it in a chamber where their wives lay, and then went to bed. Now Ruggieri by this time had gotten the greater part of his sleep over, and his draught being pretty well digested, and its virtue at an end, he awoke before morning; and, though his senses were in some measure returned to him, there was a kind of stupefaction remaining, which continued, not that night only, but for several days; yet he opened his eyes, and, seeing nothing, threw his hands about him, when he perceived himself shut up. He was consequently in the utmost amaze, and said to himself, 'What is the meaning of this? Where am I? Am I asleep or awake? I remember last night to have been in my mistress's chamber, and now methinks I am in a chest. What can it be? Sure the doctor is returned, or some other accident has happened; and she, finding me asleep, put me in here: it can be nothing else.'

Upon that consideration he lay still, and began to listen if he could hear anything stir; and, having lain for some time in an uneasy posture, as the chest was strait, and that side being sore that he had pressed so long upon, he was willing to turn upon the other, when, thrusting his back against one side of the chest, which stood upon an unequal place, he overset it, and down it came to the floor, with such a noise that the women were awakened, and so frightened that they could not speak. Ruggieri upon this knew not what to think, but, finding the chest open with the fall, he thought it better to get out if he could, rather than stay within doors; therefore he went groping up and down in the dark, to find some door or place to make his escape at. They, hearing this, cried out, 'Who is there?' But he, not knowing their voices, made no answer. Upon this they began to call their husbands, but they were so fast asleep having been awake the greatest part of the night, that they heard nothing of the matter. They were then more terrified than before, and went to the window, calling out, 'Thieves! thieves!' This brought many of the neighbours together, who forced their way into the house; and the husbands also were raised with this clamour, and seized upon poor Ruggieri, who was out of his wits almost with surprise to find himself there, where he saw no possibility of making his escape. And by this time the city officers were drawn thither, by reason of the tumult, into whose hands he was delivered, and had by them before the provost, when he was immediately put to the rack, as he was one of bad character; he then confessed that he had gotten into the house with intent to steal, whereupon the provost sentenced him to be hanged out of hand.

That morning the news was carried all over Salerno that Ruggieri was taken breaking into the usurers' house; which the lady and her maid hearing, were so astonished that they could scarcely believe what had happened the preceding night was real; whilst the lady was in such concern for her lover that she was almost distracted. At about eight o'clock in the morning the doctor returned from Malfi, when he inquired for his narcotic water, because he was then going upon his operation; and finding the bottle empty he made a terrible mutiny, telling them that nothing in his house could stand untouched for them. The lady, who had something else lying nearer her heart, replied with some warmth, 'What would you say in anything of consequence, when you make such a stir about a little water?' The doctor then said, 'Wife, you should consider this is no common water; it is water distilled to cause sleep.' And he further told her upon what account it was made. When she heard this, she concluded that Ruggieri had drunk it off, and that they supposed him therefore to be dead; and she added, 'Sir, we knew nothing of your intention, but if you please you can make more;' and he, perceiving that there was no other remedy, did so.

Soon afterwards the maid returned, whom she had sent to learn news of her lover; and she said, 'Madam, there is nobody that speaks well of Ruggieri, whether relation or otherwise, or intends to give him any assistance, but all people agree that he will be hanged tomorrow. One thing, however, I have learnt, which is new; that is, how he came into those usurers' house, which I will tell you. You know the joiner at whose door the chest stood, wherein we had put him; he has just had a warm dispute with another person, who, it seems, owned the chest, and who insisted that the joiner should pay for it: however, he replied that he had not sold it, but that it was stolen away from him. The other answered, "That is not true; you sold it to two usurers, as they themselves told me this morning, when I saw it in their house at the time Ruggieri was taken." "They are liars," quoth the joiner; "I never sold it them, but they stole it from me last night: let us go to them therefore." So away they went together, whilst I returned hither. From hence it is easy to see that Ruggieri was carried in that manner to the place where he was taken; but how he came to himself afterwards is beyond my comprehension.'

The lady now plainly saw how the case was, and told her maid what she had learnt from the doctor, begging that she would lend her assistance in promoting her lover's escape, for it was in her power at once to save his life and her honour. The maid answered, 'Madam, tell me only which way, and I will do it with all my heart.' The lady, as it was a thing that so nearly touched her, had all her wits about her, and gave the maid full instructions what she wished her to do. Accordingly she went to the doctor, and began to weep, saying, 'Sir, I am come to ask your pardon for a great crime which I have committed towards you.' The doctor asked what crime it was. She, continuing to weep, replied, 'You know what sort of a person Ruggieri da Jeroli is, who a twelvemonth ago, taking a fancy for me, obliged me, partly by violence and partly by entreaty, to become his paramour. Knowing last night that you were abroad, he wheedled me so far that I brought him into your house, and took him up into my chamber to be all night with me; when, being thirsty, and I not knowing how to get him either any water or wine, without being seen by my mistress, who was then in the hall, I suddenly recollected to have seen a bottle of water in your chamber, which I fetched, and gave him to drink, and set the bottle again where I found it; and I since understand that you have been in a great passion about it. I confess I did very ill; but who is there that some time or other doth not act amiss? I am extremely concerned for it, not so much upon account of the thing itself, as what has ensued; for it hath brought him in danger of his life. Therefore I earnestly beg your forgiveness, and that you would give me leave to go and assist him to the utmost of my power.'

The doctor, hearing this story, answered merrily, notwithstanding his former passion, 'You have reason enough to be sorry upon your own account, for instead of having a young brisk bedfellow, you had nothing but a great sluggard. You may go then and save the man, if you can, but take care you do so no more; for, if you do, I shall then pay you for all together.' Having this answer, she thought she had made a good beginning; therefore she hastened to the prison and persuaded the gaoler to let her speak to Ruggieri, when, having informed him what answers he was to make to the magistrate if he meant to escape, she went from thence to the judge, to whom she got introduced, and said to him, 'Sir, you have had Ruggieri da Jeroli before you, who was taken up for a thief; but the case is quite otherwise.' And here she related her whole story: how she had brought him into the doctor's house, how she had given him that narcotic water to drink without knowing it, and how he was put into the chest for dead; she afterwards told him what had passed between the joiner and the owner of the chest, making it apparent how he came into the usurers' house.

The judge saw that it would be an easy thing to come at the truth of this matter; therefore he first inquired of the doctor whether the story was true concerning the water, and found it exactly so; he then sent for the joiner and owner of the chest, as also the usurers; and after much examination it appeared that they had stolen the chest the foregoing night, and carried it home. Last of all he had Ruggieri brought before him, when he, being asked where he had lodged that night, replied that he could not tell where he actually did lie, but said his intention was to have lain with the doctor's maid, in whose chamber he had drunk some water to quench his most violent thirst; but what became of him from that time to the time of his awaking, and finding himself in the chest in the usurers' house, that he could give no account of.

The judge was mightily pleased with their accounts, and made them repeat their several stories over and over. At length, perceiving Ruggieri to be innocent, he set him at liberty, and sentenced the usurers to pay a fine of ten crowns. It is easy to imagine what Ruggieri's joy now was, as well as the lady's, who made themselves very merry together afterwards along with the maid, concerning the slashes with her penknife which she meant to have given him, still going on in the same mirth and pleasure from good to better – which I wish may happen always to myself, but without being put into a chest.

(1358)

Sir Arthur Conan Doyle

From A Study in Scarlet

On the very day that I had come to this conclusion, I was standing at the Criterion Bar, when someone tapped me on the shoulder, and turning round I recognized young Stamford, who had been a dresser under me at Bart's. The sight of a friendly face in the great wilderness of London is a pleasant thing indeed to a lonely man. In old days Stamford had never been a particular crony of mine, but now I hailed him with enthusiasm, and he, in his turn, appeared to be delighted to see me. In the exuberance of my joy, I asked him to lunch with me at the Holborn, and we started of together in a hansom.

'Whatever have you been doing with yourself, Watson?' he asked in undisguised wonder, as we rattled through the crowded London streets. 'You are as thin as a lath and as brown as a nut.'

I gave him a short sketch of my adventures, and had hardly concluded it by the time that we reached our destination.

'Poor devil!' he said, commiseratingly, after he had listened to my misfortunes. 'What are you up to now?'

'Look for lodgings,' I answered. 'Trying to solve the problem as to whether it is possible to get comfortable rooms at a reasonable price.'

'That's a strange thing,' remarked my companion, 'you are the second man to-day that has used that expression to me.'

'And who was the first?' I asked.

'A fellow who is working at the chemical laboratory up at the hospital. He was bemoaning himself this morning because he could not get someone to go halves with him in some nice rooms which he had found, and which were too much for his purse.'

'By Jove!' I cried; 'if he really wants someone to share the rooms and the expense, I am the very man for him. I should prefer having a partner to being alone.'

Young Stamford looked rather strangely at me over his wine-glass.

'You don't know Sherlock Holmes yet,' he said; 'perhaps you would not care for him as a constant companion.'

'Why, what is there against him?'

'Oh, I didn't say there was anything against him. He is a little queer in his ideas – an enthusiast in some branches of science. As far as I know he is a decent fellow enough.'

'A medical student, I suppose?' said I.

'No – I have no idea what he intends to go in for. I believe he is well up in anatomy, and he is a first-class chemist; but, as far as I know, he has never taken out any systematic medical classes. His studies are very desultory and eccentric, but he has amassed a lot of out-of-the-way knowledge which would astonish his professors.' . . .

They meet in the chemical laboratory at Bart's.

'Dr Watson, Mr Sherlock Holmes,' said Stamford, introducing us.

'How are you?' he said cordially, gripping my hand with a strength for which I should hardly have given him credit. 'You have been to Afghanistan, I perceive.'

'How on earth did you know that?' I asked in astonishment.

'Never mind,' said he, chuckling to himself.

(1887)

And we're off!

Dr John H. Watson had qualified MD (London) from St Bartholomew's Hospital in 1878. He had proceeded to Netley for the training course of the Army Medical Department, was shipped to Bombay as Assistant Surgeon to the 5th Northumberland Fusiliers, joined his regiment while it was fighting the second Afghan war at Kandahar, was seconded to the Berkshires for the disastrous battle of Maiwand on 27 July 1880, in which he was wounded – the bullet shattered his clavicle and grazed the subclavian artery – and 'should have fallen into the hands of the murderous Ghazis had it not been for the devotion and courage shown by Murray, my orderly, who threw me across a packhorse, and succeeded in bringing me safely to the British lines'. He got typhoid while recovering in hospital in Peshawur. Dr Watson was invalided home in the troopship *Orontes* to Portsmouth.

The day after their meeting at Bart's, the pair moved into No. 221B Baker Street. Holmes relieved his room-mate's bafflement by explaining how he knew that Watson had come from Afghanistan: a gentleman of medical mien with a military air, the tint of his face from fierce sunburn, because his wrists remained pale, haggard from sickness, and with an unnaturally stiff left arm. 'Where in the tropics could an English army doctor have seen much hardship and got his arm wounded? Clearly in Afghanistan. The whole train of thought did not occupy a second. I then remarked that you came from Afghanistan, and you were astonished.'

Not in the slightest elementary.

Watson was the worthy, bouncing twin of Sir Arthur Conan Doyle's (1859–1930) happy Baker Street event. Watson afforded the convenience and authority of a doctor's eye to the Sherlock Holmes stories; Doyle himself had qualified at Edinburgh in 1881.

Sherlock Holmes's literary model was Dr Joseph Bell, who taught Doyle at the Royal Infirmary. Bell extended the exhortation which every student hears on clinical examination: 'Eyes first and most, hands next and least, tongue not at all.' He insisted that: 'The precise and intelligent recognition and appreciation of minor differences is the real essential factor in a successful medical diagnosis.'

Bell was proud of applying this teaching beyond the pathological to the social, instantly detecting a cobbler from the bulge of his trousers and a drunk from that of his breast-pocket, and spotting a recently discharged NCO because, though respectful, he kept his hat on when standing at the doctor's desk. Bell modestly admitted later that his exceptional student was indebted 'much less than he thinks to me'.

Holmes's famed methods are a doctor's methods. 'Detection is, or ought to be, an exact science, and should be treated in the same cold and unemotional manner,' Doyle propounded. Medical diagnosis is the unromantic application of trained observation to scientific knowledge and experience – admittedly, with the help of instruments more complicated than a magnifying-glass. Thus can be logically evaluated the significance of a cardiac murmur; so can be explained the curious incident of the dog which did nothing in the night-time.

Holmes's pictorial model was the younger brother of Sidney Paget, the stories' illustrator in *The Strand Magazine*. The face which shines in public imagination as vividly as Phiz's Mr Pickwick was seen by its originator as much less kindly, razor-sharp, with small eyes set close aside a nose like a hawk's bill.

Dr Doyle practised as a GP in Portsmouth from 1882 to 1890, from Bush Villa, Southsea, which cost him £50 a year. At first he suffered the professional indignity of opening his own front door to his infrequent patients. He was making £300 a year when he ambitiously moved to Harley Street to be an oculist. He rented a consulting-room in which he waited, and a waiting-room in which nobody waited at all. In August 1891, abed with flu, Doyle calculated that he could abandon medicine for writing. 'No longer would I have to conform to professional dress or try to please anyone else. I would be free to live how I liked and where I liked.' He had rightly perceived the kernel of the literary life, tossing his damp handkerchief to the ceiling in exultation.

Doyle was knighted in 1902 for producing a sixpenny pamphlet insisting to the world that the British had not behaved barbarically during the South African war (he had volunteered, serving in a field hospital). He later became enshrouded in spiritualism, founding the Psychic Bookshop, championing mediums' rights (under a law of James I, they could be jailed), and illustrating his widespread lectures with awesome photographs of ghosts and fairies, which were unhappily revealed as someone's leg-pulls. He developed angina still a fervent spiritualist and died, possibly out of curiosity.

Doyle writes with clinical exactitude, with embracing but steadfastly relevant detail. *Sherlock Holmes, The Exploits of Brigadier Gerard* (1895), *Micah Clarke* (1889) and *The White Company* (1890) are cushioned with nearly a hundred short stories, fifteen of them about medical life. In one, a doctor got the idea of curing facial palsy by having a surgeon remove his patient's ear, to be accomplished on a blanket-draped kitchen-table by the light of two candles, which blew out. In the confusion, the struggling, shouting patient was smothered in towels, chloroformed, operated upon, and afterwards revealed as a one-eared doctor, the half-chloroformed patient having fallen under the table and been discovered asleep, hidden by the blanket. The surgeon 'was very nice about it, and made the most handsome apologies', and 'sent round his ear the next day in a jar of methylated spirit'.

This next story is a delightful send-up of a lugubrious scientist, who views our noblest thoughts and fieriest passions purely as expressions of bodily mechanics – a common failing among doctors. Both stories are very funny, though I entertain a Sherlockian suspicion that neither was intended to be.

A Physiologist's Wife

PROFESSOR AINSLIE GREY had not come down to breakfast at the usual hour. The presentation chiming-clock which stood between the terra-cotta busts of Claude Bernard and of John Hunter upon the dining-room mantelpiece had rung out the half-hour and the three-quarters. Now its golden hand was verging upon the nine, and yet there were no signs of the master of the house.

It was an unprecedented occurrence. During the twelve years that she had kept house for him, his younger sister had never known him a second behind his time. She sat now in front of the high silver coffee-pot, uncertain whether to order the gong to be resounded or to wait on in silence. Either course might be a mistake. Her brother was not a man who permitted mistakes.

Miss Ainslie Grey was rather above the middle height, thin, with peering, puckered eyes, and the rounded shoulders which mark the bookish woman. Her face was long and spare, flecked with colour above the cheek-bones, with a reasonable, thoughtful forehead, and a dash of absolute obstinacy in her thin lips and prominent chin. Snow-white cuffs and collar, with a plain dark dress, cut with almost Quaker-like simplicity, bespoke the primness of her taste. An ebony cross hung over her flattened chest. She sat very upright in her chair, listening with raised eyebrows, and swinging her eye-glasses backwards and forwards with a nervous gesture which was peculiar to her.

Suddenly she gave a sharp, satisfied jerk of the head, and began to pour out the coffee. From outside there came the dull thudding sound of heavy feet upon thick carpet. The door swung open, and the Professor entered with a quick, nervous step. He nodded to his sister, and seating himself at the other side of the table, began to open the small pile of letters which lay beside his plate.

Professor Ainslie Grey was at that time forty-three years of age – nearly twelve years older than his sister. His career had been a brilliant one. At Edinburgh, at Cambridge, and at Vienna he had laid the foundations of his great reputation, both in physiology and in zoology.

His pamphlet, 'On the Mesoblastic Origin of Excitomotor Nerve Roots,' had won him his fellowship of the Royal Society; and his researches, 'Upon the Nature of Bathybius, with some Remarks upon Lithococci,' had been translated into at least three European languages. He had been referred to by one of the greatest living authorities as being the very type and embodiment of all that was best in modern science. No wonder, then, that when the commercial city of Birchespool decided to create a medical school, they were only too glad to confer the chair of physiology upon Mr Ainslie Grey. They valued him the more from the conviction that their class was only one step in his upward journey, and that the first vacancy would remove him to some more illustrious seat of learning.

In person he was not unlike his sister. The same eyes, the same contour, the same intellectual forehead. His lips, however, were firmer, and his long, thin lower jaw was sharper and more decided. He ran his finger and thumb down it from time to time, as he glanced over his letters.

'Those maids are very noisy,' he remarked, as a clack of tongues sounded in the distance.

'It is Sarah,' said his sister; 'I shall speak about it.'

She had handed over his coffee-cup and was sipping at her own, glancing furtively through her narrowed lids at the austere face of her brother.

'The first great advance of the human race,' said the Professor, 'was when, by the development of their left frontal convolutions, they attained the power of speech. Their second advance was when they learned to control that power. Woman has not yet attained the second stage.'

He half closed his eyes as he spoke, and thrust his chin forward, but as he ceased he had a trick of suddenly opening both eyes very wide and staring sternly at his interlocutor.

'I am not garrulous, John,' said his sister.

'No, Ada; in many respects you approach the superior or male type.'

The Professor bowed over his egg with the manner of one who utters a courtly compliment; but the lady pouted, and gave an impatient little shrug of her shoulders.

'You were late this morning, John,' she remarked, after a pause.

'Yes, Ada; I slept badly. Some little cerebral congestion, no doubt due to overstimulation of the centres of thought. I have been a little disturbed in my mind.'

His sister stared across at him in astonishment. The Professor's mental processes had hitherto been as regular as his habits. Twelve years' continual intercourse had taught her that he lived in a serene and rarefied atmosphere of scientific calm, high above the petty emotions which affect humbler minds.

'You are surprised, Ada,' he remarked. 'Well, I cannot wonder at it.

I should have been surprised myself if I had been told that I was so sensitive to vascular influences. For, after all, all disturbances are vascular if you probe them deep enough. I am thinking of getting married.'

'Not Mrs O'James?' cried Ada Grey, laying down her egg-spoon.

'My dear, you have the feminine quality of receptivity very remarkably developed. Mrs O'James is the lady in question.'

'But you know so little of her. The Esdailes themselves know so little. She is really only an acquaintance, although she is staying at The Lindens. Would it not be wise to speak to Mrs Esdaile first, John?'

'I do not think, Ada, that Mrs Esdaile is at all likely to say anything which would materially affect my course of action. I have given the matter due consideration. The scientific mind is slow at arriving at conclusions, but having once formed them, it is not prone to change. Matrimony is the natural condition of the human race. I have, as you know, been so engaged in academical and other work, that I have had no time to devote to merely personal questions. It is different now, and I see no valid reason why I should forgo this opportunity of seeking a suitable helpmate.'

'And you are engaged?'

'Hardly that, Ada. I ventured yesterday to indicate to the lady that I was prepared to submit to the common lot of humanity. I shall wait upon her after my morning lecture, and learn how far my proposals meet with her acquiescence. But you frown, Ada!'

His sister started, and made an effort to conceal her expression of annoyance. She even stammered out some few words of congratulation, but a vacant look had come into her brother's eyes, and he was evidently not listening to her.

'I am sure, John,' she said, 'that I wish you the happiness which you deserve. If I hesitated at all, it is because I know how much is at stake, and because the thing is so sudden, so unexpected.' Her thin, white hand stole up to the black cross upon her bosom. 'These are moments when we need guidance, John. If I could persuade you to turn to spiritual –'

The Professor waved the suggestion away with a deprecating hand.

'It is useless to reopen that question,' he said. 'We cannot argue upon it. You assume more than I can grant. I am forced to dispute your premises. We have no common basis.'

His sister sighed.

'You have no faith,' she said.

'I have faith in those great evolutionary forces which are leading the human race to some unknown but elevated goal.'

'You believe in nothing.'

'On the contrary, my dear Ada, I believe in the differentiation of protoplasm.'

She shook her head sadly. It was the one subject upon which she ventured to dispute her brother's infallibility.

'This is rather beside the question,' remarked the Professor, folding up his napkin. 'If I am not mistaken, there is some possibility of another matrimonial event occurring in the family. Eh, Ada? What!'

His small eyes glittered with sly facetiousness as he shot a twinkle at his sister. She sat very stiff, and traced patterns upon the cloth with the sugar-tongs.

'Dr James M'Murdo O'Brien –' said the Professor sonorously.

'Don't, John, don't!' cried Miss Ainslie Grey.

'Dr James M'Murdo O'Brien,' continued her brother inexorably, 'is a man who has already made his mark upon the science of the day. He is my first and my most distinguished pupil. I assure you, Ada, that his 'Remarks upon the Bile-Pigments, with special reference to Urobilin,' is likely to live as a classic. It is not too much to say that he has revolutionised our view about urobilin.'

He paused, but his sister sat silent, with bent head and flushed cheeks. The little ebony cross rose and fell with her hurried breathings.

'Dr James M'Murdo O'Brien has, as you know, the offer of the physiological chair at Melbourne. He has been in Australia five years, and has a brilliant future before him. Today he leaves us for Edinburgh, and in two months' time he goes out to take over his new duties. You know his feeling towards you. It rests with you as to whether he goes out alone. Speaking for myself, I cannot imagine any higher mission for a woman of culture than to go through life in the company of a man who is capable of such a research as that which Dr James M'Murdo O'Brien has brought to a successful conclusion.'

'He has not spoken to me,' murmured the lady.

'Ah, there are signs which are more subtle than speech,' said her brother, wagging his head. 'You are pale. Your vasomotor system is excited. Your arterioles have contracted. Let me entreat you to compose yourself. I think I hear the carriage. I fancy that you may have a visitor this morning, Ada. You will excuse me now.'

With a quick glance at the clock he strode off into the hall, and within a few minutes he was rattling in his quiet, well-appointed brougham through the brick-lined streets of Birchespool.

His lecture over, Professor Ainslie Grey paid a visit to his laboratory, where he adjusted several scientific instruments, made a note as to the progress of three separate infusions of bacteria, cut half a dozen sections with a microtome, and finally resolved the difficulties of seven different gentlemen, who were pursuing researches in as many separate lines of inquiry. Having thus conscientiously and methodically completed the routine of his duties, he returned to his carriage and ordered the coachman to drive him to The Lindens. His face as he drove was cold and impassive, but he drew his fingers from time to time down his prominent chin with a jerky, twitchy movement.

The Lindens was an old-fashioned, ivy-clad house which had once been in the country, but was now caught in the long, red-brick feelers of the growing city. It still stood back from the road in the privacy of its own grounds. A winding path, lined with laurel bushes, led to the arched and porticoed entrance. To the right was a lawn, and at the far side, under the shadow of a hawthorn, a lady sat in a garden-chair with a book in her hands. At the click of the gate she started, and the Professor, catching sight of her, turned away from the door, and strode in her direction.

'What! won't you go in and see Mrs Esdaile?' she asked, sweeping out from under the shadow of the hawthorn.

She was a small woman, strongly feminine, from the rich coils of her light-coloured hair to the dainty garden-slipper which peeped from under her cream-tinted dress. One tiny, well-gloved hand was outstretched in greeting, while the other pressed a thick, green-covered volume against her side. Her decision and quick, tactful manner bespoke the mature woman of the world; but her up-raised face had preserved a girlish and even infantile expression of innocence in its large, fearless grey eyes, and sensitive, humorous mouth. Mrs O'James was a widow, and she was two-and-thirty years of age; but neither fact could have been deduced from her appearance.

'You will surely go in and see Mrs Esdaile,' she repeated, glancing up at him with eyes which had in them something between a challenge and a caress.

'I did not come to see Mrs Esdaile,' he answered, with no relaxation of his cold and grave manner; 'I came to see you.'

'I am sure I should be highly honoured,' she said, with just the slightest little touch of brogue in her accent. 'What are the students to do without their Professor?'

'I have already completed my academic duties. Take my arm, and we shall walk in the sunshine. Surely we cannot wonder that Eastern people should have made a deity of the sun. It is the great, beneficent force of Nature – man's ally against cold, sterility, and all that is abhorrent to him. What were you reading?'

'Hale's *Matter and Life*.'

The Professor raised his thick eyebrows.

'Hale!' he said, and then again in a kind of whisper, 'Hale!'

'You differ from him?' she asked.

'It is not I who differ from him. I am only a monad – a thing of no moment. The whole tendency of the highest plane of modern thought differs from him. He defends the indefensible. He is an excellent observer, but a feeble reasoner. I should not recommend you to found your conclusions upon "Hale".'

'I must read *Nature's Chronicle* to counteract his pernicious influence,' said Mrs O'James, with a soft, cooing laugh.

Nature's Chronicle was one of the many books in which Profesor Ainslie Grey had enforced the negative doctrines of scientific agnosticism.

'It is a faulty work,' said he; 'I cannot recommend it. I would rather refer you to the standard writings of some of my older and more eloquent colleagues.'

There was a pause in their talk as they paced up and down on the green, velvet-like lawn in the genial sunshine.

'Have you thought at all,' he asked at last, 'of the matter upon which I spoke to you last night?'

She said nothing, but walked by his side with her eyes averted and her face aslant.

'I would not hurry you unduly,' he continued. 'I know that it is a matter which can scarcely be decided off-hand. In my own case, it cost me some thought before I ventured to make the suggestion. I am not an emotional man, but I am conscious in your presence of the great evolutionary instinct which makes either sex the complement of the other.'

'You believe in love, then?' she asked, with a twinkling, upward glance.

'I am forced to.'

'And yet you can deny the soul?'

'How far these questions are psychic and how far material is still *sub judice*,' said the Professor, with an air of toleration. 'Protoplasm may prove to be the physical basis of love as well as of life.'

'How inflexible you are!' she exclaimed; 'you would draw love down to the level of physics.'

'Or draw physics up to the level of love.'

'Come, that is much better,' she cried, with her sympathetic laugh. 'That is really very pretty, and puts science in quite a delightful light.'

Her eyes sparkled, and she tossed her chin with a pretty, wilful air of a woman who is mistress of the situation.

'I have reason to believe,' said the Professor, 'that my position here will prove to be only a stepping-stone to some wider scene of scientific activity. Yet, even here, my chair brings me in some fifteen hundred pounds a year, which is supplemented by a few hundreds from my books. I should therefore be in a position to provide you with those comforts to which you are accustomed. So much for my pecuniary position. As to my constitution, it has always been sound. I have never suffered from any illness in my life, save fleeting attacks of cephalalgia, the result of too prolonged a stimulation of the centres of cerebration. My father and mother had no sign of any morbid diathesis, but I will not conceal from you that my grandfather was afflicted with podagra.'

Mrs O'James looked startled.

'Is that very serious?' she asked.

'It is gout,' said the Professor.

'Oh, is that all? It sounded much worse than that.'

'It is a grave taint, but I trust that I shall not be a victim to atavism. I have laid these facts before you because they are factors which cannot be overlooked in forming your decision. May I ask now whether you see your way to accepting my proposal?'

He paused in his walk, and looked earnestly and expectantly down at her.

A struggle was evidently going on in her mind. Her eyes were cast down, her little slipper tapped the lawn, and her fingers played nervously with her chatelaine. Suddenly, with a sharp, quick gesture which had in it something of *abandon* and recklessness, she held out her hand to her companion.

'I accept,' she said.

They were standing under the shadow of the hawthorn. He stooped gravely down, and kissed her glove-covered fingers.

'I trust that you may never have cause to regret your decision,' he said.

'I trust that *you* never may,' she cried, with a heaving breast.

There were tears in her eyes, and her lips twitched with some strong emotion.

'Come into the sunshine again,' said he. 'It is the great restorative. Your nerves are shaken. Some little congestion of the medulla and pons. It is always instructive to reduce psychic or emotional conditions to their physical equivalents. You feel that your anchor is still firm in a bottom of ascertained fact.'

'But it is so dreadfully unromantic,' said Mrs O'James, with her old twinkle.

'Romance is the offspring of imagination and of ignorance. Where science throws her calm, clear light there is happily no room for romance.'

'But is not love romance?' she asked.

'Not at all. Love has been taken away from the poets, and has been brought within the domain of true science. It may prove to be one of the great cosmic elementary forces. When the atom of hydrogen draws the atom of chlorine towards it to form the perfected molecule of hydrochloric acid, the force which it exerts may be intrinsically similar to that which draws me to you. Attraction and repulsion appear to be the primary forces. This is attraction.'

'And here is repulsion,' said Mrs O'James, as a stout, florid lady came sweeping across the lawn in their direction. 'So glad you have come out, Mrs Esdaile! Here is Professor Grey.'

'How do you do, Professor?' said the lady, with some little pomposity of manner. 'You were very wise to stay out here on so lovely a day. Is it not heavenly?'

'It is certainly very fine weather,' the Professor answered.

'Listen to the wind sighing in the trees!' cried Mrs Esdaile, holding up one finger. 'It is Nature's lullaby. Could you not imagine it, Professor Grey, to be the whisperings of angels?'

'The idea had not occurred to me, madam.'

'Ah, Professor, I have always the same complaint against you. A want of *rapport* with the deeper meanings of Nature. Shall I say a want of imagination? You do not feel an emotional thrill at the singing of that thrush?'

'I confess that I am not conscious of one, Mrs Esdaile.'

'Or at the delicate tint of that background of leaves? See the rich greens!'

'Chlorophyll,' murmured the Professor.

'Science is so hopelessly prosaic. It dissects and labels, and loses sight of the great things in its attention to the little ones. You have a poor opinion of woman's intellect, Professor Grey. I think that I have heard you say so.'

'It is a question of avoirdupois,' said the Professor, closing his eyes and shrugging his shoulders. 'The female cerebrum averages two ounces less in weight than the male. No doubt there are exceptions. Nature is always elastic.'

'But the heaviest thing is not always the strongest,' said Mrs O'James, laughing. 'Isn't there a law of compensation in science? May we not hope to make up in quality what we lack in quantity?'

'I think not,' remarked the Professor gravely. 'But there is your luncheon-gong. No, thank you, Mrs Esdaile, I cannot stay. My carriage is waiting. Goodbye. Goodbye, Mrs O'James.'

He raised his hat and stalked slowly away among the laurel bushes.

'He has no taste,' said Mrs Esdaile – 'no eye for beauty.'

'On the contrary,' Mrs O'James answered, with a saucy little jerk of the chin. 'He has just asked me to be his wife.'

As Professor Ainslie Grey ascended the steps of his house, the hall-door opened and a dapper gentleman stepped briskly out. He was somewhat sallow in the face, with dark, beady eyes, and a short, black beard with an aggressive bristle. Thought and work had left their traces upon his face, but he moved with the brisk activity of a man who had not yet bade goodbye to his youth.

'I'm in luck's way,' he cried. 'I wanted to see you.'

'Then come back into the library,' said the Professor; 'you must stay and have lunch with us.'

The two men entered the hall, and the Professor led the way into his private sanctum. He motioned his companion into an arm-chair.

'I trust that you have been successful, O'Brien,' said he. 'I should be loath to exercise any undue pressure upon my sister Ada; but I have given her to understand that there is no one whom I should prefer for a brother-in-law to my most brilliant scholar, the author of "Some Remarks upon the Bile-Pigments, with special reference to Urobilin".'

'You are very kind, Professor Grey – you have always been very kind,' said the other. 'I approached Miss Grey upon the subject; she did not say No.'

'She said Yes, then?'

'No; she proposed to leave the matter open until my return from Edinburgh. I go today, as you know, and I hope to commence my research tomorrow.'

'On the comparative anatomy of the vermiform appendix, by James M'Murdo O'Brien,' said the Professor sonorously. 'It is a glorious subject – a subject which lies at the very root of evolutionary philosophy.'

'Ah, she is the dearest girl,' cried O'Brien, with a sudden little spurt of Celtic enthusiasm – 'she is the soul of truth and of honour.'

'The vermiform appendix –' began the Professor.

'She is an angel from heaven,' interrupted the other. 'I fear that it is my advocacy of scientific freedom in religious thought which stands in my way with her.'

'You must not truckle upon that point. You must be true to your convictions; let there be no compromise there.'

'My reason is true to agnosticism, and yet I am conscious of a void – a vacuum. I had feelings at the old church at home between the scent of the incense and the roll of the organ, such as I have never experienced in the laboratory or the lecture-room.'

'Sensuous – purely sensuous,' said the Professor, rubbing his chin. 'Vague hereditary tendencies stirred into life by the stimulation of the nasal and auditory nerves.'

'Maybe so, maybe so,' the younger man answered thoughtfully. 'But this was not what I wished to speak to you about. Before I enter your family, your sister and you have a claim to know all that I can tell you about my career. Of my worldly prospects I have already spoken to you. There is only one point which I have omitted to mention. I am a widower.'

The Professor raised his eyebrows.

'This is news indeed,' said he.

'I married shortly after my arrival in Australia. Miss Thurston was her name. I met her in society. It was a most unhappy match.'

Some painful emotion possessed him. His quick, expressive features quivered, and his white hands tightened upon the arms of the chair. The Professor turned away towards the window.

'You are the best judge,' he remarked; 'but I should not think that it was necessary to go into details.'

'You have a right to know everything – you and Miss Grey. It is not a matter on which I can well speak to her direct. Poor Jinny was the best of women, but she was open to flattery, and liable to be misled by designing persons. She was untrue to me, Grey. It is a hard thing to say of the dead, but she was untrue to me. She fled back to Auckland with a man whom she had known before her marriage. The brig which carried them foundered, and not a soul was saved.'

'This is very painful, O'Brien,' said the Professor, with a deprecatory motion of his hand. 'I cannot see, however, how it affects your relation to my sister.'

'I have eased my conscience,' said O'Brien, rising from his chair; 'I have told you all that there is to tell. I should not like the story to reach you through any lips but my own.'

'You are right, O'Brien. Your action has been most honourable and considerate. But you are not to blame in the matter, save that perhaps you showed a little precipitancy in choosing a life-partner without due care and inquiry.'

O'Brien drew his hand across his eyes.

'Poor girl!' he cried. 'God help me, I love her still! But I must go.'

'You will lunch with us?'

'No, Professor; I have my packing still to do. I have already bade Miss Grey adieu. In two months I shall see you again.'

'You will probably find me a married man.'

'Married!'

'Yes, I have been thinking of it.'

'My dear Professor, let me congratulate you with all my heart. I had no idea. Who is the lady?'

'Mrs O'James is her name – a widow of the same nationality as yourself. But to return to matters of importance, I should be very happy to see the proofs of your paper upon the vermiform appendix. I may be able to furnish you with material for a footnote or two.'

'Your assistance will be invaluable to me,' said O'Brien, with enthusiasm, and the two men parted in the hall. The Professor walked back into the dining-room, where his sister was already seated at the luncheon-table.

'I shall be married at the registrar's,' he remarked; 'I should strongly recommend you to do the same.'

Professor Ainslie Grey was as good as his word. A fortnight's cessation of his classes gave him an opportunity which was too good to let pass. Mrs O'James was an orphan, without relations and almost without friends in the country. There was no obstacle in the way of a speedy wedding. They were married, accordingly, in the quietest manner possible, and went off to Cambridge together, where the Professor and his charming wife were present at several academic observances, and varied the routine of their honeymoon by incursions into biological laboratories and medical libraries. Scientific friends were loud in their congratulations, not only upon Mrs Grey's beauty, but upon the unusual quickness and intelligence she displayed in discussing physiological questions. The professor was himself astonished at the accuracy of her information. 'You have a remarkable range of knowledge for a woman, Jeannette,' he remarked upon more than one occasion. He was even prepared to admit that her cerebrum might be of the normal weight.

One foggy, drizzling morning they returned to Birchespool, for the next day would reopen the session, and Professor Ainslie Grey prided himself upon having never once in his life failed to appear in his lecture-room at the very stroke of the hour. Miss Ada Grey welcomed them with a constrained cordiality and handed over the keys of office to the new mistress. Mrs Grey pressed her warmly to remain, but she explained that she had already accepted an invitation which would engage her for some months. The same evening she departed for the south of England.

A couple of days later the maid carried a card, just after breakfast, into the library where the Professor sat revising his morning lecture. It announced the re-arrival of Dr James M'Murdo O'Brien. Their meeting was effusively genial on the part of the younger man, and coldly precise on that of his former teacher.

'You see there have been changes,' said the Professor.

'So I heard. Miss Grey told me in her letters, and I read the notice in the *British Medical Journal*. So it's really married you are. How quickly and quietly you have managed it all!'

'I am constitutionally averse to anything in the nature of show or ceremony. My wife is a sensible woman – I may even go the length of saying that, for a woman, she is abnormally sensible. She quite agreed with me in the course which I have adopted.'

'And your research on Vallisneria?'

'This matrimonial incident has interrupted it, but I have resumed my classes, and we shall soon be quite in harness again.'

'I must see Miss Grey before I leave England. We have corresponded, and I think that all will be well. She must come out with me. I don't think I could go without her.'

The Professor shook his head.

'Your nature is not so weak as you pretend,' he said. 'Questions of this sort are, after all, quite subordinate to the great duties of life.'

O'Brien smiled.

'You would have me take out my Celtic soul and put in a Saxon one,' he said. 'Either my brain is too small or my heart is too big. But when may I call and pay my respects to Mrs Grey? Will she be at home this afternoon?'

'She is at home now. Come into the morning-room. She will be glad to make your acquaintance.'

They walked across the linoleum-paved hall. The Professor opened the door of the room, and walked in, followed by his friend. Mrs Grey was sitting in a basket-chair by the window, light and fairy-like in a loose-flowing, pink morning-gown. Seeing a visitor, she rose and swept towards them. The Professor heard a dull thud behind him. O'Brien had fallen back into a chair, with his hand pressed tight to his side.

'Jinny!' he gasped – 'Jinny!'

Mrs Grey stopped dead in her advance, and stared at him with a face from which every expression had been struck out, save one of astonishment and horror. Then with a sharp intaking of the breath she reeled, and would have fallen had the Professor not thrown his long, nervous arm round her.

'Try this sofa,' said he.

She sank back among the cushions with the same white, cold, dead look upon her face. The Professor stood with his back to the empty fireplace and glanced from the one to the other.

'So, O'Brien,' he said at last, 'you have already made the acquaintance of my wife!'

'Your wife,' cried his friend hoarsely. 'She is no wife of yours. God help me, she is *my* wife.'

The Professor stood rigidly upon the hearth-rug. His long, thin fingers were intertwined, and his head had sunk a little forward. His two companions had eyes only for each other.

'Jinny!' said he.

'James!'

'How could you leave me so, Jinny? How could you have the heart to do it? I thought you were dead. I mourned for your death – ay, and you have made me mourn for you living. You have withered my life.'

She made no answer, but lay back among the cushions with her eyes still fixed upon him.

'Why do you not speak?'

'Because you are right, James. I have treated you cruelly – shamefully. But it is not as bad as you think.'

'You fled with De Horta.'

'No, I did not. At the last moment my better nature prevailed. He went alone. But I was ashamed to come back after what I had written to you. I could not face you. I took passage alone to England under a new name, and here I have lived ever since. It seemed to me that I was beginning life again. I knew that you thought I was drowned. Who could have dreamed that Fate would throw us together again! When the Professor asked me –'

She stopped and gave a gasp for breath.

'You are faint,' said the Professor – 'keep the head low; it aids the cerebral circulation.' He flattened down the cushion. 'I am sorry to leave you, O'Brien; but I have my class duties to look to. Possibly I may find you here when I return.'

With a grim and rigid face he strode out of the room. Not one of the three hundred students who listened to his lecture saw any change in his manner and appearance, or could have guessed that the austere gentleman in front of them had found out at last how hard it is to rise above one's humanity. The lecture over, he performed his routine duties in the laboratory, and then drove back to his own house. He did not enter by the front door, but passed through the garden to the folding glass casement which led out of the morning-room. As he approached he heard his wife's voice and O'Brien's in loud and animated talk. He paused among the rose-bushes, uncertain whether to interrupt them or no. Nothing was further from his nature than to play the eavesdropper; but as he stood, still hesitating, words fell upon his ear which struck him rigid and motionless.

'You are still my wife, Jinny,' said O'Brien; 'I forgive you from the bottom of my heart. I love you, and I have never ceased to love you, though you had forgotten me.'

'No, James, my heart was always in Melbourne. I have always been yours. I thought that it was better for you that I should seem to be dead.'

'You must choose between us now, Jinny. If you determine to remain here, I shall not open my lips. There shall be no scandal. If, on the other hand, you come with me, it's little I care about the world's opinion. Perhaps I am as much to blame as you are. I thought too much of my work and too little of my wife.'

The Professor heard the cooing, caressing laugh which he knew so well.

'I shall go with you, James,' she said.

'And the Professor – ?'

'The poor Professor! But he will not mind much, James; he has no heart.'

'We must tell him our resolution.'

'There is no need,' said Professor Ainslie Grey, stepping in through the open casement. 'I have overheard the latter part of your conversation. I hesitated to interrupt you before you came to a conclusion.'

O'Brien stretched out his hand and took that of the woman. They stood together with the sunshine on their faces. The Professor paused at the casement with his hands behind his back and his long, black shadow fell between them.

'You have come to a wise decision,' said he. 'Go back to Australia together, and let what has passed be blotted out of your lives.'

'But you – you –' stammered O'Brien.

The Professor waved his hand.

'Never trouble about me,' he said.

The woman gave a gasping cry.

'What can I do or say?' she wailed. 'How could I have foreseen this? I thought my old life was dead. But it has come back again, with all its hopes and its desires. What can I say to you, Ainslie? I have brought shame and disgrace upon a worthy man. I have blasted your life. How you must hate and loathe me! I wish to God that I had never been born!'

'I neither hate nor loathe you, Jeannette,' said the Professor quietly. 'You are wrong in regretting your birth, for you have a worthy mission before you in aiding the life-work of a man who has shown himself capable of the highest order of scientific research. I cannot with justice blame you personally for what has occurred. How far the individual monad is to be held responsible for hereditary and engrained tendencies, is a question upon which science has not yet said her last word.'

He stood with his finger-tips touching, and his body inclined as one who is gravely expounding a difficult and impersonal subject. O'Brien had stepped forward to say something, but the other's attitude and manner froze the words upon his lips. Condolence or sympathy would be an impertinence to one who could so easily merge his private griefs in broad questions of abstract philosophy.

'It is needless to prolong the situation,' the Professor continued, in the same measured tones. 'My brougham stands at the door. I beg that you will use it as your own. Perhaps it would be as well that you should leave the town without unnecessary delay. Your things, Jeannette, shall be forwarded.'

O'Brien hesitated with a hanging head.

'On the contrary. I think that of the three of us you come best out of the affair. You have nothing to be ashamed of.'

'Your sister –'

'I shall see that the matter is put to her in its true light. Goodbye, Jeannette!'

'Goodbye!'

Their hands met, and for one short moment their eyes also. It was only a glance, but for the first and last time the woman's intuition cast a light for itself into the dark places of a strong man's soul. She gave a little gasp, and her other hand rested for an instant, as white and as light as thistle-down, upon his shoulder.

'James, James!' she cried. 'Don't you see that he is stricken to the heart?'

He turned her quietly away from him.

'I am not an emotional man,' he said. 'I have my duties – my research on Vallisneria. The brougham is there. Your cloak is in the hall. Tell John where you wish to be driven. He will bring you anything you need. Now go.'

His last two words were so sudden, so volcanic, in such contrast to his measured voice and mask-like face, that they swept the two away from him. He closed the door behind them and paced slowly up and down the room. Then he passed into the library and looked out over the wire blind. The carriage was rolling away. He caught a last glimpse of the woman who had been his wife. He saw the feminine droop of her head, and the curve of her beautiful throat.

Under some foolish, aimless impulse, he took a few quick steps towards the door. Then he turned, and, throwing himself into his study chair, he plunged back into his work.

There was little scandal about this singular, domestic incident. The Professor had few personal friends, and seldom went into society. His marriage had been so quiet that most of his colleagues had never ceased to regard him as a bachelor. Mrs Esdaile and a few others might talk, but their field for gossip was limited, for they could only guess vaguely at the cause of this sudden separation.

The Professor was as punctual as ever at his classes, and as zealous in directing the laboratory work of those who studied under him. His own private researches were pushed on with feverish energy. It was no uncommon thing for his servants, when they came down of a morning, to hear the shrill scratchings of his tireless pen, or to meet him on the staircase as he ascended, grey and silent, to his room. In vain his friends assured him that such a life must undermine his health. He lengthened his hours until day and night were one long, ceaseless task.

Gradually under this discipline a change came over his appearance. His features, always inclined to gauntness, became even sharper and more pronounced. There were deep lines about his temples and across his brow. His cheek was sunken and his complexion bloodless. His knees gave under him when he walked; and once when passing out of his lecture-room he fell and had to be assisted to his carriage.

This was just before the end of the session; and soon after the holidays commenced, the professors who still remained in Birchespool were shocked to hear that their brother of the chair of physiology had sunk so low that no hopes could be entertained of his recovery. Two eminent physicians had consulted over his case without being able to give a name to the affection from which he suffered. A steadily decreasing vitality appeared to be the only symptom – a bodily weakness which left the mind unclouded. He was much interested himself in his own case, and made notes of his subjective sensations as an aid to diagnosis. Of his approaching end he spoke in his usual unemotional and somewhat pedantic fashion. 'It is the assertion,' he said, 'of the liberty of the individual cell as opposed to the cell-commune. It is the dissolution of a co-operative society. The process is one of great interest.'

And so one grey morning his co-operative society dissolved. Very quietly and softly he sank into his eternal sleep. His two physicians felt some slight embarrassment when called upon to fill in his certificate.

'It is difficult to give it a name,' said one.

'Very,' said the other.

'If he were not such an unemotional man, I should have said that he had died from some sudden nervous shock – from, in fact, what the vulgar would call a broken heart.'

'I don't think poor Grey was that sort of a man at all.'

'Let us call it cardiac, anyhow,' said the other physician.

So they did so.

(1894)

AUSTIN FREEMAN

Richard Austin Freeman (1862–1943) qualified in 1886 at the Middlesex Hospital and went out to the Gold Coast. He was MO to the Ashanti expedition in 1889 (*Travels and Life in Ashanti and Jamau* appeared in 1898), got malaria badly (blackwater fever), was invalided out of the Colonial Medical Service in 1891, but served in the RAMC during World War One. He had meanwhile been a prison medical officer. In 1907 Dr Freeman published the first adventures of his medical detective Dr Thorndyke, a pinch from Dr Conan Doyle. Sherlock Holmes was a doctor in all but qualification; Dr Thorndyke is a Sherlock Holmes in all but literary genius. The following story is included because of Dr Thorndyke's impressive popularity over fifty years, and for its quaintness.

The Blue Sequin

THORNDYKE STOOD LOOKING up and down the platform with anxiety that increased as the time drew near for the departure of the train.

'This is very unfortunate,' he said, reluctantly stepping into an empty smoking compartment as the guard executed a flourish with his green flag. 'I am afraid we have missed our friend.' He closed the door, and, as the train began to move, thrust his head out of the window.

'Now I wonder if that will be he,' he continued. 'If so, he has caught the train by the skin of his teeth, and is now in one of the rear compartments.'

The subject of Thorndyke's speculations was Mr Edward Stopford of the firm of Stopford and Myers, of Portugal Street, solicitors, and his connnection with us at present arose out of a telegram that had reached our chambers on the preceding evening. It was reply-paid, and ran thus:

'Can you come here tomorrow to direct defence? Important case. All costs undertaken by us. – STOPFORD AND MYERS.'

Thorndyke's reply had been in the affirmative, and early on this present morning a further telegram – evidently posted overnight – had been delivered:

> 'Shall leave for Woldhurst by 8.25 from Charing Cross. Will call for you if possible. – EDWARD STOPFORD.'

He had not called, however, and since he was unknown personally to us both, we could not judge whether or not he had been among the passengers on the platform.

'It is most unfortunate,' Thorndyke repeated, 'for it deprives us of that preliminary consideration of the case which is so invaluable.' He filled his pipe thoughtfully, and, having made a fruitless inspection of the platform at London Bridge, took up the paper that he had bought at the bookstall, and began to turn over the leaves, running his eye quickly down the columns, unmindful of the journalistic baits in paragraph or article.

'It is a great disadvantage,' he observed, while still glancing through the paper, 'to come plump into an inquiry without preparation – to be confronted with the details before one has a chance of considering the case in general terms. For instance –'

He paused, leaving the sentence unfinished, and as I looked up inquiringly I saw that he had turned over another page, and was now reading attentively.

'This looks like our case, Jervis,' he said presently, handing me the paper and indicating a paragraph at the top of the page. It was quite brief, and was headed 'Terrible Murder in Kent,' the account being as follows:

'A shocking crime was discovered yesterday morning at the little town of Woldhurst, which lies on the branch line from Halbury Junction. The discovery was made by a porter who was inspecting the carriages of the train which had just come in. On opening the door of a first-class compartment, he was horrified to find the body of a fashionably-dressed woman stretched upon the floor. Medical aid was immediately summoned, and on the arrival of the divisional surgeon, Dr Morton, it was ascertained that the woman had not been dead more than a few minutes.

'The state of the corpse leaves no doubt that a murder of a most brutal kind has been perpetrated, the cause of a death being a penetrating wound of the head, inflicted with some pointed implement, which must have been used with terrible violence, since it has perforated the skull and entered the brain. That robbery was not the motive of the crime is made clear by the fact that an expensively fitted dressing-bag was found on the rack, and the dead woman's jewellery, including several valuable diamond rings, was untouched. It is rumoured that an arrest has been made by the local police.'

'A gruesome affair,' I remarked, as I handed back the paper, 'but the report does not give us much information.'

'It does not,' Thorndyke agreed, 'and yet it gives us something to consider. Here is a perforating wound of the skull, inflicted with some pointed implement – that is, assuming that it is not a bullet wound. Now, what kind of implement would be capable of inflicting such an injury? How would such an implement be used in the confined space of a railway-carriage, and what sort of person would be in possession of such an implement? These are preliminary questions that are worth considering, and I commend them to you, together with the further problems of the possible motive – excluding robbery – and any circumstances other than murder which might account for the injury.'

'The choice of suitable implements is not very great,' I observed.

'It is very limited, and most of them, such as a plasterer's pick or a geological hammer, are associated with certain definite occupations. You have a notebook?'

I had, and, accepting the hint, I produced it and pursued my further reflections in silence, while my companion with his notebook also on his knee, gazed steadily out of the window. And thus he remained, wrapped in thought, jotting down an entry now and again in his book, until the train slowed down at Halbury Junction, where we had to change on to a branch line.

As we stepped out, I noticed a well-dressed man hurrying up the platform from the rear and eagerly scanning the faces of the few passengers who had alighted. Soon he espied us, and, approaching quickly, asked, as he looked from one of us to the other:

'Dr Thorndyke?'

'Yes,' replied my colleague, adding: 'And you, I presume, are Mr Edward Stopford?'

The solicitor bowed. 'This is a dreadful affair,' he said, in an agitated manner. 'I see you have the paper. A most shocking affair. I am immensely relieved to find you here. Nearly missed the train, and feared I should miss you.'

'There appears to have been an arrest,' Thorndyke began.

'Yes – my brother. Terrible business. Let us walk up the platform; our train won't start for a quarter of an hour yet.'

We deposited our joint Gladstone and Thorndyke's travelling-case in an empty first-class compartment, and then, with the solicitor between us, strolled up to the unfrequented end of the platform.

'My brother's position,' said Mr Stopford, 'fills me with dismay – but let me give you the facts in order, and you shall judge for yourself. This poor creature who has been murdered so brutally was a Miss Edith Grant. She was formerly an artist's model, and as such was a good deal employed by my brother, who is a painter – Harold Stopford, you know, ARA now –'

'I know his work very well, and charming work it is.'

'I think so, too. Well, in those days he was quite a youngster – about twenty – and he became very intimate with Miss Grant, in quite an innocent way, though not very discreet; but she was a nice respectable girl, as most English models are, and no one thought any harm. However, a good many letters passed between them, and some little presents, amongst which was a beaded chain carrying a locket, and in this he was fool enough to put his portrait and the inscription, "Edith, from Harold."

'Later on Miss Grant, who had a rather good voice, went on the stage, in the comic opera line, and, in consequence, her habits and associates changed somewhat; and, as Harold has meanwhile become engaged, he was naturally anxious to get his letters back, and especially to exchange the locket for some less compromising gift. The letters she eventually sent him, but refused absolutely to part with the locket.

'Now, for the last month Harold has been staying at Halbury, making sketching excursions into the surrounding country, and yesterday morning he took the train to Shinglehurst, the third station from here, and the one before Woldhurst.

'On the platform here he met Miss Grant, who had come down from London, and was going on to Worthing. They entered the branch train together, having a first-class compartment to themselves. It seems she was wearing his locket at the time, and he made another appeal to her to make an exchange, which she refused, as before. The discussion appears to have become rather heated and angry on both sides, for the guard and a porter at Munsden both noticed that they seemed to be quarrelling; but the upshot of the affair was that the lady snapped the chain, and tossed it together with the locket to my brother, and they parted quite amiably at Shinglehurst, where Harold got out. He was then carrying his full sketching kit, including a large holland umbrella, the lower joint of which is an ash staff fitted with a powerful steel spike for driving into the ground.

'It was about half-past ten when he got out at Shinglehurst; by eleven he had reached his pitch and got to work, and he painted steadily for three hours. Then he packed up his traps, and was just starting on his way back to the station, when he was met by the police and arrested.

'And now, observe the accumulation of circumstantial evidence against him. He was the last person seen in company with the murdered woman – for no one seems to have seen her after they left Munsden; he appeared to be quarrelling with her when she was last seen alive; he had a reason for possibly wishing for her death; he was provided with an implement – a spiked staff – capable of inflicting the injury which caused her death, and, when he was searched, there was found in his possession the locket and broken chain, apparently removed from her person with violence.

'Against all this is, of course, his known character – he is the gentlest and most amiable of men – and his subsequent conduct – imbecile to the last degree if he had been guilty; but, as a lawyer, I can't help seeing that appearances are almost hopelessly against him.'

'We won't say "hopelessly",' replied Thorndyke, as we took our places in the carriage, 'though I expect the police are pretty cocksure. When does the inquest open?'

'Today at four. I have obtained an order from the coroner for you to examine the body and be present at the post-mortem.'

'Do you happen to know the exact position of the wound?'

'Yes; it is a little above and behind the left ear – a horrible round hole, with a ragged cut or tear running from it to the side of the forehead.'

'And how was the body lying?'

'Right along the floor, with the feet close to the off-side door.'

'Was the wound on the head the only one?'

'No; there was a long cut or bruise on the right cheek – a contused wound the police surgeon called it, which he believes to have been inflicted with a heavy and rather blunt weapon. I have not heard of any other wounds or bruises.'

'Did anyone enter the train yesterday at Shinglehurst?' Thorndyke asked.

'No one entered the train after it left Halbury.'

Thorndyke considered these statements in silence, and presently fell into a brown study, from which he roused only as the train moved out of Shinglehurst station.

'It would be about here that the murder was committed,' said Mr Stopford; 'at least, between here and Woldhurst.'

Thorndyke nodded rather abstractedly, being engaged at the moment in observing with great attention the objects that were visible from the windows.

'I notice,' he remarked presently, 'a number of chips scattered about between the rails, and some of the chair-wedges look new. Have there been any platelayers at work lately?'

'Yes,' answered Stopford, 'they are on the line now, I believe – at least, I saw a gang working near Woldhurst yesterday, and they are said to have set a rick on fire; I saw it smoking when I came down.'

'Indeed; and this middle line of rails is, I suppose, a sort of siding?'

'Yes; they shunt the goods trains and empty trucks on to it. There are the remains of the rick – still smouldering, you see.'

Thorndyke gazed absently at the blackened heap until an empty cattle-truck on the middle track hid it from view. This was succeeded by a line of goods-waggons, and these by a passenger coach, one compartment of which – a first-class – was closed up and sealed. The train now began to slow down rather suddenly, and a couple of minutes later we brought up in Woldhurst station.

It was evident that rumours of Thorndyke's advent had preceded us, for the entire staff – two porters, an inspector, and the station-master – were waiting expectantly on the platform, and the latter came forward, regardless of his dignity, to help us with our luggage.

'Do you think I could see the carriage?' Thorndyke asked the solicitor.

'Not the inside, sir,' said the station-master, on being appealed to. 'The police have sealed it up. You would have to ask the inspector.'

'Well, I can have a look at the outside, I suppose?' said Thorndyke, and to this the station-master readily agreed, and offered to accompany us.

'What other first-class passengers were there?' Thorndyke asked.

'None, sir. There was only one first-class coach, and the deceased was the only person in it. It has given us all a dreadful turn, this affair has,' he continued, as we set off up the line. 'I was on the platform when the train came in. We were watching a rick that was burning up the line, and a rare blaze it made, too; and I was just saying that we should have to move the cattle-truck that was on the mid-track, because, you see, sir, the smoke and sparks were blowing across, and I thought it would frighten the poor beasts. And Mr Felton he don't like his beasts handled roughly. He says it spoils the meat.'

'No doubt he is right,' said Thorndyke. 'But now, tell me, do you think it is possible for any person to board or leave the train on the off-side unobserved? Could a man, for instance, enter a compartment on the off-side at one station and drop off as the train was slowing down at the next, without being seen?'

'I doubt it,' replied the station-master. 'Still, I wouldn't say it is impossible.'

'Thank you. Oh, and there's another question. You have a gang of men at work on the line, I see. Now, do those men belong to the district?'

'No, sir; they are strangers, every one, and pretty rough diamonds some of 'em are. But I shouldn't say there was any real harm in 'em. If you was suspecting any of 'em of being mixed up in this –'

'I am not,' interrupted Thorndyke rather shortly. 'I suspect nobody; but I wish to get all the facts of the case at the outset.'

'Naturally, sir,' replied the abashed official; and we pursued our way in silence.

'Do you remember, by the way,' said Thorndyke, as we approached the empty coach, 'whether the off-side door of the compartment was closed and locked when the body was discovered?'

'It was closed, sir, but not locked. Why, sir, did you think –?'

'Nothing, nothing. The sealed compartment is the one, of course?'

Without waiting for a reply, he commenced his survey of the coach, while I gently restrained our two companions from shadowing him, as they were disposed to do. The off-side footboard occupied his attention specially, and when he had scrutinised minutely the part opposite the fatal compartment, he walked slowly from end to end with his eyes but a few inches from its surface, as though he was searching for something.

Near what had been the rear end he stopped, and drew from his pocket a piece of paper; then, with a moistened finger-tip he picked up from the footboard some evidently minute object, which he carefully transferred to the paper, folding the latter and placing it in his pocket-book.

He next mounted the footboard, and, having peered in through the window of the sealed compartment, produced from his pocket a small insufflator or powder-blower, with which he blew a stream of impalpable smoke-like powder on to the edges of the middle window, bestowing the closest attention on the irregular dusty patches in which it settled, and even measuring one on the jamb of the window with a pocket-rule. At length he stepped down, and, having carefully looked over the near-side footboard, announced that he had finished for the present.

As we were returning down the line, we passed a working man, who seemed to be viewing the chairs and sleepers with more than casual interest.

'That, I suppose, is one of the plate-layers?' Thorndyke suggested to the station-master.

'Yes, the foreman of the gang,' was the reply.

'I'll just step back and have a word with him, if you will walk on slowly.' And my colleague turned back briskly and overtook the man, with whom he remained in conversation for some minutes.

'I think I see the police inspector on the platform,' remarked Thorndyke, as we approached the station.

'Yes, there he is,' said our guide. 'Come down to see what you are after, sir, I expect.' Which was doubtless the case, although the officer professed to be there by the merest chance.

'You would like to see the weapon, sir, I suppose?' he remarked, when he had introduced himself.

'The umbrella-spike,' Thorndyke corrected. 'Yes, if I may. We are going to the mortuary now.'

'Then you'll pass the station on the way; so, if you care to look in, I will walk up with you.'

This proposition being agreed to, we all proceeded to the police station, including the station-master, who was on the very tiptoe of curiosity.

'There you are, sir,' said the inspector, unlocking his office, and ushering us in. 'Don't say we haven't given every facility to the defence. There are all the effects of the accused, including the very weapon the deed was done with.'

'Come, come,' protested Thorndyke; 'we musn't be premature.' He took the stout ash staff from the officer, and, having examined the formidable spike through a lens, drew from his pocket a steel calliper-gauge, with which he carefully measured the diameter of the spike, and the staff to which it was fixed. 'And now,' he said, when he had made a note of the measurements in his book, 'we will look at the colour-box and the sketch. Ha! a very orderly man, your brother, Mr Stopford. Tubes all in their places, palette-knives wiped clean, palette cleaned off and rubbed bright, brushes wiped – they ought to be washed before they stiffen – all this is very significant.' He unstrapped the sketch from the blank canvas to which it was pinned, and, standing it on a chair in a good light, stepped back to look at it.

'And you tell me that that is only three hours' work!' he exclaimed, looking at the lawyer. 'It is really a marvellous achievement.'

'My brother is a very rapid worker,' replied Stopford dejectedly.

'Yes, but this is not only amazingly rapid; it is in his very happiest vein – full of spirit and feeling. But we musn't stay to look at it longer.' He replaced the canvas on its pins, and having glanced at the locket and some other articles that lay in a drawer, thanked the inspector for his courtesy and withdrew.

'That sketch and the colour-box appear very suggestive to me,' he remarked, as we walked up the street.

'To me also,' said Stopford gloomily, 'for they are under lock and key, like their owner, poor old fellow.'

He sighed heavily and we walked on in silence.

The mortuary-keeper had evidently heard of our arrival, for he was waiting at the door with the key in his hand, and, on being shown the coroner's order, unlocked the door, and we entered together; but, after a momentary glance at the ghostly, shrouded figure lying upon the slate table, Stopford turned pale and retreated, saying that he would wait for us outside with the mortuary-keeper.

As soon as the door was closed and locked on the inside, Thorndyke glanced curiously round the bare, whitewashed building. A stream of sunlight poured in through the skylight, and fell upon the silent form that lay so still under its covering-sheet, and one stray beam glanced into a corner by the door, where, on a row of pegs and a deal table, the dead woman's clothing was displayed.

'There is something unspeakably sad in these poor relics, Jervis,' said Thorndyke, as we stood before them. 'To me they are more tragic, more full of pathetic suggestion, than the corpse itself. See the smart, jaunty hat, and the costly skirts hanging there, so desolate and forlorn; the dainty lingerie on the table, neatly folded – by the mortuary-man's wife, I hope – the little French shoes and open-work silk stockings. How pathetically eloquent they are of harmless, womanly vanity, and the gay, careless life, snapped short in the twinkling of an eye. But we must not give way to sentiment. There is another life threatened, and it is in our keeping.'

He lifted the hat from its peg, and turned it over in his hand. It was, I think, what is called a 'picture-hat' – a huge, flat, shapeless mass of gauze and ribbon and feather, spangled over freely with dark-blue sequins. In one part of the brim was a ragged hole, and from this the glittering sequins dropped off in little showers when the hat was moved.

'This will have been worn tilted over on the left side,' said Thorndyke, 'judging by the general shape and the position of the hole.'

'Yes,' I agreed. 'Like that of the Duchess of Devonshire in Gainsborough's portrait.'

'Exactly.'

He shook a few of the sequins into the palm of his hand, and, replacing the hat on its peg, dropped the little discs into an envelope, on which he wrote, 'From the hat,' and slipped it into his pocket. Then, stepping over to the table, he drew back the sheet reverently and even tenderly from the dead woman's face, and looked down at it with grave pity. It was a comely face, white as marble, serene and peaceful in expression, with half-closed eyes, and framed with a mass of brassy, yellow hair; but its beauty was marred by a long linear wound, half cut, half bruise, running down the right cheek from the eye to the chin.

'A handsome girl,' Thorndyke commented – 'a dark-haired blonde. What a sin to have disfigued herself so with that horrible peroxide.' He smoothed the hair back from her forehead, and added: 'She seems to have applied the stuff last about ten days ago. There is about a quarter of an inch of dark hair at the roots. What do you make of that wound on the cheek?'

'It looks as if she had struck some sharp angle in falling, though, as the seats are padded in first-class carriages, I don't see what she could have struck.'

'No. And now let us look at the other wound. Will you note down the description?' He handed me his notebook, and I wrote down as he dictated: 'A clean-punched circular hole in skull, an inch behind and above margin of left ear – diameter, an inch and seven-sixteenths; starred fracture of parietal bone; membranes perforated, and brain entered deeply; ragged scalp-wound, extending forward to margin of left orbit; fragments of gauze and sequins in edges of wound. That will do for the present. Dr Morton will give us further details if we want them.'

He pocketed his callipers and rule, drew from the bruised scalp one or two loose hairs, which he placed in the envelope with the sequins, and, having looked over the body for other wounds or bruises (of which there were none), replaced the sheet, and prepared to depart.

As we walked away from the mortuary, Thorndyke was silent and deeply thoughtful, and I gathered that he was piecing together the facts that he had acquired. At length, Mr Stopford, who had several times looked at him curiously, said:

'The post-mortem will take place at three, and it is now only half-past eleven. What would you like to do next?'

Thorndyke, who, in spite of his mental preoccupation, had been looking about him in his usual keen, attentive way, halted suddenly.

'Your reference to the post-mortem,' said he, 'reminds me that I forgot to put the ox-gall into my case.'

'Ox-gall!' I exclaimed, endeavouring vainly to connect this substance with the technique of the pathologist. 'What were you going to do with –'

But here I broke off, remembering my friend's dislike of any discussion of his methods before strangers.

'I suppose,' he continued, 'there would hardly be an artist's colourman in a place of this size?'

'I should think not,' said Stopford. 'But couldn't you get the stuff from a butcher? There's a shop just across the road.'

'So there is,' agreed Thorndyke, who had already observed the shop. 'The gall ought of course, to be prepared, but we can filter it ourselves – that is, if the butcher has any. We will try him, at any rate.'

He crossed the road towards the shop, over which the name 'Felton' appeared in gilt lettering, and, addressing himself to the proprietor, who stood at the door, introduced himself and explained his wants.

'Ox-gall?' said the butcher. 'No, sir, I haven't got any just now; but I am having a beast killed this afternoon, and I can let you have some then. In fact,' he added after a pause, 'as the matter is of importance, I can have one killed at once if you wish it.'

'That is very kind of you,' said Thorndyke, 'and it would greatly oblige me. Is the beast perfectly healthy?'

'They're in splendid condition, sir. I picked them out of the herd myself. But you shall see them – ay, and choose the one that you'd like killed.'

'You are really very good,' said Thorndyke warmly. 'I will just run into the chemist's next door, and get a suitable bottle, and then I will avail myself of your exceedingly kind offer.'

He hurried into the chemist's shop, from which he presently emerged, carrying a white paper parcel; and we then followed the butcher down a narrow lane by the side of his shop. It led to an enclosure containing a small pen, in which were confined three handsome steers, whose glossy, black coats contrasted in a very striking manner with their long, greyish-white, nearly straight horns.

'These are certainly very fine beasts, Mr Felton,' said Thorndyke, as we drew up beside the pen, 'and in excellent condition, too.'

He leaned over the pen and examined the beasts critically, especially as to their eyes and horns; then, approaching the nearest one, he raised his stick and bestowed a smart tap on the under-side of the right horn, followed it by a similar tap on the left one, a proceeding that the beast viewed with stolid surprise.

'The state of the horns,' explained Thorndyke, as he moved on to the next steer, 'enables one to judge, to some extent, of the beast's health.'

'Lord bless you, sir,' laughed Mr Felton, 'they haven't got no feeling in their horns, else what good 'ud their horns be to 'em?'

Apparently he was right, for the second steer was as indifferent to a sounding rap on either horn as the first. Nevertheless, when Thorndyke approached the third steer, I unconsciously drew nearer to watch; and I noticed that, as the stick struck the horn, the beast drew back in evident alarm, and that when the blow was repeated, it became manifestly uneasy.

'He don't seem to like that,' said the butcher. 'Seems as if – Hullo, that's queer!'

Thorndyke had just brought his stick up against the left horn, and immediately the beast had winced and started back, shaking his head and moaning. There was not, however, room for him to back out of reach, and Thorndyke, by leaning into the pen, was able to inspect the sensitive horn, which he did with the closest attention, while the butcher looked on with obvious perturbation.

'You don't think there's anything wrong with this beast, sir, I hope,' said he.

'I can't say without a further examination,' replied Thorndyke. 'It may be the horn only that is affected. If you will have it sawn off close to the head, and sent up to me at the hotel, I will look at it and tell you. And, by way of preventing any mistakes, I will mark it and cover it up, to protect it from injury in the slaughter-house.'

He opened his parcel and produced from it a wide-mouthed bottle labelled 'Ox-gall,' a sheet of gutta-percha tissue, a roller bandage, and a stick of sealing-wax. Handing the bottle to Mr Felton, he encased the distal half of the horn in a covering by means of the tissue and the bandage, which he fixed securely with the sealing-wax.

'I'll saw the horn off and bring it up to the hotel myself, with the ox-gall,' said Mr Felton. 'You shall have them in half an hour.'

He was as good as his word, for in half an hour Thorndyke was seated at a small table by the window of our private sitting-room in the Black Bull Hotel. The table was covered with newspaper, and on it lay the long grey horn and Thorndyke's travelling-case, now open and displaying a small microscope and its accessories. The butcher was seated solidly in an arm-chair waiting, with a half-suspicious eye on Thorndyke, for the report; and I was endeavouring by cheerful talk to keep Mr Stopford from sinking into utter despondency, though I, too, kept a furtive watch on my colleague's rather mysterious proceedings.

I saw him unwind the bandage and apply the horn to his ear, bending it slightly to and fro. I watched him, as he scanned the surface closely through a lens, and observed him as he scraped some substance from the pointed end on to a glass slide, and, having applied a drop of some reagent, began to tease out the scraping with a pair of mounted needles. Presently he placed the slide under the miscroscope, and, having observed it attentively for a minute or two, turned round sharply.

'Come and look at this, Jervis,' said he.

I wanted no second bidding, being on tenterhooks of curiosity, but came over and applied my eye to the instrument.

'Well, what is it?' he asked.

'A multipolar nerve corpuscle – very shrivelled, but unmistakable.'

'And this?'

He moved the slide to a fresh spot.

'Two pyramidal nerve corpuscles and some portions of fibres.'

'And what do you say the tissue is?'

'Cortical brain substances, I should say, without a doubt.'

'I entirely agree with you. And that being so,' he added, turning to Mr Stopford, 'we may say that the case for the defence is practically complete.'

'What, in Heaven's name, do you mean?' exclaimed Stopford, starting up.

'I mean that we can now prove when and where and how Miss Grant met her death. Come and sit down here, and I will explain. No, you needn't go away, Mr Felton. We shall have to supoena you. Perhaps,' he continued, 'we had better go over the facts and see what they suggest. And first we note the position of the body, lying with the feet close to the off-side door, showing that, when she fell, the deceased was sitting, or more probably standing, close to that door. Next there is this.' He drew from his pocket a folded paper, which he opened, displaying a tiny blue disc. 'It is one of the sequins with which her hat was trimmed, and I have in this envelope several more which I took from the hat itself.

'This single sequin I picked up on the rear end of the off-side footboard, and its presence there makes it nearly certain that at some time Miss Grant had put her head out of the window on that side.

'The next item of evidence I obtained by dusting the margins of the off-side window with a light powder, which made visible a greasy impression three and a quarter inches long on the sharp corner of the right-hand jamb (right-hand from the inside, I mean).

'And now as to the evidence furnished by the body. The wound in the skull is behind and above the left ear, is roughly circular, and measures one inch and seven-sixteenths at most, and a ragged scalp-wound runs from it towards the left eye. On the right cheek is a linear contused wound three and a quarter inches long. There are no other injuries.

'Our next facts are furnished by this.' He took up the horn and tapped it with his finger, while the solicitor and Mr Felton stared at him in speechless wonder. 'You notice it is a left horn, and you remember that it was highly sensitive. If you put your ear to it while I strain it, you will hear the grating of a fracture in the bony core. Now look at the pointed end, and you will see several deep scratches running lengthwise, and where those scratches end the diameter of the horn is, as you see by this calliper-gauge, one inch and seven-sixteenths. Covering the scratches is a dry blood-stain, and at the extreme tip is a small mass of dried substance which Dr Jervis and I have examined with the microscope and are satisfied is brain tissue.'

'Good God!' exclaimed Stopford eagerly. 'Do you mean to say –'

'Let us finish with the facts, Mr Stopford,' Thorndyke interrupted. 'Now, if you look closely at that blood-stain, you will see a short piece of hair stuck to the horn, and through this lens you can make out the root-bulb. It is a golden hair, you notice, but near the root it is black, and our calliper-gauge shows us that the black portion is fourteen sixty-fourths of an inch long. Now, in this envelope are some hairs that I removed from the dead woman's head. They also are golden hairs, black at the roots, and when I measure the black portion I find it to be fourteen sixty-fourths of an inch long. Then, finally, there is this.'

He turned the horn over, and pointed to a small patch of dried blood. Embedded in it was a blue sequin.

Mr Stopford and the butcher both gazed at the horn in silent amazement; then the former drew a deep breath and looked up at Thorndyke.

'No doubt,' said he, 'you can explain this mystery, but for my part I am utterly bewildered, though you are filling me with hope.'

'And yet the matter is quite simple,' returned Thorndyke, 'even with these few facts before us, which are only a selection from the body of evidence in our possession. But I will state my theory, and you shall judge.' He rapidly sketched a rough plan on a sheet of paper, and continued: 'These were the conditions when the train was approaching Woldhurst: Here was the passenger-coach, here was the burning rick, and here was a cattle-truck. The steer was in that truck. Now my hypothesis is that at that time Miss Grant was standing with her head out of the off-side window, watching the burning rick. Her wide hat, worn on the left side, hid from her view the cattle-truck which she was approaching, and then this is what happened.' He sketched another plan to a larger scale. 'One of the steers – this one – had thrust its long horn out through the bars. The point of that horn struck the deceased's head, driving her face violently against the corner of the window, and then, in disengaging, ploughed its way through the scalp and suffered a fracture of its core from the violence of the wrench. This hypothesis is inherently probable, it fits all the facts, and those facts admit of no other explanation.'

The solicitor sat for a moment as though dazed, then he rose impulsively and seized Thorndyke's hands.

'I don't know what to say to you,' he exclaimed huskily, 'except that you have saved my brother's life, and for that may God reward you!'

The butcher rose from his chair with a slow grin.

'It seems to me,' said he, 'as if that ox-gall was what you might call a blind, eh, sir?'

And Thorndyke smiled an inscrutable smile.

When we returned to town on the following day we were a party of four, which included Mr Harold Stopford. The verdict of 'Death by misadventure,' promptly returned by the coroner's jury, had been shortly followed by his release from custody, and he now sat with his brother and me, listening with rapt attention to Thorndyke's analysis of the case.

'So, you see,' the latter concluded, 'I had six possible theories of the cause of death worked out before I reached Halbury, and it only remained to select the one that fitted the facts. And when I had seen the cattle-truck, had picked up that sequin, had heard the description of the steers, and had seen the hat and the wounds, there was nothing left to do but the filling in of details.'

'And you never doubted my innocence?' asked Harold Stopford.

Thorndyke smiled at his quondam client.

'Not after I had seen your colour-box and your sketch,' said he, 'to say nothing of the spike.'

(1912)

SINCLAIR LEWIS

Harry Sinclair Lewis (1885–1951), son of a Minnesota doctor, was a joyless mocker of American small-town, small-minded life. *Martin Arrowsmith* is a sustained bleak satire of doctors and academics, which awarded him the Pulitzer Prize in 1926, which he enhanced by refusing it. In 1930 he won the Nobel Prize – the first American writer to make it.

The future Dr Arrowsmith at fourteen, son of the manager of the New York Clothing Bazaar in Main Street, Elk Mills, in the Middle West, was the unofficial, unpaid assistant to Dr Vickerson. Here he is sitting in the doctor's office, which is over his father's shop, reading Gray's *Anatomy* while the doctor is out on a country call.

From Martin Arrowsmith

THE BOY RAISED his head, cocked his inquisitive brow. On the stairway was the cumbersome step of Doc Vickerson. The Doc was sober! Martin would not have to help him into bed.

But it was a bad sign that the Doc should first go down the hall to his bedroom. The boy listened sharply. He heard the Doc open the lower part of the washstand, where he kept his bottle of Jamaica rum. After a long gurgle the invisible Doc put away the bottle and decisively kicked the doors shut. Still good. Only one drink. If he came into the consultation-room at once, he would be safe. But he was still standing in the bedroom. Martin sighed as the washstand doors were hastily opened again, as he heard another gurgle and a third.

The Doc's step was much livelier when he loomed into the office, a grey mass of a man with a grey mass of moustache, a form vast and unreal and undefined, like a cloud taking for the moment a likeness of humanity. With the brisk attack of one who wishes to escape the discussion of his guilt, the Doc rumbled while he waddled toward his desk-chair:

'What you doing here, young fella? What you doing here? I knew the cat would drag in something if I left the door unlocked.' He gulped slightly; he smiled to show that he was being humorous – people had been known to misconstrue the Doc's humour.

He spoke more seriously, occasionally forgetting what he was talking about:

'Reading old Gray? That's right. Physician's library just three books: *Gray's Anatomy* and Bible and Shakespeare. Study. You may become great doctor. Locate in Zenith and make five thousand dollars year – much as United States Senator! Set a high goal. Don't let things slide. Get training. Go college before go medical school. Study. Chemistry. Latin. Knowledge! I'm plug doc – got chick nor child – nobody – old drunk. But you – leadin' physician. Make five thousand dollars year.

'Murray woman's got endocarditis. Not thing I can do for her. Wants somebody hold her hand. Road's damn' disgrace. Culvert's out, beyond the grove. 'Sgrace.

'Endocarditis and –

'Training, that's what you got t' get. Fundamentals. Know chemistry. Biology. I nev' did. Mrs Reverend Jones thinks she's got gastric ulcer. Wants to go city for operation. Ulcer, hell! She and the Reverend both eat too much.

'Why they don't repair that culvert – And don't be a booze-hoister like me, either. And get your basic science. I'll 'splain.'

The boy, normal village youngster though he was, given to stoning cats and to playing pom-pom-pullaway, gained something of the intoxication of treasure-hunting as the Doc struggled to convey his vision of the pride of learning, the universality of biology, the triumphant exactness of chemistry. A fat old man and dirty and unvirtuous was the Doc; his grammar was doubtful, his vocabulary alarming, and his references to his rival, good Dr Needham, were scandalous; yet he invoked in Martin a vision of making chemicals explode with much noise and stink and of seeing animalcules that no boy in Elk Mills had ever beheld.

The Doc's voice was thickening; he was sunk in his chair, blurry of eye and lax of mouth. Martin begged him to go to bed, but the Doc insisted:

'Don't need nap. No. Now you lissen. You don't appreciate but – Old man now. Giving you all I've learned. Show you collection. Only museum in whole county. Scientif' pioneer.'

A hundred times had Martin obediently looked at the specimens in the brown, crackly-varnished bookcase: the beetles and chunks of mica; the embryo of a two-headed calf, the gallstones removed from a respectable lady whom the Doc enthusiastically named to all visitors. The Doc stood before the case, waving an enormous but shaky forefinger.

'Looka that butterfly. Name is *porthesia chrysorrhoea*. Doc Needham couldn't tell you that! He don't know what butterflies are called! He don't care if you get trained. Remember that name now?' He turned on Martin. 'You payin' attention? You interested? *Huh?* Oh, the devil! Nobody wants to know about my museum – not a person. Only one in county but – I'm an old failure.'

Martin asserted, 'Honest, it's slick!'

'Look here! Look here! See that? In the bottle? It's an appendix. First one ever took out 'round here. I did it! Old Doc Vickerson, he did the first 'pendectomy in *this* neck of the woods, you bet! And first museum. It ain't – so big – but it's start. I haven't put away money like Doc Needham, but I started first c'lection – I started it!'

He collapsed in a chair, groaning, 'You're right. Got to sleep. All in.' But as Martin helped him to his feet he broke away, scrabbled about on his desk, and looked back doubtfully. 'Want to give you something – start your training. And remember the old man. Will anybody remember the old man?'

He was holding out the beloved magnifying glass which for years he had used in botanizing. He watched Martin slip the lens into his pocket, he sighed, he struggled, for something else to say, and silently he lumbered into his bedroom.

(1923)

F. SCOTT FITZGERALD

Poor Scott Fitzgerald! Francis Scott Key Fitzgerald (1896–1940) left Princeton in 1917 to join the army, though he never reached France. *This Side of Paradise* in 1920 was a literary hit, *The Great Gatsby* in 1925 a resounding one, turning his life into an eternal worldwide party at which he grew drunken and bored.

The hero of *Tender is the Night*, Dr Dick Diver, 'drank claret with each meal, took a night-cap, generally in the form of hot rum, and sometimes he tippled gin in the afternoons – gin was the most difficult to detect on the breath. He was averaging a half-pint of alcohol a day, too much for his system to burn up. . . . Doctors, chauffeurs, and Protestant clergymen could never smell of liquor, as could painters, brokers, cavalry leaders.' The casual truth of Fitzgerald's description: 'As if a drink were acting on him, warming the lining of his stomach, throwing a flush up into his brain,' matches Patrick Hamilton's (1904–62) equally experienced explanation 'like the effect on the body of good news, without the good news,' and Marcus Clarke's (1846–81) more elaborate analysis from the drunken clergyman in *For the Term of His Natural Life*:

> I know well what will restore me to life and ease – restore me, but to cast me back again into a deeper fit of despair. I drink. One glass – my blood is warmed, – my heart leaps, my hand no longer shakes. Three glasses, I rise with hope in my soul, – the evil spirit flies from me. I continue – pleasing images flock to my brain, the fields break into flower, the birds into song, the sea gleams sapphire, the warm heaven laughs. Great God! What man could withstand a temptation like this?

In 1920 Fitzgerald married the writer Zelda Sayre, who in 1928 developed schizophrenia (her early symptoms were frenetic ballet dancing). She spent a year in a Swiss clinic: 'I left my capacity for hoping on the little roads that led to Zelda's sanitarium.' Fitzgerald's Dr Diver is attracted to Nicole, the schizophrenic daughter of the wealthy Warrens of Chicago, herself in a Swiss sanitarium. Her family decide: 'There was no use worrying about Nicole when they were in the position of being able to buy her a nice young doctor, the paint scarcely dry on him.' Dr Diver marries Nicole, despite her own doctor's warning: 'What! And devote half your life to being doctor and nurse and all – never! I know what these cases are. One time in twenty it's finished in the first push – better never see her again!' *Tender is the Night*, its end written 'entirely on stimulant', was a critical and financial failure, but the alcoholism of its hero and schizophrenia of its heroine have poignant accuracy.

From Tender is the Night

'I WOULD LIKE – to talk to her – a few minutes now,' said Doctor Dohmler, going into English, as if it would bring him closer to Warren.

Afterwards when Warren had left his daughter and returned to Lausanne, and several days had passed, the doctor and Franz entered upon Nicole's card:

> Diagnostic: Schizophrénie. Phase aigüe en décroissance. La peur des hommes est un symptôme de la maladie, et n'est point constitutionnelle. . . . Le pronostic doit rester réservé.*

And then they waited with increasing interest as the days passed for Mr Warren's promised second visit.

It was slow in coming. After a fortnight Doctor Dohmler wrote. Confronted with further silence he committed what was for those days *une folie*, and telephoned to the Grand Hotel at Vevey. He learned from Mr Warren's valet that he was at the moment packing to sail for America. But reminded that the forty francs Swiss for the call would show up on the clinic books, the blood of the Tuileries Guard rose to Doctor Dohmler's aid and Mr Warren was got to the phone.

'It is – absolutely necessary – that you come. Your daughter's health – all depends. I can take no responsibility.'

'But look here, Doctor, that's just what you're for. I have a hurry call to go home!'

* Diagnosis: Divided Personality. Acute and down-hill phase of the illness. The fear of men is a symptom of the illness and is not at all constitutional. . . . The prognosis must be reserved.

Doctor Dohmler had never yet spoken to anyone so far away, but he dispatched his ultimatum so firmly into the phone that the agonized American at the other end yielded. Half an hour after this second arrival on the Zurichsee, Warren had broken down, his fine shoulders shaking with awful sobs inside his easy-fitting coat, his eyes redder than the very sun on Lake Geneva, and they had the awful story.

'It just happened,' he said hoarsely. 'I don't know – I don't know.

'After her mother died when she was little she used to come into my bed every morning, sometimes she'd sleep in my bed. I was sorry for the little thing. Oh, after that, whenever we went places in an automobile or a train we used to hold hands. She used to sing to me. We used to say, "Now let's not pay any attention to anybody else this afternoon – let's just have each other – for this morning you're mine."' A broken sarcasm came into his voice. 'People used to say what a wonderful father and daughter we were – they used to wipe their eyes. We were just like lovers – and then all at once we were lovers – and ten minutes after it happened I could have shot myself – except I guess I'm such a God-damned degenerate I didn't have the nerve to do it.'

'Then what?' said Doctor Dohmler, thinking again of Chicago and of a mild pale gentleman with a pince-nez who had looked him over in Zurich thirty years before. 'Did this thing go on?'

'Oh no! She almost – she seemed to freeze up right away. She'd just say, "Never mind, never mind, Daddy. It doesn't matter. Never mind."'

'There were no consequences?'

'No.' He gave one short convulsive sob and blew his nose several times. 'Except now there're plenty of consequences.' . . .

Nicole's doctor is right.

The collapse in Paris was another matter, adding significance to the first one. It prophesied possibly a new cycle, a new pousse of the malady. Having gone through unprofessional agonies during her long relapse following the birth of Topsy, their second child, he had hardened himself about her, making a cleavage between Nicole sick and Nicole well. This made it difficult now to distinguish between his self-protective professional detachment and some new coldness in his heart. As an indifference cherished, or left to atrophy, become an emptiness, to this extent he had learned to become empty of Nicole, serving her against his will with negations and emotional neglect. One writes of scars healed, a loose parallel to the pathology of the skin, but there is no such thing in the life of an individual. There are open wounds, shrunk sometimes to the size of a pin-prick, but wounds still. The marks of suffering are more comparable to the loss of a finger, or of the sight of an eye. We may not miss them, either, for one minute in a year, but if we should there is nothing to be done about it. . . .

A schizophrenic is well named as a split personality – Nicole was alternately a person to whom nothing need be explained and one to whom nothing *could* be explained. It was necessary to treat her with active and affirmative insistence, keeping the road to reality always open, making the road to escape harder going. But the brilliance, the versatility of madness is akin to the resourcefulness of water seeping through, over, and around a dyke. It requires the united front of many people to work against it. He felt it necessary that this time Nicole cure herself; he wanted to wait until she remembered the other times and revolted from them. In a tired way he planned that they would again resume the regime relaxed two years before.

He had turned up a hill that made a short cut to the clinic and now, as he stepped on the accelerator for a short, straightaway run parallel to the hillside, the car swerved violently left, swerved right, tipped on two wheels and, as Dick, with Nicole's voice screaming in his ear, crushed down the mad hand clutching the steering wheel, righted itself, swerved once more and shot off the road; it tore through low underbrush, tipped again, and settled slowly at an angle of ninety degrees against a tree.

(1939)

EVELYN WAUGH

Evelyn Waugh (1903–66), though famous on undertakers, was not interested in illness and doctors. His characters perfectly express the torments of life through its superficialities, which makes this tale of the sad, sick soldier Apthorpe the more estimable. It parallels Trollope's *Dr Thorne*, when the doctor succumbs to the alcoholic Sir Roger Scratcherd on his deathbed:

> 'Fill the glass I tell you [Sir Roger commands Dr Thorne].'
>
> 'I should be killing you were I to do it . . . you would not wish to make me guilty of murder, would you?'
>
> 'Nonsense! You are talking nonsense; habit is second nature. I tell you I shall sink without it. Why, you know I always get it directly your back is turned. Come, I will not be bullied in my own house; give me that bottle I say!' – and Sir Roger essayed, vainly enough, to raise himself from the bed.
>
> 'Stop, Scratcherd; I will give it you – I will help you. It may be that habit is second nature.' Sir Roger in his determined energy had swallowed, without thinking of it, the small quantity which the doctor had before poured out for him, and still held the empty glass within his hand. This the doctor now took and filled nearly to the brim.
>
> 'Come, Thorne, a bumper; a bumper for this once. "Whatever the drink, it a bumper must be." You stingy fellow! I would not treat you so. Well – well.'
>
> 'It's as full as you can hold it, Scratcherd.'
>
> 'Try me; try me! my hand is a rock; at least at holding liquor.' And then he drained the contents of the glass, which were sufficient in quantity to have taken away the breath from any ordinary man.
>
> 'Ah, I'm better now. But, Thorne, I do love a full glass, ha! ha! ha!'

The next night, Sir Roger was dead.

From Men At Arms

THEN OUT OF the town by a steep road to the spacious, whitish hospital, where there was no wireless to aggravate the suffering, no bustle; fans swung to and fro, windows were shut and curtained against the heat of the sun.

He found Apthorpe alone in his room, in a bed near the window. When Guy entered he was lying doing nothing, staring at the sun-blind with his hands empty on the counterpane. He immediately began to fill and light a pipe.

'I came to see how you were.'

'Rotten, old man, rotten.'

'They don't seem to have given you much to do.'

'They don't realize how ill I am. They keep bringing me jigsaws and Ian Hay. A damn fool woman, wife of a box-wallah here, offered to teach me crochet. I ask you, old man, I just ask you.'

Guy produced the bottle he had been concealing in the pocket of his bush-shirt.

'I wondered if you'd like some whisky.'

'That's very thoughtful. In fact I would. Very much. They bring us one medicine-glassful at sundown. It's not enough. Often one wants more. I told them so, pretty strongly, and they just laughed. They've treated my case all wrong from the very first. I know more about medicine than any of those young idiots. It's a wonder I've stayed alive as long as I have. Toughness. It takes some time to kill an old bush hand. But they'll do it. They wear one down. They exhaust the will to live and then – phut. You're a goner. I've seen it happen dozens of times.'

'Where shall I put the whisky?'

'Somewhere I can reach it. It'll get damned hot in the bed, but I think it's the best place.'

'How about the locker?'

'They're always prying in there. But they're slack about bed-making. They just pull the covers smooth before the doctors' round. Tuck it in at the bottom, there's a good chap.'

There was only a thin sheet and a thin cotton counterpane. Guy saw Apthorpe's large feet, bereft of their 'porpoises', peeling with fever. He tried to interest Apthorpe in the new brigadier and in his own obscure position but Apthorpe said fretfully: 'Yes, yes, yes, yes. It's all another world to me, old man.'

He puffed at his pipe, let it go out, tried with a feeble hand to put it on the table beside him, dropped it, noisily in that quiet place, on the bare floor. Guy stooped to retrieve it but Apthorpe said: 'Leave it there, old man. I don't want it. I only tried to be companionable.'

When Guy looked up he saw tears on Apthorpe's colourless cheeks.

'I say, would you like me to go?'

'No, no. I'll feel better in a minute. Did you bring a corkscrew? Good man. I think I could do with a nip.'

Guy opened the bottle, poured out a tot, recorked and replaced the spirit under the sheet.

'Wash out the glass, old man, do you mind?' . . .

There was a rattle at the door and a nurse came in with a tray.

'Why! Visitors! You're the first he's had. I must say you seem to have cheered him up. We have been down in the dumps, haven't we?' she said to Apthorpe.

'You see, old man, they wear me down. Thanks for coming. Good-bye.'

'I smell something I shouldn't,' said the nurse.

'Just a drop of whisky I happened to have in my flask, nurse,' Guy answered.

'Well, don't let the doctor hear about it. It's the *very* worst thing. I ought really to report you to the SMO, really I ought.'

'Is the doctor anywhere about?' Guy asked. 'I'd rather like to speak to him.'

'Second door on the left. I shouldn't go in if I were you. He's in a horrid temper.'

But Guy found a weary, foolish man of his own age.

'Apthorpe? Yes. You're in the same regiment, I see. The Applejacks, eh?'

'Is he really pretty bad, doctor?'

'Of course he is. He wouldn't be here if he wasn't.'

'He talked a lot about dying.'

'Yes, he does to me, except when he's delirious. Then he seems worried about a bomb in the rears. Did he ever have any experience of the kind, do you know?'

'I rather think he did.'

'Well, that accounts for that. Queer bird, the mind. Hides things away and then out they pop. But I mustn't get too technical. It's a hobby horse of mine, the mind.'

'I wanted to know, is he on the danger list?'

'Well, I haven't actually put him there. No need to cause unnecessary alarm and despondency. His sort of trouble hangs on for weeks often and just when you think you've pulled them through, out they go, you know.

'Apthorpe's got the disadvantage of having lived in this God-forsaken country. You chaps who come out fresh from England have got stamina. Chaps who live here have got their blood full of every sort of infection. And then, of course, they poison themselves with whisky. They snuff out like babies. Still, we're doing the best for Apthorpe. Luckily we're rather empty at the moment so everyone can give him full attention.'

'Thank you, sir.'

The RAMC man was a colonel but he was seldom called 'sir' by anyone outside his own staff. 'Have a glass of whisky?' he said gratefully.

'Thanks awfully, but I must be off.'

'Any time you're passing.'

'By the way, sir, how is our Brigadier Ritchie-Hook?'

'He'll be out of here any day now. Between ourselves he's rather a difficult patient. He made one of my young officers pickle a negro's head for him. Most unusual.'

'Was the pickling a success?'

'Must have been, I suppose. Anyway he keeps the thing by his bed grinning at him.' . . .

Guy supposed the summons was connected with his move-order and went to the brigadier's office without alarm. He found both the brigadier and the brigade major there, one looking angrily at him, the other looking at the table.

'You heard that Apthorpe was dead?'

'Yes, sir.'

'There was an empty whisky bottle in his bed. Does that mean anything to you?'

Guy stood silent, aghast rather than ashamed.

'I asked: "Does that mean anything to you?"'

'Yes, sir. I took him a bottle yesterday afternoon.'

'You knew it was against orders?'

'Yes, sir.'

'Any excuse?'

'No, sir, except that I knew he liked it and I didn't realize it would do him any harm. Or that he'd finish it all at once.'

'He was half delirious, poor fellow. How old are you, Crouchback?'

'Thirty-six, sir.'

'Exactly. That's what makes everything so hopeless. If you were a young idiot of twenty-one I could understand it. Damn it, man, you're only a year or two younger than I am.'

Guy stood still saying nothing. He was curious how the brigadier would deal with the question.

'The SMO of the hospital knows all about it. So do most of his staff, I expect. You can imagine how he feels. I was with him half the morning before I could get him to see sense. Yes, I've begged you off, but please understand that what I've done was purely for the Corps. You've committed too serious a crime for me to deal with summarily. The choice was between hushing it up and sending you before a court martial. There's nothing would give me more personal satisfaction than to see you booted out of the army altogether. But we've one sticky business on our hands already – in which incidentally you are implicated. I persuaded the medico that we had no evidence. You were poor Apthorpe's only visitor but there are orderlies and native porters in and out of the hospital who *might* have sold him the stuff' (he spoke as though whisky, which he regularly and moderately drank, were some noxious distillation of Guy's own). 'Nothing's worse than a court martial that goes off half-cock. I also told him what a slur it would be on poor Apthorpe's name. It would all have had to come out. I gather he was practically a dipsomaniac and had two aunts who think the world of him. Pretty gloomy for them to hear the truth. So I got him to agree in the end. But don't thank me, and, remember, I don't want to see you again ever. I shall apply for your immediate posting out of the brigade as soon as they've finished with you in England. The only hope I have for you is that you're thoroughly ashamed of yourself. You can fall out now.'

(1952)

GEORGE ORWELL

When George Orwell (Eric Blair, 1903–50) was down and out in London and Paris in 1930, he caught pneumonia and found himself in (it seems) the huge Hôpital de Vaugirard, which is near the Paris abattoirs (including the abattoir hippophagique) beside the railway lines south-west of Montparnasse. Orwell's muscular prose ripples effortlessly in the hospital wards. The performance of 'dry cupping', which he observed with critical amusement before finding it unceremoniously applied to himself, however useless was a popular treatment for pneumonia. Before chemotherapy with the suplha drugs at the end of the decade, there was nothing else. The mustard poultice in which Orwell became agonisingly encased was a 'counter-irritant' – substituting superficial pain for internal, on a principle which remains fashionable among enthusiasts for 'alternative medicine' in acupuncture. The widespread attitude – in Britain as in France – of the impersonal doctors and eager students was until the middle of the century how the poor were ill. They were considered far too ignorant to appreciate their interesting diseases, which became the hospital's property.

The reason for Orwell's 'strange feeling of familiarity' on entering the wards can be found in the item on Alfred, Lord Tennyson.

Shortly after *Nineteen Eighty-Four* appeared, Orwell died in London of pulmonary tuberculosis.

From How the Poor Die

IN THE YEAR 1929 I spent several weeks in the Hôpital X, in the fifteenth arrondissement of Paris. The clerks put me through the usual third-degree at the reception desk, and indeed I kept answering questions for some twenty minutes before they would let me in. If you have ever had to fill up forms in a Latin country you will know the kind of questions I mean. For some days past I had been unequal to translating Réaumur into Fahrenheit, but I know that my temperature was round about 103, and by the end of the interview I had some difficulty in standing on my feet. At my back a resigned little knot of patients, carrying bundles done up in coloured handkerchiefs, waited their turn to be questioned.

After the questioning came the bath – a compulsory routine for all newcomers, apparently, just as in prison or the workhouse. My clothes were taken away from me, and after I had sat shivering for some minutes in five inches of warm water I was given a linen nightshirt and a short blue flannel dressing-gown – no slippers, they had none big enough for me, they said – and led out into the open air. This was a night in February and I was suffering from pneumonia. The ward we were going to was 200 yards away and it seemed that to get to it you had to cross the hospital grounds. Someone stumbled in front of me with a lantern. The gravel path was frosty underfoot, and the wind whipped the nightshirt round my bare calves. When we got into the ward I was aware of a strange feeling of familiarity whose origin I did not succeed in pinning down till later in the night. It was a long, rather low, ill-lit room, full of murmuring voices and with three rows of beds surprisingly close together. There was a foul smell, faecal and yet sweetish. As I lay down I saw on a bed nearly opposite me a small, round-shouldered, sandy-haired man sitting half naked while a doctor and a student performed some strange operation on him. First the doctor produced from his black bag a dozen small glasses like wine glasses, then the student burned a match inside each glass to exhaust the air, then the glass was popped on to the man's back or chest and the vacuum drew up a huge yellow blister. Only after some moments did I realize what they were doing to him. It was something called cupping, a treatment which you can read about in old medical text-books but which till then I had vaguely thought of as one of those things they do to horses.

The cold air outside had probably lowered my temperature, and I watched this barbarous remedy with detachment and even a certain amount of amusement. The next moment, however, the doctor and the student came across to my bed, hoisted me upright and without a word began applying the same set of glasses, which had not been sterilized in any way. A few feeble protests that I uttered got no more response than if I had been an animal. I was very much impressed by the impersonal way in which the two men started on me. I had never been in the public ward of a hospital before, and it was my first experience of doctors who handle you without speaking to you or, in a human sense, taking any notice of you. They only put on six glasses in my case, but after doing so they scarified the blisters and applied the glasses again. Each glass now drew about a dessert-spoonful of dark-coloured blood. As I lay down again, humiliated, disgusted and frightened by the thing that had been done to me, I reflected that now at least they would leave me alone. But no, not a bit of it. There was another treatment coming, the mustard poultice, seemingly a matter of routine like the hot bath. Two slatternly nurses had already got the poultice ready, and they lashed it round my chest as tight as a strait-jacket while some men who were wandering about the ward in shirt and trousers began to collect round my bed with half-sympathetic grins. I learned later that watching a patient have a mustard poultice was a favourite pastime in the ward. These things are normally applied for a quarter of an hour and certainly they are funny enough if you don't happen to be the person inside. For the first five minutes the pain is severe, but you believe you can bear it. During the second five minutes this belief evaporates, but the poultice is buckled at the back and you can't get it off. This is the period the onlookers enjoy most. During the last five minutes, I noted, a sort of numbness supervenes. After the poultice had been removed a waterproof pillow packed with ice was thrust beneath my head and I was left alone. I did not sleep, and to the best of my knowledge this was the only night of my life – I mean the only night spent in bed – in which I have not slept at all, not even a minute.

During my first hour in the Hôpital X I had had a whole series of different and contradictory treatments, but this was misleading, for in general you got very little treatment at all, either good or bad, unless you were ill in some interesting and instructive way. At five in the morning the nurses came round, woke the patients and took their temperatures, but did not wash them. If you were well enough you washed yourself, otherwise you depended on the kindness of some walking patient. It was generally patients, too, who carried the bedbottles and the grim bedpan, nicknamed *la casserole*. At eight breakfast arrived, called army-fashion *la soupe*. It was soup, too, a thin vegetable soup with slimy hunks of bread floating about in it. Later in the day the tall, solemn, black-bearded doctor made his rounds, with an interne and a troop of students following at his heels, but there were about sixty of us in the ward and it was evident that he had other wards to attend to as well. There were many beds past which he walked day after day, sometimes followed by imploring cries. On the other hand if you had some disease with which the students wanted to familiarize themselves you got plenty of attention of a kind. I myself, with an exceptionally fine specimen of a bronchial rattle, sometimes had as many as a dozen students queuing up to listen to my chest. It was a very queer feeling – queer, I mean, because of their intense interest in learning their job, together with a seeming lack of any perception that the patients were human beings. It is strange to relate, but sometimes as some young student stepped forward to take his turn at manipulating you he would be actually tremulous with excitement, like a boy who has at last got his hands on some expensive piece of machinery. And then ear after ear – ears of young men, of girls, of negroes – pressed against your back, relays of fingers solemnly but clumsily tapping, and not from any one of them did you get a word of conversation or a look direct in your face. As a non-paying patient, in the uniform nightshirt, you were primarily *a specimen*, a thing I did not resent but could never quite get used to.

After some days I grew well enough to sit up and study the surrounding patients. The stuffy room, with its narrow beds so close together that you could easily touch your neighbour's hand, had every sort of disease in it except, I suppose, acutely infectious cases. My right-hand neighbour was a little red-haired cobbler with one leg shorter than the other, who used to announce the death of any other patient (this happened a number of times, and my neighbour was always the first to hear of it) by whistling to me, exclaiming 'Numéro 43!' (or whatever it was) and flinging his arms above his head. This man had not much wrong with him, but in most of the other beds within my angle of vision some squalid tragedy or some plain horror was being enacted. In the bed that was foot to foot with mine there lay, until he died (I didn't see him die – they moved him to another bed), a little weazened man who was suffering from I do not know what disease, but something that made his whole body so intensely sensitive that any movement from side to side, sometimes even the weight of the bedclothes, would make him shout out with pain. His worst suffering was when he urinated, which he did with the greatest difficulty. A nurse would bring him the bedbottle and then for a long time stand beside his bed, whistling, as grooms are said to do with horses, until at last with an agonized shriek of '*Je pisse*!' he would get started. In the bed next to him the sandy-haired man whom I had seen being cupped used to cough up blood-streaked mucus at all hours. My left-hand neighbour was a tall, flaccid-looking young man who used periodically to have a tube inserted into his back and astonishing quantities of frothy liquid drawn off from some part of his body. In the bed beyond that a veteran of the war of 1870 was dying, a handsome old man with a white imperial, round whose bed, at all hours when visiting was allowed, four elderly female relatives dressed all in black sat exactly like crows, obviously scheming for some pitiful legacy. In the bed opposite me in the farther row was an old bald-headed man with drooping moustaches and greatly swollen face and body, who was suffering from some disease that made him urinate almost incessantly. A huge glass receptacle stood always beside his bed. One day his wife and daughter came to visit him. At sight of them the old man's bloated face lit up with a smile of surprising sweetness, and as his daughter, a pretty girl of about twenty, approached the bed I saw that his hand was slowly working its way from under the bedclothes. I seemed to see in advance the gesture that was coming – the girl kneeling beside the bed, the old man's hand laid on her head in his dying blessing. But no, he merely handed her the bedbottle, which she promptly took from him and emptied into the receptacle.

About a dozen beds away from me was Numéro 57 – I think that was his number – a cirrhosis-of-the-liver case. Everyone in the ward knew him by sight because he was sometimes the subject of a medical lecture. On two afternoons a week the tall, grave doctor would lecture in the ward to a party of students, and on more than one occasion old Numéro 57 was wheeled in on a sort of trolley into the middle of the ward, where the doctor would roll back his nightshirt, dilate with his fingers a huge flabby protruberance on the man's belly – the diseased liver, I suppose – and explain solemnly that this was a disease attributable to alcoholism, commoner in the wine-drinking countries. As usual he neither spoke to his patient nor gave him a smile, a nod or any kind of recognition. While he talked, very grave and upright, he would hold the wasted body beneath his two hands, sometimes giving it a gentle roll to and fro, in just the attitude of a woman handling a rolling-pin. Not that Numéro 57 minded this kind of thing. Obviously he was an old hospital inmate, a regular exhibit at lectures, his liver long since marked down for a bottle in some pathological museum. Utterly uninterested in what was said about him, he would lie with his colourless eyes gazing at nothing, while the doctor showed him off like a piece of antique china. He was a man of about sixty, astonishingly shrunken. His face, pale as vellum, had shrunken away till it seemed no bigger than a doll's.

One morning my cobbler neighbour woke me up plucking at my pillow before the nurses arrived. 'Numéro 57!' – he flung his arms above his head. There was a light in the ward, enough to see by. I could see old Numéro 57 lying crumpled up on his side, his face sticking out over the side of the bed, and towards me. He had died some time during the night, nobody knew when. When the nurses came they received the news of his death indifferently and went about their work. After a long time, an hour or more, two other nurses marched in abreast like soldiers, with a great clumping of sabots, and knotted the corpse up in the sheets, but it was not removed till some time later. Meanwhile, in the better light, I had had time for a good look at Numéro 57. Indeed I lay on my side to look at him. Curiously enough he was the first dead European I had seen. I had seen dead men before, but always Asiatics and usually people who had died violent deaths. Numéro 57's eyes were still open, his mouth also open, his small face contorted into an expression of agony. What most impressed me, however, was the whiteness of his face. It had been pale before, but now it was little darker than the sheets. As I gazed at the tiny, screwed-up face it struck me that this disgusting piece of refuse, waiting to be carted away and dumped on a slab in the dissecting room, was an example of 'natural' death, one of the things you pray for in the Litany. There you are, then, I thought, that's what is waiting for you, twenty, thirty, forty years hence: that is how the lucky ones die, the ones who live to be old. One wants to live, of course, indeed one only stays alive by virtue of the fear of death, but I think now, as I thought then, that it's better to die violently and not too old. People talk about the horrors of war, but what weapon has man invented that even approaches in cruelty some of the commoner diseases? 'Natural' death, almost by definition, means something slow, smelly and painful. Even at that, it makes a difference if you can achieve it in your own home and not in a public institution. This poor old wretch who had just flickered out like a candle-end was not even important enough to have anyone watching by his deathbed. He was merely a number, then a 'subject' for the students' scalpels. And the sordid publicity of dying in such a place! In the Hôpital X the beds were very close together and there were no screens. Fancy, for instance, dying like the little man whose bed was for a while foot to foot with mine, the one who cried out when the bedclothes touched him! I dare say '*Je pisse!*' were his last recorded words.

(1946)

ALDOUS HUXLEY

Aldous Leonard Huxley's (1894–1963) *Brave New World* of 1932 contains a sharp prediction of our brave new world of 1948: a ward of the National Health Service, in which television is escapable only by death. 'Mother' was a rude word: the Savage was peculiar in having one, among a test-tube population. Soma was a delightful drug with no side-effects, which kept everybody happy. The Park Lane Hospital itself foreshadows our specialist hospices, into which families can with muffled relief tidy away their dying.

From Brave New World

THE PARK LANE Hospital for the Dying was a sixty-storey tower of primrose tiles. As the Savage stepped out of his taxicopter a convoy of gaily-coloured aerial hearses rose whirring from the roof and darted away across the Park, westwards, bound for the Slough Crematorium. At the lift gates the presiding porter gave him the information he required, and he dropped down to Ward 81 (a Galloping Senility ward, the porter explained) on the seventeenth floor.

It was a large room bright with sunshine and yellow paint, and containing twenty beds, all occupied. Linda was dying in company – in company and with all the modern conveniences. The air was continuously alive with gay synthetic melodies. At the foot of every bed, confronting its moribund occupant, was a television box. Television was left on, a running tap, from morning till night. Every quarter of an hour the prevailing perfume of the room was automatically changed. 'We try,' explained the nurse, who had taken charge of the Savage at the door, 'we try to create a thoroughly pleasant atmosphere here – something between a first-class hotel and a feely-palace, if you take my meaning.'

'Where is she?' asked the Savage, ignoring these polite explanations.

The nurse was offended. 'You *are* in a hurry,' she said.

'Is there any hope?' he asked.

'You mean, of her not dying?' (He nodded.) 'No, of course there isn't. When somebody's sent here, there's no . . .' Startled by the expression of distress on his pale face, she suddenly broke off. 'Why, whatever is the matter?' she asked. She was not accustomed to this kind of thing in visitors. (Not that there were many visitors anyhow: or any reason why there should be many visitors.) 'You're not feeling ill, are you?'

He shook his head. 'She's my mother,' he said in a scarcely audible voice.

The nurse glanced at him with startled, horrified eyes; then quickly looked away. From throat to temple she was all one hot blush.

'Take me to her,' said the Savage, making an effort to speak in an ordinary tone.

Still blushing, she led the way down the ward. Faces still fresh and unwithered (for senility galloped so hard that it had no time to age the cheeks – only the heart and brain) turned as they passed. Their progress was followed by the blank, incurious eyes of second infancy. The Savage shuddered as he looked.

Linda was lying in the last of the long row of beds, next to the wall. Propped up on pillows, she was watching the Semi-Finals of the South American Riemann-surface Tennis Championship, which were being played in silent and diminished reproduction on the screen of the television box at the foot of the bed. Hither and thither across their square of illumined glass the little figures noiselessly darted, like fish in an aquarium – the silent but agitated inhabitants of another world.

Linda looked on, vaguely and uncomprehendingly smiling. Her pale, bloated face wore an expression of imbecile happiness. Every now and then her eyelids closed, and for a few seconds she seemed to be dozing. Then with a little start she would wake up again – wake up to the aquarium antics of the Tennis Champions, to the Super-Vox-Wurlitzeriana rendering of 'Hug me till you drug me, honey', to the warm draught of verbena that came blowing through the ventilator above her head – would wake to these things, or rather to a dream of which these things, transformed and embellished by the *soma* in her blood, were the marvellous constituents, and smile once more her broken and discoloured smile of infantile contentment.

'Well, I must go,' said the nurse. 'I've got my batch of children coming. Besides, there's Number 3.' She pointed up the ward. 'Might go off any minute now. Well, make yourself comfortable.' She walked briskly away.

The Savage sat down beside the bed.

'Linda,' he whispered, taking her hand.

At the sound of her name, she turned. Her vague eyes brightened with recognition. She squeezed his hand, she smiled, her lips moved; then quite suddenly her head fell forward. She was asleep. He sat watching her – seeking through the tired flesh, seeking and finding that young, bright face which had stooped over his childhood in Malpais, remembering (and he closed his eyes) her voice, her movements, all the events of their life together. 'Streptocock-Gee, to Banbury-T . . .' How beautiful her singing had been! And those childish rhymes, how magically strange and mysterious!

> A, B, C, vitamin D:
> The fat's in the liver, the cod's in the sea.

He felt the hot tears welling up behind his eyelids as he recalled the words and Linda's voice as she repeated them. And then the reading lessons; The tot is in the pot, the cat is on the mat; and the Elementary Instructions for Beta Workers in the Embryo Store. And long evenings by the fire or, in summer time, on the roof of the little house, when she told him those stories about the Other Place, outside the Reservation: that beautiful, beautiful Other Place, whose memory, as of a heaven, a paradise of goodness and loveliness, he still kept whole and intact, undefiled by contact with the reality of this real London, these actual civilized men and women.

A sudden noise of shrill voices made him open his eyes and, after hastily brushing away the tears, look round. What seemed an interminable stream of identical eight-year-old male twins was pouring into the room. Twin after twin, twin after twin, they came – a nightmare. Their faces, their repeated face – for there was only one between the lot of them – puggishly stared, all nostrils and pale goggling eyes. Their uniform was khaki. All their mouths hung open. Squealing and chattering they entered. In a moment, it seemed, the ward was maggoty with them. They swarmed between the beds, clambered over, crawled under, peeped into the television boxes, made faces at the patients.

Linda astonished and rather alarmed them. A group stood clustered at the foot of her bed, staring with the frightened and stupid curiosity of animals suddenly confronted by the unknown.

'Oh, look, look!' They spoke in low, scared voices. 'Whatever is the matter with her? Why is she so fat?'

They had never seen a face like hers before – had never seen a face that was not youthful and taut-skinned, a body that had ceased to be slim and upright. All these moribund sexagenarians had the appearance of childish girls. At forty-four, Linda seemed, by contrast, a monster of flaccid and distorted senility.

'Isn't she awful?' came the whispered comments. 'Look at her teeth!'

Suddenly from under the bed a pug-faced twin popped up between John's chair and the wall, and began peering into Linda's sleeping face.

'I say . . .' he began; but his sentence ended prematurely in a squeal. The Savage had seized him by the collar, lifted him clear over the chair and, with a smart box on the ears, sent him howling away.

His yells brought the Head Nurse hurrying to the rescue.

'What have you been doing to him?' she demanded fiercely. 'I won't have you striking the children.'

'Well, then, keep them away from this bed.' The Savage's voice was trembling with indignation. 'What are these filthy little brats doing here at all? It's disgraceful!'

'Disgraceful! But what do you mean? They're being death-conditioned. And I tell you,' she warned him truculently, 'if I have any more of your interference with their conditioning, I'll send for the porters and have you thrown out.'

(1932)

WILLIAM SHAKESPEARE

Sleepwalking is an everlasting eerie mystery. Hippocrates, in the fourth century BC, knew 'many persons during sleep . . . rising up, fleeing out of doors, and deprived of their reason until they awake, and afterwards being well and rational as before.'

In 1686, an English aristocrat was acquitted at the Old Bailey of shooting a guard and a horse in his sleep, after fifty witnesses attested that he often so perambulated. Monks sound asleep have knifed the beds of their priors; pupils of their teachers; a sleeping Californian housewife took her dachshunds for a twenty-five mile nocturnal drive; a Sydney woman broke both legs while eloping through her bedroom window in her dreams; an English county lady, awakened and terrified unto fainting, discovered at daybreak that her sleepwalking butler had laid dinner for fourteen on her bed. Some sleepers rise to fight the furniture, some to escape from a bedroom filling with boiling water. Four million Americans are calculated to walk in their sleep, barely necessitating all-night TV. Sleeping fathers have killed their children, in 1878 and 1946.

Sleepwalkers were once seen shudderingly as the bewitched. Now they are the 'diurnally repressed aggressives', the nail-biting, stifled, anxious people of daylight. Their controlled emotions are loosed at night to prowl like cats, provoking their owners to follow.

The theatrical sleepwalking star is Lady Macbeth. She was observed by her doctor, of which there are eight in Shakespeare (1564–1616), among 712 medical references. Shakespeare's technical adviser was Dr John Hall (1575–1635) of Queens' College, Cambridge, who married his eldest daughter Susanna in 1607, became his executor and inheritor of the family home, New Place in Stratford, and whose twice-married daughter Elizabeth died in 1670 as the last Shakespearian. Hall was a 'Physician living at Stratford upon Avon in Warwickshire, where he was very famous, and also in the counties adjacent,' according to the title-page of his own publication, *Select Observances on English Bodies, and Cures both Empericall and Historicall*, written in Latin and translated by a keen Stratford practitioner in 1657.

Shakespeare, the eternal fascinator, spotlights the sleepwalking scene in *Macbeth* with his uncanny knowledge of the yet unknown.

From Macbeth

ACT V, Scene I

Dunsinane. Ante-room in the castle.

Enter a DOCTOR OF PHYSIC *and a* WAITING-GENTLEWOMAN.

DOCTOR: I have two nights watched with you, but can perceive no truth in your report. When was it she last walked?

GENTLEWOMAN: Since his majesty went into the field, I have seen her rise from her bed, throw her night-gown upon her, unlock her closet, take forth paper, fold it, write upon 't, read it, afterwards seal it, and again return to bed; yet all this while in a most fast sleep.

DOCTOR: A great perturbation in nature, to receive at once the benefit of sleep, and do the effects of watching! In this slumbery agitation, besides her walking and other actual performances, what, at any time, have you heard her say?

GENTLEWOMAN: That, sir, which I will not report after her.

DOCTOR: You may to me, and 'tis most meet you should.

GENTLEWOMAN: Neither to you nor any one; having no witness to confirm my speech.

Enter LADY MACBETH, *with a taper.*

Lo you, here she comes! This is her very guise; and, upon my life, fast asleep. Observe her; stand close.

DOCTOR: How came she by that light?

GENTLEWOMAN: Why, it stood by her: she has light by her continually; 'tis her command.

DOCTOR: You see, her eyes are open.

GENTLEWOMAN: Ay, but their sense is shut.

DOCTOR: What is it she does now? Look, how she rubs her hands.

GENTLEWOMAN: It is an accustomed action with her, to seem thus washing her hands. I have known her continue in this a quarter of an hour.

LADY MACBETH: Yet here's a spot.

DOCTOR: Hark! she speaks: I will set down what comes from her, to satisfy my remembrance the more strongly.

LADY MACBETH: Out, dammed spot! out, I say! One; two: why, then, 'tis time to do 't. Hell is murky! Fie, my lord, fie! a soldier, and afeard? What need we fear who knows it, when none can call our power to account? Yet who would have thought the old man to have had so much blood in him?

DOCTOR: Do you mark that?

LADY MACBETH: The Thane of Fife had a wife: where is she now? – What, will these hands ne'er be clean? No more o' that, my lord, no more o' that: you mar all with this starting.

DOCTOR: Go to, go to; you have known what you should not.

GENTLEWOMAN: She has spoke what she should not, I am sure of that: Heaven knows what she has known.

LADY MACBETH: Here's the smell of the blood still: all the perfumes of Arabia will not sweeten this little hand. Oh, oh, oh!

DOCTOR: What a sign is there! The heart is sorely charged.

GENTLEWOMAN: I would not have such a heart in my bosom for the dignity of the whole body.

DOCTOR: Well, well, well, –

GENTLEWOMAN: Pray God it be, sir.

DOCTOR: This disease is beyond my practice: yet I have known those which have walked in their sleep who have died holily in their beds.

LADY MACBETH: Wash your hands, put on your night-gown; look not so pale. I tell you yet again, Banquo's buried; he cannot come out on 's grave.

DOCTOR: Even so?

LADY MACBETH: To bed, to bed: there's knocking at the gate. Come, come, come, come, give me your hand. What's done cannot be undone. To bed, to bed, to bed!

Exit

DOCTOR: Will she go now to bed?

GENTLEWOMAN: Directly.

DOCTOR: Foul whisperings are abroad. Unnatural deeds
Do breed unnatural troubles; infected minds
To their deaf pillows will discharge their secrets;
More needs she the divine than the physician.
God, God forgive us all! Look after her;
Remove from her the means of all annoyance,
And still keep eyes upon her. So, good-night;
My mind she has mated, and amaz'd my sight.
I think, but dare not speak.
GENTLEWOMAN: Good-night, good doctor.

Exeunt

The Doctor has enunciated the principle of Freud's *Interpretation of Dreams* 293 years later.

'How does your patient, doctor?' asks Macbeth, on his return to Dunsinane.

DOCTOR: Not so sick, my lord,
As she is troubled with thick-coming fancies,
That keep her from her rest.
MACBETH: Cure her of that:
Canst thou not minister to a mind diseased,
Pluck from the memory a rooted sorrow,
Raze out the written troubles of the brain,
And with some sweet oblivious antidote
Cleanse the stuff'd bosom of that perilous stuff
Which weighs upon the heart?

So anticipating Freud's theory of psychoanalysis in 1895.

DOCTOR: Therein the patient
Must minister to himself.

'Throw physic to the dogs,' growls Macbeth, as thoughtlessly as he grasped the weird sisters' assurance:

Be bloody, bold, and resolute; laugh to scorn
The power of man, for none of woman born
Shall harm Macbeth.

And fatally overlooking the possibility of Macduff's Caesarean section.

(1606)

OLIVER GOLDSMITH

Whether Oliver Goldsmith (1728–74) was a proper doctor or not is a matter of professional argument. Goldsmith was a Protestant from Roscommon, his father shortly becoming curate to the rector of Kilkenny West at £40 a year. At eight, smallpox scarred his face for life. At fifteen, he went to Trinity College, Dublin, rioted, absconded, reappeared for his BA in 1749 and emigrated to America, but got no further than Cork. He took £50 from his uncle to study law at the Temple in London, but got no further than Dublin. He got as far as Edinburgh in the autumn of 1752, to study medicine, 'lodging with hardly any society but a folio book, a skeleton, my cat and a meagre landlady', at £23 a year, the cheapest digs in town. Since 13 January 1753, Goldsmith's signature has adorned the register of the Royal Medical Society of Edinburgh.

In 1754 Goldsmith sailed for Bordeaux, but was arrested at Newcastle on suspicion of recruiting for the French: luckily so, for the ship sailed on without him, and was lost with all hands. He moved to another European centre of medical excellence, Leyden – 'physic is by no means taught here so well as in Edinburgh' – then travelled to Padua and Louvain, walking from city to city, playing the flute and disputing. This was an entertainment he described as: 'philosophical theses maintained against every adventitious disputant; for which, if the champion opposes with any dexterity, he may claim a gratuity in money, a dinner and a bed for one night.' Just like TV chat shows.

Goldsmith arrived at Dover on 1 February 1756, penniless and friendless. He became a chemist's assistant at Fish-street Hill by the Monument, playing his flute to the ragged children outside his lodgings up the flagstoned ladder of Breakneck Steps from Sea-coal Lane. Then Dr Fanu Sleigh, an Edinburgh fellow-student, benevolently set him up as a physician at Bankside, south of the Thames.

Goldsmith's medical career is apparelled with three stories. The first is Reynolds': examination of his Bankside patients was complicated by the doctor having to keep his hat in his hand, deftly to hide the holes in his 'rusty, black patched suit'. On 21 December

1758, Goldsmith needed a more impressive outfit for his viva voce at Surgeons' Hall in the Old Bailey, about which he must have learned chillingly from Smollett's experiences in *Roderick Random*. Goldsmith had won an appointment to the East India Company as factory surgeon on the Coromandel coast – £100 a year, and £1,000 more, if lucky, from private practice – and needed to pass the exam for the berth of hospital mate aboard an East Indiaman, to work the passage which he could not afford. He borrowed a suit from a friend but afterwards pawned it; he anyway failed the exam and the job fell through because of fierce fighting against the French.

In 1761, contributions to Smollett's *British Magazine* had let Goldsmith move from Breakneck Steps to No. 6 Wine Office Court in Fleet Street. He then went into orbit round Johnson, becoming a founder member of 'The Club' which met at the Turk's Head in Soho, mixing with Reynolds, Burke (who was at Trinity College with him), Fox, Boswell and David Garrick, who turned down his first comedy *The Goodnatur'd Man*. It opened at Covent Garden in 1768 to take a reasonable £500, to be followed in 1773 by his smash hit *She Stoops to Conquer*.

Reynolds prudently advised him to be a doctor as well as a man of letters, so though a popular dramatist Goldsmith decided again to dabble. 'He hired a man-servant, and appeared with a professional wig and cane, purple silk breeches, and a scarlet roquelaure; thus arrayed, he would strut into the apartments of his patients, with his three-cornered hat in one hand, and his cane in the other,' writes medical raconteur John Timbs. Goldsmith complained about his costume: 'I am shut out of several places where I used to play the fool very agreeably'. He shortly had a violent argument with an apothecary over the dosage on his prescription for Mrs Sidebotham, a lady friend. To his outrage, she sided with the druggist. Goldsmith flounced out of her house in anger, telling a male crony that he was determined henceforth to leave off prescribing for friends. '"Do so, my dear Doctor," came the reply, "whenever you undertake to kill, let it be only your enemies." This was the end of Goldsmith's medical career,' says Timbs.

In 1769, Goldsmith got an MB Oxon *ad eundem*, on the strength of an MB Dublin *in absentia*. The contentious point is whether he took the Dublin exam *in absentia*, too. Doctor or not, he was fiercely against quacks, and against the universal, if reasonable, phobia about mad dogs:

> The man recover'd of the bite,
> The dog it was that died.

Though about medicine he wrote little more than about Mrs Mary Blaize:

> The doctors found, when she was dead, –
> Her last disease was mortal.

But in 1761 Goldsmith touched a medical breakthrough. He was practising the Viennese Leopold Auenbrugger's finger percussion – to locate fluid in a chest, as an innkeeper locates wine in a vat – several years before it caught on in medical London.

Goldsmith was a simple and soft-hearted man – *She Stoops to Conquer* was based on his own youthful gullibility, when a joker directed him to the squire's house for the village inn. He was only sporadically a conversation-stopping wit. Vain and accident-prone, he was a gambler who died broke, after an attack of diarrhoea and vomiting which was possibly from overdosing himself with Dr Robert James's antimony fever powder, against the advice of his doctor, William Hawes.

Garrick called Goldsmith 'scholar, rake, Christian, dupe, gamester, poet'. Everyone else respectfully called him 'Dr'. So honoured a writer, even spectrally within the medical profession, demands a snip of his widespread work.

Dr Primrose, the Vicar of Wakefield, presents a saintly fortitude to domestic disaster, and earnest improvisation in keeping his social end up. How like Mr Pooter in *The Diary of a Nobody* 126 years later, and how like Carrie Pooter is the Vicar's wife Deborah, and what fellow-feeling Mr Burchell would have had towards Mr Pooter's taciturn visitor Mr Padge.

From The Vicar of Wakefield

MICHAELMAS-EVE HAPPENING on the next day, we were invited to burn nuts and play tricks at neighbour Flamborough's. Our late mortifications had humbled us a little, or it is probable we might have rejected such an invitation with contempt: however, we suffered ourselves to be happy. Our honest neighbour's goose and dumplings were fine, and the lamb's-wool, even in the opinion of my wife, who was a connoisseur, was excellent. It is true, his manner of telling stories was not quite so well. They were very long, and very dull, and all about himself, and we had laughed at them ten times before: however, we were kind enough to laugh at them once more.

Mr Burchell, who was of the party, was always fond of seeing some innocent amusement going forward, and set the boys and girls to blind-man's buff. My wife, too, was persuaded to join in the diversion, and it gave me pleasure to think she was not yet too old. In the meantime, my neighbour and I looked on, laughed at every feat, and praised our own dexterity when we were young. Hot cockles succeeded next, questions and commands followed that, and, last of all, they sat down to hunt the slipper. As every person may not be acquainted with this primeval pastime, it may be necessary to observe, that the company at this play plant themselves in a ring upon the ground, all except one, who stands in the middle, whose business it is to catch a shoe, which the company shove about under their hams from one to another, something like a weaver's shuttle. As it is impossible, in this case, for the lady who is up to face all the company at once, the great beauty of the play lies in hitting her a thump with the heel of the shoe on that side least capable of making a defence. It was in this manner that my eldest daughter was hemmed in, and thumped about, all blowzed, in spirits, and bawling for fair play, fair play, with a voice that might deafen a ballad-singer, when, confusion on confusion! who should enter the room but our two great acquaintances from town, Lady Blarney and Miss Carolina Wilelmina Amelia Skeggs! Description would but beggar, therefore it is unnecessary to describe, this new mortification. Death! To be seen by ladies of such high breeding in such vulgar attitudes! Nothing better could ensue from such a vulgar play of Mr Flamborough's proposing. We seemed stuck to the ground for some time, as if actually petrified with amazement.

The two ladies had been at our house to see us, and finding us from home, came after us hither, as they were uneasy to know what accident could have kept us from church the day before. Olivia undertook to be our prolocutor, and delivered the whole in the summary way, only saying, 'We were thrown from our horses.' At which account the ladies were greatly concerned; but being told the family received no hurt, they were extremely glad; but being informed that we were almost killed by the fright, they were vastly sorry; but hearing that we had a very good night, they were extremely glad again. Nothing could exceed their complaisance to my daughters: their professions the last evening were warm, but now they were ardent. They protested a desire of having a more lasting acquaintance. Lady Blarney was particularly attached to Olivia; Miss Carolina Wilelmina Amelia Skeggs (I love to give the whole name) took a greater fancy to her sister. They supported the conversation between themselves, while my daughters sat silent, admiring their exalted breeding. But as every reader, however beggarly himself, is fond of high-lived dialogues, with anecdotes of Lords, Ladies, and Knights of the Garter, I must beg leave to give him the concluding part of the present conversation.

'All that I know of the matter,' cried Miss Skeggs, 'is this, that it may be true or it may not be true; but this I can assure your Ladyship, that the whole rout was in amaze: his Lordship turned all manner of colours, my Lady fell into a sound [swoon], but Sir Tomkyn drawing his sword, swore he was hers to the last drop of his blood.'

'Well,' replied our Peeress, 'this I can say, that the Duchess never told me a syllable of the matter, and I believe her Grace would keep nothing a secret from me. This you may depend upon as fact, that the next morning my Lord Duke cried out three times to his *valet-de-chambre*, "Jernigan, Jernigan, Jernigan, bring me my garters!"'

But previously I should have mentioned the very impolite behaviour of Mr Burchell, who, during this discourse, sat with his face turned to the fire, and, at the conclusion of every sentence, would cry out *fudge*, an expression which displeased us all, and, in some measure, damped the rising spirit of the conversation.

'Besides, my dear Skeggs,' continued our Peeress, 'there is nothing of this in the copy of verses that Mr Burdock made upon the occasion. *Fudge!*'

'I am surprised at that,' cried Miss Skeggs; 'for he seldom leaves anything out, as he writes only for his own amusement. But can your Ladyship favour me with a sight of them? *Fudge!*'

'My dear creature,' replied our Peeress, 'do you think I carry such things about me? Though they are very fine, to be sure, and I think myself something of a judge – at least I know what pleases myself. Indeed, I was ever an admirer of all Dr Burdock's little pieces; for, except what he does, and our dear Countess at Hanover Square, there's nothing comes out but the most lowest stuff in nature; not a bit of high life among them. *Fudge!*'

'Your Ladyship should except,' says t'other, 'your own things in the *Lady's Magazine*. I hope you'll say there's nothing low-lived there? But I suppose we are to have no more from that quarter? *Fudge!*'

'Why, my dear,' says the lady, 'you know my reader and companion has left me, to be married to Captain Roach, and as my poor eyes won't suffer me to write myself, I have been for some time looking out for another. A proper person is no easy matter to find; and, to be sure, thirty pounds a year is a small stipend for a well-bred girl of character, that can read, write and behave in company: as for the chits about town, there is no bearing them about one. *Fudge!*'

'That I know,' cried Miss Skeggs, 'by experience. For of the three companions I had this last half year, one of them refused to do plain-work an hour in the day; another thought twenty-five guineas a year too small a salary; and I was obliged to send away the third, because I suspected an intrigue with the chaplain. Virtue, my dear Lady Blarney, virtue is worth any price; but where is that to be found? *Fudge!*'

My wife had been, for a long time, all attention to this discourse, but was particularly struck with the latter part of it. Thirty pounds and twenty-five guineas a year, made fifty-six pounds five shillings English money, all which was in a manner going a-begging, and might easily be secured in the family. She for a moment studied my looks for approbation; and, to own a truth, I was of opinion, that two such places would fit our two daughters exactly. Besides, if the Squire had any real affection for my eldest daughter, this would be the way to make her every way qualified for her fortune. My wife, therefore, was resolved that we should not be deprived of such advantages for want of assurance, and undertook to harangue for the family. 'I hope,' cried she, 'your Ladyships will pardon my present presumption. It is true, we have no right to pretend to such favours; but yet it is natural for me to wish putting my children forward in the world. And, I will be bold to say, my two girls have had a pretty good education and capacity; at least the country can't show better. They can read, write, and cast accounts; they understand their needle, broad-stitch, cross and change, and all manner of plain-work; they can pink, point, and frill, and know something of music; they can do up small-clothes, work upon catgut; my eldest can cut paper, and my youngest has a very pretty manner of telling fortunes upon the cards. *Fudge!*'

When she had delivered this pretty piece of eloquence, the two ladies looked at each other a few minutes in silence, with an air of doubt and importance. At last Miss Carolina Wilelmina Amelia Skeggs condescended to observe that the young ladies, from the opinion she could form of them from so slight an acquaintance, seemed very fit for such employments. 'But a thing of this kind, Madam,' cried she, addressing my spouse, 'requires a thorough examination into characters, and a more perfect knowledge of each other. Not, Madam,' continued she, 'that I in the least suspect the young ladies' virtue, prudence, and discretion; but there is a form in these things, Madam – there is a form.'

My wife approved her suspicions very much, observing that she was very apt to be suspicious herself, but referred her to all the neighbours for a character; but this our Peeress declined as unnecessary, alleging that her cousin Thornhill's recommendation would be sufficient; and upon this we rested our petition.

(1766)

JAMES BOSWELL

James Boswell (1740–95), the eldest son of the Edinburgh judge Lord Auchinleck, had just turned twenty-two when – like Smollett twenty-three years earlier – he anticipated the advice which Dr Johnson would give him the following summer and rattled in his chaise down the high road leading to England. Boswell lodged in Pall Mall with a fellow Scotsman, the naval surgeon Andrew Douglas, and initiated without delay a fervent and lifelong relish of London's joys. Of these, the most delightful – ahead of the chaffing in the coffee houses, the quaffing in the chop houses, the theatre, the bookshops, the wags and wits – were the girls.

They swarmed all night in the Strand, the Haymarket and Whitehall, around the taverns of Covent Garden, under the trees of St James's Park, above the Thames at Westminster Bridge, in all of which sites Boswell enjoyed them al fresco for sixpence to a shilling a go. He was a doubly good customer: 'She wondered at my size, and said if I ever took a girl's maidenhead, I would make her squeak,' commended one young tart up an alley. With each of them he had 'the intention to enjoy her in armour', the prototype condoms made of sheep's gut tied on with a pretty ribbon, or of linen, which needed pre-coital soaking. But alas, 'which I found but a dull satisfaction'. The urge for full enjoyment for his money inveigled Boswell into nineteen attacks of gonorrhoea, until his urogenital system collapsed under the strain, and he died after being carried home from a literary dinner with an abscess of the prostate and kidney failure.

Boswell's tastes ran 'from the splendid Madam at fifty guineas a night, down to the civil nymph with white-thread stockings who tramps the Strand and will resign her engaging person to your honour for a pint of wine and a shilling'. But like all rakes he longed for what money could not buy: 'Indeed, in my mind there cannot be higher felicity on earth enjoyed by man than the participation of genuine reciprocal amorous affection with an amiable woman,' whom he discovered on Tuesday 14 December 1762 at Covent Garden Theatre.

His Louisa was Mrs Lewis, who had played the Queen in *Hamlet* that September. He courted her with ardent elegance, and on Tuesday 4 January she agreed to spend a night with him at Hayward's Black Lion Inn off Fleet Street.

From Boswell's London Journal 1762–1763

WEDNESDAY 12 JANUARY. At the appointed hour of eight I went to the Piazzas, where I sauntered up and down for a while in a sort of trembling suspense, I knew not why. At last my charming companion appeared, and I immediately conducted her to a hackney-coach which I had ready waiting, pulled up the blinds, and away we drove to the destined scene of delight. We contrived to seem as if we had come off a journey, and carried in a bundle our night-clothes, handkerchiefs, and other little things. We also had with us some almond biscuits, or as they call them in London, macaroons, which looked like provision on the road. On our arrival at Hayward's we were shown into the parlour, in the same manner that any decent couple would be. I here thought proper to conceal my own name (which the people of the house had never heard), and assumed the name of Mr Digges. We were shown up to the very room where he slept. I said my cousin, as I called him, was very well. That Ceres and Bacchus might in moderation lend their assistance to Venus, I ordered a genteel supper and some wine.

Louisa told me she had two aunts who carried her over to France when she was a girl, and that she could once speak French as fluently as English. We talked a little in it, and agreed that we would improve ourselves by reading and speaking it every day. I asked her if we did not just look like man and wife. 'No,' said she, 'we are too fond for married people.' No wonder that she may have a bad idea of that union, considering how bad it was for her. She has contrived a pretty device for a seal. A heart is gently warmed by Cupid's flame, and Hymen comes with his rude torch and extinguishes it. She said she found herself quite in a flutter. 'Why, really,' said I, 'reason sometimes has no power. We have no occasion to be frightened, and yet we are both a little so. Indeed, I preserve a tolerable presence of mind.' I rose and kissed her, and conscious that I had no occasion to doubt my qualifications as a gallant, I joked about it: 'How curious would it be if I should be so frightened that we should rise as we lay down.' She reproved my wanton language by a look of modesty. The bells of St Bride's church rung their merry chimes hard by. I said that the bells in Cupid's court would be this night set a-ringing for joy at our union.

We supped cheerfully and agreeably and drank a few glasses, and then the maid came and put the sheets, well aired, upon the bed. I now contemplated my fair prize. Louisa is just twenty-four, of a tall rather than short figure, finely made in person, with a handsome face and an enchanting languish in her eyes. She dresses with taste. She has sense, good humour, and vivacity, and looks quite a woman in genteel life. As I mused on this elevating subject, I could not help being somehow pleasingly confounded to think that so fine a woman was at this moment in my possession, that without any motives of interest she had come with me to an inn, agreed to be my intimate companion, as to be my bedfellow all night, and to permit me the full enjoyment of her person.

When the servant left the room, I embraced her warmly and begged that she would not now delay my felicity. She declined to undress before me, and begged I would retire and send her one of the maids. I did so, gravely desiring the girl to go up to Mrs Digges. I then took a candle in my hand and walked out to the yard. The night was very dark and very cold. I experienced for some minutes the rigours of the season, and called into my mind many terrible ideas of hardships, that I might make a transition from such dreary thoughts to the most gay and delicious feelings. I then caused make a bowl of negus, very rich of the fruit, which I caused be set in the room as a reviving cordial.

I came softly into the room, and in a sweet delirium slipped into bed and was immediately clasped in her snowy arms and pressed to her milk-white bosom. Good heavens, what a loose did we give to amorous dalliance! The friendly curtain of darkness concealed our blushes. In a moment I felt myself animated with the strongest powers of love, and, from my dearest creature's kindness, had a most luscious feast. Proud of my godlike vigour, I soon resumed the noble game. I was in full glow of health. Sobriety had preserved me from effeminacy and weakness, and my bounding blood beat quick and high alarms. A more voluptuous night I never enjoyed. Five times was I fairly lost in supreme rapture. Louisa was madly fond of me; she declared I was a prodigy, and asked me if this was not extraordinary for human nature. I said twice as much might be, but this was not, although in my own mind I was somewhat proud of my performance. She said it was what there was no just reason to be proud of. But I told her I could not help it. She said it was what we had in common with the beasts. I said no. For we had it highly improved by the pleasures of sentiment. I asked her what she thought enough. She gently chid me for asking such questions, but said two times. I mentioned the Sunday's assignation, when I was in such bad spirits, told her in what agony of mind I was, and asked her if she would not have despised me for my imbecility. She declared she would not, as it was what people had not in their own power.

She often insisted that we should compose ourselves to sleep before I would consent to it. At last I sunk to rest in her arms and she in mine. I found the negus, which had a fine flavour, very refreshing to me. Louisa had an exquisite mixture of delicacy and wantonness that made me enjoy her with more relish. Indeed I could not help roving in fancy to the embraces of some other ladies which my lively imagination strongly pictured. I don't know if that was altogether fair. However, Louisa had all the advantage. She said she was quite fatigued and could neither stir leg nor arm. She begged I would not despise her, and hoped my love would not be altogether transient. I have painted this night as well as I could. The description is faint; but I surely may be styled a Man of Pleasure.

THURSDAY 13 JANUARY. We awaked from sweet repose after the luscious fatigues of the night. I got up between nine and ten and walked out till Louisa should rise. I patrolled up and down Fleet Street, thinking on London, the seat of Parliament and the seat of pleasure, and seeming to myself as one of the wits in King Charles the Second's time. I then came in and we had an agreeable breakfast, after which we left Hayward's, who said he was sorry he had not more of our company, and calling a hackney-coach, drove to Soho Square, where Louisa had some visits to pay. So we parted. Thus was this conquest completed to my highest satisfaction. I can with pleasure trace the progress of this intrigue to its completion. I am now at east on that head, having my fair one fixed as my own. As Captain Plume says, the best security for a woman's mind is her body. I really conducted this affair with a manliness and prudence that pleased me very much. The whole expense was just eighteen shillings. . . .

FRIDAY 14 JANUARY. I then called for Lady Mirabel. She seemed to like me a good deal. I was lively, and I looked like the game. As it was my first visit, I was very quiet. However, it was agreed that I should visit her often. This elated me, as it afforded a fine, snug, and agreeable prospect of gallantry. Yet I could not think of being unfaithful to Louisa. But, then, I thought Louisa was only in the mean time, till I got into genteel life, and that a woman of fashion was the only proper object for such a man as me. At last delicate honour prevailed, and I resolved for some time at least to keep alive my affection for Louisa.

I this day began to feel an unaccountable alarm of unexpected evil: a little heat in the members of my body sacred to Cupid, very like a symptom of that distemper with which Venus, when cross, takes it into her head to plague her votaries. But then I had run no risks. I had been with no woman but Louisa; and sure she could not have such a thing. Away then with such idle fears, such groundless, uneasy apprehensions! When I came to Louisa's, I felt myself stout and well, and most courageously did I plunge into the fount of love, and had vast pleasure as I enjoyed her as an actress who had played many a fine lady's part. She was remarkably fond of me today, and sighing said, 'What will become of me if I lose you now?' . . .

THURSDAY 20 JANUARY. I rose very disconsolate, having rested very ill by the poisonous infection raging in my veins and anxiety and vexation boiling in my breast. I could scarcely credit my own senses. What! thought I, can this beautiful, this sensible, and this agreeable woman be so sadly defiled? Can corruption lodge beneath so fair a form? Can she who professed delicacy of sentiment and sincere regard for me, use me so very basely and so very cruelly? No, it is impossible. I have just got a gleet by irritating the parts too much with excessive venery. And yet these damned twinges, that scalding heat, and that deep-tinged loathsome matter are the strongest proofs of an infection. But she certainly must think that I would soon discover her falsehood. But perhaps she was ignorant of her being ill. A pretty conjecture indeed! No, she could not be ignorant. Yes, yes, she intended to make the most of me. And now I recollect that the day we went to Hayward's, she showed me a bill of thirty shillings about which she was in some uneasiness, and no doubt expected that I would pay it. But I was too cautious, and she had not effrontery enough to try my generosity in direct terms so soon after my letting her have two guineas. And am I then taken in? Am I, who have had safe and elegant intrigues with fine women, become the dupe of a strumpet? Am I now to be laid up for many weeks to suffer extreme pain and full confinement, and to be debarred all the comforts and pleasures of life? And then must I have my poor pocket drained by the unavoidable expense of it? And shall I no more (for a long time at least) take my walk, healthful and spirited, round the Park before breakfast, view the brilliant Guards on the Parade, and enjoy all my pleasing amusements? And then am I prevented from making love to Lady Mirabel, or any other woman of fashion? O dear, O dear! What a cursed thing this is! What a miserable creature am I!

In this woeful manner did I melancholy ruminate. I thought of applying to a quack who would cure me quickly and cheaply. But then the horrors of being imperfectly cured and having the distemper thrown into my blood terrified me exceedingly. I therefore pursued my resolution of last night to go to my friend Douglas, whom I knew to be skillful and careful; and although it should cost me more, yet to get sound health was a matter of great importance, and I might save upon other articles. I accordingly went and breakfasted with him. . . .

After breakfast Mrs Douglas withdrew, and I opened my sad case to Douglas, who upon examining the parts, declared I had got an evident infection and that the woman who gave it me could not but know of it. I joked with my friend about the expense, asked him if he would take a draught on my arrears, and bid him visit me seldom that I might have the less to pay. To these jokes he seemed to give little heed, but talked seriously in the way of his business. And here let me make a just and true observation, which is that the same man as a friend and as a surgeon exhibits two very opposite characters. Douglas as a friend is most kind, most anxious for my interest, made me live ten days in his house, and suggested every plan of economy. But Douglas as a surgeon will be as ready to keep me long under his hands, and as desirous to lay hold of my money, as any man. In short, his views alter quite. I have to do not with him but his profession.

As Lady Northumberland was to have a great rout next day, I delayed beginning my course of medicine till Friday night. Enraged at the perfidy of Louisa, I resolved to go and upbraid her most severely; but this I thought was not acting with dignity enough. So I would talk to her coolly and make her feel her own unworthiness. . . .

BOSWELL: Pray, Madam, in what state of health have you been in for some time?

LOUISA: Sir, you amaze me.

BOSWELL: I have but too strong, too plain reason to doubt of your regard. I have for some days observed the symptoms of disease, but was unwilling to believe you so very ungenerous. But now, Madam, I am thoroughly convinced.

LOUISA: Sir, you have terrified me. I protest I know nothing of the matter.

BOSWELL: Madam, I have had no connection with any woman but you these two months. I was with my surgeon this morning, who declared I had got a strong infection, and that she from whom I had it could not be ignorant of it. Madam, such a thing in this case is worse than from a woman of the town, as from her you may expect it. You have used me very ill. I did not deserve it. You know you said where there was no confidence, there was no breach of trust. But surely I placed some confidence in you. I am sorry that I was mistaken.

LOUISA: Sir, I will confess to you that about three years ago I was very bad. But for these fifteen months I have been quite well. I appeal to God Almighty that I am speaking true; and for these six months I have had to do with no man but yourself.

BOSWELL: But by G–d, Madam, I have been with none but you, and here am I very bad.

LOUISA: Well, Sir, by the same solemn oath I protest that I was ignorant of it.

BOSWELL: Madam, I wish much to believe you. But I own I cannot upon this occasion believe a miracle.

LOUISA: Sir, I cannot say more to you. But you will leave me in the greatest misery. I shall lose your esteem. I shall be hurt in the opinion of everybody, and in my circumstances.

BOSWELL: (*To himself*). What the devil does the confounded jilt mean by being hurt in her circumstances? This is the grossest cunning. But I won't take notice of that at all. – Madam, as to the opinion of everybody, you need not be afraid. I was going to joke and say that I never boast of a lady's *favours*. But I give you my word of honour that you shall not be discovered.

LOUSIA: Sir, this is being more generous that I could expect.

BOSWELL: I hope, Madam, you will own that since I have been with you I have always behaved like a man of honour.

LOUISA: You have indeed, Sir.

BOSWELL: (*Rising*). Madam, your most obedient servant.

During all this conversation I really behaved with a manly composure and polite dignity that could not fail to inspire an awe, and she was pale as ashes and trembled and faltered. Thrice did she insist on my staying a little longer, as it was probably the last time that I should be with her. She could say nothing to the purpose. And I sat silent. As I was going, said she, 'I hope, Sir, you will give me leave to inquire after your health.' 'Madam,' said I, archly, 'I fancy it will be needless for some weeks.' She again renewed her request. But unwilling to be plagued any more with her, I put her off by saying I might perhaps go to the country, and left her. I was really confounded at her behaviour. There is scarcely a possibility that she could be innocent of the crime of horrid imposition. And yet her positive asseverations really stunned me. She is in all probability a most consummate dissembling whore.

Thus ended my intrigue with the fair Louisa, which I flattered myself so much with, and from which I expected at least a winter's safe copulation. It is indeed very hard. I cannot say, like young fellows who get themselves clapped in a bawdy-house, that I will take better care again. For I really did take care. However, since I am fairly trapped, let me make the best of it. I have not got in from imprudence. It is merely the chance of war.

(1763)

POETS' APPENDIX

Professor Monro's painstaking *The Physician as Man of Letters, Science and Action* discovered seventy-two medical poets. But many were doctors who turned a line as relaxation from taking a pulse. Edward Jenner (1749–1823) discovered vaccination against small-pox during the summer of 1796, as a GP of the Gloucestershire countryside, and wrote befittingly untaxing rustic verses. Sir Ronald Ross (1857–1932) in 1897 discovered in human blood the mosquito-borne parasite which transmits malaria. He published in 1910 *The Prevention of Malaria*, and in 1911 *Philosophies*, a volume of verse beginning with his reflections through his laboratory window in Madras during 1881:

SIR RONALD ROSS

India

Here from my lonely watch-tower of the East
An ancient race outworn I see –
With dread, my own dear distant Country, lest
The same fate fall on thee.

Lo here the iron winter of curst caste
Has made men into things that creep;
The leprous beggars totter trembling past;
The baser sultans sleep . . .

A timely warning to both lands.

THOMAS BEDDOES, THOMAS CAMPION and GEORGE CRABBE

There are three medical poets whose work is ubiquitous and its display here redundant.

Thomas Lovell Beddoes (1803–49) was the son of the renowned Dr Thomas Beddoes, who became Reader in Chemistry at Oxford but resigned out of solidarity with the French Revolution. He then ran the not forgotten 'Pneumatic Institute' at Clifton in the West Country, for curing diseases by inhalation of the appropriate gas, his assistant being Humphry Davy. Thomas Lovell's mother was Maria Edgeworth's sister.

After Charterhouse and Pembroke, Oxford, Thomas Lovell Beddoes migrated aged twenty-two to Göttingen to study physiology under Johann Blumenbach, of the clivus blumenbachii, a slope in the base of the skull. Beddoes became MD Würzburg in 1832, then wandered round Germany and Switzerland practising and politicking, before settling as a physician at Zurich in 1835. In 1842 he fled to Berlin from rioters not sharing his liberal opinions. In 1847 he was living in Frankfurt with a baker called Degen, with whom he returned to Zurich and hired the local theatre for a night, so that his friend might play Hotspur in *Henry IV*. The pair split in May 1848, which so upset Beddoes that he attempted to bleed himself to death, then paralysed himself in Basle on 26 January with curare, the Orinoco arrow poison which a century later became an essential supplement to anaesthesia.

Beddoes' play *The Bride's Tragedy* had served him up with the taste of success at Oxford. In 1825 he began *Death's Jest-Book, or The Fool's Tragedy*, an Elizabethan-type drama:

ACT I, Scene 1

Enter ISBRAND, *the court fool.*

ISBRAND: Good morrow, brother Vanity! How? soul of a pickle-herring, body of a spagirical [alchemist] toss-pot, doublet of motley, and mantle of pilgrim, how art thou transmuted!

That style of thing. It was published posthumously in 1850.

Thomas Campion (1567–1620) from Witham, Essex, the son of

a Chancery lawyer, went to Cambridge, read law at Gray's Inn, started studying medicine aged thirty-five and became a London physician. *Cherry-Ripe* is one of his.

George Crabbe (1754–1832) was the son of a salt-tax collector from Aldeburgh in Suffolk; two of his three brothers were lost at sea. He was apprenticed to a Suffolk surgeon from 1768–74, struggled to practise back home, decided with £3 in his pocket to try his luck at writing in London, and succeeded through the patronage of Edmund Burke. In 1781 Crabbe was ordained curate of Aldeburgh, was appointed chaplain to the Duke of Rutland, picked up livings in Dorset and Lincoln and became rector of Muston, Leicester, to where he was commanded to return by the bishop in 1805 after several years' absence. In 1814 he became vicar of Trowbridge in Wiltshire, and practised medicine no more. His *Sir Eustace Grey* (1807) is a wild history of the lord of Greyling Hall, shut up in a madhouse:

> The ruins of Sir Eustace Gray,
> The sport of madness, misery's prey . . .
>
> But I had all mankind's applause,
> And all the smiles of womankind . . .

And now he suffers vivid hallucinations:

> I've served the vilest slaves in jail,
> And pick'd the dunghill's spoil for bread;
> I've made the badger's hole my bed . . .

He is beset by the fiends of darkness and shrouded shadows. It was all inspired by the opium which another doctor prescribed Crabbe for his indigestion in 1790, on which he got hooked.

ABRAHAM COWLEY

Abraham Cowley (1618–67) was the posthumous son of a London stationer, went to Trinity, Cambridge, became a fellow, but was ejected as a Royalist during the Civil War in 1643 and moved to Oxford. He was a founder member of the Royal Society in 1645, followed Queen Henrietta-Maria to Paris in 1646, performed her secret missions, was arrested in England in 1654, released on

£1,000 bail, studied medicine at Oxford and got an MD in 1657 on Government orders. He started writing poetry aged ten. He never practised.

Anacreontics

The Moon and Stars drink up the Sun:
They drink and dance by their own light,
They drink and revel all the night:
Nothing in Nature's sober found,
But an eternal health goes round.
Fill up the bowl, then, fill it high,
Fill all the glasses there – for why
Should every creature drink but I?
Why, man of morals, tell me why?

(1656)

An admirable expression of admirable sentiments.

JOHN ARMSTRONG

John Armstrong (1709–79) was born in Roxburghshire, son of the manse, and became MD Edinburgh in 1732 with his thesis *De Tabe Purulenta* (wasting away amid pus). He was a lazy, kind, buttoned-up man 'who quite detested talk'. He practised in London, and in 1736 published the poem *The Œconomy of Love*, which emulated Ovid's *Art of love* but 'in undue freedom of colouring'. It was followed in 1737 by a synopsis of the history and cure of venereal disease. In 1748 Armstrong became physician to the Hospital for Lame and Sick Soldiers behind Buckingham House, was appointed physician to the Army in Germany, retired on half-pay in 1763 at the end of the Seven Years War, and died in London after a fall. His great work, 2,000 lines of it, includes sound advice on diet, early rising, and exercise.

The Art of Preserving Health

Choose leaner viands, ye whose jovial make
Too fast the gummy nutriment imbibes:
Choose sober meals; and rouse to active life
Your cumbrous clay; nor on the enfeebling dawn,
Irresolute, protract the morning hours.
But let the man whose bones are thinly clad,
With cheerful ease and succulent repast
Improve his habit if he can; for each
Extreme departs from perfect sanity.

And on drink:

We curse not wine: the vile excess we blame;
More Fruitful than the accumulated hoard
Of pain and misery

(1744)

JOHN McCRAE

Canadian John McCrae (1872–1918) qualified at Toronto, and in 1899 became pathologist, later physician and lecturer, at McGill University, Montreal. He served in the South African War of 1899–1902, not as a medical, but as an artillery, officer. In October 1914, he sailed as MO with the 1st Canadians, in January 1918 he was promoted consultant physician to the British Armies in the Field, but caught pneumonia and died on the 28th. This poem had appeared anonymously, squashed at the bottom of a page in *Punch*, three Christmases earlier. Its mild lines express as forcefully as all literature of warfare the appalling squander of precious lives surrendered to the gambling of malevolent or stupid politicians.

In Flanders Fields

In Flanders fields the poppies blow
Between the crosses, row on row,
That mark our place; and in the sky
The larks, still bravely singing, fly
Scarce heard amid the guns below.

We are the Dead. Short days ago
We lived, felt dawn, saw sunset glow,
Loved and were loved, and now we lie
In Flanders fields.

Take up our quarrel with the foe:
To you from failing hands we throw
The torch; be yours to hold it high
We shall not sleep, though poppies grow
In Flanders fields.

(1915)

THOMAS HARDY

So painstakingly bucolic, Thomas Hardy OM (1840–1928) had little time for doctors. But here is an interesting case from Wessex of arborphobia.

From The Woodlanders

MARTY . . . GENTLY APPROACHED a bedroom, and without entering said, 'Father, do you want anything?'

A weak voice inside answered in the negative; adding, 'I should be all right by tomorrow if it were not for the tree!'

'The tree again – always the tree! O, father, don't worry so about that. You know it can do you no harm . . .'

He was better, she said; he would be able to work in a day or two; he would be quite well but for his craze about the tree falling on him. . . .

Mr Fitzpiers entered the sick chamber as a doctor is wont to do on such occasions, and pre-eminently when the room is that of the humble cottager; looking round towards the patient with a preoccupied gaze which so plainly reveals that he has well-nigh forgotten all about the case and the circumstances since he dismissed them from his mind at his last exit from the same apartment. He nodded to Winterborne, who had not seen him since his peep over the hedge at Grace, recalled the case to his thoughts, and went leisurely on to where South sat.

Edred Fitzpiers was, on the whole, a finely formed, handsome man. His eyes were dark and impressive and beamed with the light either of energy or of susceptivity – it was difficult to say which; it might have been a little of both. That quick, glittering, empirical eye, sharp for the surface of things if for nothing beneath, he had not. But whether his apparent depth of vision were real, or only an artistic accident of his corporeal moulding, nothing but his deeds could reveal.

His face was rather soft than stern, charming than grand, pale than flushed; his nose – if a sketch of his features be *de rigueur* for a person of his pretensions – was artistically beautiful enough to have been worth modelling by any sculptor not over busy, and was hence devoid of those knotty irregularities which often mean power; while the classical curve of his mouth was not without a looseness in its close. Either from his readily appreciative mien, or his reflective manner, his presence bespoke the philosopher rather than the dandy – an effect which was helped by the absence of trinkets or other trivialities from his attire, though this was more finished and up to date than is usually the case among rural practitioners.

Strict people of the highly respectable class, knowing a little about him by report, said that he seemed likely to err rather in the possession of too many ideas than too few; to be a dreamy 'ist of some sort, or too deeply steeped in some false kind of 'ism. However this may be, it will be seen that he was undoubtedly a somewhat rare kind of gentleman and doctor to have descended, as from the clouds, upon Little Hintock.

'This is an extraordinary case,' he said at last to Winterborne, after examining South by conversation, look, and touch, and learning that the craze about the elm was stronger than ever. 'Come downstairs, and I'll tell you what I think.'

They accordingly descended, and the doctor continued, 'The tree must be cut down; or I won't answer for his life.'

''Tis Mrs Charmond's tree; and I suppose we must get permission?' said Giles.

'O, never mind whose tree it is – what's a tree beside a life! Cut it down. I have not the honour of knowing Mrs Charmond as yet; but I am disposed to risk that much with her.'

''Tis timber,' rejoined Giles. 'They never fell a stick about here without its being marked first, either by her or the agent.'

'Then we'll inaugurate a new era forthwith. How long has he complained of the tree?' asked the doctor of Marty.

'Weeks and weeks, sir. The shape of it seems to haunt him like an evil spirit. He says that it is exactly his own age, that it has got human sense, and sprouted up when he was born on purpose to rule him, and keep him as its slave. Others have been like it afore in Hintock.'

They could hear South's voice upstairs. 'O, he's rocking this way; he must come! And then my poor life, that's worth houses upon houses, will be squashed out o' me. O! O!'

'That's how he goes on,' she added. 'And he'll never look anywhere else but out of the window, and scarcely have the curtains drawn.'

'Down with it, then, and hang Mrs Charmond,' said Mr Fitzpiers. 'The best plan will be to wait till the evening, when it is dark, or early in the morning before he is awake, so that he doesn't see it fall, for that would terrify him worse than ever. Keep the blind down till I come, and then I'll assure him, and show him that his trouble is over.'

The doctor departed, and they waited till the evening. When it was dusk, and the curtains drawn, Winterborne directed a couple of woodmen to bring a cross-cut saw; and the tall threatening tree was soon nearly off at its base. Next morning, before South was awake, they went and lowered it cautiously, in a direction away from the cottage. It was a business difficult to do quite silently; but it was done at last, and the elm of the same birth-year as the woodman's lay stretched upon the ground. The weakest idler that passed could now set foot on marks formerly made in the upper forks by the shoes of adventurous climbers only; once inaccessible nests could be examined microscopically; and on swaying extremities where birds alone had perched the bystanders sat down.

As soon as it was broad daylight the doctor came, and Winterborne entered the house with him. Marty said that her father was wrapped up and ready, as usual, to be put into his chair. They ascended the stairs, and soon seated him. He began at once to complain of the tree, and the danger to his life and Winterborne's house property in consequence.

The doctor signalled to Giles, who went and drew back the printed cotton curtains. 'It is gone, see,' said Mr Fitzpiers.

As soon as the old man saw the vacant patch of sky in place of the branched column so familiar to his gaze, he sprang up, speechless; his eyes rose from their hollows till the whites showed all round, he fell back, and a bluish whiteness overspread him.

Greatly alarmed they put him on the bed. As soon as he came a little out of his fit, he gasped, 'O, it is gone! – where – where?'

His whole system seemed paralyzed by amazement. They were thunderstruck at the result of the experiment, and did all they could. Nothing seemed to avail. Giles and Fitzpiers went and came, but uselessly. He lingered through the day, and died that evening as the sun went down.

'Damned if my remedy hasn't killed him!' murmured the doctor.

(1887)

THREE VICTORIAN LADY DOCTOR-NOVELISTS

CHARLOTTE M. YONGE

Magnum bonum is a large yellow plum, a choice potato, a special line of goods, and a novel by Charlotte Mary Yonge (1823–1901). She was a godly girl, the daughter of a Waterloo veteran, from Otterbourne in Hampshire. The vicar of the next parish was John Keble, who encouraged her to write *The Heir of Redclyffe*, the literary hit of 1853. Its idealistic appeal stretched from the Oxford quads to the Sebastopol earthworks. Her royalities went mostly on fitting out a missionary schooner, *Southern Cross*, for Bishop Selwyn. Charlotte Yonge wrote 160 books, bright with the stained-glass light of the High Church. For almost forty years she edited *The Monthly Packet* for children; she lived her life in Otterbourne and never wed.

From Magnum Bonum

Magnum Bonum is a thousand-page novel in three volumes (Mudie's Library in New Oxford Street dictated this format of Victorian literature, to treble its lending revenues). It is the story of an insufferably happy family. Their father, Dr Joseph Brownlow, lecturer at a London hospital, with his brass plate on a comfortable house, dies in Chapter Three leaving 'magnum bonum', a secret life-saving discovery, for development by his sons. His widow, Caroline, shortly comes into her great-uncle's fortune, and is confronted by her daughter.

'I WANTED TO speak to you, mother.'

'Well, Janet,' said Caroline, reviewing in one moment every unmarried man, likely or unlikely, who had approached the girl, and with a despairing conviction that it would be someone very unlikely indeed!

'You know I am of age, mother.'

'Certainly. We drank your health last Monday.'

'I made up my mind that till I was of age I would go on studying, and at the same time see something of the world and of society.'

'Certainly,' said Caroline, wondering what her inscrutable daughter was coming to.

'And having done this, I wish to devote myself to the study of medicine.'

'Be a lady doctor, Janet!'

'Mother, you are surely above all the commonplace, old-world nonsense!'

I don't think I am, Janet. I don't think your father would have wished it.'

'He would have gone on with the spirit of the times, mother; men do, while women stand still.'

'I don't think he would in this.'

'I think he would, if he knew me, and the issues at stake, and how his other children are failing him.'

'Janet!' – and the colour flushed into her mother's face – 'I don't quite know what you mean; but it is time we came to an understanding.'

'I think so,' returned Janet.

(1879)

Janet's choice is not 'for the sake either of the emancipation of women or of general philanthropy', and it alienates her from mother. It is upon brother Jock – 'there are golden opinions of him in the Medical School' – that mother solemnly bestows the secret of magnum bonum, 'when he has taken his degree, and is a good, religious, wise, able man, with brains and balance, fit to be trusted to work out and apply such an invention, and not make it serve his own advancement, but be a real good and blessing to all.' But by then it had been discovered two years ago by someone else.

MARY BRADDON

Mary Elizabeth Braddon (1837–1915) in 1862 wrote *Lady Audley's Secret*, which sold a million copies, made her fortune, and enabled her publisher to build a villa on the Thames, which he decently named 'Audley Lodge'. She married another publisher. She wisely wrote seventy similar 'sensation novels', including *The Doctor's Wife* of 1864. This is a politely attenuated version of *Madame Bovary*, which had appeared seven years earlier.

From The Doctor's Wife

Young surgeon George Gilbert at sleepy Graybridge-on-the-Wayverne, who 'had a tender pity for the sorrows and sufferings it was a part of his duty to behold', proposes to Isabel outdoors after a picnic enlivened by sparkling Burgundy. His father, the parish doctor, had lodged him as a medical student 'in the heart of a quiet Wesleyan family in the Seven-Sisters Road, and the boy had enjoyed very little leisure for disporting himself with the dangerous spirits of St Bartholomew's'. (An unlikely story.) This 'had left the lad almost as innocent as a girl'.

After the wedding:

'GEORGE,' SAID ISABEL, gently, when she had seen all the rooms, 'did you never think of re-furnishing the house?'

'Re-furnishing it! How do you mean, Izzie?'

'Buying new furniture, I mean, dear. This is all so old-fashioned.'

George the conservative shook his head.

'I like it all the better for that, Izzie,' he said; 'it was my father's, you know, and his father's before him. I wouldn't change a stick of it for the world. Besides, it's such capital substantial furniture; they don't make such chairs and tables nowadays.'

'No,' Izzie murmured with a sigh; 'I'm very glad they don't.'

Like Emma Bovary, 'She mistook the power to appreciate and enjoy beautiful things for a kind of divine right to happiness and splendour.' She becomes bored, and meets a poet.

Soon:

And then, like the sudden fall of a curtain in a brilliant theatre, the scene darkened, and Isabel thought of her own life – the life to which she must go back when it was dark that night: the common parlour, or the best parlour, – what was the distinction, in their dismal wretchedness, that one should be called better than the other? – the bread-and-cheese, the radishes, – and, oh, how George could eat radishes, crunch, crunch, crunch! – till madness would have been relief.

The poet understandably:

. . . met the Doctor's Wife very often: sometimes on the bridge beside the water-mill; sometimes in the meadowland which surged in emerald billows all about Graybridge and Mordred and Warncliffe. He met her very often. It was no new thing for Isabel to ramble here and there in that lovely rustic paradise: but it was quite a new thing for Mr Lansdell to take such a fancy for pedestrian exercise.

Predictably:

Poor George Gilbert was quite puzzled by his wife's headache, which was of a particularly obstinate nature, lasting for some days. He gave her cooling draughts, and lotions for her forehead, which was very hot under his calm professional hand. Her pulse was rapid, her tongue was white, and the surgeon pronounced her to be bilious. He had not the faintest suspicion of any mental ailment lurking at the root of these physical derangements. He was very simple-minded, and, being incapable of wrong himself, measured all his decent fellow-creatures by a fixed standard. He thought that the good and the wicked formed two separate classes as widely apart as the angels of heaven and the demons of the fiery depths. He knew that there were, somewhere or other in the universe, wives who wronged their husbands and went into outer darkness, just as he knew that in dismal dens of crime there lurked robbers and murderers, forgers and pickpockets, the newspaper record of whose evil deeds made no unpleasant reading for quiet Sunday afternoons. But of vague sentimental errors, of shadowy dangers and temptations, he had no conception. He had seen his wife pleased and happy in Roland Lansdell's society; and the thought that any wrong to himself, how small soever, could arise out of that companionship, had never entered his mind.

The affair had started when 'the feast of St Partridge the Martyr was close at hand'. Now, 'when the March winds were bleaker' upon their tryst:

'Going to London!' cried the Doctor's Wife, piteously; 'Oh, I knew, I knew that you would go away again, and I shall never see you any more.' She clasped her hands in her sudden terror, and looked at him with a world of sorrow and reproach in her pale face.

But, Isabel – my love – my darling –' the tender epithets did not startle her; she was so absorbed by the fear of losing the god of her idolatry, – 'I am only going to town for a day or two to see my lawyer.'

He misguidedly tries to cheer her up by continuing:

'I know I do wrong in exposing you to the degradation of these stolen meetings. If I feel the shame so keenly, how much worse it must be for you – my own dear girl – my sweet innocent darling. But this shall be the last time, Isabel, – the last time I will ask you to incur any humiliation for me. Henceforward we will hold our heads high, my love; for at least there shall be no trickery or falsehood in our lives.'

Mrs Gilbert stared at Roland Lansdell in utter bewilderment. He had spoken of shame and degradation, and had spoken in the tone of a man who had suffered, and still suffered, very bitterly. This was all Isabel could gather from her lover's speech, and she opened her eyes in blank amazement as she attended to him. Why should he be ashamed, or humiliated, or degraded? Was Dante degraded by his love for Beatrice . . . ?

The tears rolled down her flushed cheek, as she turned away her face from Roland. She was almost stifled by mingled grief and indignation. . . . A woman of the world would have very quickly perceived that Mr Lansdell's discourse must have relation to more serious projects than future meetings under Lord Thurston's oak, with interchange of divers volumes of light literature. But Isabel Gilbert was not a woman of the world.

Fortunately, her husband catches typhoid and dies. But only after his old nurse has declaimed 'in a hard cruel voice, strangely at variance with her stifled sobs, "Yes, Mrs Gilbert; and you'll be free to take your pleasure, and to meet Mr Lansdell as often as you like; and go gadding about after dark with strange men . . . you're a wicked woman and a wicked wife!"'

Then the poet is beaten up by an old foe released from prison. All ends happily, because he dies, too, and leaves Isabel his fortune, and she takes a world tour.

ARABELLA KENEALY

Arabella Kenealy (d.1938) was a doctor, who qualified at the London School of Medicine for Women, practised in London from 1888 to 1894, caught diphtheria, retired, and wrote novels. Her father was Edward Vaughan Kennedy QC, Irishman, writer, unsuccessful defence counsel at the Tichborne trial in 1873, who unsportingly afterwards attacked the judges, was disbenched in 1874, elected MP for Stoke-upon-Trent in 1875, but no fellow member would introduce him to take his seat. He had been jailed for a month in 1850 for cruelty to his illegitimate son. Arabella wrote *Dr Janet of Harley Street* in 1893, and judging by its frontispiece was a fine-looking, large-eyed, strong-chinned, well-thatched Victorian gel. She wrote fifteen novels and *The Failure of Vivisection* and *Feminism and Sex-Extinction*. She was unmarried.

From Dr Janet of Harley Street

Seventeen-year-old Phyllis Eve is to marry the sixty-year-old Marquis de Richeville, who:

. . . seizing her in his arms, he drew her insistently to him, kissing her fiercely and repeatedly upon her cheek and lips.

Uttering an amazed, horrified cry, she pushed him violently away, thrusting him back with her flower-laden hands.

Her mother points out sensibly:

'He has kissed you before, and he is to be your husband, you know.'

'Yes; but, mother, he never kissed me like that before. . . . Oh, mother, do you think he had been drinking?'

They marry, and the groom kisses the bride, who falls fainting on the floor. She instantly deserts him, and takes up medicine. Her mentor is Dr Janet Doyle, dean of the Minerva Hospital for Women:

. . . a middle-aged, genial-looking woman, of a height and figure whose ample proportions she made no effort to disguise by dress.

She was clad in a rough, loosely-fitting tweed garb – one could not call it a gown, for the skirt was of that genus distinguished by the term 'divided', and the bodice was made and worn after the fashion of a man's shooting-coat.

Janet insists over a game of patience on financing Phyllis's studies:

Phyllis, overwhelmed by this unexpected kindness, timidly bent and kissed the large hand so dexterously busy with the cards.

'You are a good angel,' she faltered . . .

Her mother, at her wish, came soon to live in London, and as Dr Janet refused, point-blank, to part with her *protégée*, for whom she had conceived a violent affection, Mrs Eve, also, was induced to make her home with the hospitable doctor.

A Minerva Hospital medical lecturer pays a call on Dr Janet, his cousin:

'Who's your little friend downstairs?' he asked later of his cousin, after they had talked awhile.

She looked sharply at him.

'You let my little friend alone,' she replied severely. . . . I won't have you make love to her – I won't have any man make love to her. I want her for myself.'

Phyllis is an earnest student. The very contemplation of amusement, over her books and beside her skeleton, makes her cry out: 'Oh, Aunt Janet, I wish you could whip me for my wickedness.'

But Phyllis grows moody on holiday in Bournemouth, and shortly falls into the lecturer's arms over her lamplit volume of *Quain's Medicine*:

He caught her back to him and kissed her passionately.

'My white dove!' he cried.

'Paul! Phyllis!'

Dr Janet stood in the doorway, watching their enraptured clasp.

Phyllis, with a timid exclamation, lifted her head from his breast. He quietly loosed her.

'It's a bad business, I know, Janet,' he said, with a gloomy look.

'Phyllis, go to your room,' Dr Doyle commanded.

The Marquis sues for restitution of conjugal rights and Phyllis is guilty of contempt of court, just like the authoress's father. Then she hears from the Marquis's solicitors that he has died – conveniently, even if she gets nothing from the will – and she marries her lecturer. Dr Janet takes it all fairly well. When Paul exclaimed before the wedding:

'I say, Janet, what a grand stroke of luck it was that brought her to you.'

'Luck for you,' she retorted; 'but I am none so saintlike that I overflow with gratitude to turn luck my way only to fill *your* hands.'

Dr Janet adds nastily that it may 'so happen that this skittish bride comes back to her aunt at the end of the honeymoon'.

Then the Marquis turns up! His solicitors have exaggerated the report of his death. The happy couple have a stillborn baby.

Luckily, after surviving a hansom smash in Bond Street the Marquis courteously shoots himself, at Dr Janet's suggestion.

Perhaps I have read too much into all this.

Thus three ladies set the style for fascinating romance against the new sanctity of medicine.

SAMUEL WARREN

Samuel Warren (1807–77) was an Edinburgh medical student for six years until 1827, when he switched to the law, became a QC, Recorder, MP and Master in Lunacy. His *Ten Thousand a Year*, the tale of Mr Tittlebat Titmouse, the draper's assistant who assumes a fraudulent fortune, was the literary hit of 1841. Warren had already enjoyed sweeping success with *Passages from the Diary of a Late Physician*, both novels being respectably serialised in *Blackwood's*. The *Diary* is that of an (unintentionally) insufferably high-minded, pompous and ineffective doctor, whose practice incurs a death a chapter. It is the precursor of Dr Finlay's and other doctors' casebooks which entertained the next century.

From Diary of a Physician

Professional indignities.

I WAS ALSO, on several occasions, called in to visit the inferior members of families in the neighbourhood – servants, housekeepers, porters, etc.; and of all the trying, the mortifying occurrences in the life of a young physician, such occasions as these are the most irritating. You go to the house – a large one probably – and are instructed not to knock at the front door, but to go down by the area to your patient!

I think it was about this time that I was summoned in haste to young Sir Charles F—, who resided near Mayfair. Delighted at the prospect of securing so distinguished a patient, I hurried to his house, resolved to do my utmost to give satisfaction. When I entered the room, I found the sprig of fashion enveloped in a crimson silk dressing-gown, sitting conceitedly on the sofa, and sipping a cup of coffee; from which he desisted a moment to examine me – positively – through his eye-glass, and then directed me to inspect the swelled foot of a favourite pointer! Darting a look of anger at the insulting coxcomb, I instantly withdrew without uttering a word. . . .

The dentist and the comedian.

FRIDAY ——18–. A ludicrous contretemps happened today, which I wish I could describe as forcibly as it struck me. Mr ——, the well-known comedian, with whom I was on terms of intimacy, after having suffered so severely from the toothache as to be prevented for two evenings from taking his part in the play, sent, under my direction, for Monsieur ——, a fashionable dentist, then but recently imported from France. While I was sitting with my friend, endeavouring to 'screw his courage up to the sticking-place,' Monsieur arrived, duly furnished with 'the tools of his craft.' The comedian sat down with a rueful visage, and eyed the dentist's formidable preparations with a piteous and disconcerted air. As soon as I had taken my station behind, for the purpose of holding the patient's head, the gum was lanced without much ado; but as the doomed tooth was a very formidable broad-rooted molar, Monsieur prepared for a vigorous effort. He was just commencing the dreadful wrench, when he suddenly relaxed his hold, retired a step or two from his patient, and burst into a loud fit of laughter! Up started the astounded comedian, and, with clenched fists, demanded furiously, 'What the —— he meant by such conduct?' The little bewiskered foreigner, however, continued standing at a little distance, still so convulsed with laughter as to disregard the menacing movements of his patient; and exclaiming, 'Ah, *mon Dieu*! – ver good – ver good – *bien*! ha, ha! – Be Gar, Monsieur, you pull one such d—— queer, *extraordinaire comique* face – Be Gar, like one big fiddle!' or words to that effect. The dentist was right: Mr ——'s features were odd enough at all times; but, on the present occasion, they suffered such excruciating contortions – such a strange puckering together of the mouth and cheeks, and upturning of the eyes, that it was ten thousand times more laughable than any artificially distorted features with which he used to set Drury Lane in a roar!

Miss Charlotte regrets.

'Why, what in the world can Charlotte be doing all this while?' she again enquired. She listened – 'I have not heard her moving for the last three-quarters of an hour! I'll call the maid and ask.' She rang the bell, and the servant appeared.

'Betty, Miss J—— is not gone yet, is she?' 'La, no, ma'am,' replied the girl; 'I took up the curling-irons only about a quarter of an hour ago, as she had put one of her curls out; and she said she should soon be ready. She's burst her new muslin dress behind, and that has put her into a way, ma'am.'

'Go up to her room, then, Betty, and see if she wants anything; and tell her it's half-past nine o'clock,' said Mrs J——. The servant accordingly went upstairs, and knocked at the bedroom door, once, twice, thrice, but received no answer. There was a dead silence, except when the wind shook the window. Could Miss J—— have fallen asleep? Oh, impossible! She knocked again, but unsuccessfully, as before. She became a little flustered; and, after a moment's pause, opened the door, and entered. There was Miss J—— sitting at the glass. 'Why, la, ma'am!' commenced Betty in a petulant tone, walking up to her, 'here have I been knocking for these five minutes, and' – Betty staggered, horror-struck to the bed, and, uttering a loud shriek, alarmed Mrs J——, who instantly tottered upstairs, almost palsied with fright. Miss J—— was dead!

I was there within a few minutes, for my house was not more than two streets distant. It was a stormy night in March; and the desolate aspect of things without – deserted streets – the howling of the wind, and the pattering of the rain, contributed to cast a gloom over my mind, when connected with the intelligence of the awful event that had summoned me out, which was deepened into horror by the spectacle I was doomed to witness. On reaching the house, I found Mrs J—— in violent hysterics, surrounded by several of her neighbours, who had been called in to her assistance. I repaired instantly to the scene of death, and beheld what I shall never forget. The room was occupied by a white-curtained bed. There was but one window, and before it was a table, on which stood a looking-glass, hung with a little white drapery; and various articles of the toilet lay scattered about – pins, brooches, curling-papers, ribands, gloves, etc. An arm-chair was drawn to this table, and in it sat Miss J——, stone dead. Her head rested upon her right hand, her elbow supported by the table; while her left hung down by her side, grasping a pair of curling-irons. Each of her wrists was encircled by a showy gilt bracelet. She was dressed in a white muslin frock, with a little bordering of blonde. Her face was turned towards the glass, which, by the light of the expiring candle, reflected with frightful fidelity the clammy fixed features, daubed over with rouge and carmine – the fallen lower jaw – and the eyes directed full into the glass, with a cold, dull stare that was appalling. On examining the countenance more narrowly, I thought I detected the traces of a smirk of conceit and self-complacency, which not even the palsying touch of death could wholly obliterate. The hair of the corpse, all smooth and glossy, was curled with elaborate precision; and the skinny sallow neck was encircled with a string of glistening pearls. The ghastly visage of death, thus leering through the tinselry of fashion – the 'vain show' of artificial joy – was a horrible mockery of the fooleries of life!

Indeed, it was a most shocking spectacle! Poor creature! struck dead in the very act of sacrificing at the shrine of female vanity! – She must have been dead for perhaps twenty minutes or half an hour when I arrived, for nearly all the animal heat had deserted the body, which was rapidly stiffening. I attempted, but in vain, to draw a little blood from the arm. Two or three women present proceeded to remove the corpse to the bed, for the purpose of laying it out. What strange passiveness! No resistance offered to them while straightening the bent right arm, and binding the jaws together with a faded white riband, which Miss J—— had destined for her waist that evening!

On examination of the body, we found that death had been occasioned by disease of the heart. Her life might have been protracted, possibly, for years, had she but taken my advice, and that of her mother. I have seen many hundreds of corpses, as well in the calm composure of natural death, as mangled and distorted by violence; but never have I seen so startling a satire upon human vanity, so repulsive, unsightly, and loathsome a spectacle, as a *corpse dressed for a ball.*

(1832–37)

John Brown

I continually quote John Brown's (1810–82) brief paragraph about medical students from *Rab and His Friends*. It is the one beginning 'Don't think them heartless . . .' on the students crowding boisterously into the operating theatre. Operations seemed 'these bloody horrors which the students so eagerly looked forward to ("A magnificent sight if Slasher does it!") . . .' as George Orwell expressed their attitude, still getting it wrong a century later.

We take up medicine from a natural pity towards human suffering and the impulse to relieve it; but focused from the emotional to the practical with the intensity of the student's microscope. If every patient becomes a puzzle, to be gratifyingly solved by the doctor's training, intelligence, dexterity, erudition and experience; if the 'bedside manner' is a sincere though superfluous solace; well, so much the better for humanity, which has more to cure its ills than witches' brews and sympathy.

Dr Brown was born in Biggar, Lanark, the son of a doctor of divinity. At eighteen he became a pupil in Edinburgh of James Syme, who 'was, I believe, the greatest surgeon Scotland ever produced', and upon whom he bestowed the timeless compliment: 'He never wasted a word, or a drop of ink, or a drop of blood'. His apprentice-fee bought Syme 'his first carriage, a gig, and I got the first ride in it'.

Though Brown's sentimentality is leashed, his humour and pathos run as loose as the dogs in this saddest of canine stories. The patient's, and her husband's, resilience, in the face of the most awesome adversity of their life is rediscovered daily by any doctor. And if the doctor's admiration and wonderment often go unexpressed, they never lessen. 'I need hardly add, that the story of *Rab and His Friends* is in all essentials strictly matter of fact,' Brown insisted in 1858, when he was a successful Edinburgh practitioner. The surgeon was Syme.

Rab and His Friends

FOUR-AND-THIRTY years ago, Bob Ainslie and I were coming up Infirmary Street from the High School, our heads together, and our arms intertwisted, as only lovers and boys know how, or why.

When we got to the top of the street, and turned north, we espied a crowd at the Tron Church. 'A dog-fight!' shouted Bob, and was off; and so was I, both of us all but praying that it might not be over before we got up! and is not this boy-nature? and human nature too? and don't we all wish a house on fire not to be out before we see it? Dogs like fighting; old Isaac says they 'delight' in it, and for the best of all reasons; and boys are not cruel because they like to see the fight. They see three of the great cardinal virtues of dog or man – courage, endurance, and skill – in intense action. This is very different from a love of making dogs fight, and enjoying, and aggravating, and making gain by their pluck. A boy – be he ever so fond himself of fighting, if he be a good boy, hates and despises all this, but he would have run off with Bob and me fast enough: it is a natural, and a not wicked interest, that all boys and men have in witnessing intense energy in action.

Does any curious and finely-ignorant woman wish to know, how Bob's eye at a glance announced a dog-fight to his brain? He did not, he could not see the dogs fighting; it was a flash of an inference, a rapid induction. The crowd round a couple of dogs fighting, is a crowd, masculine mainly, with an occasional active, compassionate woman, fluttering wildly round the outside, and using her tongue and her hands freely upon the men, as so many 'brutes'; it is a crowd annular, compact, and mobile; a crowd centripetal, having its eyes and its heads all bent downwards and inwards, to one common focus.

Well, Bob and I are up, and find it is not over: a small, thoroughbred, white bull-terrier, is busy throttling a large shepherd's dog, unaccustomed to war, but not to be trifled with. They are hard at it; the scientific little fellow doing his work in great style, his pastoral enemy fighting wildly, but with the sharpest of teeth and a great courage. Science and breeding, however, soon took their own; the Game Chicken, as the premature Bob called him, working his way up, took his final grip of poor Yarrow's throat, – and he lay gasping and done for. His master, a brown, handsome, big young shepherd from Tweedsmuir, would have liked to have knocked down any man, 'drunk up Esil, or eaten a crocodile,' for that part, if he had a chance: it was no use kicking the little dog; that would only make him hold the closer. Many were the means shouted out in mouthfuls, of the best possible ways of ending it. 'Water!' but there was none near, and many shouted for it who might have got it from the well at Blackfriars Wynd. 'Bite the tail!' and a large, vague, benevolent, middle-aged man, more anxious than wise, with some struggle got the bushy end of Yarrow's tail into his ample mouth, and bit it with all his might. This was more than enough for the much-enduring, much perspiring shepherd, who, with a gleam of joy over his broad visage, delivered a terrific facer upon our large, vague, benevolent, middle-aged friend, – who went down like a shot.

Still the Chicken holds, death not far off. 'Snuff! a pinch of snuff!' observed sharply a calm, highly-dressed young buck, with an eye-glass in his eye. 'Snuff, indeed!' growled the angry crowd, affronted and glaring. 'Snuff! a pinch of snuff!' again observes the buck, but with more urgency; whereon were produced several open boxes, and from a mull which may have been at Culloden, he took a pinch, knelt down, and presented it to the nose of the Chicken. The laws of physiology and of snuff take their course; the Chicken sneezes, and Yarrow is free!

The young pastoral giant stalks off with Yarrow in his arms, – comforting him.

But the Chicken's blood is up, and his soul unsatisfied; he grips the first dog he meets, but discovering she is not a dog, in Homeric phrase, he makes a brief sort of *amende*, and is off. The boys, with Bob and me at their head, are after him; down Niddry Street he goes, bent on mischief; up the Cowgate like an arrow – Bob and I, and our small men, panting behind.

There, under the large arch of the South Bridge, is a huge mastiff, sauntering down the middle of the causeway, as if with his hands in his pockets: he is old, grey, brindled; as big as a little Highland bull, and has the Shakespearian dewlaps shaking as he goes.

The Chicken makes straight at him, and fastens on his throat. To our astonishment, the great creature does nothing but stand still, hold himself up, and roar – yes, roar; a long, serious, remonstrative roar. How is this? Bob and I are up to them. *He is muzzled!* The bailies had proclaimed a general muzzling, and his master, studying strength and economy mainly, had encompassed his huge jaws in a home-made apparatus, constructed out of the leather of some ancient *breechin*. His mouth was open as far as it could; his lips curled up in rage – a sort of terrible grin; his teeth gleaming, ready, from out the darkness; the strap across his mouth tense as a bowstring; his whole frame stiff with indignation and surprise; his roar asking us all round, 'Did you ever see the like of this?' He looked a statue of anger and astonishment, done in Aberdeen granite.

We soon had a crowd: the Chicken held on. 'A knife!' cried Bob; and a cobbler gave him his knife: you know the kind of knife, worn away obliquely to a point, and always keen. I put its edge to the tense leather; it ran before it; and then! one sudden jerk of that enormous head, a sort of dirty mist about his mouth, no noise, – and the bright and fierce little fellow is dropped, limp, and dead. A solemn pause; this was more than any of us had bargained for. I turned the little fellow over, and saw he was quite dead: the mastiff had taken him by the small of the back like a rat, and broken it.

He looked down at his victim appeased, ashamed, and amazed; snuffed him all over, stared at him, and taking a sudden thought, turned round and trotted off. Bob took the dead dog up, and said, 'John, we'll bury him after tea.' 'Yes,' said I; and was off after the mastiff. He made up the Cowgate at a rapid swing: he had forgotten some engagement. He turned up the Candlemaker Row, and stopped at the Harrow Inn.

There was a carrier's cart ready to start, and a keen, thin, impatient, black-a-vised little man, his hand at his grey horse's head, looking about angrily for something. 'Rab, ye thief!' said he, aiming a kick at my great friend, who drew cringing up, and avoiding the heavy shoe with more agility than dignity, and watching his master's eye, slunk dismayed under the cart, – his ears down, and as much as he had of tail down too.

What a man this must be – thought I – to whom my tremendous hero turns tail! The carrier saw the muzzle hanging, cut and useless, from his neck, and I eagerly told him the story, which Bob and I always thought, and still think, Homer, or King David, or Sir Walter, alone were worthy to rehearse. The severe little man was mitigated, and condescended to say, 'Rab, my man, puir Rabbie,' – whereupon the stump of a tail rose up, the ears were cocked, the eyes filled, and were comforted; the two friends were reconciled. 'Hupp!' and a stroke of the whip were given to Jess; and off went the three.

Bob and I buried the Game Chicken that night (we hadn't much of a tea) in the back-green of his house, in Melville Street, No. 17, with considerable gravity and silence; and being at the time in the Iliad, and, like all boys, Trojans, we called him, of course, Hector.

*

Six years have passed, – a long time for a boy and a dog: Bob Ainslie is off to the wars; I am a medical student, and clerk at Minto House Hospital.

Rab I saw almost every week, on the Wednesday; and we had much pleasant intimacy. I found the way to his heart by frequent scratching of his huge head, and an occasional bone. When I did not notice him he would plant himself straight before me, and stand wagging that bud of a tail, and looking up, with his head a little to the one side. His master I occasionally saw; he used to call me 'Maister John', but was laconic as any Spartan.

One fine October afternoon, I was leaving the hospital, when I saw the large gate open, and in walked Rab, with that great and easy saunter of his. He looked as if taking general possession of the place; like the Duke of Wellington entering a subdued city, satiated with victory and peace. After him came Jess, now white from age, with her cart; and in it a woman, carefully wrapped up, – the carrier leading the horse anxiously, and looking back. When he saw me, James (for his name was James Noble) made a curt and grotesque 'boo', and said, 'Maister John, this is the mistress; she's got a trouble in her breest – some kind o' an income we're thinkin'.'

By this time I saw the woman's face; she was sitting on a sack filled with straw, her husband's plaid round her, and his big-coat, with its large white metal buttons, over her feet. I never saw a more unforgettable face – pale, serious, *lonely*, delicate, sweet, without being what we call fine. She looked sixty, and had on a mutch, white as snow, with its black ribbon; her silvery smooth hair setting off her dark-grey eyes – eyes such as one sees only twice or thrice in a lifetime, full of suffering, but full also of the overcoming of it; her eye-brows black and delicate, and her mouth firm, patient, and contented, which few mouths ever are.

As I have said, I never saw a more beautiful countenance, or one more subdued to settled quiet. 'Ailie,' said James, 'this is Maister John, the young doctor; Rab's freend, ye ken. We often speak aboot you, doctor.' She smiled, and made a movement, but said nothing; and prepared to come down, putting her plaid aside and rising. Had Solomon, in all his glory, been handing down the Queen of Sheba at his palace gate, he could not have done it more daintily, more tenderly, more like a gentleman, than did James the Howgate carrier, when he lifted down Ailie, his wife. The contrast of his small, swarthy, weather-beaten, keen, worldly face to hers – pale, subdued, and beautiful – was something wonderful. Rab looked on concerned and puzzled, but ready for anything that might turn up, – were it to strangle the nurse, the porter, or even me. Ailie and he seemed great friends.

'As I was sayin', she's got a kind o' trouble in her breest, doctor; wull ye tak' a look at it?' We walked into the consulting-room, all four; Rab grim and comic, willing to be happy and confidential if cause could be shown, willing also to be quite the reverse, on the same terms. Ailie sat down, undid her open gown and her lawn handkerchief round her neck, and, without a word, showed me her right breast. I looked at and examined it carefully, – she and James watching me, and Rab eyeing all three. What could I say? There it was, that had once been so soft, so shapely, so white, so gracious and bountiful, 'so full of all blessed conditions,' – hard as a stone, a centre of horrid pain, making that pale face, with its grey, lucid, reasonable eyes, and its sweet resolved mouth, express the full measure of suffering overcome. Why was that gentle, modest, sweet woman, clean and lovable, condemned by God to bear such a burden?

I got her away to bed. 'May Rab and me bide?' said James. '*You* may; and Rab, if he will behave himself.' 'I'se warrant he's do that, doctor'; and in slunk the faithful beast. I wish you could have seen him. There are no such dogs now: he belonged to a lost tribe. As I have said, he was brindled, and grey like Aberdeen granite; his hair short, hard, and close, like a lion's; his body thick set, like a little bull – a sort of compressed Hercules of a dog. He must have been ninety pounds' weight, at the least; he had a large blunt head; his muzzle black as night; his mouth blacker than any night, a tooth or two – being all he had – gleaming out of his jaws of darkness. His head was scarred with the records of old wounds, a sort of series of fields of battle all over it; one eye out, one ear cropped as close as was Archbishop Leighton's father's – but for different reasons, – the remaining eye had the power of two; and above it, and in constant communication with it, was a tattered rag of an ear, which was for ever unfurling itself, like an old flag; and then that bud of a tail, about one inch long, if it could in any sense be said to be long, being as broad as long – the mobility, the instantaneousness of that bud was very funny and surprising, and its expressive twinklings and winkings, the intercommunications between the eye, the ear, and it, were of the subtlest and swiftest. Rab had the dignity and simplicity of great size; and having fought his way all along the road to absolute supremacy, he was as mighty in his own line as Julius Caesar or the Duke of Wellington; and he had the gravity of all great fighters.

You must have often observed the likeness of certain men to certain animals, and of certain dogs to men. Now, I never looked at Rab without thinking of the great Baptist preacher, Andrew Fuller. The same large, heavy, menacing, combative, sombre, honest countenance, the same inevitable eye, the same look, – as of thunder asleep, but ready, – neither a dog nor a man to be trifled with.

Next day, my master, the surgeon, examined Ailie. There was no doubt it must kill her, and soon. It could be removed – it might never return – it would give her speedy relief – she should have it done. She curtsied, looked at James, and said, 'When?' 'Tomorrow,' said the kind surgeon, a man of few words. She and James and Rab and I retired. I noticed that he and she spoke little, but seemed to anticipate everything in each other. The following day, at noon, the students came in, hurrying up the great stair. At the first landing-place, on a small well-known black board, was a bit of paper fastened by wafers, and many remains of old wafers beside it. On the paper were the words, 'An operation to-day. J. B. *Clerk.*'

Up ran the youths, eager to secure good places: in they crowded, full of interest and talk. 'What's the case?' 'Which side is it?'

Don't think them heartless; they are neither better nor worse than you or I: they get over their professional horrors, and into their proper work; and in them pity – as an *emotion*, ending in itself or at best in tears and a long-drawn breath, lessens, while pity as a *motive*, is quickened, and gains power and purpose. It is well for poor human nature that it is so.

The operating theatre is crowded; much talk and fun, and all the cordiality and stir of youth. The surgeon with his staff of assistants is there. In comes Ailie: one look at her quiets and abates the eager students. That beautiful old woman is too much for them; they sit down, and are dumb, and gaze at her. These rough boys feel the power of her presence. She walks in quickly, but without haste; dressed in her mutch, her neckerchief, her white dimity shortgown, her black bombazeen petticoat, showing her white worsted stockings and her carpet-shoes. Behind her was James, with Rab. James sat down in the distance, and took that huge and noble head between his knees. Rab looked perplexed and dangerous; forever cocking his ear and dropping it as fast.

Ailie stepped up on a seat, and laid herself on the table, as her friend the surgeon told her; arranged herself, gave a rapid look at James, shut her eyes, rested herself on me, and took my hand. The operation was at once begun; it was necessarily slow; and chloroform – one of God's best gifts to his suffering children – was then unknown. The surgeon did his work. The pale face showed its pain, but was still and silent. Rab's soul was working within him; he saw that something strange was going on, – blood flowing from his mistress, and she suffering; his ragged ear was up, and importunate; he growled and gave now and then a sharp impatient yelp; he would have liked to have done something to that man. But James had him firm, and gave him a glower from time to time, and an intimation of a possible kick; – all the better for James, it kept his eye and his mind off Ailie.

It is over: she is dressed, steps gently and decently down from the table, looks for James; then, turning to the surgeon and the students, she curtsies, – and in a low, clear voice, begs their pardon if she has behaved ill. The students – all of us – wept like children; the surgeon happed her up carefully, – and, resting on James and me, Ailie went to her room, Rab following. We put her to bed. James took off his heavy shoes, crammed with tackets, heel-capt and toe-capt, and put them carefully under the table, saying, 'Maister John, I'm for nane o' yer strynge nurse bodies for Ailie. I'll be her nurse, and on my stockin' soles I'll gang about as canny as pussy.' And so he did; and handy and clever, and swift and tender as any woman, was that horny-handed, snell, peremptory little man. Everything she got he gave her: he seldom slept; and often I saw his small, shrewd eyes out of the darkness, fixed on her. As before, they spoke little.

Rab behaved well, never moving, showing us how meek and gentle he could be, and occasionally, in his sleep, letting us know that he was demolishing some adversary. He took a walk with me every day, generally to the Candlemaker Row; but he was sombre and mild; declined doing battle, though some fit cases offered, and indeed submitted to sundry indignities; and was always very ready to turn, and came faster back, and trotted up the stair with much lightness, and went straight to *that* door.

Jess, the mare – now white – had been sent, with her weather-worn cart, to Howgate, and had doubtless her own dim and placid meditations and confusions, on the absence of her master and Rab, and her unnatural freedom from the road and her cart.

For some days Ailie did well. The wound healed 'by the first intention;' as James said, 'Oor Ailie's skin's ower clean to beil.' The students came in quiet and anxious, and surrounded her bed. She said she liked to see their young, honest faces. The surgeon dressed her, and spoke to her in his own short kind way, pitying her through his eyes, Rab and James outside the circle, – Rab being now reconciled, and even cordial, and having made up his mind that as yet nobody required worrying, but, as you may suppose, *semper paratus*.

So far well: but, four days after the operation, my patient had a sudden and long shivering, a 'groofin', as she called it. I saw her soon after; her eyes were too bright, her cheek coloured; she was restless, and ashamed of being so; the balance was lost; mischief had begun. On looking at the wound, a blush of red told the secret: her pulse was rapid, her breathing anxious and quick, she wasn't herself, as she said, and was vexed at her restlessness. We tried what we could. James did everything, was everywhere; never in the way, never out of it; Rab subsided under the table into a dark place, and was motionless, all but his eye, which followed every one. Ailie got worse; began to wander in her mind, gently; was more demonstrative in her ways to James, rapid in her questions, and sharp at times. He was vexed, and said, 'She was never that way afore; no, never.' For a time she knew her head was wrong, and was always asking our pardon – the dear, gentle old woman: then delirium set in strong, without pause. Her brain gave way, and that terrible spectacle,

> 'The intellectual power, through words and things,
> Went sounding on its dim and perilous way';

she sang bits of old songs and Psalms, stopping suddenly, mingling the Psalms of David, and the diviner words of his Son and Lord, with homely odds and ends and scraps of ballads.

Nothing more touching, or in a sense more strangely beautiful, did I ever witness. Her tremulous, rapid, affectionate, eager, Scotch voice, – the swift, aimless, bewildered mind, the baffled utterance, the bright and perilous eye; some wild words, some household cares, something for James, the names of the dead, Rab called rapidly and in a 'fremyt' voice, and he starting up, surprised, and slinking off as if he were to blame somehow; or had been dreaming he heard. Many eager questions and beseechings which James and I could make nothing of, and on which she seemed to set her all and then sink back ununderstood. It was very sad, but better than many things that are not called sad. James hovered about, put out and miserable, but active and exact as ever; read to her, when there was a lull, short bits from the Psalms, prose and metre, chanting the latter in his own rude and serious way, showing great knowledge of the fit words, bearing up like a man, and doting over her as his 'ain Ailie'. 'Ailie, ma woman!' 'Ma ain bonnie wee dawtie!'

The end was drawing on: the golden bowl was breaking; the silver cord was fast being loosed – that *animula, blandula, vagula, hospes, comesque*, was about to flee. The body and the soul – companions for sixty years – were being sundered, and taking leave. She was walking, alone, through the valley of that shadow, into which one day we must all enter, – and yet she was not alone, for we know whose rod and staff were comforting her.

One night she had fallen quiet, and as we hoped, asleep; her eyes were shut. We put down the gas, and sat watching her. Suddenly she sat up in bed, and taking a bedgown which was lying on it rolled up, she held it eagerly to her breast, – to the right side. We could see her eyes bright with a surprising tenderness and joy, bending over this bundle of clothes. She held it as a woman holds her sucking child; opening out her night-gown impatiently, and holding it close, and brooding over it, and murmuring foolish little words, as over one whom his mother comforteth, and who is sucking, and being satisfied. It was pitiful and strange to see her wasted dying look, keen and yet vague – her immense love. 'Preserve me!' groaned James, giving way. And then she rocked back and forward, as if to make it sleep, hushing it, and wasting on it her infinite fondness. 'Wae's me, doctor; I declare she's thinkin' it's that bairn.' 'What bairn?' 'The only bairn we ever had; our wee Mysie, and she's in the Kingdom, forty years and mair.' It was plainly true: the pain in the breast, telling its urgent story to a bewildered, ruined brain; it was misread and mistaken; it suggested to her the uneasiness of a breast full of milk, and then the child; and so again once more they were together, and she had her ain wee Mysie in her bosom.

This was the close. She sunk rapidly; the delirium left her; but as she whispered, she was clean silly; it was the lightening before the final darkness. After having for some time lain still – her eyes shut, she said 'James!' He came close to her, and lifting up her calm, clear, beautiful eyes, she gave him a long look, turned to me kindly but shortly, looked for Rab but could not see him, then turned to her husband again, as if she would never leave off looking, shut her eyes, and composed herself. She lay for some time breathing quick, and passed away so gently, that when we thought she was gone, James, in his old-fashioned way, held the mirror to her face. After a long pause, one small spot of dimness was breathed out; it vanished away, and never returned, leaving the blank clear darkness of the mirror without a stain. 'What is our life? it is even a vapour, which appeareth for a little time, and then vanisheth away.'

Rab all this time had been full awake and motionless: he came forward beside us: Ailie's hand, which James had held, was hanging down; it was soaked with his tears; Rab licked it all over carefully, looked at her, and returned to his place under the table.

James and I sat, I don't know how long, but for some time, – saying nothing: he started up abruptly, and with some noise went to the table, and putting his right fore and middle fingers each into a shoe, pulled them out, and put them on, breaking one of the leather latchets, and muttering in anger, 'I never did the like o' that afore!'

I believe he never did; nor after either. 'Rab!' he said roughly, and pointing with his thumb to the bottom of the bed. Rab leapt up, and settled himself; his head and eye to the dead face. 'Maister John, ye'll wait for me,' said the carrier; and disappeared in the darkness, thundering down stairs in his heavy shoes. I ran to a front window: there he was, already round the house, and out at the gate, fleeing like a shadow.

I was afraid about him, and yet not afraid; so I sat down beside Rab, and being wearied, fell asleep. I awoke from a sudden noise outside. It was November, and there had been a heavy fall of snow. Rab was in *statu quo*; he heard the noise too, and plainly knew it, but never moved. I looked out; and there, at the gate, in the dim morning – for the sun was not up – was Jess and the cart, a cloud of steam rising from the old mare. I did not see James; he was already at the door, and came up the stairs, and met me. It was less than three hours since he left, and he must have posted out – who knows how? – to Howgate, full nine miles off; yoked Jess, and driven her astonished into town. He had an armful of blankets, and was streaming with perspiration. He nodded to me, spread out on the floor two pairs of old clean blankets, having at their corners, 'A. G., 1794,' in large letters in red worsted. These were the initials of Alison Graeme, and James may have looked in at her from without – unseen but not unthought of – when he was 'wat, wat, and weary,' and had walked many a mile over the hills, and seen her sitting, while 'a' the lave were sleepin';' and by the firelight putting her name on the blankets for her ain James's bed. He motioned Rab down, and taking his wife in his arms, laid her in the blankets, and happed her carefully and firmly up, leaving the face uncovered; and then lifting her, he nodded again sharply to me, and with a resolved but utterly miserable face, strode along the passage, and down stairs, followed by Rab. I also followed, with a light; but he didn't need it. I went out, holding stupidly the light in my hand in the frosty air; we were soon at the gate. I could have helped him, but I saw he was not to be meddled with, and he was strong, and did not need it. He laid her down as tenderly, as safely, as he had lifted her out ten days before – as tenderly as when he had her first in his arms when she was only 'A. G.', – sorted her, leaving that beautiful sealed face open to the heavens; and then taking Jess by the head, he moved away. He did not notice me, neither did Rab, who presided alone behind the cart.

I stood till they passed through the long shadow of the College, and turned up Nicolson Street. I heard the solitary cart sound through the streets, and die away and come again; and I returned, thinking of that company going up Libberton brae, then along Roslin muir, the morning light touching the Pentlands and making them like on-looking ghosts; then down the hill through Auchindinny woods, past 'haunted Woodhouselee'; and as daybreak came sweeping up the bleak Lammermuirs, and fell on his own door, the company would stop, and James would take the key, and lift Ailie up again, laying her on her own bed, and, having put Jess up, would return with Rab and shut the door.

James buried his wife, with his neighbours mourning, Rab inspecting the solemnity from a distance. It was now, and that black ragged hole would look strange in the midst of the swelling spotless cushion of white. James looked after everything; then rather suddenly fell ill, and took to bed; was insensible when the doctor came, and soon died. A sort of low fever was prevailing in the village, and his want of sleep, his exhaustion, and his misery, made him apt to take it. The grave was not difficult to re-open. A fresh fall of snow had again made all things white and smooth; Rab once more looked on, and slunk home to the stable.

And what of Rab? I asked for him next week at the new carrier's who got the goodwill of James's business, and was now master of Jess and her cart. 'How's Rab?' He put me off, and said rather rudely, 'What's *your* business wi' the dowg?' I was not to be so put off. 'Where's Rab?' He, getting confused and red, and intermeddling with his hair, said, ''Deed, sir, Rab's deid.' 'Dead! What did he die of?' 'Weel, sir,' said he, getting redder, 'he didna exactly die; he was killed. I had to brain him wi' a rack-pin; there was nae doin' wi' him. He lay in the treviss wi' the mear, and wadna come oot. I tempit him wi' kail and meat, but he wad tak' naething, and keepit me frae feedin' the beast, and he was aye gur gurrin', and grup gruppin' me by the legs. I was laith to mak' awa wi' the auld dowg, his like wasna atween this and Thornhill, – but 'deed, sir, I could do naething else.' I believed him. Fit end for Rab, quick and complete. His teeth and his friends gone, why should he keep the peace and be civil?

(1858)

ERICH SEGAL

Erich Segal (b.1937) of Brooklyn was Professor of Classics at Princeton then Professor of Classics at Yale. He is a Fellow of University College, London, and of Wolfson College, Oxford, and a member of the Athenaeum in Pall Mall. He wrote *Love Story, The Class, Doctors, Roman Laughter: the Comedy of Plautus*, and he edited *Euripides: a Collection of Critical Essays*, and *Plato's Dialogues*. His was a fitting pen for those academic ragamuffins – medical students – who have never changed since they took the fancy of Dickens in *Pickwick Papers*.

These individualists were admitted with amused tolerance into the pages of Thackeray (1811–63):

Rakish young medical students, gallant, dashing, what is called 'loudly' dressed, and (must it be owned?) somewhat dirty, were here smoking and drinking, and vociferously applauding the songs.

And of Shaw:

That's what makes the medical student the most disgusting figure in modern civilization. No veneration, no manners.

And of Oliver St John Gogarty (1878–1957) in Dublin:

I found out what was wrong with Anatomy; it lacked humour.

Gogarty himself became stately, plump Buck Mulligan, the cleanly medical student who opens the pages of his friend James Joyce's bafflingly venerated *Ulysses*.

The doctor whom the student mimics still fulfils a definition of 1860: 'Physicians have been coupled with priests, as beings holding a position between the two sexes.' But the intimacies of the spirit are less testing than those of the flesh.

From Doctors

'TO BE ABSOLUTELY frank, guys,' Skip began, 'that first pelvic exam is one of the scariest things you'll ever have to do. I don't care how much experience you studs have had, you've never shone a lamp a few inches from the honeypot and examined it clinically. Besides, if you don't know what you're doing, you can cause the woman a lot of pain. The first thing to remember is to warm the damn speculum. I mean, how would *you* feel if somebody put a pair of cold metal tongs into one of your orifices?'

A hand rose for a question. 'Can't we use lubricant?' asked Hank Dwyer.

'No, no. Your first job is to take clean cell samples – Pap smear, that kind of thing. Oh, yeah, and a culture for gonorrhea, too.'

'You mean we're going to be sticking our noses right into potential VD land?' Lance complained with outrage.

'Nobody said anything about using your nose,' Skip responded with a tiny smile.

There was scattered nervous laughter.

'Okay,' he continued, 'when you get the speculum in, you open it, and – if you've positioned it right – you'll be able to get a view of the cervix, which is down and posterior. You'll know when you've found it 'cause it looks like a big pink eye. Then you do your smears and gently get the hell out.'

Now a collective sigh of relief.

'Wait,' Skip protested, his arms raised like a policeman stopping traffic, 'that's only half the job. Now you can put some K-Y jelly on the second and third fingers of your examining hand' (he demonstrated) 'and do your bimanual exam. That's two fingers into the vagina – which may be a more familiar procedure to some of you.'

He waited for appreciative chuckles, but they were not forthcoming.

'Anyway, you put your other hand on the abdomen and try to assess the size and condition of the uterus – which normally feels sort of like a lemon. The secret is trying to look like you know what you're doing. The whole damn thing should take less than five minutes. Oh – and one last thing, you're going to have to keep a tight rein on your feelings because, believe it or not, the first few times it can be kinda . . . sexually stimulating.'

He paused and then said, 'Any questions?'

Hank Dwyer's hand shot up frantically.

'Yeah?' Skip inquired.

'You did say that the cervix is *pink*, didn't you?'

He nodded.

'Well,' Hank continued self-consciously, 'I've been, uh, doing a little practice. You know – with my wife –'

'Yeah?' Skip urged him on. 'And what seems to be the problem?'

'Well, I kinda flipped my lid at what you said. I mean, my wife's cervix looks – well – *blue*. Could something be wrong?'

'Well,' their expert replied, 'I can see you haven't studied your textbook, old buddy. That's called "Chadwick's sign".'

Hank's usual pallor turned white. 'Is that serious?'

'Well,' Elsas said, 'that depends on you and your wife. A blue cervix means she's pregnant.'

To which the erstwhile priest replied, 'Holy shit!'

(1988)

Richard Gordon

I am sorry about this, but the publisher insisted. Critics continually carp at authors including themselves in anthologies, but presumably if their stuff was not worth anthologising they would not have been asked to compile one. This is a faded snapshot of the domineering doctors, monstrous matrons and swigging students before the world's first health service managed medicine and spoiled the fun.

From Doctor in the House

DURING THE FOLLOWING three months I learnt a little about surgery and a lot about surgeons. I learnt more than I wanted about Sir Lancelot.

In the theatre he was God. Everything in the routine for operating sessions was arranged to suit his convenience. A white linen suit, freshly starched, was carefully warmed by the junior nurse before being laid out in his changing-room in the morning. A thermos pitcher of iced water labelled 'Sir Lancelot Spratt ONLY' was set on a silver tray nearby. He had his own masks, his own scrubbing brush, and his own soap. When he crossed the theatre floor from the scrub-up basins to the table the onlookers scattered before him like unarmed infantry in front of a tank. If anyone got in his way he simply kicked them out of it. He rarely asked for an instrument but expected the sister to guess which one to place in his waiting hand. If she made a mistake, he calmly dropped the wrong instrument on to the floor. Should she do no better at her second attempt he repeated his little trick. Once he silently reduced a whole trayful of instruments to an unsterile heap at his feet, and the sister had hysterics.

Sir Lancelot had a personality like an avalanche and a downright bedside manner that suited equally well a duchess's bedroom or the hospital out-patient department. He radiated confidence like a lighthouse through a storm. His suggestions on the removal of his patients' organs never met with their objection. The more he did to them, the greater the complications that resulted from his interference, the larger the number of supplementary operations he had to perform to retrieve his errors, the more they thanked him: there was never one but died grateful.

His teaching in the ward, like his surgery in the theatre, was full-blooded. He had a long string of aphorisms and surgical anecdotes, none of which was original or strictly accurate, but they stuck in the minds of his students long after the watery lectures of his colleagues had evaporated.

His round was held every Tuesday morning at ten o'clock, and had the same effect on the ward as an admiral's inspection of a small warship.

The preparations for his visit began about five in the morning. The night nurses started the long business of sprucing up the ward to its best pitch of speckless sterility, and when Sister and her day staff arrived at seven the energy given to preparing the long room so that nothing in the slightest way offensive should fall on the great man's eye was increased tenfold. Every article in it was scrubbed and polished thoroughly – the floor, the medicine cupboards, the windows, the instruments, the patients' faces. The bedside lockers, which usually carried a friendly jumble of newspapers, soap, jam, football coupons, and barley-water, were stripped clean and their contents buried out of sight. Even the flowers looked sterile.

The tension and activity in the ward rose together, like the temperature and pulse in a fever. At nine the senior house-surgeon, in a fresh white jacket, looked in for a worried, whispered conversation with Sister to be certain everything commanded on the Chief's last visit had been done. He didn't glance at the patients. That morning they were part of the ward furniture, or at most instruments by which the medical staff could demonstrate their abilities to Sir Lancelot.

There was one point, however, on which the patients could not be argued away from their humanity. At nine-fifteen bedpans were issued all round. The acquisition of one of these at such an hour (seven and five were the official times for their use) was usually a business comparable with catching the eye of a waiter in a busy restaurant. At nine-fifteen on Tuesdays, however, they were forced upon the patients. The nurses tripped briskly out of the sluice-room, each carrying a couple under a cloth. This was because Sister thought a request for one of these articles while Sir Lancelot was in the ward unreasonable to the highest degree – indeed, almost indecent.

The bedpans were whipped away a quarter of an hour before the Chief was due. There followed an energetic final ten minutes occupied by a process known as 'tidying' the patients. They could obviously not be allowed to disturb the general symmetry of the scene by lolling about in bed anyhow, like a squad of soldiers falling in with their hands in their pockets. They had to be fitted in to the ward neatly and unobtrusively. The technique was simple. A pair of nurses descended on the patient. First he was shot into the sitting position, and retained there by one nurse while the other smoothed and squared up his pillows (the open ends of the pillowcases always to face away from the door). He was then dropped gently on his back, so not to ruffle the smooth surface unnecessarily with his head. The bedclothes were seized at the top by the two young women and pulled taut between them like a tug-of-war; they next applied the tension upwards from the patient's feet, which brought the top edge of the bedclothes level with the patient's nostrils. In one quick motion, without releasing the tension to which the blankets were submitted, they tucked them in firmly all round. This made it impossible for the occupant of the bed to perform any muscular movement whatever, except very shallow breathing.

The ward by ten was silent, orderly, and odourless. Sister and the nurses had changed into fresh white aprons and each of them felt like Moses immediately on his arrival at the top of the mountain. Meanwhile, another focus of consternation had formed not far away.

It was the tradition at St Swithin's that the Chief should be greeted in the courtyard and lead his firm to the ward. Surgeons were met in front of the statue of Sir Benjamin Bone and physicians before that of Lord Larrymore. This form of reception resulted in everyone becoming cold in winter, hot in summer, and wet all the year round, and as it had apparently been going on for three or four hundred years this seemed an excellent reason for refusing to alter it.

We gathered for our first ward-round under the cold eye of Sir Benjamin. The differences that divided the firm, which were emphasized on Tuesday mornings, had already become obvious. The students stood in a little subdued group behind the statue. We wore our suits, with stethoscopes coiling out of our pockets and foolscap notebooks under our arms. We chatted quietly between ourselves, but would not have contemplated exchanging words with the two house-surgeons, who stood apart murmuring to each other with expressions of intense seriousness on their faces.

The third section of the party consisted only of Crate, the registrar. He was allowed to wear a long white coat like the Chief, but as he had no companion to talk to and was unable to converse with his housemen or students at such a solemn moment he had to content himself with looking at the sky in a reflective and earnest way, as if he were turning over in his mind the niceties of surgery or trying to forecast the weather.

At ten the Rolls drew into the courtyard and stopped opposite our group. Crate opened the door and wished Sir Lancelot good morning. The car was driven to its parking-place by the chauffeur and the Chief disappeared with his registrar towards the staff common room to leave his hat and put on his white coat. When they reappeared the rest of the party followed them to the wards.

Once Sir Lancelot burst through the ward door more people arranged themselves in his wake. Indeed, it was impossible for a man of his importance to walk about St Swithin's at all without a procession immediately forming up behind him.

First, of course, was Sir Lancelot, the therapeutic thunderbolt. A pace behind came the registrar, and behind him the two house-surgeons, the senior one leading. After the two housemen was Sister, her long cap trailing behind her like a wind-stocking on an aerodrome. She was followed by her senior staff nurse, who carried a trayful of highly polished instruments with which the patients could be tapped, scratched, and tickled in the aid of making a diagnosis. Sir Lancelot never used any of them and probably did not know how to, but they were produced every Tuesday nevertheless, like a ceremonial mace. Behind the staff nurse was a junior nurse bearing a thick board covered with a pad of paper, to which a pencil was attached with a piece of string. The board was marked sternly 'SIR LANCELOT SPRATT'S DRAWING PAPER'. On this he would sometimes sketch points of anatomy – not often, about once every six months, but the board had to be flashed to his hand if he asked for it. In the rear of the junior nurse, in the winter months a probationer carried a hot-water bottle in a small red blanket for Sir Lancelot to warm his hands before applying them to exposed flesh.

At the end of the party, behind even the hot-water bottle, were the students: an un-uniformed, disorderly bunch of stragglers.

The Chief spent two hours examining the candidates for the afternoon's operating list, with whom he illustated to us the principles of surgery. Sometimes he passed all morning on one case, if the patient contained a lump of sufficient interest to him; on other Tuesdays he would whip round the whole ward, diagnosing like a machine-gun. Sitting was forbidden, and towards lunchtime the students shifted heavily from one foot to the other. Sir Lancelot thought any young man incapable of standing on his own feet for a couple of hours as another disagreeable product of modern life, like socialism.

On our first ward-round we were pushed easily into place by the precision with which the rest of the troupe fell in. Sir Lancelot strode across the ward, drew up sharply, and looked over the patients in the two rows of beds, sniffing the air like a dog picking up a scent. He thundered over to the bedside of a small, nervous man in the corner. The firm immediately rearranged itself, like a smart platoon at drill. The Chief towered on the right of the patient's head; Sister stood opposite, her nurses squeezed behind her; the students surrounded the foot and sides of the bed like a screen; and the registrar and houseman stood beyond them, at a distance indicating that they were no longer in need of any instruction in surgery.

Sir Lancelot pulled back the bedclothes like a conjurer revealing a successful trick.

'You just lie still, old fellow,' he boomed cheerfully at the patient. 'Don't you take any notice of what I'm going to say to these young doctors. You won't understand a word of what we're talking about, anyway. Take his pyjamas off, Sister. Now you, my boy,' he continued, gripping me tightly by the arm as I was nearest, 'take a look at that abdomen.'

I stretched out a hand to feel the patient gingerly in the region of the umbilicus. I noticed his skin was covered with goose-pimples and twitched here and there nervously.

'Take your dirty little hand away!' said Sir Lancelot savagely, flicking it off the surface of the abdomen like a fly. He paused solemnly, and continued in a heavy tone, wagging his finger: 'The first rule of surgery, gentlemen – eyes first and most, hands next and least, tongue not at all. Look first and don't chatter. An excellent rule for you to remember all your lives. Now look, boy, look.'

I gazed at the abdomen for a whole minute but it appeared no different from any that might be seen on Brighton beach. When I thought I had inspected it long enough to satisfy the Chief, who rose uncomfortably above me, I diffidently stretched out my arm and prodded about with my fingers in search of a lump.

'*Doucemong, doucemong,*' Sir Lancelot began again. 'Gently, boy –

you're not making bread. Remember' – his finger came up again warningly – 'a successful surgeon must have the eye of a hawk, the heart of a lion, and the hand of a lady.'

'And the commercial morals of a Levantine usurer,' murmured Grimsdkye under his breath.

With a glow of relief, I finally discovered the lump. It was about the size of an orange and tucked under the edge of the ribs. We lined up and felt it one after the other, while Sir Lancelot looked on closely and corrected anyone going about it the wrong way. Then he pulled a red grease-pencil from the top pocket of his coat and handed it to me.

'Where are we going to make the incision?' he asked. By now the patient was forgotten; it was the lump we were after. Sir Lancelot had an upsetting habit of treating the owners of lumps as if they were already rendered unconscious by the anaesthetic.

I drew a modest line over the lesion.

'Keyhole surgery!' said Sir Lancelot with contempt. 'Damnable! Give me the pencil!' He snatched it away. 'This, gentlemen, will be our incision.'

He drew a broad, decisive, red sweep from the patient's ribs to below his umbilicus.

'We will open the patient like *that*. Then we can have a good look inside. It's no good rummaging round an abdomen if you can't get your hand in comfortably. What do we do then? Right – take a better look at the lump we've been feeling. Do you think it's going to be easy to remove?' he asked me, gripping my arm again.

'No, sir.'

'Correct – it's going to be most difficult. And dangerous. There are at least a dozen ways in which we can make a slight error – even though we are experienced surgeons – and kill the patient like that!' He snapped his fingers frighteningly.

'Now!' He tapped the abdomen with his pencil as if knocking for admission. 'When we have cut through the skin what is the next structure we shall meet? Come on, you fellers. You've done your anatomy more recently than I have. . . . What's that? Yes, subcutaneous fat. Then, gentlemen, we first encounter the surgeon's worst enemy.' He glared at us all in turn. 'What?' he demanded in general. There was no reply. 'Blood!' he thundered.

At that point the patient restored his personality to the notice of his doctors by vomiting.

*

Surgery was Sir Lancelot's life and St Swithin's was his home. He had given more of his time for nothing to the hospital than he ever used to make his fortune. He was president or vice-president of almost every students' club and supported the rugby team from the touchline in winter with the same roar he used on ignorant dressers in the theatre. During the war he slept every night at the hospital in the bombing, and operated on casualties in an improvised theatre in the basement as long as they came in. A team of students lived in as well and he used to play cards with them or share a pint of beer, actions which at first caused as much dismay as if he had arrived to operate in his underpants. One night St Swithin's was hit while he was operating. The theatre rocked, the lights went out, and part of the ceiling fell in. But Sir Lancelot simply swore and went on – bombs to him were just another irritation in surgery, like fumbling assistants and blunt knives, and he treated them all the same way.

The only time Sir Lancelot became at all subdued was when he talked of his retirement. It hung over him all the time I was on his firm. The prospect of losing his two days a week at St Swithin's depressed him, though he was cheered by remembering that the hospital would immediately acknowledge him as an emeritus consultant and perhaps call him in for cases of supreme difficulty. His connection with St Swithin's would therefore not be completely broken; he could go on meeting the students at their clubs, and as for surgery he could continue that in private.

One day, shortly after I left his firm, he disappeared. He said goodbye to no one. He left his work to his assistant and wrote a note to the Chairman of the Governors simply stating he would not be in again. The hospital radiologist explained it later with an X-ray film. Sir Lancelot had a cancer of his stomach and had gone off to his cottage in Sussex to die. He refused to have an operation.

(1952)

ACKNOWLEDGEMENTS

I would like to thank the following for permission to reproduce extracts: Martin Secker & Warburg Ltd and Alfred A. Knopf Inc for *The Magic Mountain* by Thomas Mann; Faber & Faber Ltd for *A Journey Round My Skull* by Frigyes Karinthy; Lemon Unna & Durbridge Ltd for *The Umbilicus* by James Bridie; The Society of Authors on behalf of the Bernard Shaw Estate for *The Doctor's Dilemma* by George Bernard Shaw; the Estate of Stephen Leacock and The Bodley Head for 'How to be a Doctor' by Stephen Leacock from *The Bodley Head Leacock*; Richard Gordon Ltd for *Doctor in the House* by Richard Gordon; the Estate of the late Sinclair Lewis, Jonathan Cape Ltd and Harcourt, Brace, Jovanovich Inc for *Martin Arrowsmith* by Sinclair Lewis; the Peters Fraser & Dunlop Group Ltd for *Men at Arms* by Evelyn Waugh; the Estate of the late Sonia Brownell Orwell, Martin Secker & Warburg Ltd and Harcourt, Brace Jovanovich Inc for *How the Poor Die* by George Orwell; Mrs Laura Huxley, Chatto & Windus Ltd and HarperCollins Publishers Inc for *Brave New World* by Aldous Huxley; The Yale Editions of the Private Papers of James Boswell and The Edinburgh University Press for *Boswell's London Journal 1762–1763*; Transworld Publishers Ltd, Ploys Inc and Dewsbury International Inc for *Doctors* by Erich Segal, US copyright © 1988 by Ploep Inc, by permission of Bantam Doubleday Dell Publishing Group Inc.

Index of Names and Works

Page numbers in italic indicate quotation, in part or in full. Works are listed by author, magazines and papers by title.